G000163293

Contents

Eight Decades

Scholars are builders, builders of the world.
— Johanan b. Nappaha. Talmud: Sabbath, 114a

Eight Decades

The Selected Writings of

W. Gunther Plaut

With an Introduction by Jonathan V. Plaut

DUNDURN PRESS
TORONTO

Copy editor: Andrea Knight
Design: Jennifer Scott
Printer: Webcom

Library and Archives Canada Cataloguing in Publication

Plaut, W. Gunther, 1912-
Eight decades : the selected writings of W. Gunther Plaut / by W. Gunther Plaut ; introduction by Jonathan V. Plaut.

ISBN 978-1-55002-861-4

   1. Judaism. I. Title.

BM45.P53 2008   296.3   C2008-904409-6

1 2 3 4 5   12 11 10 09 08

We acknowledge the support of the **Canada Council for the Arts** and the **Ontario Arts Council** for our publishing program. We also acknowledge the financial support of the **Government of Canada** through the **Book Publishing Industry Development Program** and **The Association for the Export of Canadian Books**, and the **Government of Ontario** through the **Ontario Book Publishers Tax Credit program**, and the **Ontario Media Development Corporation**.

Care has been taken to trace the ownership of copyright material used in this book. The author and the publisher welcome any information enabling them to rectify any references or credits in subsequent editions.

J. Kirk Howard, President

Printed and bound in Canada.
www.dundurn.com

Dundurn Press
3 Church Street, Suite 500
Toronto, Ontario, Canada
M5E 1M2

Gazelle Book Services Limited
White Cross Mills
High Town, Lancaster, England
LA1 4XS

Dundurn Press
2250 Military Road
Tonawanda, NY
U.S.A. 14150

THE LEGAL DIMENSION

Acknowledgements

As I look back on 2007, I realize that it was a busy year. I published one book, *The Jews of Windsor 1790–1990: A Historical Chronicle*, a project that spanned thirty years of work, and edited two books for my parents: one for my father's ninety-fifth birthday, entitled *One Voice: The Selected Sermons of W. Gunther Plaut*; and the other a genealogical book of my mother's entitled *The Plaut Family: Tracing the Legacy*, which brought her massive research on the family to the public. Thus it might have made sense to delay another project after such an exceptionally busy year.

My wife, Carol, wanted me to wait at least a year, but my sister, Judith, encouraged me to complete the projects now if possible. Furthermore, the prospect of not bringing my father's last manuscript into book form troubled me, and I knew that if I delayed, it would likely be more difficult to make the effort at a later date. I consulted Malcolm Lester, who thought that my father's manuscript of essays would be a wonderful companion to the book of sermons. I agreed and, after some soul-searching, decided that it was important to publish this book now. I want to thank Malcolm Lester, who has been most helpful in coordinating this project, for his many valuable suggestions.

Malcolm Lester and I met with Kirk Howard, president of Dundurn Press and gave him a draft manuscript. Soon after, he informed me that he had read the essays, enjoyed them, and would be most pleased to be the publisher. I would like to extend my thanks to Kirk Howard for undertaking the publication of this book, as well as *The Jews of Windsor* and *One Voice*, and to add a special thank-you to Jennifer Scott, Allison Hirst, and Margaret Bryant of the Dundurn Press team who worked with great dedication to bring this project to completion.

When we began the first project some years ago, Malcolm Lester recommended Andrea Knight as the perfect person to be the copy editor, which indeed she was. For this book, once the draft was scanned, it was apparent that it had some missing text. Andrea searched in various Canadian libraries for the missing lines and inserted them into the final manuscript. Joining her was Alison Reid, who obtained the necessary copyright permissions and also participated in the proofing process. Both of them were meticulous in their attention to detail, and my thanks to them for their efforts.

Not only were lines missing from some Canadian articles but a whole series of other articles also needed to be filled in, as my father's copies were, in many cases, incomplete. To help ensure that the texts were correct, I consulted the library at Hebrew Union College in Cincinnati for assistance in finding the original articles so each of the incomplete essays could be properly corrected. My thanks to Marilyn Krider, interlibrary loan assistant, and Noni Rudavsky, head of public services, who helped me organize the process and for finding the appropriate individuals to assist with this arduous task: Melissa Simmons, office administrative assistant at the library; Ted Appel, library assistant, who did the photocopying; Allan Satin, reference librarian; and Yarden Ginsburg, library technical assistant, who worked on finding the materials on the shelves. They all deserve my thanks for their efforts in finding the many articles. When it became clear that there were difficulties in inserting the Hebrew text, I consulted colleagues of mine, Dr. Barry Kogan and Dr. Edward Goldman, who recommended contacting Deborah Swartz at the *HUC Annual*. She suggested that her husband, Howard Stein, a fifth-year rabbinic student, would be able to do this tedious work. My thanks to him for a job well done.

Finally, I want to thank my wife, Carol, who permitted me to spend the time to engage in this project, and my sister, Judith, who strongly encouraged me to bring this project to fruition. Both of them have been a source of support for which I am most grateful.

Jonathan V. Plaut

Introduction

Writing has by now become my major occupation. During these last years, I have contributed to many a festschrift, anthology, dictionary or other collective literary enterprise, and I continue to write ... but books remained my main focus. As long as the literary muse will stand by my side I will keep on, even though she has forced me to rise earlier and earlier every morning. Or is it the secret time clock that we all carry with us? Mine seems to wake me up, as if to say to me, "Don't delay, do it now!"
 — W. Gunther Plaut, *More Unfinished Business*

Author of some twenty-five books, from scholarly works on the Bible, theology, philosophy, and human-rights issues to two books of fiction, W. Gunther Plaut has published articles in the *Globe and Mail* and, from July 1980 to December 2003, wrote a weekly column in the *Canadian Jewish News*. He has written more than one thousand articles that have appeared in encyclopedias, anthologies, and an array of learned journals, covering such topics as Bible commentary and interpretation, theology and philosophy, Reform Judaism, and a host of other issues. For W. Gunther Plaut, writing was very much a part of his daily routine and very much a part of his soul. Whenever he wrote, he felt satisfied and renewed.

As one of the greatest Reform Jewish scholars of the twentieth century, he cautioned in the second volume of his autobiography, *More*

Unfinished Business, that "speaking and writing have one major feature in common: the words that one communicates take on a life of their own. They may be quickly forgotten (by most) or long remembered (by a few), or lead a subconscious existence in someone's mind. Tradition says that words once uttered are like feathers, blown everywhere and hence untraceable." My father is a Renaissance man — a scholar, a leading authority on Reform Judaism, and a passionate supporter of numerous human rights causes.

Why, one might ask, should a collection of his articles and essays appear now when they have already appeared in other journals, *Festschrifts*, or anthologies? There is an interesting mystery connected to this question.

When my sister, Judith, and I were sorting the papers from his office at Holy Blossom Temple and from his home, we collected thirty-two boxes of material scattered throughout the two locations, including a rather thick folder with several rubber bands tied around it. On each trip I made to Toronto from the Detroit suburb where I lived, I took more of his papers back with me so that I could go through them as carefully as possible. For thirty years, my father had donated his papers to Library and Archives Canada in Ottawa and, for nearly five years, I went through the remaining papers that spanned the last ten years of his working life to organize them for his last gift.

One day, I came across the large file with the rubber bands tied around it again and began to examine the folder more carefully. In the front of the file was a handwritten letter dated May 5, 1992, addressed to Malcolm Lester, who had published two of my father's books and a book I had edited on the occasion of his seventieth birthday. The handwritten letter read, "Thanks for the visit. Enclosed is the table of contents (numbers in brackets denote estimated numbers of pages in the book). Also, the attached essay should be put into chapter 4. I forgot to mention the updated bibliography which I will provide." The file contained a listing of the essays that he had chosen for a book that he called "Seven Decades." While the letter was addressed to Malcolm Lester, it was never mailed. It remained in the front of the file folder that contained the manuscript, ready for a publisher's hand. Was there a reason the manuscript was never published? One plausible answer is that my father called Malcolm and read the letter to him before faxing it to his office. (The fax number of Malcolm's office is written on the upper-right-hand corner of the letter.) Malcolm may have told my father that he could not publish it in a timely manner, so my father put the folder in a safe place and went on with other writing projects. During this time several things occurred that may have turned my father's attention to other more pressing matters, including the scholarly research necessary to complete *The Haftorah Commentary*, which appeared in 1996.

In 2007, on the occasion of my father's ninety-fifth birthday, *One Voice: The Selected Sermons of W. Gunther Plaut* was published. The topics covered in this book range from discussions about religion, faith and God, ethics and values, being a Jew, and Reform Judaism to thoughts on Israel, age and generation, death, and his final article, which was originally published in the *Canadian Jewish News*.

This book of essays is a companion to the book of sermons. While my father titled his manuscript "Seven Decades"—as it included writings from each of the decades spanning the 1930s through the 1990s — I have selected one essay from this decade in order to encompass the full span of his literary life. Thus, the title has been changed to *Eight Decades: The Selected Writings of W. Gunther Plaut*. My father divided his manuscript into sections that cover various themes: Studies in History, Biblical Inquiries, Literature and Linguistics, Theological Questions, Moral and Social Issues, Concerning Israel, Reform Jewish Perspectives, The German-Jewish Experience, and The Legal Dimension. While my father did not select the sermons that are included in *One Voice*, he did choose all the articles for this collection — with the exception of "Prophetic Judaism Without Prophets," which was published in 2000, they are the writing selections he made in 1992.

My father was born in 1912 in the small university town of Münster, Westphalia, in the western part of Germany, not far from the Dutch border. His father, Jonas Plaut, came from the North German province of Hessen; his mother, Selma, née Gumprich, was a native of Münster. At the time of Gunther's birth, Jonas taught at the local Jewish teachers' seminary. His parents then moved to Berlin to become superintendents of a Jewish orphanage. The family resided there until the Nazi era when they were forced to emigrate.

Even though my father spent his early childhood during the turbulent years of the First World War and witnessed the rise of the ill-fated Weimar

Republic as a schoolboy, he led a rather secluded life within the confines of the orphanage his parents administered. In 1930, he became the youngest student to enter the University of Berlin's law school, graduating three years later with a Doctorate in Jurisprudence. Since the Nazis had seized power by then, he realized that, as a Jew, he would never be able to pursue a legal career in Germany.

Because his son was eager to explore other options, such as the rabbinate, Jonas Plaut suggested that he study Hebrew at Berlin's Institute for Jewish Studies with the eminent theologian Abraham Joshua Heschel. My father also enrolled in courses taught at the same seminary by the German-Jewish scholar Dr. Leo Baeck who, at that time, also was chief rabbi of Berlin.

In the spring of 1935, Dr. Baeck received a letter from Dr. Julian Morgenstern, then the president of Hebrew Union College in Cincinnati, Ohio, offering to accept five "capable and promising young German students who are now preparing for the Rabbinate in Germany, but who may desire, for one reason or another, to continue their studies at the Hebrew Union College." Urged by his parents to accept Dr. Morgenstern's invitation, my father left for America a short time later.

While studying at Hebrew Union College, he met Elizabeth Strauss, a native of Cincinnati. They fell in love and were married on November 10, 1938, unaware of the fact that on that very night all the synagogues of Germany were ablaze and that Jonas Plaut had gone into hiding to escape the Nazi action that became known as *Kristallnacht.*

My father was ordained in 1939. His first pulpit was in Chicago, where his post as assistant rabbi not only allowed him to hone his skills as an orator but also to devote considerable time to scholarly pursuits. In 1943, a few days after becoming an American citizen, he enlisted in the Chaplains' Corps of the United States Army and subsequently served overseas as a chaplain with the 104th Infantry Division.

Having been awarded the Bronze Star for distinguished military service, my father returned to Chicago in 1946. Two years later, he moved his family to St. Paul, Minnesota, to become the rabbi of Mt. Zion Temple, a pulpit he held for thirteen years. While in Minnesota, he not only began publishing his first books but also became actively involved in the community's political life and part of a circle that included such luminaries as Hubert Humphrey, Walter Mondale, Eugene McCarthy, and Orville Freeman.

In 1961, my father accepted the call to become the spiritual leader of Holy Blossom Temple in Toronto, Canada, considered one of North America's most prestigious congregations. He soon emerged as his community's leader and, before long, became the undisputed voice of Canadian Jewry. Sought after as a keynote speaker both at home and abroad, his challenging messages drew crowds wherever he went. During the dark days of the Six Day and the Yom Kippur wars, he managed to rally Jews from every walk of life with his stirring appeals for support for the State of Israel. At the same time, he never shied away from taking on other commitments. In 1971, during Soviet Premier Aleksei Kosygin's state visit to Ottawa, he led a delegation of rabbis demanding that the harsh emigration restrictions for Soviet Jews be lifted. He retired from Holy Blossom Temple in 1977 and shortly after agreed to serve a term as president of the Canadian Jewish Congress. He served as president of the Central Conference of American Rabbis from 1983 to 1985, as vice-chair of the Ontario Human Rights Commission from 1978 to 1995, and in 2000 was invested as a Companion of the Order of Canada, Canada's highest civilian honour.

My father's prime reason for withdrawing from the active rabbinate was his desire to work full time on his magnum opus, *The Torah: A Modern Commentary.* The first volume was published in 1981 and, just recently, a revised edition appeared that also includes his commentary on the Haftorah.

Until my father developed Alzheimer's disease five years ago, he spent each day writing his regular newspaper columns and magazine articles, or working on his current book. This anthology is the final publication from his pen — may its publication keep alive the spirit of this great man!

Jonathan V. Plaut
Farmington Hills, Michigan
Chol HaMoed Pesach 5768, April 2008

Preface

 $\mathcal{T}$he articles contained in this volume have been chosen for their variety, and all of them have at one time or another appeared in anthologies, *Festschriften*, memorial collections, annuals, and journals of various kinds. Some of them have been excerpted because of their considerable length, but the majority are re-published in their original format.

Any collection of this kind is in its nature eclectic and often, as here, is significantly influenced by demands for economy. I have therefore chosen to exclude (with only the occasional exception) addresses and lectures I have given, even though they were subsequently printed in various collections or yearbooks. Also, articles for newspapers, newsletters, and the like are not found in these pages, nor — at the other end of the spectrum — have I included any of my published human rights judgments, because their technical nature exceeds the objectives I have set for this book.

When all is said and done, this volume represents a small mirror I hold before my own eyes and in it see the strivings, the hopes, the changing interests, and challenges of a lifetime. In that sense the book may be seen as a supplement to *Unfinished Business*, which was published in 1981.

Jewish tradition says that on reaching the age of eighty, one reaches a time of *gevurah*, strength. Just what that strength betokens is not always clear, for in each person it represents something different. For me, it has been the ever growing appreciation of the many blessings I have enjoyed, and especially of the companionship of my beloved wife, Elizabeth. For this and all the other gifts that have been mine, I give thanks to the Source whence all blessings flow.

I want to thank Malcolm Lester for encouraging me in this project and to all the many friends who over the years by their generosity have encouraged my scholarly activity.

W. Gunther Plaut
Summer 5752/1992

Under Thirty

What are the aims, the experiences, and the perplexities of the Post-War Generation? The Atlantic *intends to find out. Space has been reserved for the best letters written by men and women under thirty. The letters should, if possible, be compassed within 650 words, and those published will be paid for. Under special circumstances, anonymity will be preserved.*

— The Editors

Testament of Exile
To the Editor of the *Atlantic*:

I am twenty-five, trying to face the complexities of a modern world. To make matters more involved, I am a Jew who spent the major part of his life in Germany.

I partook, as did the majority of my generation, in the general unrest of our time. I knew the word "peace" only from hearsay, and only in its particular connotation of "the time before 1914." I remember the war and I remember it as bringing more hardship than just reduced portions of the daily sugar supply. I remember the days when we had raw carrots for lunch, boiled carrots for dinner, and nothing for breakfast; when we arose in the middle of the winter at four in the morning to wait ten or twelve hours in line for our ration of a tiny bit of margarine; when we wore paper shoes that could not stand humidity, to say nothing of rain. I remember seeing, for the first time in my life, a piece of chocolate. That was in 1919. When it was displayed in a window in Berlin, it attracted people from many districts who gazed at it in sheer amazement.

Then came the time of my growing consciousness and with it the period of general growing unrest. Inflation and poverty followed revolutions and *Putsches*. Despair and unemployment were ravaging the country when I graduated from high school. Times had not changed when I went to the university, when I was thrown into the turmoil of unsettled ideas and political, as well as cultural, upheaval. Besides, I faced growing anti-Semitism. Then 1933 came and set a definite end to most of the things I had believed in and hoped for.

Then came America. Will this be the end of my mental and physical journeying? Shall I find in this country quiet and "peace," ideals which I have never truly known?

But America is not entirely what people abroad believe it to be. Below the seemingly smooth surface there are the same smouldering forces of unrest. America today suffers the birth pangs of social consciousness, much the same as industrial Europe did twenty and thirty years ago. The American youth of my generation begins to take not only an interest, but also an active part in the political, economic, and cultural movements of the day. He shifts from mere discussion to organization and action. The "future" is no longer conceived of in terms of generations and lifetimes. Who knows what the morrow will bring? The "future" at its best extends till the next year or two. This may be historically unfortunate, but it shows that a subconscious unrest and uncertainty have gripped the roots of American civilization. In addition, I see the gospel of Jew-hatred spread also in this country, a fact which does not add to my spiritual tranquility.

With a changing world before me, with *motion* being at the heart of things, I often wonder whether the present situation is not really the desirable one, whether one ought not to be thankful for the challenge which proves to be the stimulus to a worthwhile and responsible life. And America has, in my mind, added confidence to this outlook. For in her people I detect a keen awareness, a healthy alertness which fortunately has not yet been dulled by economic and moral exhaustion.

Thus I look at America with some bewilderment, with apprehension at times, but with hope nonetheless. And, braced by this hope, I set out to do what little I can toward the further development of this country.

W. Gunther Plaut

My Third Age

$\mathcal{Q}$uite a few years ago I reached what people now call the "third age," a semi-jocular expression which reflects a modern revision of Shakespeare's seven-ages syndrome. No longer, in today's longevous society, are elders "sans everything," but rather do they cap a new and more appropriate division in which the first stage is youth; the second, middle age; while the third elicits the comment: "You're looking well."

I used to bristle inwardly when someone flattered me in this fashion. I no longer do and accept it gracefully and gratefully. I don't "feel my age," meaning that chronologically I am one thing and biologically another. However, society only looks at the former and persists in treating people like me in stereotypical and often discriminatory fashion. It may grant us a better economic cushion, but at heart it considers us so much extra baggage.

Readers, being no doubt well versed in biblical lore, will at once recall that Holy Scripture made provision for just that kind of societal shortcoming. Such admonitions should not mislead us into believing that in ancient days elders were accorded a position of universal honour and respect: Far from it. The very emphasis of the Torah (in Leviticus, Chapter 18) that the aged and hoary-headed need to be given consideration is in itself proof that such a provision was necessary. Laws usually provide for conditions that need to be corrected; while self-evident and universally respected practice finds no place in the legal codes. Love of one's children did not need a biblical command; respect for one's parents did, and so did deference to one's elders. For someone who has long passed the biblical benchmark, the moving cry of the Yom Kippur liturgy has added significance: "Do not cast me off in old age!"

The unhappy fact is that at sixty-five years of age, society gently but firmly cuts most of us off and relegates us to the dust heap of uselessness, regardless of our ability to do a full day's job with an adequate complement of physical and mental resources. Add thereto the widespread feeling that oldsters are a drain on the public purse. Not surprisingly the elderly are now asked to carry much of their own burdens (*vide* the taxing of formerly tax exempt social security payments in the U.S. — something Canada has done all along.

All of this would not be so bad if it weren't for the fact that we elders are the butt of jokes which are funny to everyone except us. Older women are demeaned as thoroughly stupid — but then, what can you expect from "old ladies with tennis shoes"? Any woman who qualifies as an elder and still insists on exercise has obviously lost her marbles. Men are no different and are expected not only to be useless but sexless as well. Young men who have eyes for girls elicit approval, but oldsters who appreciate women are considered "dirty old men."

The very word "*old*" has a negative connotation, and only when things and people are truly antique do they fetch a higher degree of appreciation — if they are in good repair, that is. My mother is now past ninety-nine and still takes courses at the university: that gives her a special, exceptional status.

Having followed my disquisition so far the reader will no doubt interpret it as a personal *cri de coeur*. Not so. Since for many years I had realized what would await me like everyone else once I reached sixty-five, I decided to leave my employment. Though I had always been treated with extraordinary generosity, I cut myself loose and became self-employed: lecturing, writing, and accepting occasional governmental assignments. I was more than fortunate and have found my new career enormously rewarding. But precisely because I know that this is not the norm, I have also waged a passionate battle for the elderly — and compulsory retirement is one of my chief targets. (In Canada, the matter is currently before the Supreme Court as a constitutional issue and will be decided later this year.)

Growing old brings also some built-in blessings: lessened competition; a sharply decreased urge to acquire things; a newly discovered treasure trove of patience, and, popular wisdom notwithstanding, the ability to learn. There is also more equanimity regarding my final destiny and a better sense of self-acceptance than I have ever had.

I have more time than ever for my family, more time to think, and more time to be keenly aware of the kindness which Providence has bestowed upon me. In many ways, these last years have been among my very best. To Disraeli, youth was "a blunder, old age a regret." Not to everyone, thank God.

Studies in History

The First Confirmation in America

*I*n the 1915 issue of the *Publications of the American Jewish Historical Society*, David Philipson published the confirmation certificate of Hannah de Sola. Her confirmation took place in St. Thomas, on April 14, 1844, and it was henceforth commonly believed that she was either the first to be confirmed in the New World, or at least that she belonged to the first class of "confirmists" (this expression being used in the document by the performing minister, Benjamin C. Carillon). In his recently published book, *Common Ground*,"[1] Morris Lazaron, who is the grandson of Hannah de Sola and is in the possession of the original certificate, repeats and re-affirms the statement of David Philipson.

Both statements are, however, erroneous. Though indeed it appears certain that the first confirmation in America took place in St. Thomas, Miss de Sola was neither the first confirmant nor a member of the first class. She belonged to the third class that was confirmed by the adventurous Reverend Carillon, who was then minister to the little colony of Spanish Jews that belonged to the Danish crown and spoke the English language. In the original record, Miss de Sola appears as no. 14, and a glance at her certificate reveals that the same no. 14 of the protocol book also appears on the document.

The first confirmation took place on Hol ha-Moed Sukkoth, October 14, 1843, and the first entry in the record is that of a Miriam Wolff. This is not only evident from contemporary notices in the Anglo-Jewish publications, *The Voice of Jacob* and *The Occident*, but also from the original book of protocols of the St. Thomas congregation.

The following source material will tell the story and give a full picture of the first confirmation in America:

1. Confirmation for boys and girls of 14 years was ordered by the king for the Jews, in the mother country (Denmark), since 1814, and has now been extended to our island. I anticipate the happiest results from this measure, as the preparatory form of Catechism etc., will prevent, in my opinion, conversion. A severe penalty is attached to those who neglect it, they are not permitted to become citizens, hold office, marry, control the property they may get by inheritance, follow any trade, nor are their oaths taken in court.[2]

2. St. Thomas, Oct. 27, 1843. On the Sabbath of the Feast of Tabernacles seven young ladies and gentlemen were confirmed by the Rev. Mr. Carillon; that being the first ceremony of the kind performed here. It must have beneficial effects.[3]

3. Confirmation. We learn from a private letter from St. Thomas that the first confirmation among American Israelites took place on the Sabbath Hol ha-Moed Sukkoth in the Synagogue under the charge of the Rev. Mr. Carillon. The ceremony is represented as having been very imposing. The names of the confirmed are, Mrs. Daniel Wolff, Misses Miriam and Rebecca Wolff, Miss D. Cortessos, Miss De Meza, Alexander Wolff, and Jacob Benjamin.[4]

4. The following is an extract from a letter written to the author of this article.

    St. Thomas, V.I., March 16, 1938.

    ... Our Govt. Secretary has passed over to me your letter to him, of Feb. 22, 1938, for reply.

    It gives me great pleasure to inform you that we have the Original Protocol of Confirmation, by our Congregation, and in looking thru same, the very first entry is that of Miriam Wolff, performed by the Revd. B. C. Carillon, on Sunday the 21st Tish-

ri 5604 Oct. 15, 1843, bearing the original seal of
Revd. Carillon...

On that day also were confirmed:

1. The above;
2. Miriam, wife of Daniel Wolff (Daughter of Judah and Sarah Cappe);
3. Rebecca Wolff (Daughter of Aaron Wolff and Rachel Wolff);
4. Alexander Wolff (Son of the same);
5. Jacob Benjamin;
6. Deborah Simha Cortissos;
7. Esther De Meza.

On February 24, 1844, there were three more candidates for Confirmation, *viz.*:

8. Moses Benlissa;
9. Grace Constance Cortissos;
10. Abraham Ezekiel Levison.

Then on the 25th of Nissan 5604 — 14th of April 1844, were confirmed:

11. Moses Benjamin;
12. Elias Wolff;
13. Rachel Meyer Neita;[5]
14. Hannah De Sola;
15. Judith Abendanone;[6]
16. Leah Lobs;
17. Zipporah Benlissa;
18. Sarah Piza.

Nos. 19 to 27: Nine continuants were confirmed on the 30th of May, 1846; and on the 9th of April, 1847, twelve more.

This is as far as Revd. Carillon performed the rite, and it is strange that only the first entry, Miriam Wolff, bears Revd. Carillon's stamp.

The Confirmation Protocol from which this is

29

taken bears the Danish Government's Legalization
Stamp, dated: October 18, 1843 — when it became
law to have all protocols legalized ...
  (signed) M. D. Sassi, Minister

Jews in Seventeenth-Century Georgia

The source material on Jewish life during colonial times is comparatively scanty. As regards the Jews of Georgia, we are fortunate in having contemporary records from the earliest times; records which have been described and discussed by Jones and by Huehner in the *Publications of the American Jewish Historical Society*.[1]

These records mention two groups of Jews in Savannah; a Portuguese and a German. Little is known about the latter group. We owe the knowledge of their existence primarily to the notes of Reverend Bolzius, a preacher of the Salzburg Lutheran group which found refuge in Georgia.[2] In Callenberg's records of the achievements of his missionary institute[3] there are three further references to the Jews of Georgia. They represent reprints of letters written to that institute, probably by the same Reverend Bolzius, within less than five years after the foundation of Savannah.[4]

These letters — henceforth called "first," "second," and "third letter," according to their order reproduced below — shed further light upon the life of the Georgian Jewish colony. They re-assert that there was a German group among the Jews. They give us details of the relations which existed between the Portuguese and the German Jews with regard to language, services, and ritual; they present us with new aspects of the life of the Jews in general, of their liberties and of their social intercourse with the Gentile inhabitants of the colony. These new aspects can be classed as follows:

1. The second letter, particularly, deals with the German Jews and their relation to the Portuguese group. It is, however, not entirely certain that the *whole* letter deals with the German Jews. From the context, it would appear that that part, for instance, which mentions the occupations of the Jews, applies only to the German Jews. But since it is not known whether there was a physician among this group, and since all the records mention only one Jewish doctor, namely Dr. Samuel Nuñez Ribiero, we must, for lack of further and more convincing evidence, assume that the writer refers here to the entire Jewish population.

2. Huehner[5] quotes a letter which was written by the Reverend Bolzius on January 3, 1739, and in which the writer stated that the Portuguese Jews were not very particular with regard to ritual. Huehner adds:[6] "It may not be amiss to call attention to another curious note in the *Journal*,[7] bearing the date Savannah, March 23, 1734. 'There are Jews here who do not observe the Jewish regulations as to food and the Sabbath.'" This note which seems "curious" to Huehner, is now verified and amplified by another note in the second letter, reprinted below.

3. This laxity in ritual observance on the part of the Portuguese Jews, which is now asserted beyond a doubt, contains, in our opinion, the clue to the problem of their origin. It seems certain indeed that they or their families came originally from Portugal, from where they had to flee because of religious persecution. From there they probably went to England, and then on to America. Their ritual laxity can therefore be explained best by the fact that these refugees were Marranos or, at least, came from Marrano families. There were no confessing Jews in Portugal at that time, for it was before the anti-clerical movement under Joseph I (1750–1777) and before the final abolishment of the Inquisition and the

re-admission of the Jews into the country. No wonder then, that the descendants of Marrano families would not be as meticulous in their ritual observances as the Ashkenazic Jews.

4. Our second letter likewise calls attention to the type of Jewish religious service; and about this we hear for the first time. The synagogue quarrel was already known to us through the aforementioned letter of January 3, 1739,[8] but the references to the synagogue itself, to the cantor, and the peculiar reference to the "Berlin ritual" are new. Again it might seem as if the passage refers to the German Jews only; we know that it could hardly apply to both Jewish groups, for the difference in ritual was too pronounced to permit joint services. Yet we must take this statement with caution. If it was meant to apply to the *Portuguese* Jews, it was erroneous; though the mistake could be explained by the fact that a Gentile outsider would not be familiar with the differences between Sephardic and Ashkenazic rituals. If, on the other hand, it was meant for the *German* group, then it appears strange that Bolzius mentioned it at all (unless he had such a fine understanding of Jewish services that he could distinguish between South German and North German *minhagim* — and that is highly improbable). Finally, it is also possible that all Bolzius meant to say was that "the German Jews had the same service as at home." We mention this difficulty, for its understanding is important in the question of the origin of the German Jews, to which we now turn.

5. Huehner believes that these German Jews were sent over by Salvador and the London Congregation,[9] and this theory contradicted previous assumptions that it was the Portuguese group which was sent by Salvador.[10] The material which Huehner presented seemed

indeed to support his theory. Our material, however, makes Huehner's argument again doubtful, though not excluding it entirely. We are led to such a statement by a notice in Bolzius' second letter which we reproduce below and which tells us that "there are only two families who know Judaeo-German."

We possess two other notices about the language of the German Jews. First, Bolzius, in his *Journal*,[11] states that "they understand the German tongue." Second, Bolzius' letter of January 3, 1739,[12] says that the German Jews *speak* High German.

That German Jews would understand or even speak High German is nothing extraordinary. But that they, as our material states, did not understand Judaeo-German (except for two families) is very puzzling indeed. It makes it very unlikely that these German Jews had stayed in London for any length of time, if at all.

The reason for this is obvious: the language of the German Jews in London was Judaeo-German; and even had their stay in London caused them to forget their mother-tongue, it could not, at the same time, have resulted in their remembering High German, which most certainly was not spoken among London Jews. But how could they have come from Germany without knowing the common language of the Jews? This can only be explained in the following way:

These German Jews had lived in very small places, possibly as the only families in their respective villages. Their contact with fellow-Jews must have been extremely scarce. A general calamity drove a number of these Jews from the villages and forced them to leave the country. They went to England from where they were sent on by Salvador and his colleagues. This is the only way in which we can account for their linguistic peculiarity and, at the same time, retain Huehner's theory that London was their starting point for America.

6. Our second and third letters give us a good picture of the general political and social standing of the Jews. All we knew so far was that the Trustees of the colony were unfriendly to the Jews and tried to prevent their permanent stay, and that it was only because of Ogelthorpe that the Jews were allowed to remain. It appears now, however, that the attitude of the Trustees did not reflect the attitude of the Gentile settlers in general. It was probably this fact which determined Ogelthorpe's policy to a large degree. Particularly the third letter reveals such a far-reaching equality of Jews and Gentiles that the German commentator Bolzius could not help mentioning it with astonishment. The first letter, furthermore, asserts that German Jews also attended his services, a fact which is also mentioned in his *Journal*.[13] On the whole, therefore, there seems little doubt that the inimical attitude of the Trustees was not shared by the settlers, and that the credit for liberality goes to them as much as to Ogelthorpe.

The following three letters are reprints from the Callenberg collection. The *first letter* is dated from the middle of 1734; one year after the colony had been established:[14]

> Aus Georgien in America liess ein prediger der Saltzburger[15] vermelden, dass ein paar juden daselbst ihrem gottesdienst mit beywohnen …

The *second letter* was originally sent from Georgia on February 21, 1738, but it never arrived. The writer had, however, kept a copy of the letter which, mailed three and a half years later (September 28, 1741), was received in Germany on March 7, 1742, and printed in 1744:[16]

> Es gibt in dieser Colonie auch Juden, an denen man, durch die diesem Volck zum besten gedruckte Buechlein, etwas Gutes zu schaffen vermeynet;[17] es ist aber bisher von schlechtem Effect gewesen, dass sie gar gelaestert, und sich gegen uns noch mehr verhaertet haben. Sie

sind sehr boshaftig, hassen und verfolgen sich unter einander. Es klagte mir neulich einer in Savannah, dass die Spanische und Portugiesische Juden die (dortige) Teutschen Juden so sehr verfolgeten, dass kein Christ den andern so verfolgen koente; und bat mich, dass ich bey der Obrigkeit daselbst, zum (besten) der Teutschen Juden, ein gut Wort einlegen moechte. Ich ergrif diese Gelegenheit, diesem Juden zu zeigen, wie sehr sie sich versuendigten, dass sie unsere christliche Lehre nach dem Leben der meisten Christen beurtheileten, und sie um deswillen laesterten, weil die Christen boese lebeten; auch daraus schliessen wolten, sie mueste eine falsche Lehre seyn. Denn er wuerde es ja nicht wol zugeben, wenn ich aus dem Verhalten der Juden zu Savannah gegen einander, und aus ihren uebrigen missfaelligen Wesen behaupten wolte, das Alte Testament und die darin befindliche Lehre, sey falsch und boese, etc. Worauf der Jude nicht viel sagte; sondern versprach, mir einmal den gantzen Handel, der sie unter einander so erbittert mache, zu erzehlen. Sie wollen gern eine Synagoge bauen, und darin koennen die Spanische und Teutsche Juden nicht harmoniren; was die speciellen Umstaende dabei sind, ist mir nicht bekant. Die Spanische und Portugiesische Juden sind in ihren Speisen so scrupuloes nicht, als die andern; sie essen z. E. das Rindfleisch, das ordentlich aus dem Magazin zu Savannah gegeben, oder sonst verkauft wird: diese aber, die Teutschen, leiden lieber Mangel, ehe sie etwas anders, als das von ihnen selbst geschlachtet ist, geniessen solten. Sie haben in Savannah alle Freyheit, die ein ander Engelaender hat; ziehen auch, wie andere, im Gewehr, auf Soldaten weise. Sie treiben keine andere Profession, als dass sie theils das Feld bauen, theils sich auf Handlung in Kleinigkeiten legen; welches letztere ihnen leichter, als das erstere, ankomt. Es ist auch ein Medicus unter ihnen; der selbst von den Herren Trustees angenommen ist, die Leute in Savannah, die auf Kosten derselben curiret werden, zu curiren. Sie brauchen bey ihrem Gottesdienst, den sie

jetzt in einer alten miserablen Huette halten, darin auch
Maenner und Weiber gantz abgesondert sind, eben solche
Ceremonien, als ich in Berlin gesehen habe. Ein Knabe,
der vielerley Sprachen, und sonderlich gut Hebraeisch
versteht, ist ihr Lector, und wird von ihnen bezahlet. Es
koennen nicht mehr, als zwo Familien, Judenteutsch. Ob
sie von den Herren Trustees werden Freyheit bekommen,
eine Synagoge zu bauen, wissen sie selbst noch nicht;
wenigstens moechte es noch eine Weile anstehen, weil,
wie gedacht, die Spanische und Portugiesische wider die
Teutsche Juden sind, und (sie) wider einander, auch in
Ansehung der Suppliqven um den Synagogenbau, heftig
protestiren. Mit uns und unsern Saltzburgen moegen
die Juden hier gerne zuthun haben, uns auch wol bisher
manchen Gefallen in aeusserllichen Dingen gethan; in
ihrer Lehre aber bleiben sie hartnaeckig, und ist bis dato
wenig auszurichten gewesen.

The *third letter* was written on July 4, 1739:[18]

Von dem Zustande der Juden in Savannah habe ihnen
den 21. Febr. st. v. des vorigen Jahres einige Nachricht
ueberschrieben, welche ihnen wol wird zu Haenden
kommen seyn.[19] Gott erbarme sich der elenden verkehrten
Leute; und zeige uns Gelegenheit und Weise, etwas zu ihrem
Heyl an ihnen zu thun! Sie sind durch etwas, so einmal in
London gedruckt worden, sehr wider uns eingenommen:
uebrigens geben wir ihnen mit unsern Saltzburgern, so oft
wir nach Savannah kommen, ein gut Exempel; wie sie denn
mit uns und den Unsrigen lieber, als mit andern, zu thun
haben moegen; weil ihnen im Handel Wort gehalten, und
baar Geld gezahlt wird. Die Engelaender, vornehme und
geringe, halten die Juden sich gleich, und so gut, als andere
Leute; wie sie denn mit ihnen zechen, spielen, spatzieren
und alle Weltkurtzweile treiben; ja wol mit den Juden den
Sonntag entheiligen; welches wol kein Jude, den Christen
zu Gefallen, an seinem Sabbat thun wuerde.

The Israelites in Pharoah's Egypt:

A Historical Reconstruction

𝓑ack in the early 1930s, there appeared a little volume by Valerio Marcu that made an indelible impression on me and on many others in Germany who, at that time, managed to exist under Nazi rule. Every word in Marcu's book, which dealt with the expulsion of the Jews from Spain, became to us a paradigm of our fate: the author wrote about the past, while we read it as a story of the present.

It was natural, therefore, to think of Marcu's book when I received an invitation to participate in the Jewish cultural symposium scheduled for late December 1976 in Moscow. As is well known, the Soviet government forbade the conference and denied visas to the participants from abroad. Thus, history repeats itself, and the paper that I planned to read, on the Egyptian bondage, becomes a paradigm of the oppression of Russian Jewry.

I

More has been written about the exodus of the Israelites from Egypt than perhaps about any other single event in history. The bias with which nineteenth-century scholars came to that period — and indeed everything that pertained to Israel as a people — has been largely discarded by modern scholars who recognize that the core of the biblical account does represent a faithful re-creation of actual events seen from the perspective of later ages. Of course, the Bible had a distinct focus: its purpose was to show us the Exodus and God's role in it. It did not mean to give us a general history of Egypt, nor did it attempt to describe the long years of Israel's servitude. In both respects we are given the merest hints and suggestions, and if we are interested in a social and psychological reconstruction of the circumstances which preceded the Exodus, we have to rely on extra-biblical data; the available sources of Egyptian history (of which there are many); the biblical text itself, seen in the light of contemporary scholarship; and finally, the living memory of the generations which followed the Exodus. This latter source is frequently undervalued. What can the Midrash, for instance, tell us about the history of an age more than a thousand years earlier? Yet we must not forget that in biblical days — as well as much later — only very few could read; important knowledge was transmitted orally, and with astounding accuracy. Often such transmission was safer than a written document, for documents were subject to destruction by accident or by the design of kings and rulers who did not like what they read. In such cases, they had little hesitation in rewriting history — not as it actually happened but as they wanted it to be recorded.

Egyptian history prior to the Exodus is a case in point. The revolution of Akhenaton produced a wide-scale destruction of pre-revolutionary records and monuments, and the counter-revolution which followed it visited a similar fate on the monuments of the rebel king.[1] Two other famous examples belong to much later periods and feature the rewriting and careful destruction of existing records. One was the post-mortem assassination of the character of Richard III of England by the Tudors; the other, the almost successful erasure of the memory of the culture of the Chimu, whose conquerors, the Inca, portrayed themselves as the builders of that civilization. For many centuries these contributions to humanity were successfully buried by the falsifiers. But complete success evaded the suppressors of truth, and today the Chimu and Richard III have been, or are being, restored to their rightful places. Somewhere, somehow, memories survive — and if they do not survive in written form, they may survive in archaeological evidence or in folk memory. All these together must be utilized by the scholar, and no possible evidence should be rejected merely because it was not contemporaneous with the events. Thus, as we shall see, Israelite folk memory — though recorded very much later in the Midrash — can help to provide us with valuable insights into the subject under consideration.

II

We know a great deal about ancient Egypt. Written records and archaeological evidence abound. We know about its economy, about its privileged nobility and priesthood, as well as about the underprivileged classes, the proletariat and the serfs. About the latter classes André Neher writes:

> First of all there was what historians call the Egyptian proletariat. Here they are using a very modern term to designate a social group which actually existed under the nineteenth and twentieth dynasty in Egypt, showing the identical characteristics of their nineteenth- or twentieth-century European counterparts. Those who belonged to this class were destitute of everything except their hunger: "We are putrefying with hunger." That is the only language possible to describe the utter misery under Pharaohs bearing the name of Rameses. These words recur like a *leitmotiv*, like an obsession on the lips of the proletariat who have nothing else, or almost nothing else to say.
>
> Yet there were people in Egypt [whose] misery surpasses even that of the proletariat. If the proletariat remains within certain limits these are overstepped the moment we approach the serfs. Of the slaves, the Egyptian says: "They have no hearts," and here, as everywhere else in the orient, the heart signifies the personality itself. This discovery, which is as positive as a law of physics, authorizes him to treat the serf like an inanimate object.
>
> These slaves constitute one densely packed mass of humanity. In Egypt the proletariat is numerous. However, in their drawings there are spaces around the peasants and workmen who, in spite of their numbers, seem to retain a minimum of individuality. On the other hand, the scenes depicting slavery and forced labour are brutal in their massiveness. Human beings are so closely packed and piled upon each other that they appear as a single whole, yoked as such to its work, without any individuality at all.

> These human masses are the victims of the totalitarian empire of the Rameses and their passionate and fanatical cult of power. The State and its prestige demand the systematic construction of colossal depots, fortresses, palaces, temples, cities, and tombs. The slaves provide the gratuitous and inexhaustible pool of labour for this immense task.[2]

The upper classes, headed by the court and the pharaoh, ruled with absolute power, buttressed by a thought system which laid claim to ultimate truth. The king spoke with divine authority against which there was no appeal. Even Akhenaton, whose religious revolution brought Egypt close to a form of monotheism, exhorted his servants to observe his instructions by calling it "my doctrine."[3]

The biblical tradition was well aware of this hierarchy of power and it concentrated its attention on the two chief protagonists: the god of the Egyptians and the God of the Hebrews, who was represented by Moses and Aaron. Pharaoh was the human authority who ruled one of the two great powers of antiquity; he had the total resources of his empire at his command; and he could — and did — order death and bitter deprivation for the rebellious Israelites. Their resources were spiritual, and they believed that spiritual power could overcome the overwhelming pressures of the state. And they succeeded, or rather, God succeeded. At first, the demands of the Israelites were modest: give us leave to worship God in accordance with our needs and His will (Exodus 5:1ff). When Pharaoh refused, the demands were expanded and permanent emigration became the issue. "Let My people go that they may worship me" was the new request made of Pharaoh (Exodus 9:1) and, as expected, he refused again. He did not want to lose his serfs; besides, if they went, others, too, might want to escape from servitude — which was precisely what took place later on when Israel's exodus occurred. We read that, with the Israelites, a group called *erev rav*, went out, probably a mass of disadvantaged people, proletarians who had no economic future, and assorted serfs (Exodus 12:38). Pharaoh and his nobility were in the grip of their own economic system, built on exploiting cheap labour, and of their intellectual and spiritual system which declared its own viewpoint to be divine and, therefore, infallible.

The Bible, giving Pharaoh's attitude a theological name, says that "God stiffened Pharaoh's heart" which the Midrash interpreted to mean: Pharaoh had committed himself to oppression to such a degree that oppression became his way of government. Even so slight a request as the one that Moses made at first — a temporary release for the duration of three days — was considered an intolerable breach of the system — and how much more so when the Israelites requested permission for a permanent exodus. It was tantamount to drawing the whole Pharaonic world view into question. Hence, the repeated notation that while the king wavered in the face of various catastrophes — economic and otherwise — and was ready to make minor concessions (like giving the labour force a brief holiday but keeping the women and children as hostages), the final answer was always no. He would not let the Israelites go freely as they had requested. The Pharaonic system made prisoners, not only of the slaves, but of their masters as well.

III

While the Egyptian political and psychological system can be pictured with a fair degree of certainty, this is not the case when it comes to the Israelites. For instance, we are not sure precisely who were the Israelites who were in Egyptian servitude. Most certainly they were not the whole people described by the Bible as the family of Jacob. Some of the tribes apparently never left Canaan and some others seem to have left before the time of the Exodus. Thus, the Midrash tells us that thousands of Ephraimites had escaped from Egypt at an earlier time but had been killed by Pharaoh's army.[4]

Nor can we overlook the point that Joseph, who had brought his family down to Egypt in the first place, is unlikely to have lived four hundred years prior to Moses' time, as the Bible records. The figure 400 is of Egyptian origin; it played a role in the famous stele of Pharaoh Rameses II (1304–1237) and is a schematic or symbolic one. The figure 10 stood for "generation," and 10x10 meant "many generations" or "a very long time." Therefore, Israel's oppression in Egypt dated back "a very long time"— long enough to exceed the memory of anyone alive.[5] Perhaps the Israelites had come with the Hyksos invaders or had been brought in by them later on to guard the sensitive border province of Goshen. When the Hyksos were displaced, the Hebrews were de-classed and their long servitude began.

A number of questions arise — and on all of these the biblical text is silent.

Thus, we are not told how, under oppressive conditions, the Israelites were able to keep their identity alive and vital. The pressures of assimilating to Egyptian culture and thought must have been overwhelming. The history of human oppression shows that those who are degraded are likely to find their masters' civilization to be superior — why else would the masters rule? What then, made it possible for the Hebrews to resist this pressure? Remnants of religious feeling? Traditions handed on by one generation to the next? Perhaps. The Bible says nothing, but the Midrash preserves a folk memory of ancient times. It says that three practices saved the Hebrew culture from extinction: the people practised chastity; they did not forget their national tongue; and they received Hebrew names.[6] "Chastity" meant a sense of traditional purity, an intense family loyalty which caused parents to transmit to their children values which, on occasion, may have opposed the values of the ruling class.

The transmission of the love of the Hebrew language was another important factor in the struggle for identity. Such a struggle was to be repeated in many centuries of later Diaspora: when people learned and studied Hebrew they kept alive their bonds with the past and with their contemporaries elsewhere and, especially, in the Promised Land, whenever there was a strong Jewish community living there. Hebrew was the key to understanding basic oral traditions, as well as written records which assumed a sacred place only when preserved in the national language.

And finally, names. They were then, and were often afterwards, the sign that the Israelites remained proud to be who they were. For public appearances and political purposes, Joseph assumed the name of Zaphenat-paneah, but privately he remained Joseph —"I am Joseph," he says to his family (Genesis 45:3), and the Midrash adds that when he spoke to his brothers he spoke to them in Hebrew to convince them that he was authentic.[7]

To be sure, there was a time when he had tried to forget his past and his family, which explains why he never tried to get in touch with them. He had joined the ruling class and served them well, but he never could fully obliterate his identity. We may be certain that, behind his back, the Egyptians talked about his Hebrew origin, and he himself never succeeded in suppressing it fully. The visit of his brothers wiped away the veneer, and toward the end of his life he made his family promise that when, at last he would die, they would return his bones to his homeland.

IV

The homeland — doubtless the thought of it was kept alive among the people throughout their sojourn in Egypt. Someday they would return to Canaan, to the place where the ancestors were buried, where the vision of God in its pure sense was first beheld and treasured. The memory was idealized, and Canaan was thought of as the land where all human problems were solved, where the soil was rich and yielded more than enough for all of its inhabitants, and where animals could find nourishment without fear of drought or overgrazing. Memory often works like that: it emphasizes the best and most desirable and covers what interferes with hope. Why worry about hard work or crop failures in Canaan when one still lived in Egypt? So the Israelites focused — quite properly — on the most important aspect of the homeland: it represented freedom, the ability to shape life in accordance with the people's own sense of identity. It would be good simply because it spelled liberty. The material details were, no doubt, exaggerated by those who kept alive the dream of return, but the essentials were right.

Of course, not everyone is likely to have thought in the same way. There must have been the "realists" who pointed out the difficulties of crossing the desert, the delays that might occur, the enemies whom one might meet on the way. Would the Israelites be welcomed once they reached Canaan? Would things not be hard, rather than easy? Could the skills one had acquired in Egypt be used in the new land? Perhaps the period of migration and settlement would entail wars and hardships — would it not be better to stay where one was? There was enough to eat in Egypt and, while work was hard, one knew exactly what was required. That is precisely how, later on, some of the malcontents spoke: "We remember the fish we used to eat free in Egypt, the cucumbers, the melons, the leeks, the onions, and the garlic" (Numbers 11:5). The news of their discontents must have reached those who never left Egypt, and their taskmasters, hearing the same news, must have gloated and said: "We told you so."

For there were Hebrews in Egypt who never gave up their servitude. In fact, if we can trust folk memory, only a brave and adventurous minority left, while the majority stayed behind and made the best of their condition. Again it is the Midrash which has preserved this tradition. It comments on the phrase which states that the Israelites left Egypt *hamushim* (Exodus 13:18). Generally, this is understood to mean either that they left with enough provisions or that they were armed. But one tradition says that it meant that only "a fiftieth" left the country (relating the word to *hamesh*, "five").[8]

This tradition can also offer an explanation to the most puzzling of all the questions surrounding the period of Israel's stay in Egypt: why did God decide suddenly that the time had come for Israel's liberation? Was it just divine caprice or had certain conditions developed which made liberation an urgent item on God's agenda? The Bible itself is silent, noting only that Israel's bitter cries were heard by God (Exodus 2:23–25), but nothing further is said. The speculation which the Midrash puts forth on this matter is, however, worth recording. In commenting on the phrase (Exodus 6:9) that the Israelites were incapable of hearing the message of liberation, it says that they could not let go of the idolatries of Egypt — that is, the Egyptian thought-system had accustomed them to oppression, so that, having made the requisite adjustments, they were prepared to live with it.[9] When that happened, God knew that the need for liberation was urgent and He intervened to bring it about, through the agency of Moses and Aaron.

Their task was not an easy one. They told the people that God would help them to leave the country. "But they did not listen because they had no vision and because of their hard labour" (Exodus 6:10). The Egyptian system had succeeded: it had reduced a proud people to willing serfs, cogs in the machine of the state, a nation whose will power had eroded. Only the best — one-fiftieth, according to the tradition noted above — pried themselves loose from their fetters. They decided to believe in the message of freedom and risked everything they had in the pursuit of selfhood and identity. The homeland beckoned and so did their brothers who lived there.

Eventually, the Egyptian rulers decided to let them go, and when, later, they changed their minds again, they met with catastrophe. It is idle to speculate on what would have happened if Pharaoh had yielded at once to Moses' request — perhaps his kingdom would have been spared the severe jolts that it suffered during the period of the plagues (as they have become known) and later at the Red Sea. It is idle because history does not go back and try again; it is one-directional. One thing is clear from this reconstruction of the background to the biblical Exodus: the Egyptian system was brittle because of its very rigidity, and it came to grief in its struggle with a people bent on freedom — a struggle for which, at that time, there was no precedent.

Youth Movements

*J*ewish youth movements can be understood only in the setting of general historical conditions. By definition, youth movements imply a conscious revolt of youth against social, political, and cultural conditions representative of and created or tolerated by the older generation. With the progress of the nineteenth century and growing complexity of the new industrial civilization, with the development of mammoth cities, mass proletariats and a class consciousness, the cleavage between the potentialities of the age and its sordid realities in most European countries became evident and awakened in many young people the urge for a better world. They felt a desire to come once more closer to nature; they rebelled against the trend of making the individual wholly subservient to existing conventions: philosophical nihilism. Nietzschean irreverence and Ibsenian moral courage were mingled to lend their drive a sweeping, if vague urgency. Young people's movements sprang up in most European countries where an authoritarian and feudal order repressed the natural ambitions of youth. Thus youth movements found their most fertile field in Germany (where, in addition, romanticism flavoured all ideology) and in Russia, where all energies were soon directed toward definitive social and political ends, through the channels of the underground socialist parties. France and England, on the other hand, were largely unaffected.

The First World War, instead of solving the growing unrest of youth, added to their desire for reshaping the universe. Heretofore youth programs had been for the most part vaguely idealistic and individualistic;

they now gave their adherence to definite political ideologies which promised to save them from the recurrence of national and spiritual disasters. In Germany and Italy youth movements became the vehicle for the ascendance of supreme leaders (the very term "leader" is intimately linked to the structure of youth movements), and finally ended their historical cycle by enslaving those whom they had originally meant to be free. In Russia the youth movements integrated themselves completely into the new social order. In other countries, too, the erstwhile indefiniteness of ideas was replaced by political, social, and religious doctrines which were more or less committed to specific programs and parties. With the arrival of the Second World War, youth movements in the *original* sense of the word were dying and had even lost their emphasis on "youth," inasmuch as they were now inspired by adult groups and leadership. The "new" youth movements had become political rather than social and, as "party movements," had changed into youth sections of adult organizations.

Jewish youth movements reflect, in their rise and development, the general picture. Since, however, Jewish youth never became an integral part of its environs — for even in Western Europe a social ghettoization always persisted — they were affected by the general trend in a somewhat retarded measure, and did not feel the full impact of the *Wandervogel* and similar ideologies until the first decade of the twentieth century. But even when they did then, adopting many of the external features of other youth movements (as, for example, hiking and scouting), they invested them soon with a particular Jewish meaning. This was due to two reasons. Negatively, Jewish youth felt unwelcome in the general movements which strove for a certain amount of homogeneity and looked upon the Jew as an interloper and cultural stranger. On the positive side, Jewish youth, left to its own resources, discovered its own heritage and made the revival of Jewish cultural values an outstanding part of its program and a mark of distinction from other youth movements. It soon fell in with the rising tide of political and cultural Zionism, gave it its youthful impetus, and was in turn buoyed up by it. With few exceptions (notably in Germany) Jewish youth supported the Zionist program, following the lead of the German Blau-Weiss and the East European Hashomer Hatzair.

The influence of youth movements on Jewish life was immense. Practical Zionism became Halutz-borne and thereby largely a youth movement. It afforded a unique opportunity for self-realization, and produced the historically fundamental, youth-founded and youth-inspired *kibbutzim* and *kvutzoth*. At the same time, however, when youth began to leave the stage of vague idealistic pursuit and continued the realization of its program, the factionalism of the adult world entered into its endeavours. After the war, moreover, the first generation of Jewish youth had "graduated" into political and social life and become the standard bearer for the younger elements. Imperceptibly, Jewish youth movements started to be led and inspired by older leaders and their formulated doctrines. Much of the original spontaneity was lost and the young were educated along party lines — political, cultural, and religious — which the adult leaders had drawn. While a good deal of genuine enthusiasm for the attainment of social and specific Jewish ends continued to persist, Jewish youth now followed the pattern of world youth more quickly than it had done thirty and forty years before. By 1930 most youth movements had become organizations for the advancement of youth and proceeded to spend much of their energy in settling ideological controversies. They were each now affiliated with some adult organization, movement, or party, which directed its policies, set its educational standards and often supported it financially. This was particularly the fate of the Zionist youth movements, and is shown most clearly in an analysis of present-day Palestinian youth organizations.

In yet another respect had the emphasis of the movements shifted. In their inception, only those associations whose programs were moulded along lines of social and political reform were considered youth "movements." By 1930 this term was being applied also to groups which fostered purely intellectual or religious or athletic advancement — as long as the membership was composed of young people.

In the Anglo-American countries, general as well as Jewish youth movements were slow to start, owing to the absence of the autocratic systems and national minority problems which drove European and Oriental youth into rebellion. In the Western democracies, youth movements in the original sense of the term never came to full life; although beginning with the depression years a number of independent organizations arose which, however, in turn soon took their cue from adult groups existing in their own or in foreign countries. Among Jewish youth, the Hashomer Hatzair, Habonim, and similar organizations whose emphasis was on social problems were introduced into England

and America; but their membership remained small compared with that in the "new" youth movements — religions, educational, and athletic or scouting groups under the influence of parent sponsors — whose social philosophies have only a minor or no part in their programs.

After 1933 youth organizations in Germany and, with the advance of Nazism, also in other European countries, became largely survival groups, training their members for emigration and at the same time intensifying their Jewish consciousness. In this respect they performed an invaluable service. Quite naturally, Zionist youth movements experienced a resurgence of vitality and importance since Palestine was the chief centre of both Jewish thought and immigration. At the end of December 1942, most European Jewish youth movements were likely to have shared the fate of European Jewry in general. Where they still existed, they were bereft of their freedom and could carry out their program only in a very restricted manner, labouring under constant danger of annihilation.

The Canadian Experience:

The Dynamics of Jewish Life Since 1945

In many ways Canadian Jewry can be understood only in its relationship to the presence of the six million Jews in the United States, even as Canada itself cannot be discussed without constant reference to its southern neighbour. The United States and its history may be described intelligibly without constant reference to Mexico, the Caribbean, or Canada, for its existence is only marginally affected by its smaller neighbours. But for Canada it is the overwhelming presence of the United States, along the 3,500 miles at its southern border, which determines a good deal of its economy and psychology. Even its immigration patterns have been influenced, for many people unable to go directly to the United States (after 1924, when American immigration laws severely restricted access) have in the past thirty years first gone to Canada, especially in the decades before and after the Second World War. While the land mass of Canada is larger than that of the United States, its population — which has for the last generation been holding at about 10 percent of its neighbour's — is concentrated in a narrow one-hundred-mile strip north of the border, and in some ways the north-south bonds are stronger than those that tie east to west.

This very fact has also had other correlates. After the Second World War and well into the 1950s a sense of Canadian (as distinguished from French-Canadian) identity was at a low ebb, and many predicted once again the amalgamation of Canada and the United States. But in the wake of the disillusionment which swept over the United States in the latter stages of the Vietnam War, the rise of French-Canadian sentiment for secession, and a series of new federal protectionist economic measures combined to raise the level of Canadian nationalism to a new post-war high. While such favourite U.S. terms as "Americanism" and "un-American" did not have their parallels north of the border, Canadians increasingly began to define themselves less by their own character than by their desire not to be Americans — the more so since giant U.S.-controlled corporations and the all-pervasive American media, especially the electronic networks and such magazines as *Life*, *Time*, and *Reader's Digest* choked off indigenous Canadian self-expression. Even certain forms of vocal anti-Americanism could increasingly be heard, though on the whole they did not express any deep-seated popular sentiment.

In most respects the two nations remained what they had been: political and military allies, with an undefended border separating them for political and economic purposes; both subject to the same cultural pressures, so that the casual visitor might be hard put to explain in just what way the two countries were distinguished from each other. First and foremost, there was the French factor, with Francophones facing special problems of cultural attrition and isolation. But there were distinctions in the English sector as well, and they expressed themselves no less in the Jewish community. In many respects Canadian Jews were, indeed, much like their American counterparts, but on closer investigation they exhibited important differences and formed a community that had its own characteristics and played its own separate role on the stage of world Jewish life.

In 1945 there were about 12 million people living in Canada, of whom about 180,000 were considered or considered themselves Jewish.[1] The vast majority were located in Montreal and Toronto (about four-fifths of the total) while the rest were found mainly in a few urban centres such as Winnipeg, Vancouver, Calgary, Edmonton, Saskatoon, Regina, Windsor, Hamilton, and Ottawa. Most of these Jews were of East European back-ground who had come after the turn of the century. A small number had settled much earlier, the original community in Montreal going back to the middle of the eighteenth century and in Toronto to the middle of the nineteenth. Montreal's Jewry had large components from Russia and Rumania, Toronto's from Poland, and Winnipeg's from Rumania. In 1945 a significant segment of Canadian Jewry was still foreign-born and, in ac-culturation, at least one generation behind its counterpart in the United

States. Since immigrants from Germany were at a minimum (they had come primarily in the nineteenth century and had settled in the United States), the development of Reform Judaism so prominent in the United States was severely retarded. In addition, British conservatism hardly encouraged radical religious experimentation of the American kind. On the other hand, the Jews who had settled in Canada were not subject to the same assimilatory pressures as were their brothers to the south. There, the melting-pot philosophy became national policy (or at least was understood to be national policy), while the fact that Canada was the result of the co-existence, juxtaposition, and sometimes confrontation of two cultures — French and British — prevented so simplistic a pattern from developing. The very constitution of the country allowed for two distinct cultures and, by this duality, maintained the durability of ethnic differences.

There were other reasons, too. In French-Canadian cities like Montreal, Quebec City, and Sherbrooke, Jews tended to identify with the English minority and were therefore doubly isolated.[2] Further, East European Jews had come to Canada generally several decades later than they did to the United States. This delay had exposed them to the sharpened political ideologies which had come to dominate the European Jewish communities, such as Bundism and the varieties of Zionism. The Canadian Jewish immigrant tended to hold on to these ideologies much more than had been the case with immigrants who had come in earlier periods of weaker partisan commitment. Finally, in those areas of English Canada where British influence dominated the social structure (as in Toronto, London, and Vancouver), the old-country class and group distinctions persisted for a long time. This tended to "keep Jews in their place"— which, in turn, encouraged protective self-isolation on the part of Jews.

Thus there was relatively little direct pressure on Jews to abandon their folkways, and especially their Yiddish language. The Jewish community of Winnipeg was a prime example of this temper of Canadian life which gave emphasis to ethnicity rather than religion *qua* faith. Even though the two founding cultures were distinguished both by linguistic differences and by the fact that the French were largely Roman Catholic and the British Protestant, the faith elements themselves were first and foremost defined in ethnic terms. By 1945 the Jews in the United States had developed into a distinct *religious* group, on a theoretical par with Protestants and Catholics (regardless of their own practice or non-practice of religion), while in Canada the emergence of the Jew as a religious third of the Judeo-Christian complex had not yet occurred in 1945. In the United States the separation of church and state had been built into its constitution; in Canada such a separation was slow to emerge. In Quebec the Roman Catholic Church had a dominant position which was both cultural and political; in some cities in English Canada, such as Toronto, the Anglican Church over which the king or queen presided held a position of power; and in much of the countryside the amalgamated United Church was dominant. Thus the ethnic identity of the Jewish community was fairly secure, but its religious identity had a relatively low status, which as late as 1944 was expressed in Ontario by a provincial law making the teaching of Christianity in the public schools a matter of curricular obligation.

The ethnic identity of non-British and non-French minorities also made it easier to preserve existing power structures. At the end of the Second World War these structures clearly excluded Jews almost completely and often restricted their access to business and professional opportunities, to desirable living accommodations, and vacation resorts. Though anti-Semitism was no longer semi-officially countenanced (as it had been in Quebec and tolerated in the Social Credit Party in Alberta in the decades preceding), Jews found themselves clearly set apart in terms of peoplehood and not, as in America, as members of a religious faith. Their own internal organization thus favoured a comprehensive approach and made possible the effective re-establishment of the Canadian Jewish Congress as the single spokesman of Canadian Jewry — for this Jewry felt as one group, one people, a distinct minority in the world surrounding them. This became especially true after the rise of Adolf Hitler which galvanized the community into a fairly collective response.[3] In contrast, in the United States the synagogue was conceived to be the linchpin of Jewry; therefore no single comprehensive organizational structure was possible because the differences between synagogues and between religious and nonreligious institutions stood in the way. The American Jewish Conference, created to meet the war emergency, dissolved once its immediate aims had been met.

There had been notable attempts at Canadian interreligious and intercultural fraternization, but on the whole they remained marginal, so that at the end of the war the Jewish community, while living in legal freedom and with unlimited economic opportunities before it, felt itself still socially and politically isolated — a minority privileged to live in the ambience of Canadian freedom, but a minority nonetheless. It was a group which defined itself largely in terms of its ability to resist the negative impact of the outside world; consequently, it was habituated to looking over its shoulder for the approval of the Gentile or, at worst, for the effects of his disapproval. Young Jews were just beginning to graduate in larger numbers from universities and were entering the professions after their return from the war, and no one could at that time predict the phenomenal economic expansion which would benefit them in the next generation. In 1945 Canadian Jewry was emerging from its cocoon, unsure of its future but sure of its identity, experiencing a sense of continued pressure from the environment and looking for ways of dealing with it effectively. The full internal emancipation of Canadian Jewry had not as yet been completed when the war came to an end.

A number of factors combined to give post-war Canada a new look. One was the new global responsibility which the United States assumed and which perforce drew Canada into the vortex of international concerns. The formation of the United Nations was cordially endorsed by the federal government, and in time support for the world organization became a cornerstone of its policy. Lester B. Pearson, career diplomat and later to be prime minister of the country, received the Nobel Prize for his success in stabilizing international tensions in the wake of the Sinai Campaign of 1956. During the 1950s until the end of the 1960s Canada moved from being a dependency of the British Empire with narrow parochial interests to a position as a medium and mediating power on the world scene. At the same time it opened its borders to new immigrants (4 million in the next three decades, increasing its population by nearly 25 percent), pursuing a policy which recognized that a sparsely populated country could not expect to reach the acme of productivity and wealth and that, as long as the population of the nation was limited, its relatively small market would keep prices relatively high. In the years following 1945 the living standard of Canadians rose appreciably and dramatically, but it still lagged 10 to 20 percent behind that of the United States — a lag which expressed itself in high Canadian prices and lower Canadian wages.

For the new immigrants who came from southern and eastern Europe and included a sizable number of Jews liberated from concentration camps, Canada was a most desirable destination. While the United States had severely limited new immigration, Canada in comparison was wide open. It was at this point that Canadian and American and Jewish history began to diverge once again. In the United States new blood was relatively rare and in the total American Jewish population almost invisible, but on the Canadian scene the new Jewish immigrant was much in evidence. In a population of some 75,000 Jews in Toronto in 1945, thousands of arrivals with KZ numbers on their arms made an appreciable difference. In the 1950s French-speaking Jews came in large numbers from North Africa to Montreal, and Czech and Hungarian Jews fleeing Communist oppression migrated to Toronto. Some 10,000 American war resisters, among them a number of Jews, came to live permanently in Canada, and during the 1970s immigration of Soviet Jews began to increase. All the while there was migration or re-immigration from Israel, until the two largest communities in Montreal and Toronto had thousands of *yordim* (settlers from Israel) in their midst. Not all of these would admit that they desired to make Canada their permanent home, and only a portion of them were native Israelis. But their arrival made an important difference in that it added to the number of Canadian Jews who were familiar with Hebrew, even as the large-scale post-war immigration from Central Europe had greatly increased the use of Yiddish. (In the mid-1950s Melech Ravitch was writing in Montreal, and Toronto still had a Yiddish daily newspaper, but no English-language weekly — suggesting that the Yiddish-speaking minority had an important stake in their cultural past, while the English-speaking majority had not as yet acquired a compelling need for even a weekly Jewish perspective.)

The new immigrants fulfilled one other function both on the general and the Jewish scene. By the early 1960s, when they had taken root, their very presence broke through the more rigid patterns of the established community and gave it once again a multifaced aspect; they revitalized among the immigrants of former decades the emotional patterns of their European upbringing. More Jews now felt that they themselves had been liberated from the horrors of Nazism, that they themselves were, in a real way, survivors of the Holocaust. Knowledge and discussion of the Holocaust became an increasingly important subject of Canadian Jewish life. Added to this was, of course, the most important ingredient of post-war Jewish history, the establishment of the State of Israel. While it took a few years for Israel to make its full impact on the Diaspora, Canada, because of its ethnic orientation, was among the first to experience it fully, and its more recent European antecedents prevented problems of dual loyalty from emerging seriously. Love of Israel and Zionism were the accepted mode of Jewish life. Perhaps only with the exception of South African Jewry (whose agenda was somewhat different from that of Canadian Jewry) there was no country in the world in which Zionism was embraced with greater enthusiasm and Israel more deeply loved and defended than in Canada.

Most important, the new immigrants brought with them a self-assertiveness which had been largely lacking from the more staid expressions of Jewish life in the past. The war and its aftermath were thus a true watershed for Canadian Jews. In earlier immigrant phases the newcomer had tried to fit himself into an established pattern, especially into its economic traditions. The Canadian Jew himself now became an important fashioner of new social patterns and was able to participate in the enormous economic advance the country was about to experience. Frontier societies meant the opening of new and uncharted enterprises and the wide use of risk capital. The older families, whose fathers and mothers had worked assiduously at establishing a good business and had looked after fairly successful stores, were hesitant to risk the savings of one or two lifetimes in these beckoning ventures. The newcomers, on the other hand, had no such hesitation and to a significant degree it was they who, in relatively short order, anticipated the great prizes which the booming Canadian economy in the first post-war years was about to bestow. They were all desperately poor at first and many of them remained at the bottom of the social ladder, but there were others who grasped the great opportunities and participated in the nation's unprecedented growth. Their success rather rapidly broke down the old social structures. *Yichus* (family connection and background), which once had been the most important accreditation of persons, now took second place to wealth and success. In the generation after the war the Jewish community moved from a moderately situated class of citizens to a distinct middle-class and often upper-middle-class status, headed by a few barons of economic power. This was most evident in Montreal and Toronto, which was emerging as the new financial centre of Canada. It was somewhat less spectacular in other communities where immigration and economic expansion were slower, but it held true also for the West which exhibited significant repetitions of the eastern models. The numbers were smaller, but the patterns persisted.

Although the previously established structures in the Jewish community maintained their identity, there were now significant shifts within the community. This became most obvious in Toronto, which began the period as a distinct second to Montreal (where most of the national Jewish organizations were headquartered) and which in 1975 was equalling it and giving promise of surpassing it as the leading Jewish community in the country.

One effect of the new immigration was a re-emphasis on the religious aspects of Jewish life. As they did in Israel, the immigrants greatly enhanced the power of Orthodoxy which (in contrast to the situation in the United States) had a position of established strength in Canadian Jewry. Not only was this position now strengthened by immigration; it also led to the sharpening of ideological differences. While a similar development was to be experienced in some American communities (notably in New York), intrareligious cooperation there had been generally accepted as a pragmatic procedure. In Canada, however, a process of religious polarization took place. It was emphasized by the power of Israel's rabbinic establishment which exerted its influence far beyond Israel's borders. The repeated attempt to give the National Religious Affairs Committee of the Canadian Jewish Congress a format which would approximate that of the Synagogue Council in the United States met with failure because of the principled rejection of the traditionalists. They felt that their cooperation in such a venture would appear to signify implicit recognition of Conservative and Reform Jews.

Although in most Canadian communities this was not a major problem, it became one in Toronto in the 1960s because of the presence and strength of recently arrived ultra-Orthodox groups and ideologies whose persistence moved the moderate traditionalists appreciably to the right. It was a development not unlike that experienced in Israel where pressure from the Neturei Karta was felt in the Agudah, which in turn would pressure the Mizrachi, which in turn would pressure its coalition partner in the government — leading to the popular saying current in the 1960s that when the Rebbitzin Blau (wife of the Neturei Karta leader) raised her voice, Golda Meir (then prime minister) would begin to worry. In similar fashion Hungarian Hasidim (even though they themselves hardly participated in communal life) had their point of view expressed in forums far removed from their own spiritual habitat. The domino effect of international politics was operative in Jewish religious life in Canada as it was in Israel.

In fact, all religious life stood to the right of its U.S. counterpart. The Reform movement had briefly attempted a radical position when, in the 1930s, Toronto's Holy Blossom Temple had established Sunday services, buttressed by an anti-Zionist ideology. But at the conclusion of the war these ventures to the left were quickly reversed and Canadian Reform was in many ways more like American Conservatism than American Reform. Canadian Conservative Jews experienced an unprecedented growth in the post-war years and became an influential factor in the Jewish religious life of the country. They, too, moved at first to the right — but this movement was halted by the polarization which took place in the face of strengthened Orthodox ideology. Now suddenly the Conservatives were classified (by the traditionalists) with the Reformers, and a brief attempt to distance themselves from the latter was firmly rejected by the Orthodox leadership to whom they remained dissidents whose degree of dissent did not matter. In consequence, the Conservatives now made a turn to the left and liberalized their attitudes vis-à-vis the Reformers and in many instances began to stand with them. Meanwhile Conservative day schools (at first the sole domain of the Orthodox) grew apace and obtained community funding or, as in Quebec, government funding.

In 1974 Reform Jewry, too, established its first day school when the rabbis of the five Reform synagogues in Toronto helped to found the Leo Baeck Day School. Not that this path-breaking venture signified the complete erosion of an earlier liberal position which considered day schools regressive, divisive, exclusivist, and inimical to the general path of Canadian Jewish life. There were still enough people left (and not only in the Reform sector) to whom day schools were anathema. But while the Orthodox and Conservatives quickly overcame this ideological negation, this was not the case in the Reform movement where, by a long trad-ition and American precedent, day schools (also called parochial schools, with all the pejorative implications of that term) were nonexistent. At the present time, it may be predicted that Reform congregations as congre-gations will support the new school, which, however, had great difficulty in securing communal support. The reasons for this development exceed the limits of this discussion, but it could not be overlooked that the prejudices against Reform as a religious group (not against Reform Jews as communal leaders both politically and economically) were hard to eradicate. Holy Blossom Temple, long known as one of North America's prestigious synagogues, was commonly referred to as "the Church on the Hill." It was an expression which portrayed the old rejectionist attitude of much of the community toward the Liberal Jewish lifestyle and ideology. That attitude had not disappeared by the late 1970s.

Nonetheless, Reform synagogues, of which there were only three in 1945 — in Montreal, Toronto, and Hamilton — now spread throughout most Canadian cities, but in all instances they remained in the minority. The general public and the Jewish community frequently turned to them for communal leadership, but the bulk of Jewry belonged either to Conservative and Orthodox or to no religious institutions. It was a development not likely to alter perceptibly in the immediate future.

Increased immigration and the general expansion of the Canadian economy after 1945 favoured the entrepreneurial class in which Jews, by long tradition, were prominent. In the larger urban centres they now moved from the edge of poverty which they had occupied in the 1920s and 1930s into the middle class and upper-middle class, many of them becoming well-to-do in the process, especially those connected with land development and building trades. The drive for higher education proceeded apace, and soon it was an accepted fact that Jewish children, if reasonably endowed, would finish high school and go to university. However, the American hope of sending children to prestigious universities in the East or West, away from home, found no parallel in Canada. On the whole, local universities became the place where one went to school, and although McGill and the University of Toronto had a superior scholastic rating, going to university was in itself a badge of distinction and opened the way to professional advancement; one did not have to go away to become accredited at home. Only in advanced degrees was a foreign address of some significance, but this, too, was slow in coming.

This rootedness in the home base was in part a reflection of an absence of mobility. Certainly there was nothing that approached the internal post-war American migration to the West and Southwest of the United States, nor did major Canadian cities develop suburban sprawl with its dislocation of community patterns. True, Vancouver became the target of general as well as Jewish migration and its wealth rose dramatically. True also that young people increasingly left the small communities where but a few Jewish families had resided for a generation or more and went to the large city. And finally, in response to renewed nationalism in Quebec, a steady migration of Montreal Jews to Toronto and farther west decreased the Jewish base in Montreal in the 1970s. But none of this fundamentally affected the pervasive psychological status of Canadian Jews who generally were content to stay where they were and moved only because of marriage or particular business and professional interests — and in such cases the United States was usually the goal, with physicians a particularly mobile group.

On the whole, the migration to the United States was steady but minor, with a brief period of notable exception in the 1960s when people with secondary degrees were attracted to American universities and other funded institutions and organizations and left Canada permanently. Subsequently, this "brain drain," as it became known, caused Canadian universities to spend a great deal of money to reverse the trend. Their effort became successful toward the end of the 1960s when at the height of the Vietnam disillusionment and racial tensions, as well as of the increase of big-city crime in the United States, many Canadian professionals began to return. American professionals joined them and assumed significant business and university posts. By 1970 many American professors (and a goodly number of Jews among them) were found in the expanding network of Canadian universities, a fact which caused a great deal of public discussion in the face of the increasingly nationalistic temper of the country. It was not directed at Jews *qua* Jews but against Americans, and it became a facet of the trend which saw Canadians define their Canadianism to a significant degree in terms of anti- or non-Americanism. Toward the middle of the 1970s unemployment had caused sufficient concern in the country to restrict immigration in general and to restrain the free interplay of professional appointments. This brought American migration to Canada to a near halt. Moreover, reduced public funding and a government-enforced anti-inflation program caused Canadian earning power to lag behind its American counterpart. By 1978 the flow was once again from Canada to the United States, albeit at a lower rate than fifteen years before.

The most important single development in the demographic area was doubtlessly the rise of Quebec nationalism. Fanned by a sense of general economic frustration, an intellectual elite who found themselves disadvantaged by the power barons of Anglo-Saxon origin surged to new political heights in the 1960s, and there was a distinct possibility that the Parti Québécois might in fact assume power. But the victory of Robert Bourassa in the provincial elections of 1973, on a non-secessionist platform, halted this trend at least temporarily. Yet by the mid 1970s it was rising again, and the province instituted a series of measures designed to make Quebec a predominantly French-speaking province by law, with English relegated to a distinctly second-class position. This policy was concretized in the highly controversial Bill 22 and caused the Anglophone minority to reassess its status.

At this writing a new election in Quebec in November 1976 has in fact brought the separatist Parti Québécois to power. Its leader, René Lévesque, campaigned on the promise that he would hold a province-wide referendum on Quebec's independence within two years of election. The result, though it did not make Quebec's separation from Canada a certainty, created great unrest in the Jewish community. There was serious doubt among its members about a Jewish future in the province; they wondered how well Jews could integrate themselves into a society which was avowedly French and Catholic.*

Their memories of the 1930s, when the Duplessis government had not discouraged anti-Semitic expressions in the province and especially not in the countryside, were now revived once again. Heretofore Jews had largely identified with the Anglophone minority and chosen English as their primary language, a fact which was not substantially altered by the influx of French-speaking North African Jews. Jews felt that they would

---

* By mid-1976 the Lévesque government had introduced an even more far-reaching language bill (known as Bill 1 and later as Bill 101), the implications of which were perceived by many Jews to undermine their future in Quebec. As a result of spreading uncertainty, young Jewish professionals and others with economic mobility began to leave the province in increasing numbers. There was no question that the face of the Jewish community of Montreal would be permanently altered, but the full extent of these changes could not be predicted at this writing.

be the first targets of a successful Quebec separation, and significant numbers of them began to look westward to re-establish a more secure future. In many ways they came to feel that even in the freedom of Canada they were still strangers in a strange land.

But even before 1976 it had become evident that Montreal had lost its two hundred years of pre-eminence in Canadian Jewish life to Toronto.[4] National institutions were still headquartered in the Quebec metropolis, but much of the de facto leadership had moved to Toronto. That in time the national organizations would have to follow suit appeared likely, though the traditionally slow pace of change in institutional life would prevent any sudden dramatic shift. The Canadian Jewish Congress was still housed in the splendid facility named after Samuel Bronfman, its long-time president, the founder of the Seagram empire and a commanding figure in Jewish life for a generation. With his passing Montreal's hegemony also began to fade, and Congress leadership was now shared with other communities. Similarly, the Canada-Israel Committee, established after years of intraorganizational rivalries, still had its headquarters in Montreal. However, in 1976 this key institution of Canadian Jewry, which represented the total community vis-à-vis the public and the government in all matters relating to Israel, was headed by two co-chairmen residing in Toronto.[5]

Jewish patterns began to loosen and change, along with the structure of Canadian society at large. Where formerly Jews were rigorously excluded from sensitive posts and key positions in government and in universities, by the 1970s they had reached many positions of eminence. David Lewis became leader of the New Democratic Party (the third of the three major federal parties); social worker David Barrett became premier of British Columbia; a number of provinces included Jews in their cabinets, or had Jews as leaders of opposition or third parties. Thus in 1976, with the Conservatives in power in Ontario, the opposition New Democrats were headed by Stephen Lewis (David's son) and the Liberals by Dr. Stuart Smith, the former a Toronto lawyer and the latter a Hamilton psychiatrist. David Croll, once mayor of Windsor, Lazarus Phillips, and Carl Goldenberg were members of the Senate, and Windsor MP Herbert Gray had been the first Jew to join the federal Cabinet (the second, Barnett Danson, Minister of Defence, had been the founder of a Toronto synagogue). In 1961 Louis Rasminsky was appointed head of the Bank of Canada (similar in function to the Federal Reserve Bank in the United States). The judiciary also included Jews in increasing numbers on every level, culminating in the elevation of Samuel Freedman as chief justice of Manitoba and in 1974 in the appointment of Bora Laskin as chief justice of the Supreme Court of Canada.

The smaller communities had frequently seen Jewish mayors, such as in Thunder Bay (where Justice Laskin's brother was mayor for many years), in Saskatoon, and later in Ottawa itself. Eventually even in traditionally "WASP" Toronto the old pattern was finally broken when Nathan Phillips acceded to the mayor's chair and held it for four consecutive terms. After his departure from office, the city bestowed on him the unusual honour of naming its principal square after him. Nathan Phillips Square in front of the famed city hall he had helped bring into being is a vivid reminder both of a man and of a new era in the acceptance of Jews in public life. Not much later, Philip Givens, prominent Zionist activist, became the city's mayor, graduating later to federal and provincial politics and all the while remaining a vigorous spokesman of the Jewish community — a combination which would have been thought unlikely, if not impossible, only a generation before.

While all of this heralded a significant levelling of traditional differences, it did not mean a fundamental rearrangement of the power bases of Canadian life. Heavy industry and the large corporations, as well as the chartered banks, remained essentially outside the realm of Jewish influence. There was no Jewish-owned equivalent of the *New York Times* in Canada, nor was there an independent entertainment industry of sufficient impact which could dominate public taste in the manner of Hollywood. In any case, private influence in the arts was limited because of the public ownership of the Canadian Broadcasting Corporation, which itself was remarkably free of top Jewish personnel. But Jews participated freely and contributed outstandingly to science, art, and literature. Leonard Cohen and Irving Layton were Canada's best-read poets, and the stature of Abraham Klein as a major literary figure was being recognized slowly yet surely by the mid-1970s. Mordecai Richler was one of Canada's most popular novelists and certainly the one most widely read abroad; Sigmund Samuel and Sam and Ayala Zacks became Canada's foremost private art collectors and donors; and on stage such names as John Hirsch, Maureen Forrester (who had been converted to Judaism), Johnny Wayne and Frank Schuster, and theatrical entrepreneur Ed Mirvish became household words.

In the post-war years Canadian Jewry had advanced from a small and largely parochial community into a vigorous and vibrant society of Canadian citizens who were taking their place in the larger environment with great zest, and who, while making advances in the economic and public arenas, nonetheless maintained a remarkable identity as an ethno-religious unit in the Canadian fabric.

After the Second World War the inner structure of Canadian Jewry did not so much alter as it came to intensify its potential. The impact of the State of Israel was, of course, a prime factor. In 1945 many Canadian Jews still saw themselves in their traditional *Galut* role — legally free, but emotionally and practically circumscribed by the surrounding Gentile environment. This produced a relative political quiescence on their part, and when this was disturbed it occasionally tended to cause widespread unease among the Jews. Thus, the often vigorous critique of the establishment by Abraham L. Feinberg, rabbi of Holy Blossom in Toronto, was material both for newspaper headlines and for a rise in Jewish insecurity. But such misgivings yielded to increasing self-assertion, especially after the Six Day War in 1967, when proud identification with the valour and courage of the Israelis gave the Jews a new image, not the least in their own eyes.

Visits to Israel, increasing aliyah, and vigorous fundraising became a part and soon the very centre of Jewish life, and in time a new apparatus was developed by the three major Canadian organizations — the Canadian Jewish Congress, B'nai Brith, and the Canadian Zionist Federation (comprising all Zionist parties and groupings) — to represent the Jewish cause to the public, and particularly to the government. They established the Canada-Israel Committee (CIC) as the chief spokesman and agency of Canadian Jewry in all matters touching on Israel. Its most dramatic impact came in 1975 when it dealt with a proposed United Nations Conference on Crime Prevention which was to be held in Toronto in the spring of that year. The Palestinian Liberation Organization (PLO), recently given observer status at the United Nations, was slated to attend the conference, and this announcement elicited an enormous amount of reaction and resentment. A nationwide campaign, spearheaded by the Canada-Israel Committee, in time involved the premiers of various provinces, engendered wide newspaper support, and showed a country-wide aversion to the proposed participation by the PLO in the conference. After much hesitation the government withdrew the invitation to the United Nations, and the conference was moved to Switzerland. There was little question that the open and strong stance taken by the Jewish community was an important factor in this development.

Yet as late as 1976 the battle for complete self-assertion had not been won entirely. When, prior to the Olympic Games, it was proposed to hold a public Jewish memorial service for the eleven martyrs who had been slain at the Munich Olympics four years before, there was significant resistance on the part of members of the Jewish establishment in Montreal who proposed to soft-pedal the issue. In time their objections were overcome and, when the prime minister participated in a moving service which attracted 5,000 persons and worldwide media coverage, another significant step toward the formation of a firmer Jewish self-image had been taken.

A good deal of the credit for this spirit of self-assertiveness must be given to the new immigrants, and especially to the survivors of the Holocaust. They reacted quickly and vigorously (some critics claimed, too quickly and too vigorously) to any attack on Israel or on Jews in general. Thus high emotion characterized the Jewish community in its long controversy with the United Church of Canada, whose principal publication took a strong editorial stance against Israel's policies after 1967. The newcomers also reacted vociferously and strongly against outcroppings of anti-Semitism. The most famous incident in the 1960s which brought these sentiments into visible relief occurred in Toronto when a neo-Nazi party staged a public demonstration in a downtown park. Toronto Jews, led by survivor groups, came out physically to prevent such gatherings from taking place, a change from previously accepted reactions which had confined themselves primarily to briefs and presentations but had eschewed physical confrontations. The hesitant policy of the local Canadian Jewish Congress in the Allan Gardens matter brought it to its nadir of effectiveness and caused it to lose much of the internal credit it had built up in previous decades. Though the Congress would take some time recovering, the result was, in the long run, positive. Not only were the established ways of the official community infused with new vigour and pride but the more recently arrived elements in the Jewish community were given a larger voice in the formation of Congress policy.

A somewhat different controversy surrounded the proposed federal legislation which was to cope with certain public expressions of group hatred and especially with anti-Semitism. The so-called Hate Bill was helped through Parliament upon the advice of a Congress committee under the leadership of Professor (later Dean) Maxwell Cohen. But the act remained controversial. It had been opposed by civil libertarians — Jews among them — who claimed that it encroached on free speech. In the middle 1970s it was again in the limelight when it was to be applied to telephoned hate messages. The act became once more the target of newspaper editorials which raised the old arguments and, in addition, stressed that a law that had hardly been applied was useless and in fact counterproductive. It was a foregone conclusion, however, that the majority of the Jewish community would remain strongly in favour of the maintenance of such a law and be outspoken in its defence.

Related to this spirit were increasing demands for demonstrations in public places, preferably under the glare of television lights and media coverage. Nowhere did this bear greater fruits than in the events surrounding the visit of Soviet Premier Alexei Kosygin to Canada. In every community where he appeared thousands of Jews marched through the streets. In Toronto, under his window on the twenty-seventh floor at the Inn on the Park, 10,000 Jews assembled to listen to Elie Wiesel, who some years ago had first stirred the conscience of world Jewry and urged it to labour for the liberation of Russian Jews. "One, two, three, set my people free!" the marchers sang. In a memorable demonstration in the nation's capital, traffic was brought to a standstill when many thousands of Jews who had come from various parts of the country by plane, train, and bus reiterated their unshakable support of Soviet Jewry. They held midnight prayer services in front of Parliament and beleaguered Kosygin's car as it drove by. What impact this unified expression of Jewish will had on the emigration of Russian Jews, which began shortly thereafter, will not be known until the Kremlin's files are opened to future historians. But Canadian Jews felt that they had contributed to this historic turn of events and had, indeed, helped to swing open the iron gates that had imprisoned their brethren for so long. (It might be added that when, later on, increasing numbers of Soviet Jews arrived in Canada for permanent settlement, there developed a gap between the ideal and the real. As happened in Israel, the absorption of the newcomers was not easy, and but a fraction of the attention that had been focused on them while they were still in Soviet Russia was now given them upon their arrival in freedom.)

Fundraising for Israel became a major preoccupation of the Canadian Jewish community. It was said that, except for South Africa, Canadian Jewry raised a larger per capita share on behalf of Israel than any other national group in the world. Every Israeli university, many yeshivot, and other institutions had branches in the country which helped them raise capital and operating funds. It was inevitable that this outflow would sooner or later collide with the needs of the Canadian Jewish community itself, especially when federations began to replace the synagogue as the centre of power and controlled the purse strings of Jewish education, whose costs were spiralling along with expanded programs and galloping inflation. In 1975 these tensions were becoming greater rather than smaller, for the traditional emphasis on ethnicity had favoured the primacy of fundraising for Israel proper, while the cultural and social institutions of the community had a harder time gaining their due and frequently obtained their funds through being tacked on to campaigns on behalf of Israel. The satisfaction of these dual needs was still in the future and its outcome, at best, uncertain.

As late as 1957 an interdenominational commission sponsored by the Canadian Council of Churches proposed that the Protestant denominations in Canada should tackle seriously the problem of Christianizing the Jews. "We must look upon the Jewish people [it said] as individuals. They carry their burden of sin and frustrations even as the rest of us. The Jew is a person. We must treat him as such. Wherever we find him, consider him, as all others, as a potential child of God." Fewer than twenty years later such efforts at conversion were abandoned by the official churches, although small "Jews for Jesus" groups had made their appearance and briefly moved the Jewish communities to putative countermeasures.

But while conversion posed no serious threat to Jewish identity, mixed marriage did; it was steeply on the rise in smaller communities and less so in larger ones. By 1975 it was said to have reached 18 percent on a national basis, but these statistics were not conclusive. Some of the Gentile mates converted to Judaism; in Toronto alone each year some seventy-five or more non-Jews were admitted to Judaism, after passing through Conservative and Reform instructional courses. The Orthodox sidestepped the problem and referred potential converts either to New York or to Israel. The rise of out-marriages was, of course, the direct correlate of Jews moving into an open society where religious and ethnic affiliations counted for less and less. Mixed marriage was especially high in British Columbia, but no community was exempt from its increased occurrence.

In fact, the differences between Eastern and Western Canada began to level off as internal migration increased, and with the rise of Canadian nationalism and protectionism the North-South interfaces with the United States remained at their previous levels. Because of its immigration patterns Canada had not experienced the "lost generation" of the American 1920s and 1930s; instead, Canadian Jewry had progressed directly from an immigrant to a self-assertive, middle-class community. It was, in the mid-1970s, an intensely Israel-oriented and self-identified community, with larger numbers of students going to Jewish day schools, with Judaic university programs increasing, and with a few scholars like philosopher Emil Fackenheim and halachist Gedaliah Felder acquiring worldwide reputations. But the process of general assimilation went forward nonetheless, though its negative aspects were as yet less evident in Canada than in the United States. Ben Kayfetz categorized Canadian Jewry in the mid-1950s as "a community with an interest in Judaism much more self-conscious and articulate than that of 20 or 25 years ago, though not as confident and as assured of its goals." Twenty years later Saul Hayes, retiring after a distinguished career of more than thirty years as the executive director of the Canadian Jewish Congress, posed the problem facing Canadian Jewry in this fashion: "The final question is: In our post-Christian, post-Jewish society where humanism, doctrines of equality, real concern for identity and rights characterize our world, is Canadian Jewry endangered or is it strengthened as a vibrant and viable group in our present secular society? As usual, history as it unfolds alone will provide the answer."

Biblical Inquiries

The Wandering Aramean

The 26th Chapter of Deuteronomy contains the only prayers in the Torah which are fixed precisely. We are presented with two formulae which are to be spoken verbatim, one relating to first fruits, the other to tithes. The prayers are clear in intent and language, except for the opening sentence of the first, which is highly ambiguous and has received the most contradictory interpretations. It is of more than passing interest to re-open a study of this problem, for one may suspect that this, the first obligatory prayer of recorded Jewish tradition, aims at a significant statement of the Jew's relationship to God and to himself.

On offering of one's first fruits, the Jew was to speak the following:

אֲרַמִּי אֹבֵד אָבִי וַיֵּרֶד מִצְרַיְמָה וַיָּגׇר שָׁם בִּמְתֵי מְעָט וַיְהִי
שָׁם לְגוֹי גָּדוֹל עָצוּם וָרָב.

The Jewish Publication Society translates this, much like most current versions, as follows:

> A wandering Aramean was my father, and he went down
> into Egypt, and sojourned there, few in number; and he
> became there a nation, great, mighty and populous.

It is not generally recognized that this translation is a relatively recent rendering of the Hebrew, dating back only to lbn Ezra. In this interpretation the Aramean is generally said to be Jacob, for he had dwelt in Aram, and his mother had come from there.[1] The traditional understanding of the text was different. From the Targumim to Sifri, from the Haggadah to Rashi, the words ארמי אבד אבי were understood quite differently. Instead of אבי being the subject and ארמי אבד a predicative expression (as in JPS), the older tradition makes ארמי the subject, אבד a causative verb, and אבי its object.

Thus, Onkelos understood the verse to mean: "The Aramean sought to destroy my father, who went down to Egypt, etc." Targum Jonathan follows a similar line, as do many commentators thereafter. "The Aramean" is generally understood to have been Laban whose wiles nearly wrecked the life of Jacob ("the father"). The nearest thing to an official commentary on this passage is the Passover Haggadah, which follows the Targumim and explains that Laban, when he pursued Jacob (Genesis 31:22), בקש לעקור את הכל tried to undo everything that Jacob had achieved and desired. However, God appeared to Laban in a dream (just as He would later appear to Balaam) and prevented the Aramean's plans from being executed (Genesis 31:24).

Sifri, Rashi, Malbim and others support this interpretation; some, like Abarbanel, offer it as an alternative, while yet others, like Abraham ibn Ezra, Sforno, and Rashbam, feel that אבד can only be a *kal*, and never a causative form, that such a form would have read מאבד or האביד for both of which there is biblical precedent. Sifte Hakhamim, as always, defends Rashi, even though he admits the awkwardness of the grammatical construction, and Wolf Heidenheim contends that אבד is indeed a causative form, albeit of the rare *po'el* conjugation.

After listening to the arguments on both sides one cannot help but feel that no clear decision is possible on a purely linguistic, grammatical basis. On the face of it, the Ibn Ezra–JPS axis has much in its favour, but then, who would gainsay that Targum and Midrash did not have a keen ear for the meaning of the biblical text? Moreover, the Massoretic signs clearly separate ארמי from אבד אבי, as if to underscore that ארמי must be the subject of the sentence. Apparently the ancients saw no objection to אבד as a causative verb. At best, the dispute is a stand-off on this basis, and we must look elsewhere to obtain light on our problem.

Many of the commentators recognized that in some way the total text had to be taken into consideration. A Jew is to speak the formula, starting with these ambiguous words — but he is to follow them with a statement about the descent to Egypt. What does the ארמי have to do with Egypt? Much depends on whether one believes the word to apply to Jacob (or even Abraham as Rashbam suggests) or to Laban.

The "Jacob school" feels that the connection exists because he came as a poor man both to Aram and to Egypt (but he left rich, says Biur, which takes the punch out of the whole verse!); or perhaps it refers to Israel's homelessness in both instances (Abarbanel, Hirsch).

The "Laban school" finds the connection in persecution and oppression (Rashi), or in the temptation of idolatry to which Aram and Egypt exposed Israel (Lehmann), or in other fanciful and ingenious explanations.[2] The most noteworthy of these is found in the Passover Haggadah. On the phrase וירד מצרימה the Haggadah comments אנוס על פי הדבור — forced by divine command. Israel's temptation by Laban as well as his descent into Egypt were inescapable events in his life, for they were willed by God. However, this line of *midrash* still leaves the connection or the two parts of the Jacob story vague, and gives us no further insight into the meaning of ארמי אבד אבי.

To find an avenue of new understanding we must free ourselves from the traditional approaches to our textual problem and must look at the whole sentence afresh. It seems clear that somehow the Aram and Egypt episodes stand in some relation to each other, and it seems equally clear that the phrase וירד מצרימה will yield no further insights. But what of the end of the statement: ויהי שם וכו׳ "and he became there a nation great, mighty and populous?"

At first hearing, these words have the connotation of grateful remembrance. Look at what happened to the small company who went to Egypt! Look how with God's help it grew and prospered! It waxed not only גדול; it also became עצום, and even רב! It is here that we come upon the first clue to our mystery. On the surface the three terms of aggrandizement appear to have nothing further to say to us, but when we look at them more closely they leave us with an uneasy feeling that perchance something else was to be conveyed.

Let us take a closer look at the three words. גדול means "great" in the sense that we use it in English. It refers to inner stature and is usually so used in the Bible. Significantly, the Haggadah says that Israel could be called "great" because during the Egyptian sojourn the people managed to keep themselves מצוינים, distinctly separated from their environment (which is in fact an interesting side comment on what the Ba'al Haggadah considered the essence of Jewish greatness!).

On the other hand, עצום and רב carry no implication of inner greatness. They are terms of external prowess. Ofttimes the Bible — whose authors were occasionally also impressed with "bigness"— uses these words as attributes denoting success, but not always! Especially עצום has overtones of crude strength; the basic term, עצם — bone — shines through the adjective. עצום has connotations of bony, animal prowess, which was not the kind of attribute of which Israel's historians would in their best moments be proud. As a verb, עצם has a distinctly unpleasant side meaning. Isaiah uses it in the sense of "closing the eyes" (29:10; 33:15), as if being עצום and being spiritually sensitive will not go together.[3] Pharaoh is never worried because Israel became גדול — he acted only when it became רב ועצום (Exodus 1:9). To use the Haggadah's view: as long as Israel was גדול — or in modern terms, as long as it was conscious of its own nature and purpose — it was no threat to Egypt. But עצום ורב are descriptive of assimilation to foreign values, and even as Israel becomes more and more identified with them, its environment reacts with hostility.

Now it is not suggested that this is what the text says. It is suggested, however, that the ancient ear, finely attuned to the nuances of the language, heard two things, as if in a word play. גדול עצום ורב could be a progression of power (the obvious meaning), but it could also be subtle critical irony, descriptive of inner deterioration: "We were a small company when we came down to Egypt, and thereafter we became great; then our muscles swelled (at the expense of our inner qualities), and *in fine* we even became "big." What comes next is not hard to fathom: all our prowess availed us nothing and we suffered bitterly for it.

There is an ambiguity in these words for all who listen intently; and we have no doubt that the ancients heard it well. The migration into Egypt was apparently a huge success, what with royal connections and splendid, rich lands; but on closer consideration it turned out to be a "descent" indeed, a descent into spiritual alienation and loss of freedom. The Jacob-Israel who went into Egypt was an אבד, much like the Jacob of the Aram interlude.

And now we return to the original query: how are we to understand ארמי אבד אבי? The three alliterative words — like גדול עצום ורב — are a subtle play in ambiguity. There was that old interlude in our Patriarch's past which involved double deceit and flight from self. Perhaps it was all Laban's fault, but then perhaps the errant feature was Jacob's — and we can't be sure. There is the threefold backdrop of fateful history: "There is the Aramean — there is perdition (however caused) — there is my Father."[4] Make of it what you will. Buber and Rosenzweig catch the staccato quality of the text better than anyone else: *Abgeschweifter Aramäer mein Ahm.*

The solution to our problem is, then, *not to be found in one or the other of the traditionally proffered explanations, but in both at the same time,* two totally separate and distinct meanings are contained simultaneously in the text and both are meant to be conveyed. One says, "My father was nearly overcome by Aram, and later, despite all his strength, he was nearly destroyed by Egypt — but God saved him." The other says, "My father nearly lost himself in Aram, and later almost lost his soul in Egypt. But he returned to God and He turned to him."

This ambiguity of meaning has often existed in Jewish history. When calamities befell us, was it because the Aramean sought to destroy us, or because we ourselves wandered astray? When is Israel the subject of אבד, and when its object? The ear which has listened to the Prophets will not fail to detect the question behind the affirmation of this, our first fixed prayer.

In Defence of the *Erev Rav* — ערב רב

*T*he עֵרֶב רַב mentioned in Exodus 12:38 has over the centuries acquired a poor reputation. Not only is this unjustified, but on the contrary, ערב רב ought to constitute an important positive element in the liberation story of our people.

The expression is usually taken to mean the "mixed multitude" that went with Israel out of Egypt. This translation conveniently, although not accurately, turns the Hebrew adjective רַב (many or great) into a noun (multitude), and the Hebrew noun עֵרֶב (mixture) into an adjective (mixed). More properly the text should be rendered to say that "a large agglomeration," i.e., of non-Israelite peoples, left the land at the hour of midnight. This is the way the Targumim have it; they translate נוכראין סגיאין, many strangers.

The word עֵרֶב occurs four other times in the Bible in the meaning of "mixture of nations"— in Jeremiah 25:20 and 50:37, Ezekiel 30:5, and Nehemiah 13:3. Although in some of these passages the textual reading is in doubt,[1] few have advanced a sustained argument which would suggest that the ערב of the Exodus was not precisely what the Masoretic text says it was.[2]

Abraham Geiger is a major exception. He wanted to read the two words as one, ערברב,[3] which would have put it into a class with such *pe'alal* expressions as ירקרק (Leviticus 13:49), חמרמר (Lamentations 1:20), סחרחר (Psalms 38:11), and, of course, אספסוף (Numbers 11:4). Geiger's suggestion has the piquancy of onomatopoeia, suggesting the English *riffraff*, and he has the Aramaic equivalent in his favour. Both

ערברבין and ערבוביא are well-known terms, the latter having survived in current Hebrew usage, albeit in the transposed sense of "chaos."

But whether two words or one, the general meaning of the "mixed multitude" was fairly undisputed among our sages. They took ערב רב as having uncomplimentary overtones and identified the term with אספסוף, the mutinous rabble referred to in Numbers 11:14. Rashi, Ibn Ezra, and a host of others so state, and Abarbanel, anticipating Geiger, says: "These are the ערבוביא of Egypt and other nations who mingled with them, the אספסוף who were amongst them, who were not of the children of Israel." Eleazar Kalir similarly speaks of the ערב as catching Israel in their net of deceit and idolatry.[4]

But if one reads the passage without the prejudice of later conceptions, there is nothing in it which has a derogatory connotation. No indication here of riffraff, just a statement of fact: the children of Israel were not alone in the moment of liberation, others too sought and gained freedom. Who the others were we do not know. Doubtlessly there were many Israelites who had intermarried, as Ibn Ezra suggests and as the parallel use of the term ערב in Nehemiah 13:3 makes us inclined to agree. But at the time of the Exodus, marriage outside the tribes was neither unusual nor was it considered wrong, for did not Moses himself marry a foreigner? Furthermore, we may be sure that other slaves too shook off their chains in the night of liberation and that they too acquired possessions from the Egyptians.[5]

There is even a tradition that the ערב was so large that it outnumbered the Israelites. The Mekhilta records an argument between no lesser luminaries than R. Ishmael, R. Akiba, and R. Jonathan. All three are careful to relate the רב in the ערב רב to the 600,000 Israelites of the Exodus. All three sages hold that Israel was outnumbered. One rabbi puts the ratio at 2:1, the second at 4:1, and the third at 6:1! And the passage does not stand alone.

This should give us thought. There was apparently a time when the ערב was remembered as more than an adjunct, though numerous, element in the Exodus, when its role was such as to give the event a far more universal aspect than we have since come to consider it. It stands to reason that this tradition did not identify the ערב with the riffraff of Numbers 11:4. The argument in the Mekhilta and in related texts, however fanciful its figures, precludes such identification, and close attention to the Targum will make the difference doubly clear.[6]

For, as indicated, Onkelos knows the derogatory term עִרְבּוּרְבִין, but applies it only to explain אֲסַפְסֻף. He does not use it to translate רב ערב, where such translation would almost have suggested itself. Instead, he renders the latter as "many strangers"— a very proper descriptive expression without any overtones whatsoever.

What are we to conclude from this? Firstly, and obviously, that while Israel was the centre of the Exodus, its humanly and divinely motive power, there were large numbers of others who joined. There was a broader scope to the Exodus which earlier generations still sensed. Freedom had, as it always will have, a pervasive, universal appeal. It was natural that it should be heard by many who were sighing under the yoke of the Egyptian oppressor.

Secondly — and here the text speaks with the muted voice of suggestive homily — perhaps without the ערב רב the Exodus might not have taken place at all! The Midrash enumerates the likely reasons why Israel merited liberation.[7] May we not add another which is already hinted at by tradition? Moses, the Midrash tells us, literally persuaded an unwilling God to allow the ערב to join the march of liberation. Like Abraham before Sodom, he confronted the Almighty, arguing mercy with the All-merciful in behalf of strangers.[8]

Perhaps it was the thought of others which made our fathers worthy of the great moment. For is it not true that only as we think of the רב ערב, the oppressed multitudes of men, only as we include them in our prayers, dreams, and struggles, can we hope to pass through the Red Sea of our own troubles?

Pharaoh's Hardened Heart

*I*n ten different places the Torah tells us that God hardened Pharaoh's heart. The problem arising from these passages has confronted every student of the Bible. If God made Pharaoh resistant to repentance, why punish him and wherein lay his guilt? The Midrash suggests that these questions were already asked in the earliest days, for whenever the Rabbis worry about questions raised by heathens or heretics we can be sure that we deal with issues which were widely and generally discussed:

> Rabbi Johanan said (in comment on Exodus 10:1): "Does this not afford heretics a reason for arguing that Pharaoh had no chance to repent, since it says: 'For I have hardened his heart'?"[1]

What is involved, of course, is man's freedom of will and God's mercy; and the matter is further complicated through Exodus 4:21. There, as Moses is sent on his mission, he is told that Pharaoh would resist because God would encourage him to do so. Were it not for this verse we might be led to believe that Pharaoh's recalcitrance was entirely a matter of his own choice, for not until the drama has well progressed and the protagonists have taken their historic stance, do we hear again of the hardened heart. But the verse stands clearly in the way, for it has God saying: "I will harden his heart, and he will not let the people go." Divine foreknowledge is implied; God not merely directs man toward his destiny, He also knows the end thereof. How does this leave man a choice between good and evil?

Was the Egyptian episode merely staged for the benefit of history, and were Pharaoh's stubbornness, Israel's suffering, all the plagues and the drowning of Egypt's hosts but props and extras in the divine stage play?

There is, as may be expected, a good deal of comment on this problem, but on the whole, its range is rather limited. This is really not surprising. Obviously, God did what the text says He did,[2] and the question is only *why* and in *what sequence* and with what limitations. All commentators agree that man is initially free, but that this freedom can become limited and even suspended later on. Thus, the above-quoted midrash continues:

> Rabbi Shimeon ben Lakish answered: "Let the mouths of the heretics be shut ... When God warns a man once, twice, or even three times, and still he does not repent, then God closes his heart."

This line of thought is followed by most exegetes and is elaborated by Maimonides.[3] The chapter in which he deals with this question opens with the observation that Torah and Prophets contain many passages which appear to contradict the idea of man's freedom to repent, and that the verses dealing with Pharaoh's hardened heart belong in this category. Two things have to he borne in mind, says Maimonides. One, that Pharaoh had already committed grave sins, worthy of punishment, and that therefore God's announcement that He would harden Pharaoh's heart (Exodus 4:21) was a consequence of Pharaoh's previous transgressions; second, that subsequently the possibility of repentance was removed from Pharaoh. This was in itself a form of punishment and it also served to create conditions which would make the reasons for punishment plain to everyone. We have to understand similar passages regarding Sihon (Deuteronomy 2:30), the Canaanites (Joshua 11:20), or the idolatrous Israelites (I Kings 18:37) in the same manner:

> From this it is apparent that God did not predestine Pharaoh to do evil to Israel, nor Sihon to commit sins in his land, nor the Canaanites to do it in theirs, nor the Israelites to practice idolatry. They all deserved that further means of repentance should henceforth be closed to them.

Nahmanides, with his typical ingenuity, adds another view to the argument. God hardened Pharaoh's heart, he says, not against repentance but against the debilitating effects of the plagues. Pharaoh could always repent, but this repentance had to be from the heart. Had he suffered greatly from the plagues he might have surrendered to pain and inconvenience. It was therefore against those that God hardened his heart.[4]

As is often the case, Abravanel makes a point of exposing the weaknesses in his predecessors' arguments. He calls Maimonides' explanation "unworthy of God," for how can we believe that the Merciful One could ever encourage the evildoer to add to his wickedness? Does God not desire the sinner to live rather than to die? No, says Abravanel, the answer lies somewhere else. To be sure, Pharaoh and Egypt were punished for the murders of little children and the oppression they had previously committed, but while there is continuing opportunity for repentance we must remember the limitations of all repentance. God can only forgive transgressions against Himself, but he has no power to forgive sins a man has committed against his fellow man. So forgiveness and repentance are not at stake at all, for the judgment was just and Pharaoh gave no indication that he deserved special consideration. What about the hardening? God never begins by hardening the sinner's heart; at first the opportunity for free action always exists. But *events* may harden a person's will subsequently, and this is what happened here. Pharaoh's will to resist was steeled by the punishment itself and so, God is absolved.[5]

All commentators agree in their interpretation of Exodus 4:21, which foretells that God would cause Pharaoh not to listen to Moses' entreaties. What is at stake here is the reconciliation of the principle, הכל בידי שמים חוץ מיראת שמים (i.e., man's moral freedom), with the assumption of God's omniscience, of which Maimonides says that its complete resolution lies outside the realm of man's finite reason.[6] Say the exegetes: at the beginning of his mission Moses is encouraged by God to persist in the face of all obstacles, and he is forewarned that Pharaoh's hardened heart will test all his resources.

The forced, if well-intentioned, character of all this exegesis is obvious to the modern reader who responds with less than outright enthusiasm to medieval scholasticism. There remains a lingering suspicion that these giants of our tradition were themselves not entirely happy with the proffered solution.

An inquiry into the philological aspects of the problem does not prove too fruitful either.[7] At first glance (one is led to attach some significance to the fact that the Bible uses three terms to describe the hardening of the heart: חזק, קשה, כבד. Our current JPS translation, following Leeser and the King James version, uses the word "harden" for all three Hebrew words, just as the French Version Synodale uses simply *endurcir* to render all three meanings. Apparently only Buber-Rosenzweig follow the original more literally; they translate חזק as *stärken*, קשה as *härten*, and כבד as *betäuben*.[8] All these terms are used in their *pi'el* or *hiph'il* forms when God is the subject of the sentence, as if to indicate that a prior condition has to exist before God's further power can be brought into play. When Pharaoh strengthens his own heart, חזק appears in the *kal*, when God does it, in the *pi'el*. Also, there are overtones to קשה, especially in later usage, which bring out the root-meaning of the word (hard = difficult), so that Exodus 7:3, ואני אקשה, might indicate that though God might tempt Pharaoh and make it difficult for him to choose the right, such choice lies always open. The English word "harden" has a definitive connotation which the more fluid Hebrew words do not have. But this is as far as etymology will take us in this instance. The arrangement of terms and their use throughout the Bible make it clear that they are used interchangeably and that no significance can be attached to their differential inner meaning.[9]

Still, as is so often the case, close attention to language may open some additional doors to understanding. One of the terms used, כבד, has the basic meaning of weighty or heavy, and derivative meanings like honour and liver. In its verbal form it usually means either to be heavy (in the *kal*), to be honoured (*niph'al*), to honour or to harden (*pi'el* and *hiph'il*). Now biblical writing frequently uses word plays to express deeper nuances. Therefore, the twice repeated usage of ואכבדה, "and I (God) will get Me honour" (Exodus 14:4 and 17), is purposeful, as a midrash recognized long ago:

God said (to Pharaoh): "You sinner! With the same word with which you prove yourself recalcitrant, I will glorify Myself," as it is said: "And I will get me honour upon Pharaoh."[10]

This midrash performs the important function of drawing our attention — which is riveted upon Pharaoh and his problem of free will — upon the true hero in the drama, namely God Himself. Once we realize where the true emphasis of the story lies we have opened the door to a broader understanding of the text.

The first thing we must do is to keep the whole tenor of the Exodus story in mind. Above all else the Exodus epic exalts God's might, which is greater than that of the mightiest king and his magicians. The song, "Who is like unto Thee O Lord, among the mighty," is the fitting climax to the wondrous tale of salvation. The individual parts of the drama serve to let Israel, Egypt, and the world see the glory of God. The text is not concerned with philosophy or questions of free will. Rather, as Cassuto has emphasized, it is in the nature of the Bible to consider God as the source of all being. Whatever happens in this world — even what happens in the heart of man — is ascribed to the Creator of All.

God is said to have caused Hannah's sterility (I Samuel 1:5), and He may also cause involuntary manslaughter (Exodus 21:13). Behind all causes lie other causes, and behind the last cause is God's will.[11]

The text is really quite explicit about it, only we have to readjust our focus. We are so preoccupied with reading philosophical statements into a non-philosophical story that the obvious tends to escape us. The purpose of the plagues is made repeatedly plain. It is למען שתי אותותי or למען ידעו מצרים that the drama is enacted, i.e., in order to make God's supremacy once and forever an ineradicable historic reality. But it is not a Greek drama in which man is helpless in the face of the gods' whims; it is biblical drama in which man always plays his own contributory role, albeit in the framework of divinely set boundaries. Man's will is the proximate and God's the ultimate cause of human behaviour. Hence the nearly even distribution of those passages which ascribe Pharaoh's stubbornness to Pharaoh himself (as in וַיֶּחֱזַק לב פרעה) and those which ascribe it to God (as in וַיְחַזֵּק את לב פרעה)."[12]

We must retain this perspective as we approach the key verses in the flow of the story, where Pharaoh's reaction is first predicted. In contrast to our tradition which tried to explain Exodus 4:21 away, or nearly so, we consider it basic. The verse is part of the charge which God gives to Moses. The latter is given all the signs and symbols of divine might, he is to be in every way a messenger of the One who sent him. But Moses hesitates, he fears this role which has so suddenly been thrust upon him. How can he be "in God's stead" (4:16) — he, a mere human? The prospect is overwhelming; he flees, he makes excuses and submits only after God's anger is kindled against him. Still, he is half-hearted and fearful. Once again he is instructed: Be sure you persist and act in My stead, and be not afraid, for when you will come face to face with Pharaoh and the drama will begin, I myself will be, as it were, an actor. *I Myself will strengthen his heart and he will resist.* The text makes the emphasis crystal-clear. There would be little other reason to stress the "I" of God in this verse, but there it is, by way of contrast: ואני אחזק. It is the text's way of underlining, of making clear the supremacy of God in the developing tragedy. Moses acts in God's stead, but God does not relinquish His role as the *spiritus rector* of history.

Lest this fail to carry the point, the next time the issue arises it is put into the sharpest possible focus. In 4:16 Moses acted in God's stead vis-à-vis *Aaron*; in 7:1 his role is extended: "See, I have set thee in God's stead to *Pharaoh*; and Aaron thy brother shall be thy prophet. That is strong language, "thy prophet." Moses will indeed appear to the Egyptians (who were familiar with god-kings) as a divine figure with an inspired prophet to communicate his words to earthly beings. But never is Moses to forget that he is only the vessel, not the source of the divine will, and neither are Pharaoh, Egypt, Aaron, Israel, in fact the world, to forget the unchanged supremacy of the Lord. Hence again the unusual emphasis, ואני אקשה, "and *I* will harden Pharaoh's heart...and the Egyptians shall know that I am the Lord." (7:1, 3.) There follows immediately, almost oppositionally, the addition (inexplicable in itself but quite clear in the context): "... when *I* stretch forth My hand upon Egypt and bring out the children of Israel from among them." This is to say: You, Moses, do the apparent stretching forth, you use the rod — but in reality, it will be I, the source of All, who will be the motive power. Again, in 10:1, we find the same constellation. This time the third verb is used, and once more in now familiar emphatic fashion: ואני הכבדתי, "For *I* have hardened his heart, and the heart of his servants, that I might show these signs in the midst of them." God, and God alone, is the author of Israel's salvation; He is the One who in the First Commandment will proclaim Himself for all time not merely as God, but as the God of the Exodus.

In this light the textual phrasing of the finale, based on the above-mentioned word-play, on כבד as "harden" and "get honour," assumes its proper place. "And I will strengthen Pharaoh's (Egypt's) heart ... and I will get Me honour (4:4, 17).[13] Never does the story veer from its major theme, to elevate God's power above all else. Free will is never at issue, for no doubt man's ability to make moral decisions would be wholly at variance with all biblical thought. Moses' comparison of Pharaoh's and Israel's free volition should be enough to reassure the reader: "Behold, the children of Israel have not hearkened unto me, how then shall Pharaoh hear me...? (6:12 and the related passage in verse 30).

To sum up: the traditional discussion of the moral and ethical implications of "hardened heart" passages is essentially misplaced. Of course, the Bible does not deny man his moral choice, not here nor elsewhere. But all of history stands under the purpose of God's will, and all men — be they Pharaoh or Job — can only move within the framework of His plan and will. The Exodus is the hinge of Israel's fate, and ultimately God alone brings it to turn. It provides the foundation for the theophany at Sinai, and thus is part of that manifestation which reaches all the way into the conquest of Canaan. Therefore, it is natural for the biblical idiom to phrase the story of the defeat of the Canaanites in the same way the Exodus was told (Joshua 11:20): "For it was of the Lord to harden their hearts...." How else could it be? God had promised the land, as He had promised freedom from bondage, and the fulfilment of this promise involved the lives, the thoughts and actions of men and nations.

The Pillar of Salt

$\mathcal{T}$he sad fate of Lot's wife is recounted in what probably is the briefest of all short stories, a single-sentence account in Genesis 19:26: ותבט אשתו מאחריו ותהי נציב מלח.

But his wife looked back from behind him, and she became a pillar of salt.

The proverbial image of the pillar of salt belongs today to all languages on which the Bible has had a commanding influence. It also has been and still is part of the folk tradition in the Dead Sea area. Flavius Josephus claimed to have seen the pillar with his own eyes,[1] and until this day there is a place called Mt. Sodom which is filled with saline columns whose changing and often statuesque appearances give credence to Josephus' account and help to reinforce old legends.[2]

Of course, there is some question whether the biblical account preceded the legend of the woman-turned-salt, or whether the changing aspects of the terrain gave rise to the story in Genesis. Many scholars, amongst them so traditional an interpreter as Benno Jacob, hold the latter view and therefore spend no time on examining the story on its own level. They are impressed with the fact that various aspects of the folk legend are not unique to Israel. A salt woman is known as far away as among the Pueblo Indians; the Mexicans had an image of the Goddess of Salt; and the Greeks told the story of Eurydice, who slipped back into Hades' domain when her lover Orpheus offended against the command not to look back.[3]

But whatever the origin of the biblical account, it makes a claim to be taken seriously simply by being where it is — and a closer look reveals that our short-short story contains problems and hints at matters well worth a detailed query.

Note that our tragic heroine (if she may be so called) has no name. This namelessness occurs occasionally in the biblical text, and when it does, as in the story of Potiphar's wife or the Kushite whom Moses had married, there is a crisis afoot and our attention is focused on questions which lie below the surface. The Midrash must have sensed this when it called Lot's wife עדית (Edith), a name derived from עדה, which means symbol or witness.[4] Of course, as a pillar she stands as permanent witness, for the word נציב has this meaning.[5] But witness to what? Merely as a reminder that she turned around? And why a pillar of *salt*?

To be sure, the angel had warned Lot not to turn around. (Had he warned her also? Verse 17 does not say, but with our commentators we may assume that she was included in the prohibition.) However, after she had been rescued from Sodom and had been forgiven her previous association with evil, how could the divine mercy be abrogated now for an apparently minor transgression? This is the heart of the question.

Two of the Aramaic translations of the passage only confound the problem. Says Targum Yerushalmi:

> Because Lot's wife was of the children of the people of Sodom, she looked behind her to see what would be the fate of her father's house, and she remains as a pillar of salt until the time of the revival of the dead.

Does concern for her father's house appear as so ignoble a sentiment that it evokes the direct punishment? Targum Jonathan ben Uzziel is even less helpful:

> And his wife looked behind the angel to see what would be the end of her father's house (for she was of the daughters of Sodom), and because of the sin of salt, at the betrayal of the poor, she became a pillar of salt.

It is quite obvious that Jonathan is hard-pressed for a satisfactory comment. According to him, the woman sinned on several counts. He, too, has her look back at her father's house; but the addition, that she did this because she was from Sodom, hardly qualifies as a cause for capital punishment. So Jonathan brings up an old legend about an act of inhospitality which she was said to have committed; she had betrayed the presence of strangers in Sodom by asking her neighbours for extra salt; or, as another version went, she had been angry at her husband for showing them hospitality (of which the offering of salt was symbolic).[6] This legend, of which the Bible knows nothing, explains little about the salt pillar, and nothing about her guilt. For even if some such event had happened, this was all in the past. She was in Zoar now; she had been saved. Would she now, suddenly, be punished for an old transgression?

Jonathan is apparently aware of the difficulty, for he introduces a third reason for punishment: she looked "behind the angel." Now the Bible says nothing of this, yet it must be admitted that the suggestion has some merit, for the text is ambiguous, to say the least.

Look at the order of the sentences. Verse 23 speaks of Lot arriving at Zoar in the morning. Verse 24 tells of brimstone and fire raining upon the wicked cities; verse 25 of God overturning people, cities, and vegetation. Then comes our short story, which speaks of "his wife" (although Lot has not been mentioned as an immediate antecedent reference) and then says ותבט...מאחריו, that she "looked back from behind him." Most interpreters refer "behind him" to Lot, but of course the text is not unequivocal.[7] Some suggest that we should read מאחריה, "behind her," but this too is of little help, for it does not tell us why she looked back, what she looked at and what her sin was. Therefore, Targum Jonathan's suggestion that she looked at the angel, or the Divine Presence, has at least the virtue of plausibility, and many commentators follow his lead.[8]

The argument implies that the prohibition issued in verse 17 means: Do not look back, for if you do, you will see God at work, and no man can see the Shekhinah and live, as the Bible tells us repeatedly.[9] But there are objections. Abravanel points out that the Zoarites looked on and were not punished; further, that all Israel saw the Divine Fire for forty years and were not consumed. He could also have pointed to Jacob who saw God and lived. And so the argument goes.

There have even been suggestions that it was not Lot's wife who turned into a pillar of salt. The text says "she became" but does not specify who "she" is. Perhaps the reference is to the Plain or to Sodom, so that the verse would read: But Lot's wife looked back and saw the Plain turned into a pillar of salt. This suggestion was made by Ralbag, and indeed it cuts through all our problems — except that all our tradition stands in the way, as does the subsequent story of Lot and his daughters, a story which would be hard to believe if Lot's wife had still been alive. Abravanel felt so strongly on this point that, with a display of bad temper, he called Ralbag's interpretation "the teaching of a deceiver."[10]

Without indulging in his extreme language, we must agree with the angry statesman-commentator that the plain meaning of the text speaks of Lot's wife from beginning to end. We will have to admit, also, that the meaning of "behind him" in our context will ultimately remain uncertain. Perhaps Lot was not even forbidden to look *back*, but rather to look at what would come *after him*, to contemplate his future — for אל תביט אחריך (in verse 17) could have that meaning. From this possibility one commentator draws the startling conclusion that the sin of Lot's wife consisted in her being concerned about her husband's future (אחריו) and hence her own. Now that they were reduced to poverty, what would become of the stipulations in her wedding contract?[11] If this seems naive and slightly amusing, it is at least a thoroughly human explanation. Who knows what went through the mind of a woman who yesterday was rich and well settled with a large family, and who the next day, without preparation, had become a wanderer whose abode would be a cave (see verse 30)!

The very vagueness of the text makes it most likely that we deal here with a figurative expression altogether. We are not told at what Lot's wife looked because *she was simply "looking back"— not at anything specific, but at that which was left behind: her family, her possessions, her whole yesterdays. "Do not look back" was a command not to the eye but to the spirit.* She could not live in approval of and longing for Sodom and be permanently saved. Her looking back revealed a condition of mind which continued to identify her with the evils of the society in which, apparently, she had lived all her life. She had a chance to liberate herself from her past, but she would not or could not do it. The angel had taken her out forcibly (verse 16), for the sake of her husband; but, like an animal which runs back into the flaming barn, she could not resist returning on that level which now counted most: in her soul. She perished — just as did later the generation of the desert who never ceased to yearn for the fleshpots of Egypt.[12]

For Sodom was not only wicked, it was rich, "like the garden of the Lord, like the land of Egypt" (13:10) — a telling parallel. It was richer than any other city, says the Midrash. The streets of Sodom, its very soil, were gold; and, lest strangers would share this wealth, the Sodomites flooded the approaches to their city to isolate themselves from unwanted intruders — a sort of physical immigration restriction.[13] No wonder that Lot himself hesitated to leave such opulence (verse 16),[14] and that later, in the mountains of Zoar, he drowned his misery in drink. But apparently he fell short of "looking back," while his wife succumbed. For her there was no future; she died with her past.

There remains the symbol of the pillar of salt. Why salt? The popular naturalistic interpretation that Lot's lingering wife was caught in the catastrophe and became salt-encrusted (much like the people of Pompeii)[15] is not satisfactory. It cannot account for the fact that Lot's family had already arrived in Zoar, well out of the range of the destructive elements.

If the first part of verse 26 is to be taken figuratively, we may conclude that the last part —"and she became a pillar of salt"— ought to yield symbolic meaning also. This is the more plausible since salt is rich in associative meaning, and especially so in Jewish tradition.

Salt was a *sine qua non* at sacrifices; it was in fact called the "salt of the covenant." This may reflect a pre-Mosaic concept which regarded sacrifice as a meal of God, but in later years the addition of salt as a prerequisite in the sacrificial cult had purely symbolic value.[16] A field "sown" with salt was thereby rendered unfruitful (Judges 9:45; Deuteronomy 29:22). Salt land was equated with wilderness (Job 39:6), or uninhabited country (Jeremiah 17:6).[17] Of course the preserving faculty of salt was also well known. S.R. Hirsch concludes from this that the symbolism of salt was dual: it had the connotation of a preservative, and it made things unfit for other usage — hence salt invested sacrifice and covenant with the qualities of permanence and holiness (in its aspect of separation).[18]

Salt also denoted the essence of a man or a thing, as in "the salt of the palace" (Ezra 4:14) or in the talmudic saying that "the salt of money is to decrease it" (by spending it for charity, for only then will it truly increase).[19] We too speak of salt money when we use the word salary (*salarium*, from *sal*, i.e., salt): the giving of salt money carries the implication of giving of one's substance.[20]

Finally, in the environs of the Dead Sea, at the southwestern corner of which the old Sodom was located, salt remains descriptive also of the countryside itself. The sea has high salt content, and the hills around it have crystalline, saline gloss. The Talmud knew of Sodom salt, which was said to have been mined in the area and had an especially pungent quality.[21]

Salt, then, was a word rich in connotation: it evoked pictures of permanence and aridity; as the salt of the covenant it spoke of sacrifice; it stood for the essence of things, and it reminded one of Sodom itself. On which of these themes does our story play? A definite answer is impossible; we can only guess. Certainly the "pillar of salt" was to the ancients a "pillar of Sodom"; and doubtlessly it conveyed also the notion that looking back to Sodom was an arid, futile, and destructive enterprise. Or perhaps to contemporaries more alert to the nuances of symbolism than we are today, the salt pillar was not merely *reminiscent* of Sodom; it represented its very *essence*. Lot's wife had desired Sodom, now her wish was fulfilled: for all eternity she became the salt of Sodom itself.

In Greek mythology, it was Midas whose craving for gold nearly became the instrument of his undoing.[22] But while Midas was saved by Dionysius from starving in the midst of his golden opulence, there was no second chance for Lot's wife. She looked back, for she wanted Sodom above all else. Her wish was granted and she became a symbol of the city, a pillar of Sodom, warning future generations of the dangers of desiring the empty pleasures and immoral practices which beckon men in every age.

Why Love a Stranger?

*T*hirty-six times does Scripture warn us to treat the גר, the stranger,[1] in kindly, generous, and loving fashion. R Eliezer Hagadol, to whom the statement is attributed, knew his Bible thoroughly and the figure may be checked.[2] Our sages were already aware that this was an unusually high degree of repetition. Was it because of human weakness that one had to be so frequently warned about this matter? Or was there another reason?

The answer which R. Eliezer gives us is unfortunately rather cryptic, which caused a good many headaches to our sages who wrestled manfully with the great rabbi's explanation. The Torah, said R. Eliezer, warns us so often about the stranger, מפני שסורו רע.

Now, if we would only know what this means! Alas, it is an almost oracular reply and it naturally elicited a flood of commentaries, some of them highly ingenious and others frankly emendatory.

Rashi, for instance, emends שסורו רע to שאורו רע, by which he means the swelling of the genitals (i.e., the evil inclination).[3] According to him, R. Eliezer's expression means: the Torah warns us so often about the גר because of his evil inclination — a rather prejudicial reference to the presumed unreliability of the stranger or proselyte. Elijah Mizrahi, in his commentary on Rashi, quotes Eleazar ben Samuel of Metz (the RAM), in reading שצורו רע, "because the stranger's god is evil,"[4] and he defends his emendation on the grounds of euphemistic necessity, which hardly improves on Rashi.

Bertinoro does better, but only because he uses his imagination more freely.[5] He understands R. Eliezer to refer to the stranger's bad smell, for when you oppress him the odour of oppression will give him away and will make your ill treatment of him only too obvious. All of which is likely to leave the reader puzzled and unconvinced.

Whatever R. Eliezer's explanation, Scripture doubtlessly had its good reasons for repeating the injunction concerning the stranger so many times. It was not easy then, nor is it easy now, to withstand the temptation of exploiting the weak amongst whom the stranger, the widow, and orphan inevitably are found. And when it comes to loving the stranger who lives in our midst — how much more difficult is this than loving one's neighbour, which is hard enough! (Some will of course assert that it is easier to love strangers than neighbours.)[6]

Actually, the frequency of repetition presents only a minor problem. A much more serious question arises from the fact that the Torah repeatedly tells us why we should respect and even love the stranger. Three of the best-known passages will illustrate our dilemma:

> You shall not wrong a stranger or oppress him, for you were strangers in the land of Egypt. (Exodus 22:20)
> The stranger who resides with you shall be to you as one of your citizens; you shall love him as yourself, for you were strangers in the land of Egypt: I the Lord am your God. (Leviticus 19:34)
> You shall not oppress a stranger, for you know the heart of the stranger, having yourselves been strangers in the land of Egypt. (Exodus 23:9)

The Torah apparently founds the mitzvah on two reasons: one is historical כי גרים הייתם בארץ מצרים and the other compassionate or, if you will, psychological אתם ידעתם את נפש הגר. One needs to think but little about these stated reasons to appreciate that they do not really supply us with an effective motivation.

The psychological motivation occurs only once, although it appears to be the more powerful. Jews of past and present have indeed known "the heart of the stranger," having themselves been strangers in many lands. This reminder of our past bitter experience presumes that this remembrance makes us empathetic with regard to others. Alas, while this is true for some, it fails as a social and psychological device with all too

95

many. In fact, often men will revert to oppressive behaviour in direct proportion to their former depressed condition. Still, the argument is sound for some, and perhaps this is why it is given only once.

But over and over we are told that the major reason for not wronging the stranger is historical. We ourselves were strangers once, therefore do not do to others what has been done to us. All present-day homilies aside, Egypt and Exodus belong to the far distant past. Will the rehearsal of this historic incident produce moral rectitude and even lead us to the well-nigh unreachable goal of loving a stranger? Should we not expect the Torah to tell us that the real reason for treating the stranger decently is that this is the right thing to do, since he is our brother?

The problem did not escape our ancient commentators. The Mekhilta, in commenting on Exodus 22:20, says that the phrase "You shall not wrong a stranger" לא תונה applies to wronging him with words, while "nor oppress him" לא תלחצנו applies to money matters. From this, R. Nathan deduces that the stated reason "for you were strangers in the land of Egypt" applies to verbal offences only, for one should not reproach a fellow man with a shortcoming which is one's own מום שבך אל תאמר לחברך.

Having once been strangers themselves, Jews should not now taunt others with being strangers. The Talmud further illustrates this by quoting an earthy proverb: "Whoever has someone in his family who was hanged should not say to the vendor: 'Hang a little fish up for me.'"[7]

This solution — if it may be so called — apparently appealed to Rashi who repeated it in various places,[8] but even his devoted disciples who in turn elaborated on his commentary could not see eye to eye with him in this matter. The argument was forced and it did not say anything about the passage in Leviticus where we are asked to love the stranger since we ourselves were strangers once in Egypt. R. Nathan's pragmatic advice hardly matches this exalted command.

Ibn Ezra also contributes little to the elucidation of our problem, especially since he muddies the discussion by assuming that גר means proselyte. The גר, he says, now accepts the rejection of idols, hence do not oppress him just because you have the power to do so. What makes Ibn Ezra's comment invaluable, however, is his homiletical aside on the fact that in verse 20 the Torah addresses us in the singular, in verse 21 in the plural, and in verse 22 in the singular again. Says he: everyone who sees another person oppressing the weak and does not help them, thereby is himself reckoned as an oppressor.[9] All of which is splendid for sermons but does not explain the introduction of the historical reasons into the essentially moral command to treat the stranger decently and lovingly.

The Ramban does not hesitate to reject Rashi's and Ibn Ezra's explanations outright. ואין בכל זה טעם בעקר he says. Why then the reminder that we were slaves in Egypt? Because it draws your attention to the fact that God hears the cry of the oppressed and saves them, as He saved Israel in Egypt. "For you know the heart of the stranger" refers to the same central point. You know what you did and felt when you were slaves, you cried and redemption came (however, as Ramban is careful to add, it came not because of your cry but because of God's mercy).[10]

Abravanel follows a similar line and explains the difficulty as follows: "Just as you were strangers there (in Egypt) and I made My name known to you and guarded you, so now for the goyim who live amongst you, I am their God."[11]

Perhaps just because Rashi's commentary was in this instance so obviously strained and, in fact, plainly unsatisfactory, it was left to those who in turn commented on him to recognize the textual difficulty most clearly. Of the major annotators of Rashi, only Mordecai Jaffe fails to deal with the problem, but Mizrahi and the two *gedolim* from Prague, the Maharal (גור אריה) and Shabbetai Bass (שפתי חכמים) expose the heart of the matter.

Mizrahi states flatly that כי גרים הייתם cannot be the reason for the command not to oppress the stranger, but is merely a historic reference,[12] and the Maharal with his usual perception simply says: The Torah commands us to love the stranger, and not to despise him — and that is it, no reasons need to be given.[13]

Bass sums up his predecessors' insight in this fashion: Love itself is commanded, but not because we were strangers in Egypt. "For the fact that (Jews) once were strangers does not form the basis of their obligation to love the stranger."[14]

What then is the basis of the obligation? The key lies in Leviticus 19:34. Just as the difficult command to love one's neighbour is rendered comprehensible only by the climactic ending אני ה״ so the command to love a stranger is climaxed by the reminder אני ה״. Without this, the command has no foundation; the fact that God is God is the final reason for human love. And conversely, "the esteem for and love of the stranger is the true touchstone of your fear and love of God," as Samson Raphael Hirsch remarked.[15] The expression, "for you were strangers in the land of Egypt," is designed to keep alive the awareness of God's role in Israel's history and thereby to re-emphasize that the foundation of our moral law is the existence of God.

Here, and here alone, lies the answer to our question. If Hermann Cohen says that the alien is to be protected because he is a human being, he is of course right. But when he goes on to say: "In the alien, therefore, man discovered the idea of humanity,"[16] he tends to be misleading. For in the alien the Jew was first and foremost bidden to discover the presence of the redeeming God, and thereby he was to reinforce his bonds with all men.

The best summation of this solution is already found in the Torah itself, in Deuteronomy 10:17–19:

> For the Lord your God is God supreme and Lord supreme, the great, the mighty, and the awesome God … [Who] loves the stranger, providing him with food and clothing. You too must love the stranger, for you were strangers in the land of Egypt.

Literature
and Linguistics

The Origin of the Word "Yarmulke"

*I*t is strange that the word *yarmulke* — describing as it does the distinctive religious head covering of the Jew — should have such uncertain origin.

Aleksander Brückner[1] cites a Polish source from 1608, in which the word *yarmulka* occurs, but no reference is made to any Jewish association of the word.

Max Vasmer[2] traces *yermolka* to the fifteenth century, and follows its use to the eighteenth. Vasmer takes it to be of Osman origin, *yarmuluk*, which means "rain cover." Here, too, however, there is no specific association with Jewish usage.

Shlomo Noble finds it to be a widely held opinion that the word is "of Slavic origin," occurring "in Russian, Polish, Ukrainian, and, possibly, other Slavic tongues.... The term occurs frequently in the early Hassidic literature, that is, in the eighteenth century. It may also occur in earlier writings. It was used in Eastern European countries, in the Ukraine, Lithuania, and Poland. I have heard it as far west as Frankfurt-on-the Main. In that instance, it may have been a carryover from Eastern Europe."[3]

Other explanations derive the word from Hebrew and German origins.

The alleged Hebrew source is said to be *yere melakhim*.[4]

For a possible German origin the word *Jahrmarkt* is adduced. The word — often dropping the final "t"— is used in Polish and Russian to describe a county fair. It has been suggested that the distinctive headgear of the Jew was called *yarmokke* or *yarmolke* because of their wearers' frequent attendance at the fairs,

While etymology cannot rule out any of these explanations as impossible, it is evident that all of them suffer from one or another serious defect.

Brückner's and Vasmer's *yarmulke* has no specific relation to Jews. But *yarmulke* in today's usage refers not just to a certain headgear worn by Jews, but to the cap which they wore at home or at prayer, and whose usage *distinguished* them from their neighbours. The explanation using the German *Jahrmarkt*, while having a possible Jewish connection, has no religious connotation. The assumption that the Hebrew *yere melakhim* is its origin is laboured and ill-founded. *Yere melakhim* would never refer to God, and is not the type of term which through frequent usage might give rise to a popular derivative. It is a late and etymologically unsound use of unrelated terms, which is always striking at first sight, but erroneous nonetheless. It reminds one of the "obvious" derivation of "cap" from the Latin *capere*, "quia quasitotum capiat hominem"; or the derivation of the Yiddish *davenen* from the English "dawn."

A study of the distinctive headgear imposed generally on the Jews since the days of Innocent III and Charles V (but in use before that time in many Christian lands), shows that while the word *yarmulke* is not found in any edicts prior to the middle of the nineteenth century, the headgear used may point up clues to our etymological question.

In Ofen the cap was referred to as a *capucium*,[5] and when the requirement of wearing it was revoked in 1520, the ordinance called it "capucium quod vulgariter cuclya vocatur."[6]

In Germany it was known as *Judenhut* (*cornutum pileum*), or *Gugelhut*, and occasionally as *Kappe*.[7] Now it is worth noting that *Gugeln* were special caps which reached (like a cape) down over the back and shoulder.[8]

A Polish edict of 1538 also uses the terminology of a priestly vestment, the *Bireta*, to describe the Jewish cap;[9] and in various Spanish countries the prescribed Jewish headgear was a cowl-like cape.[10] This general type of gear is portrayed by Ulysse Robert[11] and further underscores its striking resemblance to certain church vestments.

What was the comparable church garment which the Jewish cap resembled, without, of course, duplicating it?

It was the *amice* (or *almuce*), a cape which covered the shoulder and which was worn by the priest until he arrived at the altar.[12] Rabanus Maurus' opinion that the *amice* originated in the biblical *ephod* is no longer held;[13] but it appears most likely that in later days it gave rise to a Jewish word — our *yarmulke*.

The Latin word for amice (or almuce) was *almucia*.[14] Most scholars agree that the German *Mütze* is derived from *almucia* or its related forms, *aumucia, armutia*.[15]

The earliest German forms were *almutz* and *aremutz*, and there is also an interesting Portuguese variation, *mursa*. Since these forms go back to the thirteenth century, it is likely that they recall the original shape of the *almuce*, namely, a cap separate from the hood. At first only the clergy wore this garment, but in time it was taken over by the laity — and it was then that *Mütze* in Germany, *mursa* in Portugal, and *mutch* in Scotland came into greater use.

The word *almucia* had a diminutive form *almucella* or *armucella*.[16] It should be borne in mind that the Latin pronunciation of the "c" varied considerably, and was quite often consistently pronounced as a "k." It is suggested, therefore, that "the small amice," or *armucella* gave rise to the use of the word *yarmulke*. The transposition of the "l" and "c" is a common phenomenon in linguistic derivation. It appears plausible to assume that *almucia* was an often-used term in medieval Germany; hence its adoption into everyday language, taking later the form of *Mütze*. This same process then gave rise also to calling the small Jewish cap by this term; and the Jews who took their medieval German with them to Eastern lands probably also took the word *armucella* along. With them it travelled as far east as Turkey; and we suggest that the Osman term came from the West — either through the mediation of the Jew, or more directly in some similar way. It is entirely possible that the ultimate adoption of the word in its present popular form was hastened by a "re-inoculation" from Slavic or other languages; and it is equally possible that the word *yarmulke* came into prominence amongst the Jews because their neighbours used it to describe the Jewish cap.

To sum up: in our opinion all previous explanations fail to establish the connection between the term and the specific Jewish or religious use of the cap.

We suggest that the religious headgear of the clergy, called *almucia* (or *armucella*), which gave rise to the German *Mütze*, the Portuguese *mursa*, and the Scotch *mutch*, also was the source for the Jewish *yarmulke*, the Slavic *yermolka* and probably also the Osman *yarmuluk*.

A Hebrew-Dakota Dictionary

*A*mong the treasures of the Minnesota Historical Society students may inspect a manuscript which surely belongs to the more unusual curiosities of the past. It is a Hebrew-Dakota dictionary, compiled by Samuel W. Pond in 1842. Samuel Pond was a man who for devoutness and sacrificial spirit had few equals anywhere. Largely self-learned, he in time mastered not only the Indian tongue better than most of his more studied contemporaries, but occupied himself with classical learning and took up the study of Hebrew in order to understand fully the Word which had sent him forth. Samuel and his younger brother Gideon were in their twenties when they arrived in the rugged climes of the Minnesota hills and forests — and a rugged land it was indeed. They came from old Puritan stock and were soon to prove their hardiness in the virgin territory of a land which was settled almost entirely by Indians. The Pond brothers represented no human agency, no board of missions; they were what were then called "volunteer missionaries"; that is, they had come completely on their own initiative and had to look entirely to their own resources. This meant that they had to support themselves by hard manual labour, which in turn left them little enough time to pursue the real purpose of their life. But such was their spirit and devotion that nothing stood in their way — they acquired friends, learning, and, after some years, their first converts.[1] Only many years later did the official Dakota Presbytery recognize their work by ordaining them officially and making it possible for them to assume regular pastorates.

Samuel's ability to learn new languages bordered on the phenomenal. It was not long before he was able to assist in the preparation of the first translation of the Bible into the native tongue. In order to do this, the brothers had to invent a system of phonetics — a system which with small changes remained the basis of all subsequent Dakota literature. In 1840, six years after he had first come to Minnesota, Samuel Pond wrote a letter to his sister in which he said:

> I have spent a little time lately in studying Hebrew. I think I can learn to read the greatest part of the Bible in that language without much difficulty.[2]

This newly won facility evidently inspired him further, and in his unbounded enthusiasm he apparently projected a Bible which would be translated directly from Hebrew into Dakota. The preparation of a Hebrew-Dakota dictionary was his first step. Whether he also hoped that some day the Indians might study Hebrew is hard to say, for no ideals seemed beyond reach to this man. As it turned out, Pond never got beyond the Hebrew-Dakota dictionary. To us it remains a monument of devotion, and a fascinating detail of the building of the American Northwest.

The manuscript consists of 142 sheets, about six by four inches in size, sewed together at the end, and without cover. Some of the sheets are written on one side only. The manuscript contains an astoundingly large number of words — about 4,400. Its arrangement is exceedingly simple. On the left side of the page a Hebrew word is noted and is then followed by one or several Dakota translations. Thus, the first entry reads:

אָב [ʻab]   aṯ [ate] & ḥ ḵ ḥ .

A distinguishing mark of the dictionary are the vowels. Dakota was ordinarily written in Latin characters, and the five vowels were usually given their German value equivalent. However, Pond resorted in this dictionary to a novel and space-saving device. He used the Hebrew vowels even in their Dakota translation. The vowel "a" is represented by a horizontal line under the consonant it follows (corresponding to the Hebrew *pathaḥ*; "e" by two horizontal dots one next to the other [the Hebrew *ẓere*]. The German vowel equivalent "i" is represented by a single dot (the Hebrew *ḥirek*); "o" by a slanted line going from lower left to upper right (representing generally the Hebrew *ḥolem*). The vowel "u" is represented by a line running in the opposite direction (connecting the three dots of the Hebrew *ḳubbutz*). Ba, be, bi, bo, bu would therefore look as follows:

ḅ   ḅ   ḅ   ḅ   ḅ

[Where the Indian vowel had a certain nasal quality, Pond indicated it by adding a dot to the vowel, as in ḥ ḳ ḥ.]

Forty-five years after the compilation of the dictionary, Pond wrote in pencil on the back of the manuscript:

> This is a translation of Hebrew words into Dakota in which the Dakota vowels are written under the consonants done by me in 1842.
> SWP 1887.

No credit is given to Gideon, and there is every reason to believe that Samuel, who was the more brilliant of the brothers, did the entire manuscript by himself. Certainly there is no variation in handwriting, either in Hebrew or the Dakota. Pond's Hebrew penmanship was unexceptional — it was as clear and meticulous as his English — and perhaps even more so, since doubtlessly he felt less inclined to take any liberties with the letters of the Hebrew alphabet.

Pond of course worked from some dictionary in his possession.[3] Just what this was can only be surmised. That it is likely to have been a Gesenius-based dictionary can be deduced from a number of instances. Where the Hebrew word has several meanings, Pond followed the arrangements in Gesenius, which in themselves are often somewhat arbitrary. A good example is the Hebrew word רַחֲמִים [*raḥamim*]. This is rendered by Pond in the following order:

> *Tan make,*   *xupe,*   *wowaoxida*

These three Dakota words in their order signify:

> womb (*tamni*; or *tanmahen*, in the body); entrails; goodness (*wowaxte*).

Gesenius has precisely this order of meanings; and these examples could be multiplied. The dictionary is reasonably complete, but does not attempt to list any proper names. This is not surprising, because Pond evidently prepared the manuscript for his own use and needed no translation for proper names. On the other hand, *hapax legomena* are included. Grammatical derivatives are almost entirely omitted — occasionally do we find the mentioning of *hiph'il* or *niphal* forms; but then he evidently knew what these forms would be and only gave their translations. Thus, for instance, he lists:

| אָמַן [*'aman*] | *yuha, suta* | *waciye, pica, wicaka* |
| *hiph* | *waciya,* | *wicada* |

It is difficult to say just how far Pond had penetrated into the knowledge of Hebrew grammar and syntax. His vocalization is on occasion quite bad; he particularly confuses the usage of *pathah* and *kamaz*. The *dagesh* is rarely used. The manuscript has no other contents except the straight listing of Hebrew words and their Dakota meanings, and does not contain cross references. It is altogether a tremendous individual effort and must have taken the author many months to complete.

When we turn to the translations themselves we are confronted with a peculiar problem. Dakota had not been standardized in its literary form when Pond compiled this dictionary; and therefore reference to the later printed Dakota-English lexicon by Stephen Riggs does not always prove too enlightening.

Fortunately, we have access to another manuscript, this one a Dakota-English dictionary compiled by both brothers Pond; a 559-folio-page work which was finished some time after the Hebrew dictionary. On its fly leaf Samuel Pond wrote in 1890:

> This dictionary was finished about 40 years ago. It is almost exclusively the work of my brother G.H. Pond and myself....

In order to ascertain then the meaning of the Dakota words in the Hebrew-Dakota lexicon, we should refer not to the later dictionary by Stephen Riggs, but to this manuscript dictionary which reveals to us, we are sure, with reasonable accuracy, the meaning which Samuel Pond meant to give to his Hebrew words. This is then the procedure which we followed: The Dakota translation of the Hebrew word was checked against the Dakota-English manuscript of the two Ponds; and all meanings given below are derived from this manuscript exclusively.

In the rendering of specific Hebrew words into Dakota, we are of course interested in those terms which are singularly expressive of biblical theology and ethics.

First, let us look at the terminology for the divine being. How did Pond render such terms as ʿEl, ʿElohim, ʿAdonai, and YHWH?

The first striking fact is that Pond gives no rendering at all for ʿElohim and YHWH. This may have been due to his treatment of these words as proper names (he no doubt would have followed the King James in rendering YHWH as Jehovah),[4] but it may also have been due to certain convictions regarding the Dakota religion as Pond understood it.

Pond renders the word ʿEl, where it refers to the Divinity just as ʿAdonai, as *Wakan Takan*. Just what *Wakan Takan* was to the Indian is a matter of speculation and the subject of widespread disagreement. The term *Wakan* is the key in this controversy. Gideon Pond thought that "*Wakan* signifies anything which is incomprehensible." With others he shared the belief that Indians were pantheists in the sense that "…there is nothing that they do not revere as God."[5] *Wakan* is the mysterious, the inexplicable, and anything that is *Taku wakan* (that which is *wakan*) is therefore godlike. Gideon Pond believed that *Taku wakan* was indigenously Indian, but that the Dakota did not conceive of a "Great Spirit" similar to the Jewish-Christian God. He held that the term *Wakan Takan* was invented by the Indians only after their contact with Christian missionaries. Henry Sibley, who was no theologian, agreed with Pond in this respect.[6]

According to Samuel Pond,[7] the chief Dakota object of worship was *Unkteri*; they revered thunder as the voice of a gigantic bird; and they were much impressed by the mystery of motion, to which they assigned a specific term, *Taku-shkanshkan*. They had their ghosts; sun and moon played a role in their myths, and they believed in various gigantic or fabulous beings (Heyoka, Unktomi, and others); but, according to Pond, "Of such a being as the Creator or Preserver of all they have no knowledge."[8]

Wakan Takan, he says, was the God of the whites, and the "Great Spirit" played no role in Indian ritual or mythology. Franz Boas, in taking the sum total of Indian religion, describes their God concepts in general as immanent rather than transcendent.[9] William H. Forbes called them deists,[10] and James Owen Dorsey, too, doubted the existence of monotheistic concepts.[11]

On the other side, we find James Lynd who maintained that the Dakota were believers in a supreme being, a Creator who existed from all time. Confronted with the difficulty that this Creator played no role in their cult, Lynd claimed that they thought him too far away; that he was not concerned with human affairs and therefore prayer to him was not indicated. He construed his power to be latent and of a negative rather than a positive fashion. Lynd hotly argued that the Great Spirit originated with the Indians and not from contact with the whites and that this was equally true of the Algonquian *Maneto*.[12] To him the Dakota approach to the holy was the same as that of the Hebrews; and he got support in this opinion from no less an authority than Edward Neill.[13]

Samuel Pond, in his omission of several Hebrew terms for the Deity, may have proceeded from the conviction that Indian equivalents were not available for these concepts.

His method of dealing with words, for which there are no Indian terms, varies. Sometimes he leaves the word untranslated, like בְּרִית [b'rith]; on other occasions, he translates the Hebrew word into English instead of Dakota. This of course may be due in part to the fact that he simply did not then know such words; but in some of the cases the equivalent was simply lacking. He lists, for instance, for the corresponding Hebrew words, the following in English only:

> Prison, consumption, compass, kingdom, mortar, destiny,
> Manna, yoke, to impose a fine, usury.

Other translations of characteristic nature are the following:

Hebrew	Dakota	Equivalent of Dakota Word
צֶדֶק [zedek]	wowaxte wicowotana (?) (wicowaxte =)	goodness happiness
חֵטְא [het']	wowantani	transgression or neglect of

		superstitions, rules, and observances; sin
חָטָא (*sic!*) [ḥata]	boxna	to miss in shooting;
	wartani	to transgress or neglect or to observe any of the superstitions, rules, or ceremonies of the Indians; to sin
	wakiyuxna	to offer a sacrifice
	kajuju	to erase, knock in pieces, cancel, pay
	wartaniya	to carve, to wartani
	yaxica	to injure, spoil, defame
סְגֻלָּה (*sic!*) [s'gullah]	woyuha	a vow, a relation

תּוֹרָה [*Torah*] is rendered by Pond as *wokicuze*. This word is not found in the brothers' Dakota-English manuscript dictionary; however, *wakicunza* is given as "decide, judge, enact laws."

שָׂטָן [*Satan*] is translated as *toka*, which is an enemy — one of a hostile nation. This is indeed the basic meaning of the word; and since Pond does not list the additional meaning of "the arch-enemy of God" as rendered in Job, it may be assumed that in those passages he would have rendered it as a proper name.

Other translations of interest are:

קֹדֶשׁ [*kodesh*]	(No Dakota word, only:)		holiness
קָדַשׁ [*kadash*]	womnaxni		pure, clear
(also)	wakan		
תְּשׁוּבָה [*t'shubah*]	hdipi	(hdi=)	to return home
		(pi=)	good
	woayupte		an answer
תְּשׁוּעָה (*t'shuʻah*)	wonikiye		(not found in Dakota-English dictionary)
	wooltiye		victory

111

It is hard nowadays to picture this man almost alone at the very outpost of civilization, braving winters as rugged as forty below zero, in some inadequate quarters, and by the light of a poor lamp working on a task such as this. There is no doubt that he acquired the thorough admiration of both natives and white settlers. Perhaps it was because of his interest in Hebrew that he set a standard for later translations of the Bible into Dakota. For these were rendered not, as might have been expected, from English into Dakota; but, like Thomas Williamson's and Stephen Riggs', directly from the Hebrew.

The purpose for which Pond laboured so hard, at least the immediate purpose, was not achieved. He himself did not translate the Bible. But such was the fascination of the holy tongue and so sacred the meaning of the biblical word, that nothing less than perfection would do. With his zeal he inspired others — and at least to this one student of his little manuscript he leaves the challenge of an undaunted spirit — "Thou shalt meditate therein day and night."

Long-hand with Buber

(a review)

THE BOOK

$\mathcal{L}$et me say it right at the outset: the first of three planned volumes of letters written by, and to, Martin Buber is the most exciting book I have read in years.[1] I finished its six hundred pages at two sittings, and only unavoidable duty prevented me from reading it all at one time. It is literature, history, criticism, Zionism, Germanism, Hasidism; scores of the famous and the near-famous speak in its pages or are addressed by Buber; war and peace, the hopes and tragedies of the Jewish people appear in the ever-changing kaleidoscope of its letters.

The book is, above all, the superb, unselfconscious autobiography of a man who set out to teach Jews and ended up teaching Gentiles more than his own people. You may know little or much about this man; you may belong to the *cognoscenti* who savour the intricacies of *Daniel* and the origins of the Scholem-Buber controversy over the true nature of Hasidic lore; or to you the man may be a mystery, the lover of the Written Torah who rejected the Oral Law. No matter; this exchange of letters will be fascinating to initiate and non-initiate alike. Add to this the finest available short biography and evaluation of Buber that has been written to date (140 pages, by Grete Schaeder who edited the volume); and, further, a corpus of notes, indices, and biographies of Buber's letter partners, and you have the kind of book which comes along only once in a while — for its true subject is history itself, mirrored in the minds of some of the age's most perceptive men and women. The era covered in this first volume is

1897–1918 and it focuses, above all, on the rise of Zionism and the first act of a bitter tragedy: the dissolution of the German-Jewish symbiosis. But there are many other images which appear and re-appear, depending partly on whether Buber kept copies of his own correspondence or whether his correspondents made his letters to them available.

FAMILY

Buber's family surfaces rarely in these letters, except, of course, for his wife, Paula, who, by all odds, was a remarkable woman, an independent creative spirit whom Buber met at the University of Zurich in 1899 (he was twenty-one at the time and she a year older):

> In those days [writes Schaeder] a woman student was still a rarity. In addition to her birthright of great intellectual endowment she possessed apparently a strong urge for personal independence. From Theodore Lessing's auto-biography we knew that even before becoming a student Paula Winkler lived away from her parents' home, in an artists' colony in Southern Tyrol, a "wild elf-like creature" he calls her, "persistent, brilliant, daring;" another time he calls his pupil (who studied Latin with him) "fabulously bright and of dominant will." (p. 34)

Occasionally, Buber's grandmother, Adele, whom he loved deeply, and his grandfather, Solomon, the famous *ba'al ha-midrash*, make their appearance in this volume:

> Whenever I get together with Zionists I am asked how Grandpa is, how he is getting on, how his work is pro-gressing, etc. Never am I introduced to anyone who does not ask me if I am related to Solomon Buber. Recently I was in Breslau and gave a talk before the Zionists there at a celebration of the Maccabeans with more than 600 people in attendance. The Rabbi (Dr. Ferdinand Rosen-thal) came to congratulate me warmly, told me that he

agreed with my opinions and asked me to give regards to Grandpa. Wherever I talk I hear Grandpa's name. From this you can see how deeply the Zionists feel about Jewish literature and how enthusiastic they are about men who, through their work, exalt the crown of Judaism and who, with their whole life, witness to the unbroken vitality of our people. (Letter 7)

Buber's father, a successful businessman, had neither Solomon's scholarship nor understanding for Martin's developing interest in Hasidism:

I would be happier if you would forego your interest in the Hasidic movement and the Zohar. These can only corrode the soul and have dreadful effects. Too bad that you waste your talents on such fruitless matters and use up so much work and time for things that the world cannot utilize. (Letter 124)

But, some years later, after Buber had published his *Daniel*, the father accorded his son reluctant admiration:

We have read the magazine with great interest, and if people will say about your work only a portion of what Landauer writes, you can be rather satisfied. We ourselves are filled with joy and happiness that your endeavours have had such success. I am afraid only that such great intellectual work will be too much for you, and I would be happy if you would occupy yourself with less complex problems and return to some easier work. (Letter 215)

THE JEWISH PEOPLE. ZIONISM

Though born to an East European tradition, Buber had become a Westerner in Germany where he had studied and would continue to live until the Nazis forced him to leave. He must have thought of his own background when he saw a trainload of emigrants pass through Berlin. He wrote to his wife:

> Yesterday at the railway station I saw a special train with a sign: "Russian Emigrants." The people looked out of the window — they were all Jews. One asked me, "What kind of town is this?" None of them knew where he was, all they knew was that they were going to America. How lost they were! They were alone, without guidance. In Hamburg an agent expects them. What it is they will be doing "there" they did not know. They are like things thrown into an empty room. The officials treat them like animals.... One of the emigrants asked us, "You are labouring here?" He could not imagine that one can go to a strange land except to engage there in some form of heavy labour in order to make a meagre living. (Letter 11)

To Buber, America could never be the answer to the Jewish question. He was a spiritual Zionist by religious tradition, a cultural Zionist by inclination, and a political Zionist by dint of circumstance. The leaders of the movement were quick to recognize the unusual literary capabilities of the young man, and Theodor Herzl asked the twenty-two-year-old to take on the editorship of *Die Welt*, the chief organ of World Zionism. Buber answered the great man with respect but not without independence:

> Your invitation gave me great pleasure, coming as it did as proof of your confidence and holding out the possibility of splendid work. If, nonetheless, I tie my acceptance to conditions, you will understand that this is not based on personal motives. I do have a single desire, namely, that the comparative independence which existed at the time of Feiwel's editorship will continue to be safeguarded. I also must ask for an increase in the honorarium paid to writers who assist in the various issues. I have the intention of staying with average fees, but I must have the right to go beyond them if necessary. (Letter 18)

Herzl's trust was not misplaced:

> Esteemed and dear friend! *Die Welt* is splendid. I read
> the last and the current numbers with deep satisfaction
> and pride. I know that though I am tired out, there are
> new people to take my place. (Letter 24)

At the Zionist Congress, Buber had joined Chaim Weizmann's
Democratic Faction, which earned him Herzl's bitter critique. The young
man defended himself vigorously and he labelled the accusation that
Herzl levelled against him "uncalled for and even offensive":

> Nothing is further from our minds than a sense of regret:
> in fact, we are ready now and always to reaffirm what we
> have said and done. I am surprised that in your debates
> you utilized basically impermissible means which cast
> doubt on your opponents' rational sense. (Letter 62)

A year later, the Founder was dead. Buber wrote to his wife:

> You have doubtless heard of Herzl's death; tomorrow
> is the funeral. It came dreadfully unexpected and I
> cannot grasp it. For him, of course, it was the best time
> to die: at the height of his achievement and prior to
> the unavoidable disappointment and defeat. I cannot
> imagine what form our movement will now take on, but
> I can hardly think of that, for the human aspect itself
> moves me too deeply. (Letter 81)

The demise of the leader left the movement bereft of its driving force
and divided against itself. Weizmann, too, was greatly disheartened:

> Now, dear Martin, as far as political intentions are con-
> cerned I have become very pessimistic of late. During
> the summer I was in Vienna for the meeting of the Ac-
> tions Committee and left it with such disgust that until
> today I have not been able to overcome it. After Herzl's

death these people have become even worse. With whom can we work? Have you got people available? If you can name them, fine; I myself do not know any. (Letter 83)

Buber continued to participate in Zionist politics for a while, but he was not cut out for it. He was too introspective; too much the thinker and scholar to fit the role of doer and mover who would jockey for position and would have to disregard the sensitivities of others if that were the only way to success. There was also within him a highly self-critical, almost Hamletian streak which made him, on occasion, indecisive. He planned to settle in Palestine, but delayed even a visit to the land. Then the First World War broke out and, along with his associates, Buber was caught up in its complexities. He was thirty-five years old then; he volunteered for the army but was rejected because of his health. To Hans Kohn he wrote:

> Never have I felt the meaning of [German] "peoplehood" as much as during these weeks. Jews, too, experience this deep and serious sentiment almost to a man. (Letter 250)

A few months later, Hugo Bergmann [now Shmuel Bergman, philosopher at Hebrew University] wrote to him from Vienna in a similar vein:

> Now that we have battled for German culture, we sense more than ever what this culture means to us and how we are tied to its spirit.(Letter 263)

Before long, however, Buber began to develop serious doubts about the war and all supra-patriotic sentimentalities. He knew the difference between truth and propaganda:

> There is nobody today who can dare to say, "The truth about the war is thus and so, and nothing else." Presently we do not even have the most elementary preconditions which would enable us to determine the most "objective" fact. Until we have them, all accusations are empty talk. (Letter 264)

More and more, Jewish fate after the war became Buber's chief concern. He founded a new magazine, *Der Jude*, which was published until the mid-twenties and in its short life earned for itself the reputation of being the world's outstanding forum of Jewish letters. Part of it was devoted to contemplating the tension between Germanism (*Deutschtum*) and Judaism which he, himself, considered "a dynamic and tragic problem, an agony of the soul, which, however, can become creative like every agony." Religious non-Jews, too, felt the pull of contrary forces, but for them it was Germanism and universalism or, as in the case of Hermann Hesse, messianism:

> As far as I am concerned [he wrote to Buber] I have it easier: the conscious acknowledgement of peoplehood is strange to me. Since I react with the pulse of the Gospels I see here the presence of a Messianic mankind which even now exists in the seed, that is, in all the individual believers to whom God is more important than any nation. But I have neither the gift nor the practice to express such thoughts, with which I live as a stranger in my daily existence. But in your writing, even where perhaps you meant it differently, I found here and there some endorsement of my thoughts. (Letter 334)

To some Jews, conversion seemed one way to resolve the tension. A well-known judge had written that he knew of nothing which should keep him from accepting Jesus as the Messiah who had redeemed Israel from idolatry. Buber replied:

> The world is unredeemed — do you not sense this in every drop of blood as I do? Do you not sense as I do that "Messianic" is not a past event, is nothing in a certain spot of the historical past where it can be localized, but only that to which we look in infinity and for which we wait in eternity? A supra-empirical ideal, something toward which we work every hour, directly confronting us, yet untouchable like God Himself and indubitably alive like Him — in other words, the absolute future? Is

it possible that this primeval Jewish sense which is the root of Jewish religiosity, the belief in the fulfilment at the end of days which eschews the ephemeral but yet may, and must, work through the ephemeral, has been torn from your heart? I said that the chasm in this regard is unbridgeable. I mean to say: from me to you there is no bridge at this point. But from you to me, is there one? Would you not ask your own heart? (Letter 372)

But renegades, potential and otherwise, were not the only ones who tested Buber's mettle. For years he carried on a spirited exchange of letters with Stefan Zweig, whose universalism pitted him against Buber's Zionism. Zweig had been asked to contribute to *Der Jude* but felt that he could not commit himself:

However, the goodwill is there and I hope you will believe me. Never have I felt as free — and precisely because of my Judaism — as I feel now, in this time of national delusion. I am separated from you and what you stand for only because I have never desired that Judaism would become a nation once more and thereby debase itself in the competitiveness of reality. I love the Diaspora, and I say yes to its essence of idealism, its world-embracing all-human call.

...My tragedy *Jeremiah* will take a long time finishing. What its fate will be is no longer important to me; I only know that the two years of labour (bitterly wrought from the duties of the military) have purified and saved me. If I survive the war, nothing more can happen to me. I have put behind me all literary ambition and know that I will utilize my power, whatever worth it may have, only on reality itself. I respect you as an old confidant of my beginnings and I feel for you the same moral respect as ever. Whenever you will call me to do something and I feel free to do it, I will follow you. (Letter 333)

Zweig considered himself — precisely because he was a Jew — as a guest everywhere, an intellectual and spiritual mediator. As a classic liberal he embraced his Diaspora as a blessing:

> This supra-national feeling of freedom from the crazy delusion of a fanatic world has saved my soul during this time and I am grateful that it has been Judaism which has made this supra-national freedom available. I actually consider the idea that Judaism should concretize itself [as a nation] a come-down and a rejection of its highest mission.
>
> Perhaps it is its purpose to show throughout the centuries that a community can exist without soil, by common blood and spirit alone, by word and by faith. To forego this singularity would mean for me to resign voluntarily from the high office which we have accepted from history and to close a book which is written on a thousand pages and has yet room for more thousands of years of wandering....
>
> Even though I personally have no faith in the concretization of a community of [Jewish] people who want to rebuild an old nation into a new one, I am still not without respect for those who will create it or devote themselves to the attempt. (Letter 362)

When the issuance of the Balfour Declaration (at the end of 1917) foreshadowed the realization of Zionist dreams, Zweig was more than ever convinced that this represented a regression in Jewish history:

> I am entirely clear about my decision to love the painful idea of Diaspora the more the dream [of Jewish national-ism] appears to come closer to realization — that dan-gerous dream of a Jewish state with cannons, flags, and decorations. For I love Jewish destiny more than Jewish comfort. This people never did find comfort and ful-fillment to be of value, it found its strength only under pressure in the dispersal of its togetherness. When it will

gather in one place it will burst asunder from within. What is a nation except destiny transposed, and what remains of it if it escapes its destiny? Palestine would be the terminal point, the return of the circle to itself, the end of a movement which has deeply touched Europe and the whole world. It would be a tragic disappointment like every repetition. (Letter 384)

Buber replied in words to which his own life would later bear witness:

> Only this today: that I know nothing of a "Jewish state with cannons, flags, and decorations" — not even in the form of a dream. What will be depends on those who will create it, and precisely because of this those must come to help who, like myself, have a human and humane orientation. (Letter 385)

The future founder of *Ihud* speaks here, the passionate lover of Zion who does not want to see his ideals spoiled by the crass politicians and "pragmatists." He wrote to Bergmann early in 1918:

> A few days ago I had a talk with Dr. [Viktor] Jacobson about what is to take place in Palestine. At its conclusion I was near to melancholy. "As quickly as possible and with every means we must create a majority in the land"— the argument made my heart stand still. What can one answer on that same level? We must not deceive ourselves that most of the leading (and probably also most of the led) Zionists are today entirely unscrupulous nationalists (following European models), imperialists indeed, subconscious mercantilists and admirers of success. They talk of "rebirth" and mean "enterprise." If we are not successful in creating an authoritative counter-balance to them, the soul of the whole movement will be spoiled, perhaps forever: In any case, I am determined to do my utmost until the very end, even if

all my personal plans will have to suffer because of it. (Letter 386)

On the same day he addressed to Franz Oppenheimer a letter which outlined his intention to tackle the problem on an intellectual plane:

> I plan a collection of essays against the advance of imperialism, mercantilism, and other spiritual negotiations in Palestine. The collection is not to be primarily polemical in character but, of course, it should point out the threatening danger and give a picture of the community as we understand and want it. (Letter 387)

Buber was not alone in his doubts. Arnold Zweig, who, unlike his namesake, was a staunch Zionist and socialist (he was to make aliyah in 1953, return after the war, and live in East Germany) wrote:

> The real Zionist struggle will begin only after the war. The sense of *golus* will also emigrate to Palestine and we have to be very careful to uncover all its masks, and especially so the mask of Orthodoxy which will be inimical to culture and fight as un-Jewish everything we want to take with us of the great European cultural values. I see a whole knot of problems, but in my good hours I also see, with equal clarity, the spiritual solutions. (Letter 379)

As the war was nearing its end, Buber made his final decision to retreat from political Zionism into scholarship. Was it his growing disillusionment or his basic nature which forbade his active involvement? Perhaps both:

> As far as I am personally concerned, I want at last to take a look at the land, and do it as soon as possible after the war. But probably a number of years will still go by before I can think of settling there. For to start with, I can no longer begin by working the soil and I do not as yet see for myself any possibility of economic

independence. Secondly, and that is the most important thing, there is a reminder by my doctor, who has given me to understand that for the next few years I must give myself entirely to the final formulation of my thought system which of late has matured, and that I must create the possibility of concentration and do so with some care, which means, amongst other things, that I should keep myself back from all public activities....

...I have (at a recent public address) experienced the sense of *limitation*; I can no longer talk "to Jews," in fact, no longer "to...." *Incipit vita nova*. (Letter 400, the last in Volume I)

THE EDITOR

Throughout these early years, after his formal studies had come to an end, Buber had been engaged in literary enterprises. He was forever planning collections and magazines, and in his official capacity as an editor for a leading German publishing house he was in touch with writers and scholars of many persuasions. Life-long associations were formed on more than one occasion after Buber had issued an invitation to submit an article or essay to some collection or to *Der Jude*. In this way he came to know both Rosenzweig and Kafka. To the former he wrote, at the end of 1915:

> Honoured Sir: Beginning next January, together with some friends, I will be editing a monthly magazine called *Der Jude*, which will not be subject to any party philosophy and is meant to treat of Jewish problems in depth and to provide an adequate exposition of Jewish reality as well as an unswerving and insistent emphasis on Hebrew. I have agreed to edit the magazine during the war and during the period immediately afterward, and I would be happy to count you amongst our co-workers. I would like to publish meaningful and relatively brief essays in addition to short comments on the happenings

of the day. I would be very grateful for an early answer
and any terms you would suggest. (Letter 280)

Kafka, long before even the *cognoscenti* had discovered him, was
singled out by Buber as someone whom he wanted to publish. At about
the time when the United States was joining the Allied war effort, Kafka
wrote from Prague:

> Many thanks for your kind letter. Well, I will be published
> in *Der Jude* after all, even though I have always thought
> it impossible. Please do not call my pieces "parables," for
> they are not really parables. If they are to have a joint
> title, then perhaps one should call them "Two Animal
> Stories." (Letter 359. The stories appeared under this
> title in Volume II of *Der Jude*, pages 188 and 559ff)

Editing frequently involved Buber in the unpleasant task of refusing
contributions. He could be very harsh at times, as he was with young
Werner Kraft who was desperately searching for Jewish meaning but
found himself repelled by the Jewish people. Buber was not satisfied
merely to reject the article which Kraft had submitted:

> I do not suppose you will understand what I have said
> of Jewish matters, for you yourself say that it is "the
> Jews who prevent you from appreciating Judaism."
> Apparently you have not occupied yourself at all with
> the latter. As for me, Jews prevent me as little from an
> approach to Judaism, as human beings ... prevent me
> from being human.
>   To say it in your own language: "I do not have the
> courage to publish your writing in my journal;" or, to
> speak in my own tongue: "I do not believe that what you
> have to say matters at all." (Letter 345)

Kraft was deeply hurt but persisted in his search, and, in time, became
Buber's admirer and disciple. In 1933, he settled in Palestine and, in 1966,

published a noteworthy volume of Buberiana in which he reported on years of conversations with the master.

But when Buber admired someone he admired deeply, and when he loved he loved passionately. Is there a more perceptive evaluation anywhere of Shmuel Josef Agnon than what Buber wrote about the man who, a half century later, would receive the Nobel Prize in literature:

> You would like to hear from me a word about our friend Agnon. Not many words, just one! Here it is: Agnon has a sacred relationship to Jewish existence. There are others, who like him know about it, but their knowledge is meagre. Then there are still others who feel like him about Jewish existence, but their sentiment is vague. Agnon is one of the few who have a sense of sanctity about the components of Jewish life. This sanctity is neither cold nor sentimental, it is glowing and firm — that is Agnon. Sanctity: not false, conceited, and shot through with pose, but one which is right, quiet, humble, loyal. That is Agnon. He is destined to be the poet and chronicler of Jewish life, both of that which dying today and is in a state of metamorphosis: and also of that which is in the state of becoming and not yet known. Agnon is both from Galicia and Palestine, he is Hasid and pioneer, and he carries in his loyal heart the essence of both worlds in balance and in sanctity. Shall I tell you how we esteem him? We love him. (Letter 299)

The sampling could go on and on — but then the whole book is a sampler from which, at times, one tastes delicious tidbits (as when Agnon — who instructed Buber's son in Hebrew — inquires whether the latter remembered anything), and at times savours a full course (as in the correspondence with Gustav Landauer, Buber's close friend whose life was ended by a political assassin).

Ernst Simon, in his Preface, tells us that even as an old man Buber continued writing his letters by hand. It did not come easy; he had to work at it as he did with any personal relationship, and he was aware that (as Simon writes) "of all means of communication a letter is most particularly exposed to misunderstanding, because it is both direct and mediated speech." Matters became even more complicated because Buber achieved wide fame at an early age and was considered, as he himself noted, "an oracle." Letters to and from an oracle are soon touched by the mystery of prescience — and occasionally one begins to taste its flavour even in this first volume.

Grete Schaeder, herself a friend and longtime interpreter of Buber's, has made this selection from a prodigious amount of material available at the Hebrew University, and the result is a book extraordinary in every respect, which leaves one looking for the early appearance of its two successor volumes. Simon's hope that they be accorded adequate attention will not be disappointed.

Assessing the Jewish Mind
(a review)

"*J*ews are just like any other people, only more so." I do not know when or where this well-worn saying originated, but I rather suspect it has its roots in the nineteenth-century North American ideology which held that all people were more or less alike, their cultural differences accidental, and distinctions an invention of the devil.

Jews especially were anxious to proclaim that the peculiarities which popular prejudice ascribed to them were either nonexistent or exaggerated. Radical reformers among them pressed for a concomitant change of religious practice which would unmistakably express this view: they rearranged their synagogue pews and pulpit, making the latter — in Protestant style — the focus, replacing the old centre platform from which Scripture and liturgy were traditionally read. They removed their head coverings, reduced the amount of Hebrew in the service, and introduced responsive prayers and English hymns. It was done, Jewish Orthodox criticism notwithstanding, not for the purpose of giving up the ancestral faith, but to make Jews acceptable to the Christian majority. Strange as it now sounds to most Jewish ears, the approbation of non-Jews became an important part of the Jewish agenda. When a visitor to the synagogue exclaimed with genuine surprise, "Your worship is so much like ours," it was, to the Jews, an indication that this recognition of basic similarities in religion would soon be followed by social, economic, and political acceptance. The rise of anti-Semitism rudely shook this anticipation and restructured the Jewish psyche fundamentally.

An inquiry into the specific characteristics of Jews and Jewish attitudes is today neither a putative justification for Gentile discrimination nor a vehicle for anti-defamation, but a legitimate subject for scholarly effort. One must therefore be grateful to Raphael Patai for attempting a comprehensive approach to what clearly is a complex subject.[1] For in exploring it one needs to traverse such diverse matters as Jewish intelligence, giftedness, genuine and special talents, personality and character, physical and mental health, alcoholism, overeating, drug addiction, the world of values, self-hate, and, in addition, become familiar with the outlines of Jewish history.

Of course the basic question is whether in fact a "Jewish mind" can be said to exist at all:

> Social psychologists and anthropologists have found that the plurality in any given population share certain motives, traits, beliefs, and values. In a large aggregate, such as a nation, the sum total of these shared mental traits is referred to as "national character" or "basic personality." In other words, when a social scientist speaks of, say, the "Polish national character" and states that the "Polish mind" is characterized by traits A, B, and C, he does not mean that every Pole exhibits them, but merely that these traits are found more frequently among Poles than, say, traits D or E. It is with this qualification in mind that we shall discuss "Jewish" intelligence, "Jewish" talents, "Jewish" character traits, etc., as well as differences between the "Jewish mind" and the "Gentile mind."

These considerations are adequate as far as they go. They do not, however, fully deal with a related problem (and the book as a whole barely touches on it): that *individual* Jews may often not exhibit the traits which pass as "Jewish" and that only in the aggregate, when they are subject to mass psychology and group pressure, can these traits be said to emerge. In other words, the characteristics described as Jewish may not be the characteristics of any significant group of individuals *per se*, but only aspects of mass psychology.

This observation does not of course restrict itself to Jews. For instance, during the Hitler period the average German could probably not be found to exhibit any traceable degree of murderous instincts or inhumanity which could be measured and be seen to set the German significantly apart from any individual elsewhere. But as a nation, subjected to mass hysteria and incitement, and given certain sets of circumstances (such as fear of the Gestapo), Germans did as a nation what as individuals they probably would not and could not have done. To be sure, this is an extreme example, but the underlying dynamics are operative elsewhere, certainly among the Jews. To use one example: Patai's discussion of Jewish charity is an admirable exposition of what motivates the individual Jew and what his tradition has contributed to making charity a prime demand on every member of the people, but the author does not touch at all on the influence of group pressure, which has a measurable effect on the funds raised for charitable purposes. It may well be that the individual Jew when compared to his neighbour is more "charitable"; but the extent of his charity is influenced by peer factors to a degree perhaps found nowhere else in comparable social structures.

The underlying thesis of Patai's book is related to Arnold Toynbee's concept of Challenge and Response. (One should not wonder that this is nowhere acknowledged, for Toynbee had little appreciation for the dynamics of Jewish history.) Patai's basic approach is stated early in his book: "The Jewish mind has for two thousand years been exposed to two equally powerful forces — the Jewish tradition and the Gentile influence. And it is itself a product of the tension between the two; by contrast to the Gentile mind, it is, to a much greater extent, exogenous. For this reason it is evidently not possible to discuss the Jewish mind without constant reference to the Gentile environment whose impact so greatly contributed to its formation."

The desire to explain the Jewish situation as a response to the challenge of external circumstance occasionally leads Patai into some dubious assessments. In his discussion of the essence of Jewishness, he considers the antique Jewish self-image (which he describes as highly particularistic and withdrawn into itself) as a natural response to the overwhelming pressures of Greek and Roman rule. As an example, he quotes the statement of Simon the Just (about 200 BC) recorded in the

Ethics of the Fathers: "The world stands on three things: on Torah, on worship and on charity." Patai then supplies the following commentary:

> When using the expression "the world" [Simon] did not, of course, mean the world-at-large, which bore no relationship to the Torah and to the Temple service, but the Jewish world. One must therefore interpret this saying as meaning that the existence of Jewry depended on the study of the law, the performance of the Temple ritual, and the practice of charity. Against this view which assigns a pivotal place to ritual, as one would expect of a sage who was also a priest, Rabban Shim'on ben Gamliel [first half of the second century AD] stated that the three things on which the world [that is, again, Jewry] stood were justice, truth and peace — three moral features which were "Jewish" only inasmuch as they were made into fundamentals of Jewish existence.

It seems to me that this misses the mark. Of course it cannot be denied that Patai's interpretation is *possible*. But it is not convincing, for it overlooks entirely the outer-directed nature of Jewish morality and the basic conception of the Covenant, which is an essential part already of the prophetic stance. To be sure, the pursuit of justice is commanded to Jews, and it is also true that "Love thy neighbour" first meant the person next door, or the member of the village or the tribe. However, it was not long before these concepts opened out into larger vistas. For at the root of the Jewish image of self was also a conviction that God had placed this singular people at the core of history, that He wanted its partnership in the task of salvation, and that therefore the world at large was indeed dependent on Israel. Detractors of Judaism may view this as a thoroughly arrogant conception, a form of historical self-idolization, but even this assessment will not take away from its existence in the Jewish mind: what a member of the people did was considered pivotal to human existence. In a manner of speaking each person could help to save the world.

This conception is part of the idea of Jewish centrality. Whatever its objective "truth" may be, its subjective existence cannot be doubted, and as such it became a dynamic factor in Jewish history; for what one believes contributes to one's character, philosophy and action. Simon the Just, as well as Simon the son of Gamliel, certainly believed that the world (that is, humanity itself) depended on Israel's performance. A people faithful to the Covenant could help to bring salvation to this world, a people disloyal to it would delay the coming of redemption. The framers of the Torah were aware of this ideological sweep. This is why they began the story of Israel's Covenant and the exposition of the Law with the story of Creation itself, for Sinai cannot be understood without Creation. God spoke and the world came into being, and again God spoke and the foundations for a moral humanity were delineated, as His own people, the servants who would bring His divine purposes to fruition, came into existence.

I have a further problem with Patai's conception that according to the ancient rabbis the crucial distinction between the nations and Israel lay "neither in ritual, nor in the credal, but in the moral realm." No such distinction existed in the talmudic mind between ritual, credal, and moral conceptions. Halakhah (the pragmatic practice of God's will as expressed in daily life) did not know, at least in its essential features, a distinction between form, faith, and ethics. Rather, Jewish ritual was by nature ethical, and the very fact that it was God's will made it an aspect of morality. But there can be no disagreement with Patai's summation of what he calls the core of Jewishness, "the belief in the one God; the belief in the special relationship between God and Israel; the duty toward God; and the duty toward one's fellow man."

In so wide-ranging a work one is bound to find passages of exceptional strength and others that one would wish to have been phrased differently. Patai's discussion of "Who is a Jew?" is excellent and lucid; but despite his awareness of fundamental ideological differences between various religious groups, these differences are not really exposed. Apparently, a consideration of what constitutes the specific reasons for one person to become Orthodox, another Conservative, and a third Reform was not part of the author's plan. Nonetheless, the absence of an adequate consideration of these vital movements and their social and psychological impact on the formation of the contemporary Jewish mind seems to me a serious lacuna. There was more to the result of Enlightenment than the numbers of Jews leaving their people and constituting a large brain drain. Also, not surprisingly, in Patai's book Canada is merely a small footnote to the United States.

The author comes to some conclusions which will doubtless arouse vigorous opposition. Chief among these is his firm conviction that Jews are indeed, or have become in the course of centuries, more intelligent than other people. The reasons are various, but his conclusions are simple. Jews are not by accident preponderant in intellectual and artistic enterprises; the Jewish mind has developed along certain ways, and the payoff has come in the free world. He extends this conviction to those groups of Jews who are currently not exposed to full opportunities for mental development, and he conjectures that the Sephardim, given their chance, will prove to have the same superior IQ as (he claims) have their Ashkenazic brethren elsewhere.

> Having reached the end of our road, with what final thought can we leave the reader who has patiently followed thus far? Perhaps this: Our examination of the Jewish mind disclosed the *homo Judaeus* to be a human specimen with great and many internal variations and with significant differences everywhere between him and his Gentile environment. Some of these differences show him to be superior to the Gentiles; in others he is inferior to them. On balance it would seem a pity, and a loss to humanity as a whole, if Jewish assimilation should lead to a state where the Jewish mind would in no way differ from the Gentile mind. Conversely, it appears that mankind would be better off if it could acquire more of the characteristics of the Jewish mind than it has done heretofore.

All in all, Patai's book represents an interesting, informed, and well-written, though often selective, analysis of what constitutes the Jewish mind. As the first serious full-length study of the subject, it has broken ground in an area that was hitherto reserved for specialists on the one hand and anti-Semitic charlatans like Theodor Fritzsche or

Alfred Rosenberg on the other. We should not be surprised, however, if each new inquiry will yield somewhat different data, for the Jewish mind, whatever it may be, is subject to radical change both in Israel and in the Diaspora.

Theological Questions

What I Believe

1. In what sense do I believe the Torah to be divine revelation? In no sense and in every sense. The answer is meant to be neither paradoxical nor evasive; it is conditioned by my understanding of the two key expressions "the Torah" and "divine revelation."

Divine revelation is a self-disclosure of God. It requires God as well as man to give it reality, for all revelation is a form of communication. To reveal need not imply speaking and hearing — perhaps it never does; it always means the communication of selfness and essence. Divine revelation is God's-accessibility-and-man's-knowing.

To know the Other One is to grasp part of His reality. It is a knowledge based on greater certainty than that accorded our sensual or logical apprehension. When we "know" a person or a thing or a situation in this sense, we commit not our skill but our selves to this knowledge. We grasp it and are grasped by it. "I know that my Redeemer liveth" expresses such certainty. And to the man who can say this, God has revealed himself.

Orthodoxy believes that such revelation has, in Torah and Prophets, implied a verbal communication. I do not believe this. I do not believe that man's spiritual reach exceeds the knowledge of God's being and essence. This is what Rosenzweig meant when he said that at Sinai God revealed no words, no commandments, only *Anokhi*, "I am." The rest was, literally, commentary — human commentary, the attempt to translate the apprehension of God's being into the imperatives of human behaviour. "God spoke" is a figure of speech, denoting, "This is what I know God wants of me." It is the consequence of revelation, not the revelation itself.

Every communication is conditioned by the way in which the communicants interpret the message. Divine revelation is a direct relationship between man and God; when it is communicated to others and reduced to speech or writing, it becomes interpretation. Torah and Prophets are records of Israel's interpretation of divine encounters.

The plural is used advisedly. Revelation is not a single act but a process, a succession of events culminating in the supreme experience of knowing, which in turn, in the very attempt to prolong the experience and to interpret it, yields to elation-and-agony, certainty-and-doubt. The consequences of revelation are both the healing and the hurt: the concomitant of divine knowing is divine doubt. The possession of things brings in its train the fear of losing; friendship and love carry the potential of painful separation; and thus, when man has heard the divine question, *Ayekka?*, "Where art thou?," he at once, having answered, *Hineni*, "Here I am," feels constrained to ask in turn, *"Where art Thou?"*

Revelation is, by its nature, neither confined to one time, nor to one man, nor, for all I know, to one people. Applied to the relationship of God and Israel, revelation was not limited to Sinai, even if Sinai represents, as I believe it does, not a single place but a series of events. Each generation stands at Sinai; each generation has the opportunity of "seeing the thunder," as the process of knowing God is so tellingly called in Exodus.

This understanding of revelation precludes my giving assent to the proposition that the Torah (i.e., the five Books of Moses) *is* divine revelation. It is the mirror of God's presence, but not the presence itself. The mirror is flawed because it is human; it is recapitulation of the essence but not the essence itself. This is why I said in the beginning that the Torah can in no sense be called divine revelation.

Yet not only *the* Torah, but Torah in the wider meaning (denoting Israel's progressing, ongoing encounter with God) represents what record we have of our people's spiritual reach. All of Torah, down to our day, wrestles with confrontation and turning away, with what was and what is, with reality and potential, with certainty and doubt. While the Torah *is* in no way revelation, it does *manifest* it in every way. It is record and failure to record, *mitzvah* understood and misunderstood, God known and God forgotten.

This is, of course, a liberal's approach. It implies the need for human judgment, my judgment, with its potential and its limitations. It carries the burden of choice: it speaks of freedom which must forever guard against the temptation of convenience. The 613 commandments are my starting point: I observe what I, listening for the voice, can hear as being addressed to me. What I hear today is not always what I heard yesterday, and tomorrow may demand new *mitzvot*, for I may be capable of new insights, a wider reach.

Time was when *Taryag*, the 613, represented a consensus, the evolutionary agreement of how the record of revelation was to be read and interpreted. The mainstream of Judaism ran clear and strong as long as this consensus existed. Since it ceased, in the wake of Enlightenment and Emancipation, the waters of revelation have rarely broken through the surface rock of indifference and doubt. Since then, we have all become searchers for the living waters, each of us in his own way, each with his own divining rod.

Today, a newly emerging consensus among the non-Orthodox is slowly taking form. It will be some time before it becomes clearly discernible. When that time comes, the people as a whole who have hidden themselves from God may once again, together with their traditional brethren who have guarded the old way, bear witness to the incursion of the divine into the realm of Israel. Until then, I listen to and take counsel with those who, liberals like myself, strain to be what they must be as Jews, and I seek their guidance. This joint and yet individual hearing, weak as it may be, is my only channel of understanding. There is none other, at least not for me.

2. Having devoted an entire book to the subject of chosenness I will touch on only a few relevant aspects.

I affirm chosenness, albeit in a special sense. I know little about the *content* of chosenness, except that it cannot — any more than the content of any other relationship — be static. The burden at Sinai differed from that of the prophets; Israel in Babylon had a task different from that it faced in Auschwitz. The world is not what it was, despite Koheleth's assertion to the contrary. In facing our world we meet challenges indigenous to our age. It is the task of each generation to search for the meaning of its chosenness, the "perhaps" of its existence.

The use (and misuse) to which choice and chosenness have been put is of historic and political interest only. From a theological viewpoint it is irrelevant. In any case, *atta v'hartanu* has nothing to do with superiority, even if Jews and non-Jews have at times so construed it. And despite Toynbee's vocal asseveration, the sins of chauvinism and racism were not fathered by the Jew.

Chosenness does not imply limited access to God; there are many ways of serving Him. Nor is Israel by definition a limited people. It is so by dint of history and circumstance. Israel's unique way of serving God is open to all who would join in.

3. Is Judaism the one true religion? A strong strain in our tradition answers this question in the affirmative, despite the oft-quoted meliorating dictum that "the righteous of all nations have a share in the world-to-come." Agreeing for a moment that Judaism can be classified properly as a "religion," and holding subsequent thereto that it is *a* true religion — i.e., a true way of serving God — I cannot believe that it is the only way of serving Him. For the Jew it is; for him the covenant provides the framework of his divine and human relationships. For those outside of the *b'rith* there are many other opportunities.

What distinctive contribution can Judaism make to the world? Itself. The Jewish way of serving God is not the only way; it is, for humanity's sake, an *essential* way. The presence of the Jew and his tradition, his mood, his stance, his special accent on life — all these have a pivotal role in the society of men. The believing Jew sees himself as a child of the covenant and hence always *sub specie aeternitatis*. That he does so both as an individual and as a member of a people gives his striving a unique dimension. The believing Jew is always engaged in the salvation of the world rather than of his own soul; in doing so he pursues *mitzvot* rather than proclaiming a system of thought.

4. All religion, it has been said, begins with mysticism and ends in politics. At this late date one need hardly affirm that Judaism is deeply concerned with the condition of the *polis*. Consequently, Judaism has something to say on all political matters which involve moral judgments.

The Jew, like everyone else, ought to make his decisions out of the moral imperatives that govern his life. I act on the basis of Judaism, as

I understand it. For me, a particular political viewpoint is in most cases a particular moral viewpoint backed (for often less than moral reasons) by a political party or personage. Judaism, being the foundation of my moral existence, urges me to a certain position — but it is not an abstract "Jewish imperative," it is *my* imperative based on *my* understanding of what Judaism demands of me. There are many who read the divine script differently, but that may be my error, not theirs.

Could then a "good Jew" (I am not sure what this means) be a Communist or a Fascist? No, if such political conviction endorses the policy of preventing a man from fulfilling his potential; if, for instance, it means to make it impossible for a Jew to live as a Jew; or if the Communist or Fascist state declares the striving after God to be an antisocial pursuit. No, if being a Fascist or Communist means favouring the abridgment of human rights in any form; if the interests of the community by definition and practice submerge the liberties of the individual.

Yes, if Communism could denote, as it does for some, merely economic or political ideas which deal with the ownership and distribution of wealth and its administration. Such separation of theory from practice is hard to maintain nowadays, which makes the yes rather theoretical, if not academic. As for Fascism, I am unaware of any acceptable description of its system which does not contain approval of violence as a means of obtaining and maintaining power, and of justice supine before the state.

5. "God is dead": any discussion involving man's idea of and relation to God has relevance for me. There were and are many to whom God was dead at Auschwitz; there are many today who, while they consider themselves to be Jews, yet cannot bring themselves to affirm the God of Judaism. No rabbi I know deals lightly with this contemporary dilemma. Nor is it the first time Jews have faced it.

Haskalah and post-Haskalah wrestled with it and so already did the talmudic sage who had God say of Israel: "Would that they had forsaken Me but had kept My commandments!" There is a strong implication here that Israel, as long as the *mitzvot* are recognized and kept, could conceivably get along without God. The separation of God from man has been repeatedly contemplated as a divine (and human!) possibility.

The Jew, of course, was never caught in the narrow confines of a triune affirmation. He had a hundred different terms for God, fitting every mood and every divine aspect, and in a way also fitting most philosophies. God was Father, Friend, Husband. As "Master of the Universe" He might seem far removed from man, yet He was ever so close to him in the equivalent Hebrew appellation, *Ribbono shel olam*. He was King of the Kings of Kings, and He was also *Du*; He was and is Presence, Place of the World, God of the Fathers, and, always, God of Israel.

I suspect that the "God is dead" philosophers face a primarily Christian problem. For the Jew, God, Israel, and Torah are one, hence the absence or denial of God undermines also one's existence as a Jew. Theology and peoplehood dwell close together in Jewish life, while the *mitzvah*-directed, this-worldly orientation of Judaism gives all matters of belief and faith a less than central position. Jews have been occupied for a long time with the problem of survival. The time has not yet come when this preoccupation appears antiquarian.

The most serious challenge to Jewish belief is neither this particular constellation of thought nor philosophy and science as disciplines. It is, rather, *scientism*, the elevation of science to the position of arbiter of all human enterprises, the yardstick of thought and action. In this conflict with scientism, Judaism can have the devoted assistance of men in universities who themselves are scientists and yet are rigorously opposed to all dogmatic asseverations, scientific or religious. Scientism has become the pied piper of our younger generation whose hearts and minds we stand in danger of losing unless we can learn to speak to them with words and concepts they can understand, and face them with human tasks to which they can wholly give themselves.

The Sabbath as Protest:

Thoughts on Work and Leisure

in the Automated Society

I

A Change of Concept

The difficulty of approaching our subject lies to no small degree in the fact that all its important terms — Sabbath, work, leisure — have undergone changes of meaning. These changes are not merely semantic novelties. They contain changes of subtle or not so subtle emphasis revealing shifts in cultural outlook. One of the great problems of any contemporary discussion involving religion and society is that such changes of terms and concepts are not always sufficiently recognized. Let me give you an example which will serve as an opening illustration.

A few years ago a young woman called at a home in an upper-class neighbourhood. She represented a university-sponsored survey to gather materials for a family study. The surveyor was courteously received by the lady of the house who, having been assured that complete anonymity of the respondents would be observed, gave her answers with total frankness. She answered questions about her parents and children, and about sexual relationships with her husband as well as her and his extra-marital ventures. The interviewer then asked, "Incidentally, what is your husband's income?" The answer: "Now listen, aren't you getting a little personal?"

This story, which I am assured is not apocryphal, tells us not only about the way in which sex and money may or may not be discussed in our time, but also reveals something far more significant: where formerly the family sphere defined the man and his status, and his finances were an external additive, today money, that is, possession and the social status which derive therefrom, primarily describe a man. Which is to say, the meaning of the words *private* and *public* has changed because the very structure of society which defined these terms has undergone revolutionary changes.

So it is with the terms *work* and *leisure* with which I am concerned in this lecture. Everyone seems to be quite clear when he is told by someone else, "I have little leisure." Yet, the speaker may convey something altogether different from what his counterpart, using the same words and the same sentence structure, would have meant one hundred years ago. What is "little" today would have been "much" then; and "leisure" itself has changed its content.

We no longer live in Puritan times when idleness was considered one of the seven deadly sins and the word *sloth* a favourite opprobrium. Today idleness appears, to many, as one of life's most desirable blessings and, when it is achieved, often as its greatest threat. I do not know whether a Puritan could have understood the term *killing time*, but we certainly can.

Similarly with the term *work*; if the story of the Garden of Eden means anything, it means that work was at one time considered a curse — although later Jewish and Christian theology strenuously denied this and turned it in fact into its opposite, so that work became the very essence of living and labour its own fulfillment. We shall have more to say on this later on, but let it be noted now that work no longer has this implication today. For most of us it is a means to an end; it implies not life but livelihood. And if the latter can be obtained in some other way, by investment or pension, then most of us would like to be done with working, only to tackle the even more difficult problem of leisure.

Even time itself is a relative concept, and not merely since the days of Einstein. It has had different meanings in successive ages and often in different places and cultures at the same time. In our society, we save time, spend time, waste time, in the same way in which we waste, spend, and save money. In fact, time is money. But it is not so for everyone.

A study of contemporary Greek society reveals this analysis:

> Greeks "pass" the time; they do not save or accumulate or use it.... The clock is not master of the Greek: it does not tell him to get up, to go to the field.... At church the people

are not impatient while waiting for Mass to begin; and the church fills only gradually. They know when to go to church; yet when a foreign visitor inquires as to the time of a certain Mass, the subject creates a discussion; and eventually the answer will be something like: "Between 2 and 3." And when Greeks who follow their traditional ways invite, they say, not: "Come at 7 o'clock," but: "Come and see us." To arrive to dinner on time is an insult, as if you came just for the food. You come to visit, and the dinner eventually appears…. For the Greek traditionally, to work against time, to hurry, is to forfeit freedom. Even in the cities, people are called "Englishmen" when they turn up on the dot at meetings or appointments.[1]

Examples can be multiplied. When I went to university in Germany, a distinction was always made between standard time and academic time. When you said "two o'clock" without any additive, you meant two sharp. When you said "two o'clock academic," you meant 2:15. Every Jew knows that we have, or at least had in the very recent past, something called "Jewish time." A Jewish fraternal or Zionist meeting may be called for 8:30 p.m., but it is understood that it will not start until 9:00. There are still some people in Toronto who are shocked to find that when they come to my synagogue at 6:30 p.m. for a wedding that has been called at 6:00, the ceremony is already over. Not a few have been quite incensed over this breach of what they consider a Jewish cultural convention. In Toronto a dinner invitation for 7:00 p.m. on a weekday, means 7:00 sharp or shortly thereafter; on a Saturday night it would be perfectly alright to arrive at 7:45 or even 8:00.

What I have been trying to say in this somewhat lengthy prolegomenon is that in approaching the problems and opportunities of the Sabbath we must be aware that we are dealing with variables. Further, if we are to make a radical reassessment of our time and value structure, as I believe is urgently necessary, it is both instructive and useful to take the Sabbath as paradigmatic. The revolution which it set off when it first made its appearance amongst the Jews has not yet ended and its potential function may yet be as great as it has ever been. For the Sabbath is indeed a ubiquitous institution. In one form or another, it now exists amongst all people in the West. Its neglect, misuse, and abuse are in themselves significant bellwethers of social problems, even as its radical reassessment may become a window of hope and progress.

· II

The Sabbath in History — A Partial Survey

Much has been written on the relationship between the biblical Sabbath and the Babylonian *shappatu*, which was considered an unlucky day on which certain labours and procedures were proscribed. Just what the connection was between these taboos and the work prohibition of the Bible is no longer clear. Suffice it to say that somewhere in history there appeared a revolutionary observance of religious time which was not dependent on any natural phenomena in the heavens or on earth.

The significance of the Sabbath as opposed to the earliest festivals in Israel and in all nations was precisely that it was not dependent on the position of sun or moon, on planting or harvest time. To be sure, both in Genesis and Exodus, the Sabbath is related to Creation, that is, to a cosmic event. But its celebration week after week becomes remembrance and is not based on contemporaneous observations or happenings. Thus, the Sabbath becomes God's time, the God who created the world and also created Israel. Every Sabbath, when the Jew lifts his Kiddush cup for blessing, he remembers the One who created the Universe out of primeval darkness and led His people from the night of Egyptian slavery.

At a later age the Sabbath became "humanized," if one may so call it. It became social time devoted to the liberation of every man from the fetters of work, a liberation which included the freeman as well as the slave. Thus the Sabbath acquired a dual aspect which it has maintained throughout the centuries and which can best be explained by the differences between the Ten Commandments in the Books of Exodus and Deuteronomy.

The command in Exodus (20:8) opens by saying *zachor*—"Remember the Sabbath Day." Remembrance is an act of cognition, of reason, of the mind. The Deuteronomic command (5:12) begins with *shamor* —"Observe the Sabbath Day." Man is here called to an act of will rather than reason. Thus cognition and obligation form the twin aspects of this day, which is God's time and man's time and finds a place for both.

Or put it another way. *Zachor* demands spiritual effort, *shamor* physical observance. We may state here the distinction which Isaac Arama made centuries ago. "Remember," he said, is a reference to rest as sanctification; "observe" to rest from physical labour.[2] We shall return to this proposition at a later time, but lest the differentiation is driven too far, I may also quote another tradition, which emphasizes the need to consider *zachor* and *shamor* as two sides of the same coin: "The two commandments 'Remember' and 'Observe' were spoken by God in one single moment."[3]

Like any vital religious system, Judaism became deeply concerned with the need to translate the Sabbath command into Sabbath reality. The Talmud developed thirty-nine different categories of labour, with many subdivisions arising therefrom, so that to the superficial observer it might appear that the Sabbath was indeed a great burden laden with taboos and prohibitions. Prohibitions there certainly were and many of them, but a burden? No — that the Sabbath was not— at least not in those days when work and rest still meant what since biblical times they had meant. Only when the cultural environment, in fact the whole context of civilization, changed to such a degree that labour and idleness, leisure and work, assumed different meanings, only then were the ancient categories of the Talmud first drawn into question and then largely abandoned by the multitudes of the Jewish people.

It is not essentially different with the Christian observance of the Sabbath. We here in North America are to a large degree inheritors of the Puritan tradition, and while the younger generation may recall Blue Laws only from the history books, we older ones still remember them very clearly. A mere nine years ago when I moved to Toronto you could not see a movie on Sundays, a prohibition which has since been abandoned. In many American states there are similar leftovers, covering sports events or the purchase of alcohol.

The disappearance of the Blue Laws signals the abandonment of certain old ideas and values. It highlights the breakup of traditional society, just as the dissolution of the Jewish ghetto was highlighted by the disregard of the thirty-nine categories of forbidden Sabbath labour.

Here too, then, the Sabbath has become paradigmatic. It has heralded the shattering of personal observance. Not by coincidence, attendance at Sabbath services is falling to ever-lower levels.

People concerned with the religious enterprise are, however, quite mistaken when they believe that attractive services, fine music, comfortable pews, air-conditioned halls, and other esthetic and physical stimuli will return church and synagogue to their erstwhile pre-eminence. Nothing of the sort. People will return when the Sabbath and what it means become important to them, not the other way around. And in our day the Sabbath cannot become important to people until it has been radically restructured, its foundations re-examined and its opportunities thoroughly reassessed in the modern context. The old Sabbath may be alive for the few; for the many it is a shell without substance. A new Sabbath observance must begin with real and realistic relationships, with people where they presently are in their daily lives.

III

New Approaches

Quantitatively, the work week is constantly getting shorter. In Canada a union recently demanded that its work week be reduced from thirty-two to twenty-eight hours. While such demands will be made and granted more and frequently in the next decade, they no longer form the major concern of the working public. No longer will it be the right not to work which people will worry about, but the right to work. The very concept of a negative income tax indicates this inversion. Fifteen years ago it was estimated that there were 500 billion leisure adult hours to be disposed of in the United States. Now, the figure may easily be double.

Concurrently, leisure has become a problem. Where formerly man was concerned with surcease from work, he now wonders how to get surcease from leisure. Furthermore, our rapidly increasing geriatric population needs everything except physical rest. Doing nothing was for centuries the acme of pleasure, and too much work a curse; now too much leisure is a curse and doing something a pleasure.[4]

In 1952, Josef Pieper called leisure one of the foundations of modern Western culture, and claimed that we had entered a new era in which one would have to set aside the prejudices that come from over-valuing the sphere of work. Work alone, he emphasized, could no longer define our concept of human life. Leisure had to be recognized as a source of value and perhaps its primary source.[5] A few years after Pieper first gave the concept of leisure a new dimension, the Jewish Theological Seminary of America called a Conference on the New Leisure and subsequently published a volume of its findings.[6] Leisure, the conference held, must now be incorporated into the theological and philosophical thinking of church and synagogue.

What these new approaches tried to do was to remove work from the centre of our attention and put leisure in its place. They intended to replace the traditional work ethic of Western culture with a leisure ethic. But despite all the quantitative changes in our work-and-rest habits we still continue — at least for the present — to consider work as central to human existence. The important change which has taken place is that it is the *quality* of work — and no longer its quantity — which determines the structure of our civilization. The question that men ask is no longer "How long do I have to work?" or "How much leisure can I get?" That is the surface question which is asked in labour negotiations. The human question below, however, is asked with ever greater urgency: "How can I do significant work? How can I do work which fulfills not only the needs of my pocketbook, but also the needs of my ego?" French young people were recently asked, "What is most important in choosing your job?" The answers were as follows: the job must be interesting — 65 percent; it must pay a high salary — 24 percent; it must provide much leisure — 10 percent.[7]

Pieper and his successors were of course right in one important area and therein lies their chief contribution: leisure *is* a potential source of significant living, and this is the area to which we now turn.

We can begin with an old definition, to which I have already alluded, that of Isaac Arama who differentiated between Sabbath rest and sanctification. This definition was taken up in the nineteenth century by the Jewish religious Reformer Samuel Holdheim and his successors.[8] Definitions, of course, do not a Sabbath make, and so the rabbinical Reformers had little success in rescuing the Sabbath from neglect, for they approached its problems in an ideological rather than a structural way — that is to say, they believed that by providing their new definition they could also radically alter the habits of their contemporaries. That was a delusion which we ourselves must take care not to emulate.

But it is important to realize that all living consists of doing and not doing, of positive acts and of abstaining. The opportunities of the Sabbath still lie in turning doing and not doing toward rest and sanctification. Only we must understand these opportunities in the context of our time. We still need rest, but not primarily from work. Rather, *we need rest from unrest*. We do need sanctification in our lives and particularly a *sanctification of freedom*, the cry for which is urgent in our time.

Two questions arise here. For one, why must rest and sanctification be linked to the Sabbath? Young people especially suspect that tying these objectives (of which they generally approve) to one particular day, is another way of shoring up the institutional religious enterprise. I do not deny my hope that such might indeed be a result. But the argument needs to be met on its own merits. Now, experience teaches that while occasional and intuitive actions are in fact often more authentic religious responses than the regular and patterned practices of traditional religion, the former will tend to occur so rarely that their effect on one's life becomes negligible. The repetitive occurrence of the Sabbath is more likely to encourage rest and sanctification than the once-in-a-while, whenever-it-may-be spontaneity which sounds ideal and turns out to be Utopian.

Second, must our response be couched in prescribed acts and abstentions? Alvin Reines, in opposing such codification, pleads for an "open symbolism," a framework vague enough to permit each person his own understanding of and response to the opportunity, because the set responses of traditional religion are most likely no longer meaningful to him.[9] However, in the Jewish context group observance has its own motive force in addition to its indigenous merit: it is good for the enhancement of Jewish identity and in turn encourages others to join in these particular forms. But Reines is right when he suggests that there must be openness, and indeed, contemporary guides to Sabbath observance should emphasize choices and opportunities.[10]

IV

Rest from Unrest

If the Sabbath is to have any significance it must confront one of modern man's greatest curses, his internal and external unrest. This unrest arises from the fact that today he leads a life without goals and, as a consequence, that he is involved in competition without end.

1. Life without Goals

Formerly, both the physical and spiritual goals of man were clear. He needed to survive physically and do everything and anything that would help him achieve this goal. He tried to survive in nature's as well as in society's jungle. He had to fight the devils of sickness and starvation and whatever else was his lot. If only he could survive he had achieved life's major physical goal. Spiritually, the matter was even simpler. With Jew, Christian, and Mohammedan, living the good life or the life of faith was sure to bring some form of salvation: Paradise, Heaven, or Life in the presence of God. It was happiness postponed, but as a goal it remained quite clear.

In today's Western society purely physical survival is no longer the clearly defined physical goal (although for a good portion of mankind it still is, and therefore their Sabbath needs would be entirely different from ours). For us, to keep from starvation is no longer the problem. Rather, if I may so put it, the problem is that we no longer know what the problem is. We no longer know what life's physical goal might be or even if there is one altogether. Further, except for those who truly believe in salvation in the old sense, few men are sure what life's spiritual goals are. So they talk of happiness or use similar empty phrases with which to cover their aimlessness.

I often ask young people who come to me to discuss their marriage plans just what their goals are. The two outstanding answers are "happiness" and "security" (the latter is the preferred answer of women). But when I press my visitors further and ask what they mean and how they aim to achieve these goals, they become very vague. The fact is that, like their parents, they have no clear goals, a lack of which from the outset is a built-in cause of marital unrest.

Added to the general conundrum is the ever-increasing infantilization of our culture. The child wants his satisfactions now and not later. The "now" dimension has become the overriding aspect of our youth culture and has increased their sense of unrest (which in turn affects their elders), because the moment now is experienced another now is at hand. Thus now becomes never, and never is the feeding place of restlessness.

I therefore view the Sabbath as potentially an enormous relief from, and a protest against, these basic causes of unrest. Once a week it provides us with an opportunity to address ourselves to the who-ness rather than the what-ness of life, to persons rather than things, to Creation and our part in it, to society and its needs, to ourselves as individuals and yet as social beings. This is what Pieper called "the inner source of leisure," the setting of goals which are both realistic and within one's reach, yet also beyond one's self.

I rarely find a better place for such redirection than a religious service, whose major function ought to be not just the repetition of well-worn formulae but the celebration of human goals, setting them within the context of Creation. If nothing happens to us during this or any Sabbath experience except an enlarging of our vision, we will have gained a new perspective of life's meaning and will have diminished our sense of unrest. That will be Sabbath rest, in the sense required by our time.

2. Competition Without End

Endless competition is a specific form of goal-lessness. Formerly there was probably not as much economic competition as there is today, but however much there was had a clearly defined objective. For most people it was to gain a livelihood. In today's Western civilization that is simply no longer enough.

Nowadays, everything is competitive, but the end is never quite defined. Our culture asks us to acquire and acquire ever more, but we are never told when we will have enough. Women are urged to beautify themselves, for the sake not only of other women but also of other men, but are never told to what end such competition is entered into.

I view the Sabbath as a surcease from and a protest against all forms of competition, even when they come in attractive packages marked "self-advancement" or "self-improvement." I view the Sabbath in this respect as a "useless" day. Our forefathers had a keen understanding of the fact that sleep on the Sabbath day was a form of coming closer to God. We must once again understand that doing nothing, being silent and open to the world, letting things happen inside, can be as important as, and sometimes more important than, what we commonly call the useful.

I am often asked why we have more than the necessary number of Torah scrolls in the synagogue. Actually, only one single scroll is needed; two, and on rare occasions three, are useful in the sense that when various passages are required to be read at the same service the congregation need not wait until the single scroll is rolled back and forth. But many congregations have ten, fifteen, twenty, or even more scrolls in the Ark, more than they can possibly use — and these scrolls are considered the prize possessions of the synagogue. That to me is a marvellous example that the House of God is essentially not useful. Besides, it does stand empty a great deal of the week, its facilities are not always used, nor are the activities that take place there useful in the ordinary sense.

Formerly, a person who did not work was considered useless; what we need now is a *purposive uselessness,* an activity (or non-activity!) which is important in that it becomes an essential protest against that basic unrest which comes from competition without end.

In the Jewish context I would therefore suggest that on the Sabbath one ought to abstain from everything which on one level or another is considered *usefully competitive.* For instance, going to the hairdresser's on the Sabbath is in my view a form of sexual or social competition and ought to be left to other days. Equally, going to classes at night to advance oneself usefully would fall into the same category of Sabbath prohibition. Let there be some special time during the week when we do for the sake of doing, when we love the trivial and in fact simply love, when we do for others rather than for ourselves and thus provide a counterbalance for the weight of endless competition that burdens our every day.

V

The Sanctification of Freedom

The Sabbath gives us a quantity of free time and thereby a quality potential of freedom time, when a man can be himself and in some area do for himself and for others what in the workaday world he cannot. Such Sabbath observance is a sanctification of freedom.

Part of the hopelessness of our age is our sense of imprisonment. This comes not merely from the increasing complexity of society and our experience of marginality, but from the ever-growing importance of machines and the advance of automation. Everyone can add to the stories that illustrate this experience. For example, this exclamation by an adult: "See that beautiful flower! It looks as perfect as if it were artificial!" Or the marvel of child who upon seeing a pianist says, "Look, Daddy, he is playing with his own hands!" Automation not only removes men further and further from their work, but also from the opportunity of making decisions. And a man who makes no decisions is ultimately a man who is bereft of a basic freedom.

It is for this reason that, on the whole, spectator sports and other spectacles which now fill much of men's free time too often represent missed opportunities. True, when we sit and watch we may celebrate the uselessness of the day. But is this the only way to escape the time machine, or can we put something else in its place? There ought to be occasions when free time becomes sanctified freedom time.

In contemplating these matters I have come to wonder why baseball, formerly America's favourite spectator sport, has lately fallen from grace. Is it because it is too slow for today's taste? Perhaps — but there may be another, subtler reason. Over the decades the record book has become such a major factor in the game that it has begun to overwhelm spectator and player alike. What a man does is at once measured against the performances of the book; his own individual effort in the framework of the game is frequently dwarfed by the record of the ages. And somehow, somewhere, deep down in the public's mind there may be some doubt that their own needs of escaping from the machine and its pressures are sufficiently served by this constant recourse to statistics.

It is perhaps this very fact (if I may continue in this vein) which attracts so many to the game of golf, both in the doing and in the watching. For here a man competes ultimately not for the money (that is reserved to the few professionals) and not even primarily against others, but essentially against himself and his own potential. Thereby he opens up a measure of freedom which may give him some relief of the soul —

despite the ulcers and other frustrations which the game may otherwise produce. (Of course, I am not unaware that people might come to any game or program "with many different attitudes and approaches. And what might look like the same activity because it has a similar format, might have an entirely different value with respect to whether the person is increasing his or her personal freedom through the experience.")[11]

The words *sanctification of freedom* imply yet another dimension. It has to do with that hope which attempts to make possible what is apparently impossible. There is a special kind of freedom which enables us to strive for the perfection of the essentially imperfect and thereby to enter the dimension of the Divine into a segment of human time. Abraham J. Heschel speaks of Judaism as "a religion of time aiming at a sanctification of time. Unlike the space-minded man whose time is unvaried, iterative, homogeneous, to whom all hours are alike, qualityless, empty shells, the Bible senses the diversified character of time. There are no two hours alike. Every hour is unique and the only one given at the moment, exclusive and endlessly precious. Judaism teaches us to be attached to holiness and time; to be attached to sacred events, to learn how to consecrate sanctuaries and emerge from the magnificent stream of the year. The Sabbaths are our great cathedrals.... Jewish ritual may be characterized as the art of significant form in time, as architecture of time."[12]

To the religious person God is the source of holiness, and the Sabbath therefore a truly sanctified segment of hope which lights up the dark horizon of pessimism. It is not only useless time, but non-rational time, for in the final analysis hope like faith is non-rational (to be distinguished from irrational).

A fascinating number of parallels suggest themselves, especially from the world of psychology.

The English psychologist R. D. Laing, for instance, has suggested that man's true liberation might have to come from a temporary retreat into schizophrenia. That is to say, with the world being what it is, one must experience unreality in order to both understand and master reality. In order to be oneself one must, so to speak, learn to get outside oneself. In his book *The Divided Self*,[13] Laing suggests a retreat into simulated insanity as the extreme means of liberation, to propel us out of the box in which we are imprisoned. I am in no position to comment on these latest theories, but it occurs to me that since ancient times religious people have often been closely linked to what were considered the crazy and the insane — only we used more pleasing words such as *vision* and *mystic trance* for otherwise dubious experiences.

However, we do not have to go to extremes of religious apprehension to understand that the religious man who escapes from the machine does indeed escape from the normal. The man who attains freedom on any level in our day is, in effect, abnormal when measured against the normalcy of automation. Because it encourages this kind of non-rational escape the Sabbath may therefore be described as an opportunity for "religious schizophrenia," a pious *meshuggas* which R.D. Laing would find a source of real hope. I use this terminology only to indicate again how closely the concerns of religion may be related to those of psychology and how closely the prescriptions resemble one another.

In pursuing yet another avenue of psychological inquiry one can consider all religious ritual a kind of sacred play or game, a retreat into the "as-ifness" of our soul. Johan Huizinga describes three qualities which religion and play have in common: both strive seriously for perfection; both have specially assigned spaces with their own rules and sanctions; and both religion and play rely on symbols, pageantry, vestments, and special languages.

Both religion and play, we might add, are important retreats from the realness of the machine and the pressure of the everyday and are on their level avenues of hope — whatever that hope may be: either to win a game, or to score, or perchance to win salvation. To put it yet in a different way, prayer may be regarded as a form of sacred recreation — and saying this does not demean either prayer or recreation. Frequently, study belongs to the same category. Judaism has always encouraged study in every form and on every level. Study for its own sake and not for the sake of self-advancement is basically an exercise in "as-ifness," a sacred kind of game where thought takes wing and imagination replaces automation.

For where hope exists decision exists, and where decision exists there is freedom. And freedom comes in many packages. It comes alone or in groups, it comes in effort and doing, or it comes in openness and in silence. It comes in retreat from men as protest against the oppression of man and machine. It may fill a day or only a portion of it. However much or little, it is a precious time to sanctify freedom. And for him who knows this day to be beloved of God it is indeed a very special day with special opportunities. To celebrate it let a man do those things which liberate him from the ordinary and give him areas of free decision, of doing for himself and for others those things he wills to do rather than those which he must do; where he indulges in recreation both sacred and other which will help him to escape from the oppression of our civilization.

VI

The Protest

I titled my lecture "The Sabbath as Protest"—but it is not only the Sabbath which does the protesting; it is also that which it represents, namely, the religious venture of man. For religion itself at its best is a protest. It is the unusual that denies the ordinary; it is standing still and sitting down; it is doing something and nothing; it is hoping and being. The Sabbath can be the paradigm of this understanding of the religious quest.

Two French psychologists, André Virel and Roger Frétigny, talk about four states of human consciousness: imaginative, active, reflexive, and contemplative.[14] The two middle states (activity and reflexive response) characterize our automated society; the two other (imagination and contemplation) are the redeeming features which make life livable. These are the qualities to which the Sabbath addresses itself, for imagination is a form of freedom, and contemplation is rest from unrest.

I have spoken from the vantage point of a Jew, but the problems and the opportunities are not Judaism's alone. Every man, and not just a Jew, needs rest from unrest, needs surcease from goal-lessness and endless competition, and in the face of automation needs to sanctify his free time as freedom time. In the process, work and leisure will have to get themselves new vestments so that the increasing quantities of free time which society will have in the years to come may become true freedom time for many — until that day when the protest will no longer be necessary and when the Sabbath will have become the antechamber to the Messianic era. Until then, I fear, it will have to be a protest against what is, and a celebration of what may yet come to be.

Toward a Higher Morality

*I*f there has been a conspicuous failure of Western man to achieve the higher morality to which our religious systems have challenged him, the failure lies not entirely with recalcitrant mankind. It must lie at least in part with us, the professed agents and harbingers of this morality. Also, we must seriously rethink certain premises which we who are religious representatives have accepted, and I suggest that this can be done without disturbing the basic suppositions upon which Judaism, Catholicism, and Protestantism are based.

Anthropology teaches us that primitive man was essentially a group man. He lived and reacted, thought and behaved primarily in terms of group standards. His individuality was strictly subordinated to the needs of the family, clan, or tribe. Today, too, the tribesmen are of little significance as individual persons; they achieve full human status only from membership in their group.

During the last fifty years we have begun to understand that this co-operative existence of primitive man is indeed a genuine aspect of both physical and psychological evolution. This stands in contrast to the original Darwinian concept that war and destruction and the elimination of the weak by force are the inherent thrust of evolutionary survival. We now know that this is true on a very limited scale only. Today, the early ideas of Kropotkin and many others who followed him have gained an ever-wider range of acceptance. The original pattern of survival is based not on conflict, but on co-operation. Only those organisms survive which succeed in establishing the best system of co-operation and mutual helpfulness. Biologists follow this trend from the cellular level and even the sub-cellular structure through the animal kingdom to the behaviour of anthropoids.

GAIN IN INDIVIDUALITY AND LOSS IN GROUP COHESION

The evolvement of man is in effect bound up with the evolutionary establishment of his identity and the loosening of the bonds which tie him to the group. Biblical man is the emergent individual. In pre-biblical society the children's teeth were always set on edge because of the deeds of their fathers. There is a long struggle which leads to the pronouncement of Deuteronomy and Ezekiel on individual responsibility.

Biblical man represents the first great human tension. He is still a creature of his group, but he struggles to gain his selfness. This development took place in what Karl Jaspers calls "the axial age of human history."[1] Israel's prophets regarded the tension between the group and the self as existentially necessary. They called for balance, not for the abandonment of one in favour of the other. Actually, there was a price to be paid for this "axial" phase of man. What he gained in personal identity he lost in group cohesion. He learned that God had regard of him, but in social morality man began to face an ever-greater struggle to maintain his concern for the group.

Christianity further polarized this tension. Its theology took man away from his national and group moorings and anchored him in a universal concern. It made the individual the supreme object of divine love. Man was essentially and primarily the one and only in the sight of God. It was total universalism based on total individualism that brought the universal church into being. This made possible diverse social and religious forces: the acceptance of the hermit as a servant of God and the creation of monastic orders. In modern times it fathered a rugged individualism and the doctrine of laissez-faire, and in its Puritan form it encouraged the development of capitalism, as well as Stirner's anarchism.

Of course, nowhere did this chain of events liberate man completely from his group. He always remained part of some tradition, be it his guild, his liege, or his religion. But the dynamism of the church was theological, not social. It was natural, therefore, that the church became a socially conservative force which was satisfied to keep men within their traditional economic and social settings, but which at the same time insisted that man was a unique individual and that his relationship to God was independent of the restrictive settings of which he was a part.

THE CURRENT PROCESS OF REVERSAL

The confluence of emancipation and the industrial revolution began the dual destruction of traditional group patterns and of the doctrine of the supremacy of the individual. It has produced two evident philosophic opposites: modern democracy, socialized capitalism, and the welfare state on the one hand, and communism and fascism on the other. But on every plane except the philosophical and religious, the contrast is less pronounced than political antagonisms would have us believe. The social and psychological condition of man on both sides of the Iron Curtain is similar. The individual is in retreat in the West; his retreat is complete in the East.

Even capitalist democracy, ostensibly dedicated to personal liberty, has brought in its train mass-produced conformity, mass neurosis, the stultifying features of other-directed society, and the *MasseMensch* who is alienated from himself, the man who, in Tillich's term, lives with the anxiety of non-being. If the process remains unchecked by the kind of counterforce which religion can muster, a full cycle will have been drawn: the new primitive man of the twentieth century will return to the condition of the pre-biblical primitive. The group and its values are everything, the individual counts for little. Once again society will be the measure of all things.

In this process of reversal which has now gone on for 150 years, our religious groups have been on the defensive. The religions of the West have been slow in re-integrating group values with their cherished individualism. Christian theology continues to exhibit a wide acceptance of fundamentalist and evangelical teaching which emphasizes its overriding concern with individual sin and individual responsibility. The social gospel is today less at the centre of the church than a generation ago. Judaism has fared somewhat better in this regard; its holy day liturgy still says, "We have sinned, we have transgressed, we have done perversely." But neither has Judaism resolved the challenges of the closing cycle. Its natural preoccupation has been with the survival of the Jewish people. Only of late have the universal aspects of social salvation on the one hand and individual salvation on the other become a central issue in our re-created Jewish theology. When one's life is at stake, theology takes second place, and this has been the existential position of Judaism for all too long.

NEO-BIBLICAL MAN MUST EMERGE

It is our proposition that the cycle from the primitive man of yesterday to the primitive man of today threatens to close once again. We may therefore wonder whether the time has not come to have a neo-biblical man emerge. If we are to achieve a higher morality, it must take the direction of integrating personal and social values. But since history, contrary to Ecclesiastes, is irreversible, it cannot be biblical man who will be our emerging or re-emerging goal. He arose out of the group and struggled to obtain individual selfness.

The neo-biblical man's spiritual quest is different. *He struggles to maintain his hard-won individual selfness and must now attempt to re-acquire compatible group values as an essential part of his being.* Our task is to save man from being overwhelmed, but also to make him fully human. Without this confluence there can be no salvation. Without social values there can be no personal salvation, and without values of the individual there can be no social values. Here lies the road to higher morality. Religious leadership must not be toward a society of mere individuals, it must be toward the human being who is nothing alone, yet everything as the single one, who has no worth except he be his brother's keeper.

SOCIAL CONSCIOUSNESS AND MUTUAL ACCEPTANCE

From this I draw two conclusions which in my theology seem cogent and seem to me necessary avenues of practical procedure.

1. The church and the synagogue must re-acquire social consciousness and hence become political. I take the word here in its original meaning,

the meaning which Martin Buber had in mind when he said that religion starts in mysticism and ends in politics. I think of the term as *politeia*, as concern for society, rather than its application to partisan politics. The preachment of articles of faith, destined to provide individual salvation, must be supplemented by an equally strong set of ideals which lead us to the acceptance of group responsibility. The responsibility for achieving higher morality for man lies essentially with the church and synagogue, at least in the West. Unless we as religious leaders make the social order and the attendant human questions our prime concern, we will have every reason to share the guilt of returning the world to its primitive mass existence.

Churches which do not make slum clearance and unemployment their prime concern are not fulfilling their potential, nor are they fulfilling their duty. Churches which equivocate on questions of human equality and racial amity are not fulfilling their divine function. Furthermore, religious bodies which do not make the elimination of prejudicial attitudes a major part of their program are sadly neglectful of the duty entrusted to them.

2. Churches and synagogues must go beyond this and must make societal individualism part of their active teaching. It is not sufficient to give lip service to something called pluralism, and all the while strive to eliminate it by making our tradition dominant in what would doubtless become another monolithic society. Of course, we are asking our individual members not only to become aware of his neighbour, but to integrate his own needs with those of others, to preserve his individuality as precious but at the same time do this only in a differentiated, pluralistic, social framework. *But what church and synagogue ask of their members they must also ask of themselves.* We must begin our climb toward higher morality by truly accepting each other as religious groups.

EXCLUSIVE TRUTH AND SOCIAL POLICY

I ask for more than a mere recognition of each other's existence. Neither our much-heralded dialogues nor real social morality are possible on that level which can never go beyond mutual toleration. But we must go beyond it, however hard it may be. For us, the next level of higher religious morality lies on the level of active acceptance of each other as legitimate searchers for the differentiated reality of a complex non-monolithic Truth.

What about our cherished idea that we have the only key to salvation? What about the doctrine of exclusive truth and the right and duty to advocate this truth through mission? I would not disturb the doctrine, though I do not hold it. Neither would I infringe upon the privilege of mission. I would zealously defend it as an inalienable right of persuasion, inherent in this open society. *But the doctrine of exclusive truth must remain a personal conviction and not become a social policy.* In the arena of the community the full acceptance of religious pluralism must become part of religious advocacy.

We must cease to be concerned with our own exclusive rights and prerogatives. Just as Marxism is bent on an establishment of its philosophy as the only force for human salvation, so have we in turn been led down the traditional road of individualism and have made our personal and church individuality central to the world. Sooner or later it must be said that our critics are not altogether wrong when they claim our *religious institutions today are providing the last great fortress of social divisiveness in our society.* Our pious preachments of understanding have meant nothing or little, because we ourselves did not really believe them.

That today's churches, two thousand years after Jesus, have not succeeded in eradicating a religion-based anti-Semitism, is sinful and nothing else. And while Jews may claim that outward pressures are responsible for certain of their mental attitudes, it must also be stated that our attitudes towards non-Jews and our theological relationship to Christianity leave much to be desired. All too many Christians are encouraged by their churches to look at Jews with jaundiced eyes, and all too many Jews are encouraged by their synagogues to look at Christians with blind eyes. We may continue to believe that, were humanity at our feet, our own religious system would be the footstool to the throne of God.

THE STAKE IS HUMAN SURVIVAL

Meanwhile, it should be our task to be concerned less with what could be at the end of days, but with what must and can be in our times; not with our right to exclusive salvation but with our duty to contribute to the world's salvation now, as partners in a divine enterprise of utmost urgency. In our days, if I may quote Jaspers once again, "it is not on the basis of revelation that men can come together; the basis of solidarity can only be experience."[2] We must finally recognize that the world will not believe us if, in the name of God, we cannot live peaceably and constructively with each other as religious people.

We need a frank dialogue and frank recognition of each other and a franker understanding of our position, and the knowledge that we must not only tolerate each other but work with each other. The stake is not just higher morality, but morality altogether. We cannot save man for himself, unless we save him within the context of society; we cannot save society unless we can save the individual man. None of us can do this alone.

In sum, we cannot achieve the higher morality, unless we as religious people and bodies, in concept and concerted action, achieve a higher level of living and working with each other. These are harsh times; the time for the continuation of pious platitudes has passed. If we desperately need the emergence of neo-biblical man, we may not expect him to descend from heaven or emerge full-blown from the head of religious institutions. We will have to labour before we give birth; we will have to re-fashion our goals.

The stake is human survival.

Moral and Social Issues

The University and Society

*T*he phrase "ivory tower" first made its appearance in 1869 when C.A. St. Beuve used it with respect to Alfred de Vigny, who unfortunately was dead by then and could not defend himself. However, the major application during the last few generations has been not to poets but to the university. Quite clearly, it has been meant to be a pejorative, and therefore a judgment on the university rather than *by* the university. It might be well to spend a few moments examining the reason for such characterization and ask: what precisely does it mean? What have been reasons for making the assessment? Was it justified? And finally, is it still justified? Or perhaps: should this judgment, even if pejorative, be cherished by the university as both necessity and desideratum?

Ivory tower was (and is) the image of a place apart. Yet apartness alone does not describe the image fully. Let me take an example from the Bible. In the Book of Numbers we are told of a pagan prophet by the name of Balaam who had his reputation unjustly diminished because he rode an ass that was, so we are told, miraculously gifted with speech. Balaam was a hired hand; the Moabite monarch, King Balak, had engaged him to curse the people of Israel whom he feared. So Balaam mounted a promontory and looked down on the hapless folk over whom he was about to pronounce one of his famous maledictions. (Under such circumstances, cursing was considered quite *salonfaehig*.) Well, the great Balaam wanted to do one thing, but God made his tongue issue blessings instead of curses. One of the laudatory phrases Balaam uttered about Israel was this: "Lo, there is a people that dwells apart and is not counted

167

among the nations." Clearly, apartness here was seen as something positive, as uniqueness; and Jewish tradition in later centuries built a whole philosophy of existence around it and made apartness a condition of serving the Lord fully. Unless there is some degree of separation, so it was argued, assimilation would eventually ensue and, therewith, an ultimate inability to carry out the function of serving God in a special way. Apartness thereafter had a double value: it was in time seen as a negative by the outside, and Jews received derogatory characterizations such as clannish, snobbish, and exclusive. But from the inside, the picture was different. There the value was positive, and separateness was, at least to some degree, considered desirable and necessary.

This excursion into the field of my particular interest does, I think, shed some light on the questions I asked. If ivory tower — as a judgement of others — meant to describe the university's apartness from the rest of society and was given a negative connotation, the same description could be found inside the university, but with a positive accent. Yes, we are apart, and we need to be; else we cannot do our job properly. Study is not a majority occupation nor is it undertaken to please anyone. Ideas, in Platonic language, have an existence of their own, and like them teachers need to have an independent perspective. If ivory tower means apartness, then it is an adequate, or at least partly adequate, description of a necessary premise to make the university function at its best. But, of course, that isn't all the expression means to convey. If the university was merely to be characterized as *the Jewish people of the intellectual world*, that would not be bad at all — forgive me my prejudice in this regard. However, ivory tower also implies lack of real knowledge of society, the kind of knowledge which comes from empathy and concern. The guy in the ivory tower, so the implication seems to be, is interested in himself and his facts, but not in people. He is there, shut away; we are here, where life is.

I suppose this is what John Milton meant when he called the university "a stony-hearted step-mother," or take Governor Jerry Brown's California assessment: "Never has education been more irrelevant to more kids." Given such judgement by others, we proceed to ask, what has prompted it? A number of answers spring to mind.

1.   The university has generally appeared as a place where the relevant
     and the irrelevant (seen from a popular perspective) are all too
     freely mixed. Medical schools or engineering colleges will never be
     classified as ivory towers; they relate to the here and now and satisfy
     the perceivable needs of society. But philosophers or archaeologists?
     They chase analytical constructs or broken pottery which many people
     believe to be more or less the same thing. A learned paper on the
     ritual bath in the Qumran community will engage the rapt attention
     of but a few cognoscenti; and while the media have made a valiant
     attempt to infuse an element of sensation into the finds at Ebla, the
     photograph of Paolo Matthiae poring over ancient fragments, elicits
     in most people the regrettable reaction, so what? North American
     society, suffering from the emphysema of pragmatism, is constantly
     concerned with the practical, the workable, the manageable. All else
     is considered expendable, and that includes the arts which usually
     are the first to feel the shrinking of the public purse.

2.   Ah, Mammon has raised its ugly head! Be not surprised or offended
     at the number-two reason for dubbing the university a place apart.
     Ordinary people have a work week of thirty-five or forty hours,
     with two or three or, rarely, four weeks' holidays during the year.
     The professor is seen not to teach during a large part of the year; he
     goes on sabbaticals; travels here and there; and gets paid for lectures
     in addition to his regular salary. College teachers will of course
     have ready answers for such odious comparisons: they will point to
     the necessity for preparation; administrative work; the exhausting
     demands which mental labour makes, etc. I am not about to judge, I
     merely report: that is what they say out there.

3.   They say more, and Mammon again is urging them on. (The economic
     determinists in the audience will applaud me for saying this; after all,
     do they not hold that opinions are primarily shaped by economic
     considerations?) They say out there: ordinary folk are pawns in the
     tug-of-war between labour and industry, and between both and
     government; they face unemployment at the drop of a dollar. But you
     professors? You have, or live for, tenure. We have to perform all the
     time or we are out of a job; or we lose our investment in the corner

grocery; and we make no commission on sales that fizzle. But you? You can teach well or badly; your students may love you or hate you; learn something from you or be bored to death — no matter. Like civil servants (about whom we are also not too enthusiastic) you get your pay cheques from the public trough. Of course, you will point out how necessary tenure is, because it protects freedom of thought (although I must tell you that there are unthinking people who claim that such freedom could nowadays actually survive without tenure; but it is obvious to one and all who care about hard-won privileges that it would be better if such thoughts remained unexpressed).

4. The university, they say, tends to promote elitism in what should be an egalitarian society. This is one argument that needs to be taken especially seriously. All the other criticisms can be argued, adjusted, or otherwise mediated — for while they pose some valid questions, they also have some valid answers. In most cases both sides are right to a degree. After all, the university is part of life, and life knows the necessity of imperfection and of compromise. But the issue of elitism points up the essential polarity inherent in the societal process. The long and short is that elitism is both a threat to democracy and its salvation at the same time. In theory it should not have to be with us, in practice it must.

We are rapidly approaching the point of no return. Education for all is workable up to a point, although professors of English aver that we haven't begun to crack the thick epidermis of illiteracy. If everyone is expected to graduate from high school (as is the case in numerous American and probably Canadian places as well), then such graduation means little; for school standards have been sufficiently lowered to make it possible. The more people go to university, the more will its level be depressed. Quantity has an effect on quality.

It is of course a truism to deny that people are created equal, as the American founding document would have us believe. In fact, our endowments differ vastly, and a society that does not find the means of raising its best members to positions of social, technical, industrial, and — last but not least — intellectual influence will tend toward the tyranny of mediocrity. This is not a contradiction of the basic tenets of democracy, far from it. Our democratic system requires that the university be accessible to all regardless of station (although that too is an ideal that will not be realized, for accessibility is frequently a function of social inheritance and expectation). But the principle is valid nonetheless. The university is open to all, but those who attend it should be the best we have. *The best* — that does not necessarily mean an acquiescence to the superiority of English or French traditions; the best of our native people too can and must find their place at the university.

I repeat: *the best.* Sooner or later, and I hope it will be sooner, we must relocate our courage and say it out loud: if the university cannot reach for excellence, its reach is short indeed. Excellence does not mean perfection; it does mean, however, striving for it. That goes for students, for professors, and those who are entrusted with the administration of the institution. Publius Ovidius Naso said it two thousand years ago: *nulla nisi ardua virtus.* There is no excellence without difficulty.

We who care about universities have other battles to fight as well. There are three that come to mind, and they will be a convenient conclusion to my disquisition.

1. In a goal-oriented society, an education which does not produce a measurably higher income has diminished status. Yet the phenomenal success of evening and extension programs shows how great is the hunger of many people for learning. They want an education for its own sake, and not in order that they might get something tangible in return. I would therefore like the university to raise these courses in the scale of importance. Who has decreed that only the education of largely unwilling and frequently incompetent youngsters must be the locus of the university? Why not also — or perhaps more so — the teaching of men and women whose maturity permits them to discern the true goals of learning: study for the joy and thrill of it? That will mean, of course, a severe reduction of undergraduate courses and a redistribution of available funding to mature education. The result will be that the level of cultural appreciation in our communities will rise perceptibly.

2. Such a course will also require the university to do something it ought to be doing in any case: go out into the community, where

the people are. Elitism does not require intellectual narcissism or snobbery. You will be surprised to see how much untapped talent is out there waiting for you to offer your very best and not, Heaven forfend, some condescending pap. It also means that your lecture platforms ought to be open to people who can think, and not merely to colleagues from other schools, whom you invite in the merry-go-round of the back-scratching circuit.

Appoint lay fellows to your colleges and don't be afraid to use them. The university must be, and must be seen to be, a part of the community. Social studies are possible only if their bottom line is concern for people. Professors who flee the demands of humanity in its concrete forms injure society and at the same time the credibility of their school.

3. And finally, there is the battle for the humanities. The natural sciences which once had to fight the strictures imposed by religion, have nothing to fear but expansion and the absence of a moral framework, though these are by no means negligible dangers. But the humanities are in deep trouble. We are not sure what a liberal education is supposed to be, and our best minds are wrestling with the question. For us there is another and equally pressing task: to make sure that the humanities are not eviscerated by the cutting scalpel of a pragmatic government which sees itself as the enunciator of the popular will. Don't be afraid to assert the vital importance of the intellectual pursuit for its own sake. There is no such thing as *obscure knowledge*, for if it is knowledge it is not obscure, and the quantity of those who care about its results is immaterial. There is, in this sense, no difference between important and unimportant knowledge.

Yet it is also clear that at a time when the whole fabric of society is in danger of being rent asunder, there must be some, if temporary, priorities. Universities should deal with truth itself, but unless there is a community in which it can be taught, truth will have no takers. The health of the social weal is, and must become, much more distinctly a primary objective of the university, and therefore it is not unbefitting an academic institution to admit values into its hallowed precincts. It is not enough to turn out students (using Dr. Gregory Bateson's words) who "perpetuate our way of life, and on the whole aggravate its pathologies, its greed, its hatred of nature and its hatred of intellect." Our schools must help students be both critical and caring.

To take just one example: the need to give of oneself to the community is a matter not just for home and Sabbath school, it is worthy of the most serious study in Academe.

In fine, the ivory tower should open some of its portals, but it should not be torn down. We do need that *place apart*, though the *ivory* has lost both its ecological and social desirability. Brick will do; besides it will have become resistant because of its exposure to firing, and with the proper mortar it will withstand the vicissitudes of shifting priorities, inflationary pressures, and budgetary convolutions. For we need the *tower*.

We need it as refuge for the spirit and as the secure training ground of the mind; and we need it as the watchtower against the onslaught of pragmatism and goal orientation. An ancient Hebrew saying went: "The day is short, the labour is much, and the Master is pressing. It is not given thee to finish the work, but neither are you permitted to desist from it." And another asked: "If not now, when?"

The Morality of the Calley Trial

"This Calley business," said a friend of mine, "is a can of worms. Leave it alone." But I can't help it; the outcry which the judgment has raised doesn't leave me alone. Memories crowd me, troublesome memories.

The sight of the Vietnamese officer shooting a prisoner right there in front of me on my television screen. I remember it clearly. I was eating supper and I should have vomited it up, but I finished it calmly. That is one memory that will not leave me alone.

And Nordhausen concentration camp, my confrontation with evil incarnate; twenty-four hundred dead lying unburied in the streets and in their bunk beds. Two disembodied feet still sticking out of the oven with the smoke trailing away. "O, ye chimneys," Nellie Sachs was to write later, and like her I remember the stench. The good burghers from the town, just a stone's throw away, came, looked, and disclaimed all responsibility. "We didn't know; we had no idea."

Only one man was overcome. "No, no, no," he shouted, then threw himself on the nearest corpse and kissed him. The others turned away, horrified. Later, in a preliminary inquiry, a burgher said, "I only did what I was told to do." He turned directly to me: "What would you have done?"

What, indeed? Of course, I know what I should do. My religious tradition is unequivocal in the matter. It demands me to suffer death rather than kill an innocent person. "Perhaps his blood is redder (that is, more worthwhile) than yours," says the Talmud. Yes, I remember that. But knowing what it means to deface God's image in man is one thing, doing another.

Horror attracts and repels. Sometimes you dream about it, then wake up from the nightmare and say, "Thank God it didn't really happen." How can you make My Lai go away like a nightmare? You can deny it, of course, but that won't do. The facts are clear and they drip with the blood of innocents. So you call on Fate Inevitable and proclaim (as Billy Graham does), "War is hell. I have never heard of a war where innocent people were not killed." You ask, is there a nation, ancient or modern, that has been without it? There have been a thousand My Lais in history. As long as men will insist on war as a means of solving their problems there will be other My Lais.

To many it therefore seems only logical to conclude that to blame it all on some young chap who did his job is a ludicrous and pious sham. Admiral Edward C. Owtlaw speaks for this point of view: "Lieutenant Calley may not have been a hero, but he represents that sort of young man who has always been the salvation of our nation when the chips were down." Meaning: he may have overdone it a bit, but at the core he is sound, as honest and brave and whole as the American dream. If patriotism has any meaning it is "My country, right or wrong" (isn't it?), and so you've got to stand with Calley and applaud the president, or even defiantly sing the Battle Hymn if you feel strongly about it. If you're down on Calley, you betray the country and besmirch the flag, and you say to the draftees, "Wait until we get you, too."

So some draft boards draw the consequences. They close down and refuse to induct any more likely victims of future courts martial. For who, finally, is Lieutenant William Calley? He is you and me, the average man. We could have been in his shoes. What if the order had been given to us? There but for the grace of God stand we, little, ordinary folk. No Eichmanns who helped plot the extermination of millions, but decent men caught in a web not of their making, frightened and confused, numbed by the habit of pulling the trigger in self-defence, and compelled by orders either given or implied, "Waste 'em!" So you do, and your men are safe, and tomorrow you may die yourself and lie crushed in a ditch. Murderer? If he is one, you say, then I am too, real or potential. Inevitably, others come forward: "If you condemn him you must condemn me also."

So the little man in the street rises up and defends the little man of the bar. "Rusty," they call him, and the newspaper says that "he has no

175

history of anything more violent than water skiing." In retrospect he is sorry that he did it. "I had been told what war is like," he is quoted as saying, "but I never knew until I got there, I was never taught the tragedy of war. After seeing war you just sit down and cry…. I'll be very proud to have been in the U.S. Army and fought at My Lai if it shows the world just what war is."

When you look at it this way you are inclined to weep with Calley as much as with the dead. If there was evil it is reduced, attenuated to a shadow. One does not have to be wicked to shoot a submachine gun. Even Adolf Eichmann (keeping all differences duly in mind) had exhibited none of the characteristics commonly associated with killers. He, too, was the little man, picked by fate. This is why Hannah Arendt had called the Jerusalem trial an exposition of the banality of evil.

The little man understands, or thinks he does, anyway. In Indiana, and Alabama, where Middle America is still alive, the people understand: the sharecroppers and the blue-collar folk, and the storekeepers and the hard hats to whom Spiro Agnew appeals in a way northern sophisticates can't comprehend (and therefore laugh it off with ready-at-hand contempt). Lester Maddox and George Wallace understand. Calley is their man who, like them, is crushed by the brass and the big shots in Washington. "All power to the people," they too cry — if it's the right people, like Calley.

Which brings us inevitably, sadly, to the core of the matter. All the legal, moral, and quasi-moral considerations must take their place before the ultimate and ugly reality. You cannot comprehend the reason for the convulsion which the affair has produced unless you face up to the unpalatable issue: Calley's trial might not have caused a ripple had he been black and his victims white. Everyone (or nearly everyone of "us") would have seen a conviction to be just and necessary. But Calley is "our" kind and the dead at My Lai were not the sort of civilized people who would know a Pinto from a Cadillac, or the need for indoor plumbing, high-rise apartments, and superhighways, and who certainly could not be relied upon to understand the honour and respect due a Southern lady. Take your choice: you could either say it never happened or, if it did, they deserve it. You can't compare "them" with real folk; they only look like them. There isn't any basic difference between South and North

Vietnamese; in either case we're ahead when they are ditched. Only for the body count it matters, and the rule (as a veteran put it) is simple. "If it's dead, it's VC — because it's dead."

"It"— that is no accident of language. The GIs in the last war never talked that way about Germans; the French called them Boches and hated their guts but never doubted that withal they were equals. In the American Civil War, when the atrocities at the Andersonville prison camp came to light, retribution was firm against the offending officers. No Calley outcry then — how could there have been? The victims were Americans (especially since they belonged to the victorious North) and justice had to be done.

And here is the cruel parallel between Eichmann and Calley. Not in the extent of the evil. There is no comparison. Not in the genocidal intention — Calley certainly had none and neither had nor has the American government, all Communist and other rhetoric notwithstanding. Eichmann and his ilk had been indoctrinated with the idea that Jews (and gypsies and, to a lesser degree, Poles and some other nationalities) were subhuman. Killing them was desirable and even necessary in the framework of Nazi ideology. The fact that the victim was innocent hardly mattered; "it" had to be dispatched for the good of the army or the Reich or whatever. "It" had no more bearing on feeling than did animals in an abattoir. One could get sick from the bloody mess but one was not likely (unless one had special sensitivities) to get a bad conscience from it.

Calley's framework of reference was different in degree but not in nature. The young platoon leader had only the vaguest sort of guidance. What he knew came from the environment of war with an enemy whom one seldom saw and always feared for his stealth and cunning like a clever and ferocious jungle beast — but did not consider an equal. "Waste 'em" was an order that fitted this framework. Morality was not involved, only survival and expediency, the same kind of expediency which has led to the establishment of body counts and "permanent free-fire zones" (anything that moves is free for the kill). One GI, recollecting his presence at My Lai, reflected on the basic unreliability of the experience. "Everything is backwards. Any other time you think. Here you can go ahead and shoot for nothing…." (Today things have changed, at least to some extent. Now there are lectures about the need to treat civilians and soldiers in accordance with the Geneva Convention.)

So the circle inevitably widened and the masses who cheered Calley and Wallace and Maddox understood instinctively. What was on trial and what has been judged was they themselves, people afraid of having their racial proclivities challenged. If lynchers can be heroes, then how much more so Calley, whose bravery at My Lai was dressed in American fatigues.

Still, widening the circle has dangers of its own. Not because it would bring to the judgment people that need to be judged, the soldiery who ordered or knew of or encouraged or suppressed the knowledge of indiscriminate killings. There is no turning back here. They, too, must come to stand in the dock, however exalted their position, but speak primarily of the crime of government and of the American people in general, of racism which breeds excess, and you create the ultimate Frankenstein: everyone is responsible, which is to say, no one is by himself. This was the point which Eichmann's lawyer, Robert Servatius, made in Jerusalem in 1961: "The accused (he claimed) was in no wise different from his environment. One must see him as part of an existing civilization and therefore subject to its dynamism." The court disagreed and firmly held to the proposition that where there is individual freedom to choose there is individual responsibility. Similarly, the Calley jurors were unanimous in their judgment that Calley was free not to kill — however restricted this freedom was by orders, or fear, or VC-phobia. If one takes the view that Calley was faced not by "its" but by people, he was guilty of murder. Other soldiers found themselves in similar situations, but did not turn their battles into My Lais. And thousands of others practiced love in unparalleled fashion, caring for the injured and the desolate, adopting children, staying to help even after they were mustered out.

"But he only did his duty. He followed an order like any good soldier." That, certainly, is one aspect of this bitter business which should at last be clear. Even Field Marshal Wilhelm Keitel admitted at Nuremberg, "It is tragic that I did not understand ... that there is a limit even to how a soldier may fulfil his duty...." And Justice Moshe Landau, speaking for the Eichmann court: "In civilized countries the rejection of the defence of 'superior orders' as exempting completely from criminal responsibility has now become general." It should have, anyway.

One should also be careful not to mix too many questions together. For instance, if Calley is guilty, is not also the aircraft bombardier who releases his load over a civilian target, knowing that innocents will be maimed or killed? Or the stockholders of the corporation which manufactured the bullets, or the workers in the factory in Canada where death-dealing parts are made? How far do you go? Where does moral argument become sophistry? The matter is worth pursuing, but one need not wait for one verdict to determine the other.

The pendulum swings to the other side, too. Calling Calley guilty must not lead us into all sorts of generalized comparisons. My Lai was no Auschwitz, and not only because of the difference in numbers. It is well to recall that Sir Hartley Shawcross, chief British prosecutor at Nuremburg, emphasized that while every war provides acts of violence and excess (and on both sides of the conflict), they are generally accidental, unorganized, singular excesses. They must not be compared with what the Nazis were accused of: the systematic, organized extinction of whole groups and populations.

Careful also that U.S.-baiting, the world's most popular sport, does not get the best of the argument. Canadians may not be so different in this matter. An open-line program in Ottawa, dealing with the trial, had 80 percent of the callers express a strong pro-Calley sentiment. So beware of the valorous sophisticate who loves to examine My Lai as another example of Uncle Sam's deviltry, but is blind to the national fortitude which has permitted such a trial in the midst of a war. (In 1902, when General Jacob Smith stood trial for the massacre of Filipinos at Bahangiga, the war was over.) After all, it was from the den of all wickedness, the Pentagon itself, that approval came for holding a trial bound to call the whole military establishment into question. And not all Americans consider Calley a hero; far from it. The final vote is not yet in, as former president Harry Truman remarked wisely. The real hero of the affair may turn out to be Captain Aubrey M. Daniel III, Calley's prosecutor, whose courageous letter to the president may instruct a future generation in the nature of the judicial process and the rule of law as the foundation of democracy.

Wherever you touch the case, it seems to turn another side to you. Each question answered raises another. Seeing the matter only in black and white does not do it justice. Condemn Calley and none is finally exempt from judgment — no person, no nation which has ever fought an ugly war, man against man. Who can say of his own religion or cultural or national group: "My people are blameless; we have known no

My Lais?" Look again. Righteousness is a noble goal, self-righteousness a dangerous trap.

Condemn Calley and you might imply that more remote killings of civilians, from afar or from the air, are, in fact, legitimate; that war and morality can be neatly separated. Or does the considered judgment of his peers mean that even in the midst of organized brutality each person must salvage a little humanity and snatch it from the ashes of sin? Perhaps that is it, and that is why Calley must stand condemned.

In the end, you come back to yourself and your memories. You know, again, that laws and courts deal mostly with the framework of action and not usually with its blood. And you know at last that it is you, yourself, who stands with Calley at the bar of final judgment, that you are judging while being judged, that you are condemning while being desperately unsure what you might have done yourself. War turns the most decent and thoughtful into something they had not thought possible. "We stopped being human beings," an anonymous soldier writes of another war. "Everyone's face is set in a snarl and there's a deep growl coming from your belly. You want to kill and kill…. You think all the time of your own family, but they are just insects to be killed. Until afterwards, then you realize that they have families, too…." If only afterwards could have come earlier.

So even though I say an emphatic yes to Calley's conviction, I feel sorry for the man who is called out to kill, sorry for myself, and sorry — what a weak, denatured word for it! — for the old and young lives snuffed out beyond recall at My Lai and so many other places on the map of history. For history itself is on trial again, the whole human enterprise. Man's frail humanity is in the dock and it is America's turn to bare its soul. A lacerated country, this is its latest (though most likely not its last) attempt to purge itself from the tragedy of Vietnam. For this it should be honoured, not condemned. The mirror it holds up to its own soul is held up for Everyman. Let him look at it squarely and with as little self-righteousness as he can manage. Let him look hard and he will find Lieutenant William Calley looking over his shoulder.

The Curse of Literalism

*T*here is a curse abroad in this world of ours. It is not new, but especially in our days it is a prominent affliction which has its influence on the activities of individuals as well as nations. It is the curse of literalism. By literalism I mean an approach to life which leaves no open ends, which believes that all problems have an "either-or" solution, that every situation demands either affirmation or denial. I call this literalism, because it stems not infrequently from the literal application of a text or dogma that is considered identical with Truth, and it is assumed that this Truth must of needs be victorious in the end. This is an ancient disease and we have not been able to find its cure. It is in effect an infantile residue coming to us out of prehistoric days. Let me begin my discourse by applying this outlook to the principal problems of the current political scene.

You are all familiar with Marxism and its expressions in modern communist countries. You know that they are built on certain texts and dogmas. Deviation from the text, from the literal application of the dogma, is in effect a crime against the state. In Soviet Russia and China today no greater epithet can be hurled against a political non-conformist than that he is a deviationist — one who deviates from the literal or the dogmatic. The only other epithet in competition with deviationist is revisionist. Of course, when a person is accused of being a revisionist, he himself calls his accuser a literalist, for which in the Marxist lingo there is also a word, namely, dogmatist.

Lest we believe that we in the West are exempt from this disease, let me hasten to assert that in our way we are just as subject to its affliction; of course we use different terms. We believe that there is a rigid distinction to be made between good and evil, that certain things are good and therefore other things must by definition be evil. This is but an application of the type of literalism that afflicts our society. Applied to everyday politics, it comes down to a belief that there must be an "either-or" solution in history. We come to believe that democracy will have to win and will eventually overcome the Marxist concept and the communist society.

Khrushchev has a little earthier approach to these complex questions and puts it in a more memorable form when he says, "We will bury you." We are a little more genteel about it, a little more indirect, more polished — but it amounts to the same thing. We say that we will bury them, and they say that they will bury us. We are both literalists in this sense. We both believe that there must be in history a clear-cut solution, that right (that is, what our side considers right) must triumph over wrong.

The different textbooks tell us clearly what the future will hold. Of course, it depends on whether these textbooks are the *Communist Manifesto*, the works of Lenin or Engels, or whether they are our Bible, the BNA Act, or the American or French constitutions. These are our documents and they determine who will be victorious and what, in the long run of history, will end in defeat. But as anyone acquainted with even a small aspect of history can attest, life does not necessarily work this way.

CHRISTENDOM AND ISLAM

In 1683 the Turks were halted at the gates of Vienna. Up to that point there was a belief that the world of the future would belong to either Christendom or Islam. The secular empires built upon these religious philosophies were locked in a life-and-death struggle which began in the eighth century when the Moors first invaded Spain. The Crusades were part of this struggle. Somehow it was obvious to both parties, the leaders of Islam as well as the leaders of Christianity, that the future could belong to only one of them. In 1683 this literalist interpretation of history was dashed on the rocks of reality. The battle between the giants was a standoff. The representatives of Islam retreated and since that day Christendom and Islam have turned to other pursuits and to other kinds of disagreements — and agreement as well.

History will not be written in the "either-ors" of Christianity or Islam.

In my opinion the same is true for East and West today, for communism and democracy. In a way Marx was right when he taught us that history was not static, that it was in flux, that men could have a share in moulding it, which after all was the essence of his creed. There is a dynamism in history, he said; classes are not fixed and rigid forever, wealth and its distribution are not God-given. Here, Marx, the determinist, left his fixed philosophic base and became kin to Western idealism, which held that men and the thinking of men have an impact on history. The moment you say this, you state that history is open-ended. Strange as it may seem, in this so dissimilar fashion, Marxism and Western idealism find a riverbed of confluence. To both, in this sense, history is subject to man's will. To be sure, Western idealism reserves to man a greater area of freedom because the open-ended society is to Western man a goal in itself. There remains enough area of agreement to make it possible today to speak of co-existence not only as a temporary device for the alleviation of immediate and acute tensions, but to go beyond this and to say that co-existence is a philosophic and therefore also a political need as well as a possibility.

FEDERALISM AS ANTI-LITERALISM

You may wonder what all this lengthy and circuitous introduction has to do with World Federalism. But to me the conclusion is obvious. I believe that World Federalism is built on the realization that a literal interpretation of history is erroneous, that history need not resolve itself into an "either-or" solution, and that tensions not only will persist, but are needed to drive man forward.

The question is: how do we handle these tensions? Will we utilize them constructively in order to drive man forward to new heights of achievement, or will we allow these tensions to deteriorate into political and military chaos? World Federalism in its very terminology recognizes not only diversity but also the infinite philosophic need for the coexistence of various kinds of approaches to political life. In this sense World Federalism is thoroughly anti-literalist.

Those who would interpret the movement as an ultimate in mono-lithic structure misread this program entirely. Were this the program of World Federalism I would be the last to join the organization. I do not wish to live in a monolithic world; I do not wish to live in a world governed in a unitary fashion, allowing no diversity of opinion and development, a world which would demand the same political system to be imposed upon all human society. It would not only be a dull world, it would be intolerable.

I am deeply committed to certain prophetic visions, but these visions do not foresee a realistic society in which there will be no injustice at all. That can be the vision of "Kingdom come," but not of an ordinary human society. As long as there are men, there will be justice and injustice, there will be hatred and love, and there will be force and counterforce.

The question is: how can we marshal and control these varying elements so that society can resolve its controversies in a non-violent, peaceable, and orderly fashion? World Federalism to me is the very incarnation of non-literalism in history, the recognition that ours is a complex, diversified, and forever tension-filled society, which nevertheless needs means and ways to live non-violently and constructively together. This can only be done under the rule of law.

SIGNS OF A WORLD CONCEPT

In many ways the world concept which is ours is already recognized by multitudes of people who have never heard the term World Federalism. I am not now speaking of the UN, which is our basic instrument and the starting point of our practical endeavours. I am speaking of the unseen progress which our thoughts have made. These are part and parcel of the forward thrust of our time, greater than many of us realize. Let me illustrate this in reference to three areas of the contemporary political scene.

Take South Vietnam. Quite aside from the military shifts and needs, there is one problem in this still faraway country that has gripped our interest and our compassion. It has to do with the struggle of the Buddhist for religious equality. The fact is that most people in the Western Hemisphere are not Buddhist, yet nonetheless feel a tremendous sense of identification with these men who sacrifice their lives for the sake of an idea. We have a bond with people far away. In that sense it is quite uninteresting to us that this happens in South Vietnam, and despite all the publicity which has attended the tragic developments in that country, only the most sophisticated among us have more than a vague idea about its variegated and complex problems. What is important is that even though we do not know much about Vietnam's economy and even though its political intricacies hold only the remotest interest for us, nonetheless there is a problem which we consider ours, namely, the problem of religious freedom. We live in the same world and we feel that the law that applies to us in this regard should also apply to the Vietnamese.

Or take Birmingham, which is closer to home. The other day Prime Minister Pearson said that Birmingham was our Canadian problem also, for when human rights are diminished in Birmingham they are diminished in Canada as well. This, I believe, signified tremendous progress. It is a great forward step for a Canadian prime minister to say, "Birmingham is my problem." A little while ago this would have been impossible; nobody would have dared to say it. And mind you, he said it in the United States, and he said it to Secretary of State Dean Rusk, and over American television. A foreigner, from their point of view, comes to their country and says, "Your problem is my problem." The huge audience applauded wildly simply because the concept that we are in effect one society, that certain ideas belong to all of us, has already been widely accepted — only it has not as yet been encased in the kind of world law which we hope some day we may call ours.

A third problem, close to me, and I am sure not unknown to you, is the problem of the Jews in Soviet Russia. American senators, the United States House of Representatives, and legislatures in various other lands are concerned with the fate of a relatively small religious minority in the vast Soviet Union. There are some 220 million Soviet citizens and probably between 3 and 5 million Jews. The latter's religious rights are being abridged, the Jews are being singled out for special economic and sociological persecution. Is this our business? It is now the business of the American Congress, it is the business of foreign embassies, and it is the subject of official inquiry. One could only wish that thirty years ago more countries would have made it their business to inquire about human rights in Germany. Perhaps the ghastly slaughter that ensued might not have happened.

Instance number three belongs to the same calendar of progress, not because it happens in Russia, but because of our attitude toward it. Because we recognize that this is our problem and that for the first time we are bold enough to say, what about it? An answer such as "This is within our borders" no longer suffices. Mr. Pearson can come and say to Mr. Rusk in Cleveland, "Your problem is our problem," and we in Canada are collecting funds to send south of the border. In the same manner today, we can go to the Russians and say, "Your Jews and your treatment of religious minorities are our problem." Whether they will act upon it is yet another question, but the very fact that we have already progressed to this stage is enormously hopeful, because it indicates our range of world problems and draws the fences more broadly around the courtyards of human life.

Or take the United Nations, where significant progress has been made despite all the pessimism and despite all those who would denigrate the work of that organization. Even in its peacekeeping activities we have made great progress. From the days of the Palestine peacekeeping force, which was only designed to keep parties apart and to prevent further incursions, we have progressed to the days of the Congo. I don't know what you think about the Congo affair. I am sure you all share with me the sense of frustration and bewilderment over some of its failures, but one thing stands out. In the UN Congo operation something new has happened, for there the forces of the UN have acted as an independent police force and not just as a buffer between contending parties. Whether this was wise or unwise is not the subject at this point, but the fact that many nations have managed to accept this as a legitimate extension of peacekeeping activities is highly significant.

We are indeed a smaller world. Greater pressures are being brought to bear upon all of our problems, and therefore I believe we will see more and more of the expansion of a world concept in the next few years. There is a greater ground sweep that works in our favour. Recently a conference was held in Denver that brought people together from various countries with the announced purpose of calling a World Constitutional Congress. Recently professors of law assembled in Athens, Greece to deal with the philosophy of world law. These are more than straws in the wind. There is no question that the acute dangers which developed in the aftermath of the Cuban crisis have hastened the urgency for developing these concepts more fully and more effectively.

BEGINNING ON THE MOON

I am not facetious if I say that world government is closer to us now than ever before, even though we may have to begin world government on the moon. A year and a half ago, when he spoke about the U.S. race to the moon, President Kennedy emphasized that America must be first, that being first was part of the country's philosophy. But you also know what he said recently when he offered to the Soviet Union and to others to make common cause in the race to the moon. Suppose this comes to pass as a by-product of the present detente. If the Soviet Union and the United States put a man on the moon together, you would then have your first world government. To be sure, it would come to us from far away, but we would have it nonetheless. If that should happen, the billions and billions of dollars and rubles that will have been spent on the exploration of space and on the manning of capsules to reach the moon will indeed have been very well spent.

May I also say at this point that because of all of this we are becoming a very respectable organization. This bothers me, as a matter of fact. Sometimes I feel it is good to be non-respectable because then you are a little bolder and what you say finds readier ears. But I will not quarrel with this newly acquired respectability. Only ten years ago we were under investigation from Senator McCarthy. Ten years later McCarthy's closest henchman is in deep trouble and under investigation himself and we who were then suspect have become highly legitimate.

Presidents of various nations and prime ministers quote the World Federalist ideal as if they had always thought of it. We are very happy with this. We do not arrogate to ourselves the distinction of being sole possessors of a patented idea. We are satisfied to leave our ideal quite free for public use. I am very happy with the kind of further advance which Mr. Pearson has proposed to the United Nations in his suggestion for a more effective and extended peace force. Our president, Professor Burchill, has submitted to us what he calls a Canadian initiative. This goes even further and underscores the fact that the middle nations not only have a role to play but have a potentially decisive opportunity in international affairs. I would buttress Professor Burchill's very imaginative statement with a philosophical or perhaps moral consideration. At the present time, Canada has limited political power. This is in fact our greatest advantage in the world today, because the nation that acquires political power becomes enmeshed in the day-to-day opportunistic needs of applying its power to a diversity of conflicting situations.

There was a time two generations ago when the United States was the great moral power in the Western world, but when it acquired actual political and military power after the First World War and in a vaster measure after the Second World War, its moral influence disappeared in direct proportion to its economic and military influence.

Or take the example of India. As little as twenty years ago, was there a greater moral force in the world than India? But when India assumed its own power stature and started to apply this power to the immediate needs of everyday political life, its moral force diminished until it has today become of the same order reserved for the great nations.

The middle or small powers still possess moral influence which the large powers do not wield, because their economic and military establishments make their morality suspect however genuine it may be, suspect and therefore unacceptable. This is why a Canadian or middle-power initiative would have a real chance for success, because it would also be borne aloft by that moral strength which is still ours.

CONCLUSION

In a sense it is very fortunate that the World Federalists of Canada are a relatively small group. I do not believe we will ever be a mass movement. I do not believe that this will be necessary. Matthew Arnold said some fifty years ago that the world is pushed forward by minorities; it is the individual or the small group with great imagination which by the force of ideas and the power of personality propels the world to new areas of progress.

I believe this is the task of the World Federalists: to infect the world with our enthusiasm for the possibility of the rule of world law. For we live in a world in which ultimately progress will not be achieved by force and deterrence, but by ideas. We have hold of a great idea, the greatest idea in political life there is. Stemming from the ancient days of the prophets, it remains an idea which will yet be the prophecy and reality of tomorrow.

Concerning Israel

Why Is Israel Different?

$\mathcal{T}$he voices are many and dissonant: I love Begin — I hate Begin (Menachem, that is, not Monique). Ariel Sharon was innocent of any complicity in the Beirut massacre — he was guilty and therefore had to go. Settlements on the West Bank are our only permanent defence — settlements must stop because they hinder the peace process. An independent Palestinian state will spell the end of Israel — such a state is inevitable, and its teeth can be pulled in advance. All Israelis agree — no Israelis agree on anything. Yasser Arafat is a moderate who wants peace — yes, the peace of an Israeli cemetery.

Etcetera.

"Back to the 1967 borders!" is the United Nations' demand. But before the Six Day War it was "Back to the 1947 borders!" On November 29, 1947, the UN divided what was then Palestine into a Jewish and an Arab state. Jerusalem was to be internationalized. The Jews accepted and proclaimed Israel within the specified borders. The Arabs demurred, and five of their armies invaded the land. For a long time the fate of the tiny new nation hung in the balance, but in the end its fortunes turned. One percent of its population fell in the battle (imagine 250,000 Canadians dying in a nine-month war). The conflict re-drew the borders, people fled and were displaced — the unhappy consequence of any war. Germany invaded Poland in 1939. When it was over, 10 million Germans had to leave their homes and are now settled in the rest of Germany. No one suggests that Poland should resettle them and act as if 1939 never happened.

But it is different with Israel, everything is, and it worries me.

After thirty-five brief years of existence she has fought five wars. Except for Egypt and Lebanon, no Arab nation recognizes her, and most governments in Asia and Africa follow the Communist line and have no diplomatic relations with her (though many of them are happy to receive her technology, her goods, and even her weapons as long as they are imported via a third country). If there is any agreement among nations West and East about Israel, it is one thing: she alone of all the nations in the world must observe ideal standards of international ethics and internal social justice, standards neither demanded of nor achieved by any nation on the globe, Canada not excepted. When I travelled to Australia recently, I was thunderstruck to find that Canadians are portrayed primarily as heartless killers of innocent baby seals. I got nowhere talking about the Canada I know and love. We are not all seal hunters, I argued. There is really more to us than that.

That's the way it is with Israel. Every mark against the nation — real or invented — makes it, so to speak, into a nation of sealers. Responsibility for the three hundred tragic victims of Christian Phalangist murderers — Arabs themselves — was laid at the door of Israel. This magazine [*Maclean's*] headlined a memorable issue on the subject with a cover stating, ISRAEL ON TRIAL. But no one was on trial when, in the seven years previous, at least 60,000 Lebanese were slain in the course of the civil war. The loudest cries came (and come) from the Left, both here and abroad, that same Left whose silence about Afghanistan marks it for a special prize in political hypocrisy — the same people who condemn US imperialism but find no fault with Soviet expansionism or Cuban mercenaries. "No country must keep territory acquired in war," they proclaim, meaning Israel but not, of course, the Soviets' acquisition of the Baltic states of Lithuania, Estonia, and Latvia.

Yet withal, the little nation of Israel has looked to its ethics while the real slayers of Sabra and Shatila have not been apprehended by the Lebanese (much less tried). Because its own citizens so demanded, Israel felt compelled to put its entire government on trial to determine whether there was any action that was morally reprehensible and could be construed as complicity or even knowledge. In consequence this nation ousted its most admired war hero and sacked two other generals — for ethical reasons, not for failure to have performed valiantly.

The Palestinian problem will not go away. Israel's first president, Chaim Weizmann, once said that it represented the clash of two national rights. It must be resolved and it could and would if a Palestinian leadership, Syria, Jordan, and the other Arab states would sit down with Israel and talk about it in rational terms rather than through terror and constant war. Thus, while Israel needs and wants peace desperately, Syria, the Soviet Union's chief client state in the Middle East, does not want it at all. On the contrary, the country's minister of planning declared recently that Syria has thrived in its permanent state of war. For some strange reason — which appears logical to the purveyors of 1984 — that attitude is said to be best rectified by putting even more pressure on Israel to make further concessions.

Israelis themselves are not agreed on their own politics, which are raucous and verbally violent, for democracy and dissent are the very lifeblood of the country, and that alone should make it appealing to those of us who are aware of the shrinking perimeters of democracy in a world that counts only twenty-eight or twenty-nine nations that deserve this ascription.

Israelis discuss the fate of the Arabs in their midst, the future of the West Bank, the rightness of adding new settlements, the peace process, the justification for the Lebanese war. Most believe that an independent Arab state on the West Bank would pose a great danger to Israel. Yet, while they want to give the Arabs the greatest autonomy possible, they do not consider independent statehood to be the only avenue for realizing cultural and national aspirations. In this respect they are no different from Canadians with regard to Quebec.

Israel is thirty-five years old. Transposed into Canadian history, that would bring us back to 1902, a world away from today's realities. In 1902 the world demanded little of Canada, but of Israel it wants everything — total justice and total righteousness. It isn't there of course — but there is more of it than in many, if not most, places if one is willing to take a dispassionate look.

The land needs a little patience, a little peace, and a little love. I believe that given half a chance they will do the right thing by the Arabs and by themselves, unless of course one thinks that the right thing is Israeli suicide. That was Gandhi's advice to the Jews of Europe in the 1930s: collective suicide. There must be a different way.

A Eulogy for the Israeli Martyrs
of 1972 at Munich

"To everything there is a season and a time to every purpose under the heavens ... a time to weep and a time to laugh, a time to mourn and a time to dance."

Tonight is the time for weeping and for mourning. Weeping over eleven men who were raised to young manhood, rejoicing in the strength of body and the fullness of will with which nature had endowed them and which their own persistence had brought to full fruition. Men who had fathers and mothers, men who had wives and children, men who gloried in being alive and who looked to men from other nations so that they might be friends together, strive together, compete with one another, and match their prowess and their skills. Men cut down in the flower of their youth, killed mindlessly and savagely not for deeds they had committed but for what they were: because they were members of their people, a people upon whom modern history has forced the sword of self-defence, but whose watchword has been and remains *shalom* — peace.

Especially now, four years later, it is a time to mourn for these eleven young men (and for the German policeman who died attempting to protect their lives and who deserves to be remembered in this hour as well). To mourn, however, is more than to weep, for mourning is ultimately invested with the quality of remembering, and remembrance is the stuff of history. Without remembrance we are forced to live our yesterdays all over again, without understanding, without purpose and without goals. But when we recall the past, we can, if we wish, be instructed and warned. Thus four times a year Jews stand up in the synagogue and proclaim to their Creator that they are remembering the past, as they remember their own dear ones and the martyrs of their people. But more than this, Jews call upon God Himself to remember, to make sure that the structure of the world retains its ethical continuum. God, too, must remember, and this is what we say tonight: *Yizkor Elohim et yakirenu ha-kedoshim.*

Olympic martyrs, we weep for you who died in pursuit of peace, striving for the Olympic ideals of friendship. We weep for the years you were not allowed to live on this earth and enjoy the fullness thereof. We weep for your widows, your children, your parents, your brothers and your sisters, we weep for your people — nay, our people — so sorely tried; we weep with all men and women whose hearts can still distinguish between good and evil, right and wrong.

We mourn, but our mourning is suffused with more than tears. Our mourning also contains the resolve that if your deaths are not to have been entirely in vain, we must redeem your memories with our deeds.

You were slain in Munich, a city identified by history with the rise of Hitler. It is also the place where appeasement found its ultimate expression, where a nation was sacrificed to the appetites of the predator, where two proud and cultured nations caved into terror and tyranny and thereby sacrificed their own best youth to the inevitability of a world war yet to come. Therefore, in 1972, Munich was the place where memory was to be redeemed by a new age. Yet, new memories, new tears, new regrets were to be shaped there once again, because terror was still alive, because the nations of the world had not yet resolved to stamp it out. We mourn today because the spirit of Munich still roams the world.

Therefore we say to you, the slain heroes of Munich, we will do more than weep, we will do more than mourn. The biblical text goes on to say, "There is a time to keep silence and a time to speak." This is a time to speak, yea, to cry out to the world on your behalf and on ours: "Awake, lest it be too late! The terror that stalks by night must be exposed to the full light of human conscience and resolve. The time is past for mouthing pious words. If there is no action, there will be no community left to take action. If the world does not rise to the need to stamp out terrorism once and for all, there will be no world community left in which to breathe freely and without fear. If Munich is not to happen once again, then the umbrellas of caution must be folded up. There should be no airport in the world that allows terror to find a home; and if there is, let no civilian airline fly there any more. There must be no nation left in the world to give succour to those who hold others hostage at the point of a gun and at the thrust of a bomb; and if there is, let the rest of the nations shun it like the plague.

This is the bitter lesson of Munich and it is the cogent lesson of Entebbe. It is no accident that in both these encounters Jews were the focus of extermination. Alas, we know all too well that when we are isolated and marked for killing, the world that calls itself free will also lose its license to live freely. Its liberty, too, will be murdered, for in the course of history Jews have been the bellwether of human freedom. At Munich, civilization itself was threatened, and at Entebbe, civilization itself was rescued. For how long? That is the question we ask tonight. Unless there is an answer that comes from the nations of the world, the clouds will form once again and beyond Entebbe there will be other Munichs.

Our tradition says, "The day is short, the labour is much ... and the Master of the house is pressing." "The day is short"— yet we also know that in this nation of Canada there are burgeonings of hope. The very presence tonight of the nation's leaders, men and women who are distinguished representatives of democracy, gives hope that the time for silence is past, and that a time for speaking has come. Yea, more — a time for doing!

Your presence here bespeaks your will and your determination. May the Lord of history, He who remembers, uphold your hands, and may the world take note of these moments when weeping and mourning, words and deeds, are blended into one resolve. Eleven men died at Munich, but Israel lives; eleven men died in the pursuit of an ideal, but in this country — now preparing to play host to the same ideal — freedom lives and resolve has been strengthened. Thus, out of the ashes of yesterday a better tomorrow will be fashioned, when men shall sit each one under his fig tree, when swords shall be turned into ploughshares, when nation shall not lift up sword against nation, nor shall they know war any more.

Yizkor Elohim, may God remember the dead and may He remember the living, so that the glory of His name shall be exalted and the radiance of His presence illumine the world.

Amen

The Un-public Relations of
Our National Bodies

*E*ver since I came to Canada some years ago I have been struck by what appeared to me a peculiar, Old World mentality of Canadian Jewry — especially when it came to politics. At first I dismissed this observation as prejudice and probably grounded in my ignorance of, and unfamiliarity with, the Canadian scene. But as the years passed, my original impression was reinforced rather than weakened.

I do not delude myself into thinking that what follows will be immensely popular, quite the contrary. In fact, I hope that it will arouse some vigorous discussion, for thereby we can make some fresh advancement on the road to political emancipation.

I hold that in the most important aspects and methods of public relations the national Jewish bodies in Canada are hopelessly moored in nineteenth-century attitudes. For many decades now the leading public relations bodies, namely, Canadian Jewish Congress, B'nai Brith, and the Zionist organizations, have almost exclusively relied on a number of old and tried methods. These consisted of submissions and briefs, representations to government, luncheons with political leaders and other outstanding figures, articles in newspapers and magazines, carefully phrased answers to letters which appeared in the mailbox columns of various journals, the occasional good spot on a radio or television program, and the like.

There is of course no reason to denigrate these methods; they have their place, they are policy-shaping, they help to create what the national organizations like to think of as "the image" of Canadian Jewry.

What does "the image" try to convey? That we are law-abiding citizens, that we put Canada first, that we are loyal, but that we are also Jews and that (with your permission, honoured gentlemen!) we also have certain Jewish interests which now we would like you to be good enough and kind enough and generous enough to consider.

Often things work out the way we planned. This in turn reinforces our beliefs that our old and tried methods are really very good, and that if we fail occasionally we need merely try harder next time. So we intensify our activities with submissions, briefs, representations, luncheons, speeches, letters, and interviews to shine up the public image.

The underlying theory is a very simple one: a good image of Canadian Jewry will make it easy for our policy makers to accede to our legitimate wishes, for a good image has political force. Within the framework of such thinking everything is logical and watertight. As I said, there is good reason to pursue this method, for it has advantages and within definite limits it is successful and in conformity with Canadian political tradition.

But the emphasis must be on the words "within limits" and these limits are very narrow indeed. What applied fifty, sixty, or eighty-five years ago simply no longer applies. The Jewish community has grown both in numbers and in stature, although it has not as yet grown in appreciation of its own potential.

The fallacy of nineteenth-century methods is the belief that a public image creates a public policy. The belief was of course erroneous some years ago, even as it is erroneous today, but the glaring inconsistency of goals and methods is more sharply delineated in our age when we have a much deeper appreciation of politics and when hundreds of excellent analytical studies and much experience in the political field itself should teach us differently.

Public policy is not primarily a matter of image-making — it is a matter of politics, pure and simple, and our public relations bodies will have to awaken to this fact. They may continue their submissions, briefs, representations, interviews, and letters, but they also must finally and at last enter the twentieth century of political life, and become frankly, openly, and courageously political, with new methods that reflect this appreciation.

Now is the time. Walter Lippmann once said that it takes fifteen to twenty years after a major cataclysm for leaders to emerge who will properly assess and utilize the new powers which have been unleashed by the upheaval. We have now travelled this distance since the European Holocaust and the time has come to turn our un-public relations into truly public relations and policies.

This article is being written in the midst of the 1965 national election campaign. I have been present at enough discussions of various bodies to set down the following as observations of Jewish psychology in Canada.

There is an enormous fear of the words "Jewish bloc." These words, as is well known, were created by anti-Semites and, whatever else they may have contributed to public life, they have thoroughly frightened the Jewish community. Everyone piously beats his breast and proclaims that there is no Jewish bloc in a Canadian election. If this be piety it is nothing but pious nonsense. If there were an issue on which Jews felt strongly — for instance, if a declared anti-Semite were to run in a certain riding — would there be any hesitation on the part of Jews to vote against this man because they considered him a menace to their own security? Would they not have a perfect right to translate this feeling into their votes? An anti-Semitic candidate in a riding would by his very presence and activity create a "Jewish bloc." And there would he nothing wrong but everything right if Jews en masse voted to defeat this candidate.

Every voter is motivated by a whole series of psychological and social "blocs": he belongs to a labour union; or to a manufacturers' association; he is a farmer who favours the sale of wheat to Red China; or he is in the automotive industry and favours the loosening of tariff restrictions; he is of Indian ancestry and would like a new deal for the Indian community; he is a Negro and wants a national fair-housing law; he is a doctor and is against compulsory Medicare; he is a French-Canadian and wants a new approach to French culture and tradition.

Everyone recognizes these aspirations as legitimate and intimately interwoven with the structure of Canadian public life. They represent realities and "blocs" in any election. Not only is there nothing to be afraid of in such power groupings, but without these various pressures and counter-pressures nothing like a national will can ultimately emerge. What is a parliament except a collection of men of diverse interests and opinions who in session assembled try to arrive at some form of consensus? Behind this consensus lie pressures as well as convictions, and together they form the precarious checks, balances, and exigencies of the public will. *This is the nature of politics; it has always been so and certainly in a democratic society this is the way it will always be.*

While these realities are generally recognized, there is a visible hesitation to identify any issue as having Jewish import. It is permissible to have labour import, capitalist import, farmer import, French-Canadian import, or whatnot; but a Jewish import is something from which Jews themselves instinctively shrink.

A prime example in the current election has been the approach to the hate literature conundrum. There have been repeated suggestions to confront candidates across the nation with some of the problems arising from this situation, to ask them, for instance, whether or not they could agree with the principles of a bill which would preserve free speech, but which on the other hand would make the public dissemination of racial and religious hatred a criminal offence. No such confrontation has occurred except in individual instances. There is a general hesitancy to put "pressures" on the candidate, because "it might make a bad impression."

In the opinion of this observer such an attitude reveals a second-class citizenship approach to Canadian life. Nobody goes into politics expecting it to be a rarefied form of teach-in. Politics is a strange mixture of moral conviction and public pressure. Forceful representation always contains both a promise or a threat: that the voter might or might not cast his vote for the candidate. *And is it not really closer to the true meaning of democracy to confront each candidate squarely with certain issues so that the voter may then be in a position to determine whether or not he should and will cast his ballot for this particular candidate?* It need not at all mean that a Jew would, for instance, vote for a man who favours a strong hate-literature law, for he may find this candidate unsuitable for other reasons. But then again, this particular stand may make all the difference to the voter.

In these respects I have observed a distinct difference between the attitudes taken by Jews in the United States and those in Canada. In the United States there has been no hesitation in the past few decades to make the strongest possible representation before political conventions, to have planks include positive statements regarding Israel and to have politicians commit themselves in advance to certain basic attitudes. Jewish organizations have not hesitated to invite candidates of both parties to debate their viewpoints publicly and to ask them for definite commitments if they felt so inclined.

In Canada, where there are no such platforms created prior to an election, but where the campaigning is much more individual, different methods are, of course, called for. But the principle remains the same: a true public confrontation of each candidate with the issues at hand is necessary and desirable. Yet Canadian Jewish organizations have shied away from this normal process of democracy and have thereby underlined a basic anxiety which stems from unforgotten yesterdays. It has no longer any place today.

It will be said that, after all, Canadian Jews are not in the same position as their brethren south of the border. We here are not as many, and consequently cannot wield the same kind of influence as can American Jews. But this very argument reveals a sense of inferior citizenship. A first-class citizen does not think of himself merely in terms of numbers, he thinks of himself as having certain rights which he will use within the framework set by the democratic process. He is unafraid to think freely and to say freely what he thinks. If others want to label a particular position he takes as "pressure," he will gladly take this risk, if a risk it be. There is nothing wrong with any group within society turning from time to time into a pressure group in pursuit of ideas and policies which it deems necessary for the public weal.

Anybody who has read President Truman's memoirs knows what he said about his decision to recognize the new State of Israel in 1948. He frankly speaks of "Zionist pressure." Is there a question in anyone's mind that without such pressure the United States would have hesitated to act? Would we rather that the Stephen Wises and the Abba Hillel Silvers had been silent and written lengthy submissions and briefs and made polite reply by writing letters to the editor?

The first-class citizen acts on behalf of what he thinks is right. This is a privilege which Canada confers on all who dwell within her borders. Not to use the privilege within proper legal and moral limits is, in effect, a betrayal of these very rights.

Some feel that the advocacy of such procedures will bring about a clash between morality and politics. Nothing of the sort! I hope that as Jews we will always be moral, and not for one moment would I advocate the use of political pressure for any aims except moral aims.

I happen to think that Jews at their best represent the moral conscience of society, and therefore what they advocate is usually congruent with the public good. The old-time Jew who looked at a public pronouncement by some political figure and instinctively asked, "*S'iz goot fer Yidn*?" had an instinctive reaction which in the context of total Jewish history was quite appropriate. In the context of Canadian public politics, he was closer to reality than those who make submissions, briefs, representations, and letters their demi-gods.

We must get away from the misconception that using the power tools of politics is by itself immoral. It will be immoral if method or purpose are immoral; but power politics requires power tools, and hand tools of the Model-T era are simply ineffective today.

What is needed therefore is a vigorous rethinking of our approach to public relations. The Jewish community across Canada was jarred by the events following the so-called Allan Gardens riots earlier this year.[1] The real result of those events was a re-evaluation of the place which public demonstrations could have on public policy. Everyone regretted of course that violence entered the picture, but that a new element had also become part of the Canadian Jewish community was unmistakable.

There are apparently enough people in the community who feel instinctively that new methods adequate to our age might be employed to bring about more vigorous action by our politicians. This recognition may yet prove to be a turning point in our general attitude toward matters of public policy.

In a recent article the noted Jewish publicist M. Z. Frank criticized Jewish organizations (he had the American Zionist organizations particularly in mind) for failing to see that they must be thoroughly home-based. He argued that an American Zionist organization had to be anchored in American public and political life and in American Jewish realities. His ideas can easily be transferred to Canada because they are equally applicable. Congress, B'nai Brith, and the Zionist organizations must be thoroughly home-based, by which I mean that they must be grounded in the realities of Canadian political life.

The ideal of human brotherhood and decency, to which we all subscribe, must be translated into the home-based, hard facts of political life; else they will remain pious pronouncements. The ideal of a strong and peaceful Israel pursuing the great goals of its founders must be taken out of Zionist publications and be translated similarly into the hard facts of Canadian public life. All these organizations need a thorough revision of their political action programs which will take into account the proper method of political persuasion and the compatibility of morality and political action.

And we need new direction from the top. We will never lose sight of the fact that we want to represent moral issues morally and do so by the proper method of persuasion. But we simply cannot overlook the fact that on political issues there must be political realism within the framework of our moral conviction. Only this understanding will turn the un-public relations, which we have been following with minor success in the past, into real public relations adequate to our time.

Foreword to S. Zalman Abramov's
Perpetual Dilemma

"*When* you enter the land that the Lord your God has given you as
a heritage and you occupy it and settle in it ..."— thus begins a weekly
portion in the Book of Deuteronomy. It is one of those passages in which
the Torah anticipates what would or should happen once the people
occupied the Promised Land and sets forth ethical and social rules for the
governance of its society. In these and similar prescriptions the overriding
idea of the Torah is that once the people set up their own independent
government in the land which was to become the inheritance of Israel,
they would organize a theocracy imbued with justice and compassion.
It would be a land ruled not by priests (or later, rabbis), kings, or other
appointed or self-appointed men, but rather by the invisible God of the
Covenant and of the Torah which gives expression to His will.

Such was the hope and the record, but practice proved otherwise.
Where the Torah provided that idolaters and idolatries were to be rooted
out, the people of Israel instead assimilated the inhabitants and often
were assimilated by them. Idolatry continued to play an important role
in Jewish history and was for hundreds of years the target of prophetic
ire. Contrary to the desires of Samuel, the people forced him to accede to
their request for converting the theocracy into a monarchy. Subsequently
the priesthood served not only the Temple but also the temporal and
political powers. It became allied with government and was controlled by
— and sometimes controlled — its uses and abuses. In turn this gave rise
to the spiritual opposition of the prophets, who were often suppressed or
at other times ignored, and who on the whole were acclaimed only after

their death. Their revolution lay frequently in the seeding of ideas rather than in immediate political changes.

In the fifth and fourth centuries, in consequence of the efforts made by Ezra after the return from Babylonian exile, a new attempt was made to establish a theocracy. Here began the development of what today we call Halakhah, a body of rules which developed the laws of the Torah in systematic and structural fashion, and here also, through the Great Sanhedrin and the authorities which arose in later times, the idea emerged (though it was not at once accepted) that the orderly growth of Halakhah was a direct continuation of the divine inspiration derived from Sinai. But the progress of these ideas was not at all smooth, nor did it follow a direct line. Political and social upheavals, wars and rebellions and foreign oppression combined to alter the course of the Jewish tradition violently from time to time. In the end, toward the latter days of the Second Temple, the religious structure of ancient Israel showed a new dichotomy: there was a priesthood which was generally, although not always, allied with the ruling political powers; and there arose populist reform movements which attempted to chart a different religious course for the people, one that was both more inward and more private. While the priesthood emphasized the Deuteronomic insistence on the centrality of the cult in the sanctuary in Jerusalem, various brotherhoods and Pharisaic parties, while not denying the importance of the Temple cult, aimed to privatize religion significantly. They did this through self-isolation in retreats, or through the development of a new class of religious leaders, rabbis, who functioned outside of the Temple and shifted the basis of authority — from the political to the scriptural. It was because of them that, when the Temple was destroyed, law and tradition, Halakhah and Minhag, could become substitutes for the vanished, visible presence of God in the sanctuary. As long as the Temple had stood, these populist reformers had been generally supportive of its cult as the manifestation of public religion, but when the sanctuary lay in ashes, the privatism of Judaism gained the upper hand. It was a salvational process with its imperfections built into it from the beginning.

For while the Halakhah had the effect of making Judaism a portable religion and made the continued spiritual viability of the faith possible, it also separated itself by force of circumstance from the original major locus of Judaism, namely, the Land of Israel. To be sure, there always were Jews in the land, and they would remain there in smaller or larger numbers throughout the centuries, but never again, until 1948, would they have complete control of their own political destiny. With statehood denied them, the external government of their society, both in the land of Israel and in the Diaspora, became a function of the sovereign power under whom they lived. In earlier centuries of occupancy in Palestine, they had had to grapple with national, economic, military, and social pressures and to fashion the political organs of their society. They had to take care of their own internal system of security and their external international relations. Now, as a minority in a foreign-ruled Palestine as well as in the Diaspora, their portable religion became divorced from these considerations. The privatism of Judaism became complete and with it its Diaspora nature. While there were still ancient treatises dealing with sacrifices and ownership in the Holy Land, and pious souls continued to study them in anticipation of the day when Israel would return to the land at the time when the Messiah would come, they had very little relation to life as it was. For the years between 70 and 1918 CE, Judaism was a Diaspora religion, and remained so essentially even in the years of pre-state settlement after 1880. The law book of Judaism which summarized and codified the centuries of earlier tradition, Joseph Caro's *Shulhan Arukh*, regulated every vestige of personal life, but had not a single chapter on the administration of an army or police force. For both in Safad where Caro wrote and throughout the lands of dispersion, these considerations were not relevant to the Jewish community. Foreign powers administered these areas of public life, and it was no different in 1517 under Turkish rule or a hundred years later when the British took on this responsibility.

Nothing demonstrates this gap more clearly than the Shemittah controversy of the 1880s. It had to do with the biblical rule that the land was not to be worked in the sabbatical year, that is, once every seven years. By common consent of the tradition, the law was applicable only to Eretz Yisrael, but now that the settlers had returned, it suddenly became evident that either the ancient rules had to be enforced or adjusted or they would be disregarded altogether. The very process and ultimate resolution of the controversy made it clear that while some groups of immigrants came to the land in the hope that all problems could be met on the basis of a Diaspora-based and developed Halakhah, others arrived with different concepts of how religious precepts were or were not to be realized in Eretz Yisrael.

What ultimately determined the development of this inherent tension were a number of factors which sometimes were related and at other times were not. The primary one was *who* immigrated and *when*, for each new wave of settlers brought along a set of religious and social ideals which on occasion were in sharp contrast with each other. In addition, the political struggle (first against the British and then against the Arabs) determined to a significant degree the external environment in which such developments were taking place.

Important aspects of this constellation were the original settlement (the so-called Old Yishuv), in both its Sephardic and Ashkenazic components; the fact that the New Yishuv was mostly socialist and usually atheistic in conviction, foreshadowing the ultimate conflict or at least continuing tension between the state and the synagogue; the relatively late arrival of German Jews with their components of the Liberal religious element; the presence of Holocaust survivors for many of whom the traditional framework of life had been emptied of meaning; the large-scale immigration of Oriental and North African Jews who transposed both their religion and culture from medieval context into the twentieth century; and last but not least, a small but significant aliyah from countries with a Western industrial background. This mixture is what modern Israel presents today. The country was not subject to a slow, organic development of many centuries; it was an instant society with components both ancient and new, both rigid and flexible, autocratic and democratic. It thus became a nation of great piety and impiety, of magnificent social vision on the one hand and crude acquisitional instincts displayed at times on the other.

This book, after a brief Introduction, concerns itself with the way in which the people of Israel have attempted to deal with the realization of varying and often conflicting religious ideologies, theologies, and anti-theologies, the tensions between the state and its religious institutions. The latter was frequently expressed in law both legislative and judicial, and because a large area of public and private life was given over to official Orthodoxy, the book shows how the traditional approach to Halakhah has met or failed to meet these challenges. The work puts into bold relief the important ways in which the conflicts between state and synagogue have surfaced, and especially so in the application of the Law of Return, and the question "Who is a Jew?"

What emerges is a picture of law and history intimately intertwined in a manner hardly duplicated in any other country or perhaps any other time, and for this reason alone the book presents a landmark. It should be of interest not only to the people of Israel or students of law and politics, but also, and especially so, to the Jews of the Diaspora. They must be intimately concerned with its subject matter, for the religious and social influence of Israel upon Diaspora Jewry far exceeds the borders of the land. Every religious divorce granted, every conversion performed outside of Israel must at present stand the scrutiny of the rabbinate in Israel, and the status of whole families is thereby determined. Every Jew in the Diaspora is a potential settler in Israel and therefore his own religious or nonreligious convictions as well as his status may ultimately have a bearing on or be subject to the realities of Israel. On the other hand, Orthodoxy in Israel itself and its allied Orthodoxies of the Diaspora must ultimately make their peace with the existence of vigorous Reform and Conservative movements in the lands of dispersion, and these in turn will have their influence on the life of Israel and its emergent dissident religious expressions. One cannot understand the land and its people as they are today without comprehending the complexity of its religious life.

This book therefore has its particular fascination. It is enhanced by its scholarly grounding and the unique qualifications of the author, who brings to the subject a wide range of information and historical comprehension. Not every aspect of the problem has been covered, but that is the nature of the subject, which in itself is changing from day to day. The ultimate conclusion which the author presents to us more implicitly than explicitly is clear: the future of the land lies not in the reintroduction of a theocratic or semi-theocratic society, however much it is desired by those who support it, but in the openness and mutual respect of varying religious convictions. Such openness does not exist at the present time, but it will have to be achieved if Israel is to have a religious future which is fundamentally different from that of a transplanted ghetto. This book, it is hoped, will contribute to this development.

We Are Jews

(A speech delivered at a demonstration in Toronto following the outbreak of the Yom Kippur War in 1973)

I must confess that these last seventy-two hours have been nightmarish for me, as I know they have been for you. Somehow the prayers for Yom Kippur were jumbled in my mind, and while in the anxiety of my soul I prayed with great urgency. I did not always know the words I was saying. In my mind's eye, I saw the boys and girls once again marching off to war. I saw the young men climbing into airplanes in civilian clothes and manning the tanks. I could not help but feel that they, like the rest of us, had that sinking sense of déjà vu, of historical repetition. "Here we go again,"— four times in twenty-five years. "Enough, Lord," I cried on Yom Kippur, "let there be an end."

Yom Kippur — how little they know us who suggest in cruel jokes that Jews would go out to battle deliberately on the holiest of holy days! Abba Eban called it an odious blasphemy and precisely that is what the allegation represents, a total misreading of our Jewish sensitivities and sensibilities. How little they know us!

We are schooled in trial and in sorrow. We know what it means to lose loved ones in war as well as peace, for even when there has been peace for others there has not always been peace for us. Alas, the furnaces of the Holocaust were first stoked in times of peace, when the world looked away.

I am a Jew. I believe in God and I believe that in his wisdom He has set aside a special role for us which is assigned to us for the sake of mankind. We are the People of the Covenant. This covenant exists today. No war, no international forum, no resolutions or vetoes will affect it. We stand before history as a people who since ancient days have preserved the knowledge of a compassionate and righteous God. We do not always know what our task may be for the moment, but Torah and tradition point the way for us.

The world may not fully understand us. No matter. Of course we would like to be loved and understood, who would not? But it has not been our fate to be loved and understood, nor have we been many in numbers. We have always been in the minority. Seen in the full context of history, it is no accident that billions of people are today allied against us — Russia, China, India — without cause, without reason.

We do of course understand why the Arabs are arrayed against Israel (although we can neither understand nor condone the evil they have committed in using a national conflict for fostering anti-Semitism). Count those who are lined up against us and they likely add up to a majority of men as represented by their governments — if their governments indeed represent them.

But Jews have never counted heads nor felt that majorities were naturally right. Had we done that, we would have folded our tents long ago and would have disappeared into the mists of history. We did not. When all the world went spiritually one way, we went another.

The Midrash explains the word *Ivri* (Hebrew) by explaining it as "ever" (on the other *side*), meaning Abraham stood apart from the rest of mankind. When all the world looked to a pantheon of gods, we looked to the One and Only One of Israel. When all the world exalted war as a normal accompaniment of human existence, we listened to the voice of Isaiah; we promised that some day, inspired by a knowledge of God, men would beat their swords into ploughshares and their spears into pruning hooks; that some day men of every nation and every creed would sit under their vines and fig trees and none would make them afraid.

When all the world shouted "Power!" we listened to the prophet who said, "Not by might and not by power, but by My spirit, saith the Lord." When all the world shouted for force, the Jew said "Shalom" when he came and when he went. The Jew identified the very words of Torah with Shalom, proclaiming that all its paths are peace.

No wonder that a people whose vision has been trained on the salvation of man and on eternity, a people preoccupied with their obligations under the Covenant, should be a thorn in the side of those who conceive of life in different terms. It is no accident that of all the nations in the world Israel is the only one whose right to existence is still debated a quarter century after its birth. We do not hear about Togo or Bangladesh. War and strife have carved them out, but here they are, their selfhood is their passport to international acceptance. Not so with us.

Colonel Qaddafi, Libya's head of state, who is rich enough that he can offer to support the Arab war effort single-handed and who is used to speaking his mind, said unequivocally that neither the 1967 ceasefire lines nor the occupied territories are the real issue. President Sadat said the same. The issue, they said, is Israel's existence, which remains an offence to the Arabs.

Nothing but our disappearance will satisfy them and many like them. The world does not listen to this warning because it does not want to listen. But we Jews cannot forget, for in the larger sense we have always fought and battled for the existence of our people and our ideas.

We are Jews. We are a small people, but we are large in compassion and in love. Our brothers in Israel are forced to take up arms, but it does not make them into a warlike people. The announcers speak of tanks lost and planes downed, while our people worry more about the black boxes in the Israeli newspapers which announce the deaths of the country's youth. Young people, full of promise, who leave behind families in desperate bereavement and who themselves are forever cut off from the fullness of life. We grieve for them, but we are a people who grieve for the Arab youth as well. They too have families, they too wanted to live and now they die needlessly because their leaders have pushed them into a battle they will not and cannot win.

We are Jews. We do not hate. Others, alas, have invoked the evil passions of anti-Semitism once again against us, so that throughout the Arab orbit as well as in Soviet Russia, the word "Jew" is once again a battle cry for hatred. We, in return, hate no one. Our tradition says, "I do not desire the death of the sinner, but that he turn from his evil ways and live." God, says our tradition, does not hate the sinner, but the sin. We hate no Arabs, we hate no Russians, we hate no Chinese, we hate no Indians — our people stretch out their hands to the world and say, "Work with us!" But the world should also know that even if we are rejected we do not despair. On the contrary, we know that the Lord of Hosts is with us in the long haul of history.

We are Jews. In the midst of war, we remember that people must be cared for. We remember that our brothers still must be rescued from Soviet Russia, and that even in the presence of war we must bring them to the Land of their Fathers, settle them, make them welcome, provide them with jobs and housing and welfare services. We know that there are poor people in Israel whose standards must be raised, whose hopes for a good and better life must continue so that they may become productive and full partners in the economy of tomorrow. It is war now, but even the loud clashing of the cymbals of destruction will not drown out the still small voice.

This is what it means to be Jews. Jews in Israel, and Jews also in Canada. Everyone who lives in this great and wonderful land of Canada, with its open spaces and its reality of freedom, has a deep sense of gratitude toward the gifts it has granted. Yesterday was Thanksgiving in our land, and I am sure that every Jew was keenly aware of the marvellous opportunity that was his. That opportunity is not only social or economic or political. All this of course — but the main point is something else. *A Jew in Canada can be himself, a Jew at his best and highest level.* Canada says to the Jews as it says to all her children, "Be yourself, for by being yourself, you can make your greatest contribution to Canada."

I give thanks that I can be a Jew in this land, to be myself, to know my tradition, to learn what it means to work for the good of every man, of whatever race, colour, and creed. That I can make my contribution to society as a Jew — this is the genius of Canada, and for this we owe profound and abiding thanks. We strengthen this thanks with the determination to make this an ever-more glorious and wonderful land, rich especially in human, spiritual, and intellectual resources.

Living here in Canada, we Jews are deeply aware what it means to have a State of Israel across the sea. I lift my head higher because there is Israel, my pride of selfhood is greater because there is Israel. There are young people here who do not remember what it meant to live before 1948, what it meant to live before and during the Holocaust. They do not know what it meant when one could not go to Palestine or anywhere except by permission of other governments, when one had to stand in line before foreign consulates to try and get a visa to get to somewhere, somehow, in order to flee. Ask me, I know. I remember the long lines that wound around blocks before every conceivable consulate. How slowly the lines advanced, how few got visas, for so many lands did not want the burden of Jewish immigration. I remember what happened when it came to 4:30 in the afternoon, when the sign was hung on the door, "Closed for the afternoon, come back tomorrow," and how we came back and stood and saw the sign again, "Closed for the day, come back tomorrow." And how Jews stood and stood, until the enemy came and took them to the camps for extermination where there was no tomorrow. I remember.

And I remember what it meant when 1948 came, when suddenly the burden of anxiety was lifted from our hearts. We knew then that whatever happens, there would be a place to which a Jew could go. There would a place in which Jews could build there own culture and do so in freedom, where they could live not by permission but by right. Then we knew that the Shoah, the Holocaust, would never again threaten the existence of our people. That in part is the meaning of Israel to every Jew.

Thank God there is Israel today, and across the ocean stretches a bridge of love. They are my family and we are theirs. What happens to them happens to me. When they threaten my brothers in Israel they threaten me. We want to tell the people in Israel that we belong to them and that they can count on us. Fear not, we shout to them — fear not!

But we also want to tell them that it is not only Jews who stand with them. Many non-Jews in all parts of the world — and thankfully in Canada as well — stand with them also. Those who are here tonight are a representation of the multitudes whose hearts and souls are bound up with us and our brothers in Israel. We thank them all and we thank you especially who are here. We Jews know what it means to be alone, and therefore know the full meaning of friendship.

So here we are tonight in this demonstration of solidarity. You have already heard what is required immediately — to give of your substance and to do so now. For if not now, when? So go outside and do your share. Go and do it well.

But still more is required of you. We require of you also persistence, courage, unflinching will and eternal readiness. Do not bend your neck to the yoke or fatigue. Stand up and stand straight. Be Jews, be Jews not only in your hearts, but also in your actions. Let righteousness and justice be the guide of your lives, let knowledge of Torah and tradition, of Jewish history and of Hebrew, let all of these be aspects of your striving so that you may be Jews to the fullest extent, as Canada allows and encourages you to be. Be Jews NOT ONLY IN NAME, be Jews in knowledge, be Jews in spirit. Be Jews in deed and be Jews also toward the world outside. Let them know who you are and say in proud proclamation, "I am a Jew!"

And when the call comes, say as Abraham did, "Here I am," so that together with friends who care for us and with our brothers in Israel whom we love, we may always say, "The people of Israel shall live, forever and ever and ever...."

Reform Jewish Perspectives

The Sabbath in the Reform Movement

Only once in over fifty years did our Conference take time out to devote itself to the subject of the Sabbath. Such silence and self-restraint practiced by our usually vocal and often volatile body have surely not been accidental.

Was it because there were other, more pressing problems? Hardly. Our discussions have dealt with the esoteric as well as the ephemeral and the marginal.

Was it because the Sabbath was so secure in our midst that, like Motherhood, it needed only a friendly nod? Hardly that — and besides, we did discuss Motherhood from time to time.

Or was it because we deemed the Sabbath issue beyond our power of confrontation? The suspicion persists that this motivation was not altogether absent. We talked on matters surrounding the Sabbath: attendance at services; bar and bat mitzvah; dances and committee meetings on the Sabbath; we discussed how to deal with school and social parties on Friday nights; we deplored that stores were open — and we returned to debating how to increase attendance at services. Attendance: there has been at least this one consistent concern. But the student of the record must note that even this concern touched primarily on issues other than the Sabbath: we spoke about prayer and its place in modern life, about social habits, about attractive sermon topics, stimulating forums and pleasant Oneg Shabbats.

But we avoided the Sabbath *qua* Sabbath. We did not ask questions of substance and, since 1937, when our colleague Israel Harburg dealt with the matter, the Sabbath question as such has not appeared on our agenda — not once.

What becomes then of the sentiment which Ahad Ha-am phrased so memorably: יותר משישראל שמרו את השבת, השבת שמרה אותם – "More than Israel has guarded the Sabbath, the Sabbath has guarded Israel"?[1] For one thing, we emended the axiom officially. Our Union Prayer Book now proclaims as a self-evident truth: "Even as Israel has kept the Sabbath, so the Sabbath has kept Israel." [2] It is a quid pro quo, and has a sad, penitential ring. But the older saying was closer to reality. The Sabbath has done more for us than we for it. In fact, it continues to exercise this guarding function, more so than we realize.

It is to an exploration of this problem that our paper is devoted, i.e., to the mutual relevance of Sabbath and Reform Judaism. We will not undertake an exposition of the traditional Shabbat, its history, its Halakhah, its customs, its special mythos and midrash, except where such investigation may help us arrive at a better understanding of our own present situation and potential. We will, in fine, attempt to present notes toward the definition of a liberal, realizable Sabbath for our time.

I

Whether the Sabbath as an institution preceded the idea of the Sabbath is a philosophical, not a historical, question. It has to do with our conceptualization of historic processes. Jost and Graetz differ fundamentally from Dubnow and Baron, even as Ranke and Treitschke, in their approach, see history differently from Mehring and Toynbee. It still was a matter of great importance to Kaufmann Kohler "whether the Hebrew Sabbath was from the beginning based upon the fixed institution of the week, which certainly rests on Babylonian astrology, or whether it originally corresponded with the four lunar phases, so that the 7th, 14th, 21st, and 28th of each month were the days of the moon's 'stand-still,' that is, Sabbath days."[3] Of course, Kohler's concern was in part apologetic, which is to say, political; for he laboured in the shadow of the Bibel-Babel controversy and was anxious to prove that Israel's Sabbath was not a derivative of the Babylonian *shabbatu*, a *dies nefastus*, but a conscious development of the natural phenomenon of חודש into a spiritual day of the Lord.

Kohler spoke as a child of nineteenth-century idealism who could, without raising an intellectual eyebrow, believe in "conscious" development — a concept which today, a mere fifty years later, no member of this Conference could possibly accept. To him, as to the earlier Reformers, the *original* ideas of the Sabbath, the *origins* of the day, were more important than what Israel had done with it over the centuries. If one could only show that once upon a time, in Mosaic or even pre-Mosaic days, the institution had had a certain character, one would have ample foundations for a contemporary decision. Holdheim and Wechsler had already argued along these lines during the first rabbinic conferences in the mid-1840s. Their neo-Karaitic fervour proved ultimately nothing, except that they managed to assuage their minds with scientific-sounding historical disquisitions. Having done that they proceeded to do what they wanted to do in the first place. Their considerable scholarship provided them with a rationale fit for their time. It is no longer fit for ours.

I will therefore eschew the opportunity of reviewing for you the conclusions of present-day scholarship with regard to the history of the Sabbath. We have gained new insight into the antecedents of our biblical institution and into their relation to the early Israelite Shabbat. We know more about the ancient Near East and about ancient Israel than did the generations before us. We also have a more modest view of what biblical criticism can reveal, and we can better assess the interlocking significance of the Exodus and Deuteronomy passages, as well as the numerous other prescriptions and references in the Tanakh.[4] We no longer take the simplistic view of earlier days which portrayed the Prophets as anti-ritualistic and conveniently overlooked their scathing condemnation of those who failed to observe the holy days properly, and especially the Sabbath.[5] We have become slightly embarrassed with our biblical eclecticism and now look for stronger staves to lean upon. We can learn much from our past, to be sure, but we must not, as our predecessors were wont to do, choose only a part of this past — and the more distant the better — and pretend that it is still normative. Our past is alive, our *whole* past.

II

Our approach to the contemporary Sabbath must therefore take into account the full fertile field of Sabbath thought and practice, without regard to historic sequence. The ancient rabbis doubtlessly understood less about biblical scholarship than we do, but they knew much about the dynamics of Jewish life when they took the Torah as whole and confidently proclaimed: אין מוקדם ומאוחר בתורה. There is no historic sequence when it comes to a consideration of Torah. So it must be with us here. אין מוקדם ומאוחר בשבת, we might say. A multitude of practices have enriched a series of ideas and have in turn been enriched by them. I will briefly treat of these Sabbath ideas since usually they receive much less attention than the Sabbath practices.

I spoke of a *series of ideas* and that is precisely what they are: antithetical thoughts which have found their reflection in the mirror of a people's practice. But these ideas are bound to a specific day which is hallowed by Israel in the name of its God. Shabbat is not, as Holdheim and his successors mistakenly assumed, *merely* a group of ideas which could easily be affixed to another day. He and others forgot the reality of Israel which has been the culture in which יום השביעי became יום השבת, and in which these ideas grew and flourished. Some of them are new, some old; none stands by itself but stands in contrast to another; none can be seen except in the full colour scheme of this spiritual כתונת פסים.

Creation and Exodus

1. Foremost among the Sabbath theme, because most obvious, has been the contrast between the decalogues in Exodus and Deuteronomy. Issuing at once from this duality have been the two reasons given for the observance of the Sabbath. In Exodus we are bidden to rest because God rested from His universal task of creation; in Deuteronomy, because He led us out of Egypt. The Sabbath thus encapsulates the essence of all of Jewish life: the tension between the universal and the particular, the uniqueness of God's love for Israel joined to His love for all creation. On the Sabbath the Jew contemplates the vastness of the universe and his own special place in it; he reconciles the seemingly irreconcilable: how he can say רבון כל העולמים and at the same time address Him as אוהב עמו ישראל. The Sabbath in this sense testifies to the divine possibility of joining the existence of the world to the existence of Israel, and thus the Torah could proclaim: אות הוא לעולם. No wonder our sages concluded that the קריעת ים סוף

was a pre-existent condition for the creation of the world. The world cannot exist without us: this is the improbable affirmation which we make week after week. On the surface it makes no sense, but then, does Israel's existence "make sense" on any level?

2.   The contrast of the two decalogues has also given rise to other themes. The text in Deuteronomy: "Remember that you were a slave in the land of Egypt and the Lord God freed you ... therefore the Lord your God has commanded you to observe the Sabbath day," may be taken to emphasize a social demand. The slave too deserves consideration, for every man is entitled to the divine dignity of rest. The Sabbath, said our late teacher David Neumark, combines the ethical and the cosmological element and thereby expresses perfectly the true nature of Judaism.[6]

3.   The third theme springs immediately from the second. To gain recognition of God and His universal order is a task of personal, individual growth. It relates me to the universe, its order, its purpose, and speaks to me of my place in the vastness of the creative process. It focuses my eye on God, on my God, however I perceive Him. The recognition of God as the guarantor of human dignity relates me to society and imposes social obligations. Exodus stresses the cognitive aspect of the Sabbath, Deuteronomy projects obligation. Exodus addresses me as an individual, Deuteronomy as a social being. The Jew who meditates alone or who sees God in nature's revelations about him, lacks an essential element in his Sabbath observance. At some time on that day he must, together with others, re-affirm his obligations as a member of the כלל.

שמור *and* זכור

Countless are the comments which have grown up around the differential exhortations introducing the two decalogue versions. One says זכור את יום השבת, the other says שמור. From this our tradition has deduced, for instance, that זכור demands a spiritual effort, while שמור demands physical observance. Remembrance is a function of the soul, observance a function of the body. Isaac Arama saw in זכור a reference to the obligation of rest and sanctification, in שמור to the

221

prohibition of work, a distinction which the early Reformers revived with great energy.[7]

Merely to remember the Sabbath is a mitzvah. One must speak, eat, even dress differently, says the Talmud, and if one is too poor to change one's garment one should at least make some change in it to remember the day.[8] One can and should remember the Sabbath every day of the week; observance, says the Hofetz Hayyim, is abstinence from work on the day itself, while remembrance takes place both on Sabbath and weekdays. For it is on the latter that one must prepare for Shabbat. Without weekday preparation in work and thought there cannot be proper Sabbath observance.[9] Throughout our traditional literature runs the thought that both remembrance and observance are necessary aspects of the command, a sentiment already anticipated in the statement: זכור ושמור שניהם בדבור אחד נאמרו.[10]

עשה and לא תעשה

The third group of antipodal Sabbath aspects has to do with laws and customs of עשה and לא תעשה, of what is commanded and what is forbidden. Into this area fall the practices of Sabbath worship and study, of Oneg Shabbat and Sabbath rest as the chief מצוות עשה, and the traditional thirty-nine categories of prohibition, the negative commands. It is here that observance and non-observance can be most easily measured, and it is here especially that we will attempt to separate fact from fiction in the context of contemporary Reform Jewish life. For the moment it is well to keep in mind that doing and not doing, positive as well as negative commands, have consistently formed the two prongs of Sabbath celebration.

Some commands and the activities issuing therefrom partake both of the positive and the negative, and the two are not always easily distinguishable. Rest is both sanctification and abstinence, relief and restriction at once. It is hard to say whether the man who sleeps on Shabbat afternoon — this, as you know, is a hallowed custom which rabbis especially should practise assiduously — is, in a theological sense, resting "positively" or "negatively"; that is, whether his sonorous slumber is Sabbath sanctification or merely a function of his soma, whether he loves to sleep and considers doing so during the bright day a special

Sabbath luxury or whether he is merely tired from his morning activity
— preaching, listening to the preacher, or doing חס וחלילה, forbidden
work.[11] But whether difficult to separate or not, the two elements of עשה
and לא תעשה are always present, and they will form an essential basis for
our own evaluation.

The Blossoms of Sentiment

In the catalogue of ideas which have enriched and penetrated the traditional Sabbath there remain the countless blossoms of divine sentiment
which flowered on the seventh day. To remember them, even merely to
read of them or, as in Jerusalem especially, to observe them today, elicits
a flood of nostalgia. It also evokes, I must admit, a sense of deep regret
and frustration that in our own time and environment such sentiments
and practices are gone and, for us at least, beyond recall.

We can sing of שבת המלכה, but she is no longer Queen nor Bride in
the old sense. We can speak of the נשמה יתרה,[12] but we have difficulty
perceiving its entrance into a contemporary home.

Turn to Heschel's tribute to the Sabbath or to any autobiographical account of days gone by — even in the reminiscences the flavour of uniqueness can be tasted. Turn to the old and not-so-old interpretations of biblical
texts and the special glory of the Sabbath crown illumines the pages.

To take but one example, Abravanel takes the passage אך את שבתתי
תשמרו (Exodus 31:13) to refer to two types of Sabbath: a this-worldly and
a trans-worldly Sabbath, one that belongs peculiarly to man and one that
is, as it were, God's own.[13] Or one may note that the passage introduced
by אך follows the prescriptions for the building of the Tabernacle. The
fulfilment of this latter mitzvah, carried out in all its resplendent detail,
was evidently then as now a potential diversion from the true purposes
of worship. Hence, after the building is finished and dedicated, the text
returns to the needed essentials: אך את שבתתי תשמרו — *nevertheless*,
fine building or no, you shall observe the Sabbath.[14]

Again, why does it say שבתתי, in the plural? Because if Israel would
only observe two Sabbaths it would at once be redeemed. The exile is
drawn out, said Moshe Hayim Luzzatto, because Israel has separated
itself from its roots, for did not the Talmud say that if Jews would

observe two Sabbaths faithfully they would thereby grasp the essence of their heritage which would be tantamount to instant redemption.[15]

Or, why does it say "*My* Sabbath," when the prophets remind us that God hates Sabbaths and festivals? The reason is, that if man perverts the Sabbath and makes it a day to serve human ends, God hates such pseudo-celebration. For, He says, I have not asked you to keep *your* Sabbaths, but *Mine*.[16]

The list can be prolonged ad infinitum. It speaks of the Sabbath as the source of all blessings[17] and finds its apotheosis in the midrashic exclamation: שקולה שבת כנגד כל המצוות, "The Sabbath outweighs all the other commandments together."[18] It speaks of a world of spiritual affection which was matched by centuries of loving practice. But, for better or for worse, that world is gone for us, and it is well to remember in our discussions that in Western lands it has in large measure been gone for over one hundred years. In fact, the beginnings of our movement are tied to the founders' concern over the Sabbath, for they felt then, as we feel today, that we remain the guardians of the spirit which found the holiness of the Sabbath at the core of Jewish life.

III

In its earliest years Reform was concerned primarily with worship improvement and education. Alterations in the traditional modes of prayer had aroused the most violent opposition from the Orthodox, which in turn led the proponents of Reform to believe that, if only the prayers were shortened, beautified, and translated, Judaism could make its full adjustment to the new era. The liberalizers were of course mistaken. Forces were at work which did not and could not yield to mere worship reform. This applied especially to the Sabbath. Already at the Breslau meeting of the liberal rabbis, in 1846, the discussions concerning the Sabbath occupied a major portion of the conference.

There was no question about the need to do something. The Sabbath was being violated, people were working, stores were open, and services were poorly attended. Valiantly the Reform rabbis tried to maintain the principle of Sabbath rest, but there were no quick remedies to be had. The new principle was: *Maintain the Sabbath according to tradition if you can; but if you are unable, do what you must.* "Where it is a question of one's total material welfare, where one's total possessions or the means of one's future existence are in question or threatened, a Jew (said Bernhard Wechsler) would not be transgressing a religious duty if he takes remedial measures and, where others cannot assist him, attends to them himself."[19] He quoted the rule of tradition: מוטב שיחלל שבת אחת ואל יחלל שבתות הרבה, "It is better to desecrate one Sabbath so that one should not be forced to desecrate many Sabbaths"[20] — but alas, no argument availed and many Sabbaths were desecrated. Nor could the ingenious *pilpul* of a Samuel Adler prevail — the same Adler who later came to New York as rabbi of Temple Emanu-El — who tried to rescue the Sabbath on the shaky distinction of כל מלאכה and כל מלאכת עבודה. His effort was as ineffective then as it would be today. It was, in fact, already then an anachronism.[21]

Whatever one may think of Samuel Holdheim and his many aberrations, he certainly had ideas. He resuscitated the dual emphases on מנוחה and קדושה, on Sabbath rest and sanctification. The former he declared to be of symbolic and therefore of time-bound importance; only the latter, the sanctification of the Sabbath, was to him a timeless command. Sabbath holiness was the goal, Sabbath rest a means to achieve the goal. The goal was unvarying, the means was not. If necessary, the latter could be altered or dispensed with altogether. How to hallow the Sabbath was therefore left to the individual Jew: "We must leave it to his conscience how far he will by himself try to reach the purpose of religious exaltation on the Sabbath, even though he does not celebrate it as a general day of rest, and we must avoid judging him in this respect."[22]

Not only did Holdheim thereby give sanction to complete הפקרות, which some naively called eclecticism, but he drew a further conclusion: the command, he said, merely asked that man sanctify himself *once a week*. To do it at *some* time was centre of the demand; the actual day of sanctification was quite secondary in importance. If it no longer could be the seventh day, let it be the first day of the week. To Holdheim and his Berlin Reform Association it mattered not when but that the spiritualization of time took place. Holdheim became the father of the Sunday services which in the 120 years of their existence have had a chequered and often embattled career.

But for the time being, in Germany as in North America, the old Sabbath remained the problem child. In 1871 the Augsburg Synod proclaimed its brief Sabbath amendments to the Shulhan Arukh. They are worth repeating for on the whole they represent the position which now, a hundred years later, is taken by the Conservative movement:

> If the distance from the residence to the house of wor-
> ship, or age and delicate health prevent attendance at
> divine service, it is permissible to remove this obstacle
> by riding to the place of the communal worship on Sab-
> bath and holidays, either on the railroad or in a vehicle.
>   This permission extends also to the practice of charit-
> able acts in such cases where delay would be dangerous.
>   The same permission holds where the purpose is
> educational or recreative.
>   An Israelite is permitted to play the organ in the
> house of worship on the Sabbath.[23]

While in mid-nineteenth-century Germany the Reformers had already given up on such questions as work and business activities on the Sabbath, and restricted themselves to the more malleable Halakhot which surrounded synagogue worship, their American colleagues still had high hopes for some more thoroughgoing observance. Bernard Felsenthal, first rabbi of Chicago Sinai Congregation, concerned himself less with prayer innovations and instead attempted to tackle the "widespread evil," as he called it,

> ...that Sabbath and holy days which ought to be dedi-
> cated to the life of the spirit are also used as business days
> and thereby these days miss their purpose altogether. To
> be sure, some people visit religious services for one hour
> during the morning, but then hurry into their stores and
> offices and attend to their business.... Here in America
> ... it is possible for everyone to find his livelihood with-
> out making the Sabbath into a weekday.... It is possible to
> observe the religious law, to withdraw the Sabbath from
> weekday work and to utilize it for the advancement and
> sanctification of the spirit, and therefore it must be ob-
> served. If one knows and recognizes this law and yet to
> disregard it, if observance is possible, merely shows rot-

tenness in his spiritual nature. For that act is immoral and unethical, which is in contrast to our convictions.[24]

That same year Isaac M. Wise and Max Lilienthal motivated several Cincinnati businessmen — Reform Jews all of them! — to sign a public resolution which stated that they would unite their influence

> to persuade all businessmen of our creed in this city, to observe the Sabbath by abstaining from all business transactions.
>
> RESOLVED, that we in signing our names ... declare that we pledge our word to each other and to all, to keep our places of business closed during every Sabbath of ours; to transact no business ourselves, nor allow any of our clerks, bookkeepers, or any other person in our employment to transact business for us on that day on our premises.[25]

There was only one condition. This compact, forerunner of a modern חבורה, was to take effect only if twenty-five wholesale houses which were not presently observing the Sabbath would join themselves to the signatories. I have reason to believe that the full twenty-five were never found, which spelled the end of a noble venture. It also marks the one serious effort on record to find a new voluntary discipline for Sabbath observance within our movement. Perhaps it is decreed by fate that we should make another effort a century later in this very city.

For a hundred years now the question of how to return the Sabbath to a day of rest, a day on which no labour would be done, has been avoided by Reform leaders. Even our official platforms are vague on the subject and with obvious embarrassment look the other way.[26] Instead, we attempted to tackle the one aspect of the observance which seemed to lie within our rabbinic reach, and that was attendance at Sabbath worship. The pews were emptying or empty, and no rabbi could overlook this all too obvious fact. Two radical remedial measures were the consequence of this dilemma, and both were for some time the cause for bitter intramural controversy. I refer to the institution and ultimate rejection of statutory Sunday worship (which was a sort of negative rescue, if you will), and the other was the innovation of holding Sabbath services on Friday night.

Isaac M. Wise claimed for himself the distinction of having first proposed the institution of Sabbath eve lectures and services at a fixed time. Whether this is so or not I do not know; in any case no one else came forward to dispute his claim. But while Wise may have thought of it first, he did not succeed in the beginning to persuade his own congregation to adopt his idea. Benai Yeshurun turned down its rabbi's request, but two other Reformers, Leopold Kleeberg of Louisville and Jacob Mayer of Cleveland, introduced the innovation in their communities, apparently with good results. By 1869 the board of K.K. Benai Yeshurun relented and permitted Wise to establish a 7 p.m. Friday night service. For some years thereafter Wise advocated the experiment with great vigour, describing its advantages in detail, suggesting topics for discussion and even tackling the already pesky problem of members attending theatre parties on Friday nights.

> It has been objected [he wrote] that many prefer the theater and the opera to the Temple, and will go to those places of amusement in preference to the house of worship. Good-bye to you, ladies and gentlemen, we will see you again. Persons who have no higher than fictitious ideals, who prefer play to reality, self-deception to self-elevation, fiction to truth, amusement to instruction, the fleet shadow of the moment to the rock of eternity, persons who worship selfishness in lieu of the Eternal God, will go almost anywhere. But we do not suppose we are mistaken in the bulk of our coreligionists, if we maintain that the vast majority of them will visit the temple, when opportunity offers and go to hear artists some other evenings, if they wish to hear them. Managers of theaters and operas will have to put off their gala evenings from Friday to Saturday evening.[27]

In his enthusiasm Wise thought of every conceivable argument to bolster his new project. He reminded his readers that in ancient Jerusalem sacrifices were held at the twilight hour, that during the summer months the morning heat was oppressive, that Gentiles too could come at night, that working people could not come in the morning, that a fixed hour was advantageous, and finally he was led to exclaim that in any case "evening services are much more impressive and solemn than the day service."[28] He encouraged the use of Friday nights for adult educational lectures[29] and was pleased to record a few years later that the Sabbath eve worship idea had been widely accepted and, in his congregation at least, was a success. Already in 1873 Wise, who was then engaged in battling against the rising tide of Sunday services, exhorted his readers with this apotheosis: "Take care of Friday evening, and it will take care of Judaism to be preserved intact."[30] We who have taken care of Friday night can, alas, no longer be as sanguine about the Jewish future as was Wise.

Not everyone was, incidentally, enamoured of the great innovation. That the Orthodox would ridicule it was to be expected,[31] but they were not alone in opposing it. Wise claimed that only the supporters of the Sunday-Sabbath would have no part of the Friday night service, but he also failed to convince men like Joseph Silverman and Kaufmann Kohler who even in this century thought that our total effort should continue to be directed toward strengthening Sabbath morning worship.[32] In this respect these men remained closer to the European tradition. There, Friday night services neither achieved the prominence they had in America, nor did they replace the morning worship as the chief service. The Guide Lines of 1912 — which were German liberalism's Pittsburgh, or rather Columbus, Platform — still stressed total Sabbath observance and counselled that "all workday labor must be avoided," where possible.[33] A rabbi in a small community suggested that all members of the community should voluntarily assume a "Sabbath watch" and promise to attend one particular Sabbath morning a month, thus assuring the congregation of a minyan."[34]

The historic fight over the Sunday-Sabbath which began in America during the 1860s and lasted for fifty years was, if one was to believe the proponents of the shift, an attempt to rescue Jewish worship and thereby Judaism itself. They claimed that, with daily prayers having disappeared and Saturday services ever more poorly attended, the only recourse was to attract Jews to a Sunday service. Holdheim was the father of this idea, but while in Europe he found almost no supporters, the Sunday service movement spread in the United States and Canada. While the opponents did not deny that one could get larger attendances on a Sunday morning, they believed that once Reform instituted Sunday as the chief worship day, two consequences would be inevitable: whatever little was left of

Shabbat would be further attenuated, and there would be a real danger of Reform Judaism becoming a schismatic sect. Moritz Loth, a founder and the first president of the UAHC, was so emphatic on this point that he advocated the adoption of

> a code of laws which are not to be invaded under the plausible phrase of reform; namely ... that the Sabbath shall be observed on Saturday and never be changed ... that any Rabbi who, by his preaching or acts advises ... to observe our Sabbath on Sunday has forfeited the right to preach before a Jewish congregation, and any congregation employing such a Rabbi shall, for the time being, be deprived of the honor to be a member of the Union of Congregations.[35]

On the other side were equally sincere advocates of regular Sunday services. Some, like Hyman G. Enelow, took up the old Holdheim argument and argued for an official transfer of the day of rest to the first day of the week. To this Conference he quoted the midrashic rule: לא מן השבת מתירא אלא ממי שפקד על השבת, "Fear not the Sabbath but Him who instituted it."[36] Others who advocated Sunday services did so from pragmatic rather than theological motives and, while they wanted to retain the seventh day as Shabbat, nonetheless felt that it would be — as Kohler said at the Pittsburgh Conference — "the most cruel and stubborn, the most stupid and fanatical blindfoldness of mind and heart to deny these hundreds of thousands of poor Jewish employees (who have to work on Saturday) the privilege of divine service and religious instruction on Sunday.... The responsibility of their religious and moral shipwreck falls upon us."[37]

For some years the argument surged back and forth, occupying this Conference for more than a decade. The discussions make instructive reading even today for much that was said then can be and is being said today, and while for us the issue is not the Sunday-Sabbath, it is the neglect of Jewish practice and it is the same Judaism with the survival of which we are occupied. Especially rewarding is a study of the long and carefully reasoned address by Jacob Voorsanger, who reported as chairman of a special committee on the Sabbath question.[38]

In the end it was not our Conference but our congregations who saved us from the horns of the Sabbath dilemma. The Conference agreed to publish a special separate prayer service for Sunday worship and in fact proceeded to do so. But either the pamphlet, separated from the Union Prayer Book, appeared as a sectarian offshoot, or the Sunday movement had already passed its peak; in any case our only official attempt at a Sunday prayer book found no favour, the booklet saw no second edition and instead was given an unostentatious burial in our Reform cemetery of experiments. Sunday services continued, of course, but in ever diminishing numbers. This did not, alas, betoken a revival of the Shabbat: the seventh day remained as little observed as ever. The outcome of the Sunday controversy meant, however, two things: one, that Friday night had (literally speaking) carried the day; and two, that Shabbat remained for us, in principle at least, the weekly day of holiness. "However we may interpret the statement of its divine holiness," said Voorsanger, "that institution is indissolubly interwoven with other elements that make up our religious system."[39] In the sixty years which have passed since then, this Conference has not changed its position.

But while we have not changed we have also not done anything about it. I have already indicated that only once in this time span did we put the complete Sabbath question on our agenda. In 1936 Felix Levy, then president of the CCAR, recommended that the matter be studied,[40] and the following year, in Columbus, Israel Harburg delivered an address which occupied twenty-five pages of the *Yearbook* and which I recommend to you for most profitable reading.[41] He traced the reasons for the silence of our movement on the subject, and he made a number of cogent observations which are as relevant today as they were then. "First and foremost," he said, "we should free ourselves and others of the prevailing notion that Sabbath observance means exclusively attendance at Temple service." He reminded us that more than worship, practice, or ceremonies was at stake, but our whole attitude toward mitzvah and Halakhah. The Sabbath was the keystone of Jewish life, he reiterated, and what we did or did not do with it would spell out the success or failure of our movement.

Perhaps it was because in 1937 we were concentrating on our new Platform (which speaks politely of the need for the preservation of the Sabbath), or because Jewish existence in Europe was rushing toward its nadir, and because the cataclysmic events of the next decades left little room for truly fundamental reconsiderations of the type which Harburg had submitted, that we turned our collective face almost entirely away from שבת קדש.

Almost, but not entirely; two apparently disparate developments, each representing an important aspect of the Sabbath, occupied us in the intervening years.

One was the dramatic and unforeseen return of Sabbath morning services to our Reform movement. They came dressed in the garment of the bar mitzvah and presented us with new and different problems. We did not and do not always like what comes along with this reincarnation, but I say frankly that it may turn out to be the formerly unwelcome bar mitzvah who with his breaking voice, imperfect Hebrew, and his many relatives and friends has given us an entirely new lease on Sabbath celebration. The least he will have done is to have given us a new basis for development, for he has reopened the doors to the synagogue on Sabbath mornings and, even more important, has caused Jews to remember the Sabbath in ways they had not remembered it for some time. This situation has also pointed up sharply what we have known for some time: that we no longer have the same people in our movement as we had sixty years or even thirty years ago, and that we therefore have opportunities of which our predecessors could hardly dream.

The second development is closely related to the first. It is the great increase of interest in guiding principles for Reform Jews, highlighted by the growth of our responsa literature and, specifically, of responsa concerning the Sabbath. The *Yearbooks* of our Conference bear less testimony to this than the writings of our teacher Solomon Freehof.[42] Jews still — or is it, again? — want to know whether certain procedures are allowed or forbidden, whether one may or may not keep a gift shop open or whether committee meetings are permissible on Friday night, and so forth. "Allowed," "forbidden": we have not heard these words for along time in the meetings of the CCAR. We have heard that some practices were beneficial and others were not, that some were in the spirit of Judaism and others were not, but we shied away from calling anything "forbidden" if we could possibly avoid it. Now the concept is back in Reform Jewish life and it is back for the Sabbath also and gives it a dimension it has not had for us in a hundred years. It is none too early.

IV

These then are the history, the ideas, the problems which have formed the Sabbath as we have it today. Before we can speak of the future we must first properly ask: just where are we now? How much or how little is really observed in our movement? We all have of course our impressions and I have the feeling that perhaps we prefer not to know with too great precision what our people do or do not do. But now that the matter is once more before us we have to look at the contemporary observance of the Sabbath by Reform Jews as it is, and not as we think, hope, or fear it is.

To give us some basis for discussion I prepared a brief, one-page questionnaire which I sent to 350 colleagues who were selected at random. I only made sure that all American states, as well as Canada and Central America, were included and that enough congregations in small towns were represented. Perhaps because of its brevity or because of the urgency of the subject matter, I received a 43 percent response without any kind of follow-up. Briefly, here is my analysis of the answers to the three questions.[43] I must remind you that this survey is in no wise scientific, nor does it pretend to represent anything more than the opinions of 150 colleagues. But it does say something about how they view the present situation in their own congregations and, perhaps equally important, it says something about their own views.

The first question dealt with home observances. Most rabbis instruct their congregants and especially their children in some observance, and according to the survey about 80 percent of our congregants (at least those with children) observe something. Women light candles, with or without blessings, wine is served, with or without a ברכה, a family dinner is eaten, with or without any ceremony. Havdalah is practised rarely. This is the extent of it. If it is not yet *reductio ad absurdum*, it is *reductio ad minimum*.

The second question concerned Temple attendance. The majority of the rabbis stress Friday night over Saturday morning, but they do not necessarily like to do so. Do they ask people to attend because it is *demanded* or because it is desired, and therefore merely *suggested*? While our colleagues do demand it of children and especially confirmands, only a few consider religious services in the synagogue as a requirement that has to do with God and as a demand that can be made on adults. Why do rabbis suggest attendance? Because it is good mental health: it promotes peace of mind, is good for Jewish affirmation and unity, and generally is portrayed — in our col-leagues' words — as beneficial to man. There is almost no mention of God or holiness — we hold such concepts in reserve until the worshipper enters the Temple. And people who do not think that synagogue worship does anything measurable for them are therefore free to stay away or, when on occasion they do come, evaluate the experience as they would any lecture, concert, or entertainment. The synagogue's Nielsen ratings would be very low; our survey shows the percentage of regular attendance to be 10 per-cent of the potential in the larger congregations (or 20–25 percent if once a month is deemed "regular"); it is a little higher in the smaller ones — and some allowance must be made for rabbinic double vision which is the result of overwork, frustration, and incurable optimism.

The final question read as follows: do you instruct your children and/or adults in the Sabbath observance of any מצוות עשה and מצוות לא תעשה, and if so, which? The majority chose to overlook this question altogether. Some filled the space with question marks. One asked, "What is this, an Orthodox questionnaire?" Another wrote, "Whom are you kidding?" The rest mention study, visiting the sick, and rest under מצוות עשה, and abstinence from chores, from visiting the hairdresser and public parties or such under the heading of לא תעשה. The number of people whom our colleagues surmise to be practicing any observances is modestly respectable for מצוות עשה, mainly because the respondents included anyone who made Kiddush or kindled Sabbath lights at home. When it comes to things that Reform Jews do *not* do on Shabbat, the percentage drops sharply, near the zero point. In other words, there is hardly any observance of כל מלאכת עבודה לא תעשה; in this respect there is for our people no difference between שבת and חול. What rest there is, may be termed North American leisure, but not שבת מנוחה.

Throughout the answers runs a sense of quiet desperation, and for good reason. Fortunately for us there are many other "activities" to bring our people to Temple and many other problems to take our minds off the central issue — which however is thereby not rendered any less pressing.

I must confess that I experienced a fleeting temptation to withhold these figures from publication, lest those who wish us ill would use them as a means of attacking the validity of our movement. But not only are others in circumstances which are basically similar, we at least choose to face our dilemma head on, for only a frank confrontation with the full extent of the corrosion of Sabbath consciousness will make it possible for us to chart our course for the future. We must be done with all fiction and begin with the facts.

V

The facts spell out a significant failure in the two areas of Sabbath worship, Sabbath rest and sanctification. The failures are related, but they are far from identical.

The weakness of Sabbath worship is of course only in part attributable to our neglect of Shabbat. It is our whole modern attitude toward prayer which is involved, our theology and deology, our ambivalent relation to our own sense of worth, our externalization of values — in short, the decline of worship is a fundamental aspect of our Western civilization. We Jews who live at its periphery react more quickly to the swing of the wheel, we are less rooted and therefore, spiritually as well as physically, the most mobile element in our society. This is the subject which our new Joint Commission on Worship will tackle. It would be presumptuous for me to anticipate its research and recommendations, but some matters must be obvious to all of us.

One is that the fond dream of the founders — that a beautiful understandable service will bring the Jew back into the synagogue — has not and will not become reality. It was based on the misconception that esthetics and philosophy, properly presented, are the bases on which worship is founded. It was as fallacious as the talmudic prediction that it would always be rainy on Friday and sun-bright on Saturday[44] (although some rabbis still believe this is so and thus explain the poor Friday night turnout). We will of course revise our prayer books from time to time, our liturgy committee will carefully scrutinize each word, rabbis will worry about their sermons and think of many ways to attract the multitudes, they will have baby namings and installations and boy scout nights and Oneg Shabbat and forums, concerts, and films and youth dances — in vain, none of these hallowed devices will by itself produce worshipfulness and devotion. The malaise lies deeper.

We will get farther perhaps if we ask not why we *fail* but why we *succeed* on any level. Why *do* some people come to Temple on Shabbat? In part because of various external stimuli, certainly; in part also because they do have an inner urge to satisfy their spiritual hunger, however ineffectively they manage to do this at our services. But there is one other reason, and it is often overlooked. *Many people come to Temple because it is Shabbat.* They may not be aware of it at all times; still, they often have a residual sense of obligation. Have you not heard the most recalcitrant absentees of your congregation say, "Yes, I know I ought to be there, but…." There is more of a sense of ought in our members than we realize. Search deeply enough and you will find that the knowledge of mitzvah is still present on some level.

I hold therefore that strengthening our feeling for worship is only one side of the coin. Strengthening the feeling for the Sabbath is the other. In fact, we would have little worship left were it not for Shabbat. It is not, in my opinion, our worship which has saved the Sabbath, but exactly the reverse: it is the Sabbath, weak and emaciated though it is, which has saved our worship. (The few surviving Sunday services, based on local traditions and attractive lectures, do not prove the contrary.) We have been entirely too one-sided in our approach. We have said, make the service attractive and people will return to the Sabbath. Now I present the other side: make the Sabbath attractive as a precondition for people returning to the services. This point of view has a direct bearing on the recommendations we will make.

Before I turn to them, however, I must address myself to a related matter, an additional reason which has determined our Sabbath failures. I refer to the erosion of the concept of mitzvah, of any sense of obligation vis-à-vis the Sabbath. We are reaping here the fruits of permissiveness which have grown, ripened, and have inevitably turned rotten. Our own awareness of Halakhah is so attenuated that it is hardly alive at all. Out of the 150 replies to the questionnaire there were not ten who made a demand of Sabbath observance — and some of these added in a postscript: what good would it do? They are right, of course. Short of some resolve by this Conference to introduce a level of Halakhah into Reform Jewish life, short of some understanding that even Liberals must submit to obligation, be it theological, historical, national, or even congregational in origin — short of this there will be only frustration and further decay. Our "mental health" approach to the Sabbath is a failure. The fact is that the rabbi's opinion of Sabbath observance as "desirable" and "good for the Jew" has not been convincing. Why not recognize this? Of course, the rabbi cannot suddenly make Sabbath demands when the foundation for making *any* demand has not been laid.

Has the time not come, my colleagues, to make the turn which has been overdue for a hundred years? It is my suggestion that this Conference which will ineluctably proceed to a reconsideration of Reform Halakhah begin its labours in the field of Sabbath observance. For I hold that with all the erosion which has taken place, there remains — along with the total residual power of the Sabbath — a basic respect for Halakhah which we have utilized all too rarely. But when we do we are aware that there are possibilities.

Let me refer you to two familiar aspects of לא תעשה. None of you officiates either at a funeral or at a wedding on the Sabbath. If your members complain of inconvenience, you say no. You would perhaps not mind making הבדלה while it is still light, but you will wait with קידושין until it is dark. You yourself may smoke, ride, shop, work, or violate the Shulhan Arukh in a hundred ways, but you will not assist in a celebration of nuptial holiness or say the relevant blessings on Shabbat. Why? Because you don't want to write a כתובה you don't use anyway? Because suddenly you don't want to assist in a business transaction? Or because you don't want to transgress the principle אין מערבין שמחה בשמחה?[45] Yet you say no and firmly so and, *mirabile dictu*, your members respect your stand. You say "It is Shabbat," and the people understand. They may not know the word Halakhah, but they respect it vaguely if you will help them respect it. Perhaps there is something in the midrashic text which says: אין שבת בטלה מישראל, "The Sabbath will never disappear from Israel" (because God called it "a sign forever").[46]

Let me summarize this section by repeating its main propositions:

1. The weakness of Sabbath worship is only in part due to the weakness of worship feeling in our time. It is due also, and in greater measure than usually recognized, to the erosion of שבת קדש. Conversely, what feeds the existing observance of Sabbath worship is only partly the pervasive human need for prayer, or the various time-bound attractions provided by rabbi and synagogue, but in greater part than realized the residual strength of Sabbath feeling. It is the Sabbath which keeps communal worship alive as much as worship keeps the Sabbath alive.

2. The attenuation of Sabbath observance is related to the popular confusion of Reform Judaism with extreme permissiveness, which is in turn caused by our failure to formulate a Reform Halakhah. What is true in general is true for the Sabbath. But here as elsewhere there does remain a rudimentary respect for Halakhah which, when we bring it into play, has surprising depth. There still is Sabbath law, and perchance it can be of regenerative power.

VI

What then can we do? Does the future hold any promise for us? Two premises are necessary for any kind of program: we must have definite goals, and these goals must be realistic.

Premise one. We must resolve that the Shabbat problem is of lasting concern to us and not merely of passing interest. It is inconceivable to me that we should continue to disregard this question and thereby contribute by our silence to the neglect of the Sabbath. Shabbat must remain on our agenda. I suggest that this Conference resolve to establish a permanent committee to define goals for the observance of Shabbat and to delineate ways and means to approach these goals. After some years of thought and discussion we may be ready to suggest to the UAHC the establishment of a Joint Commission. It should be clear that the new Joint Commission on Worship is not the agency to deal with the Sabbath. The problem of worship exceeds the limits of the Sabbath, and vice versa.

Premise two. Our goals must be meaningful in the context of Reform Jewish life. We do not aim at the re-creation of the traditional Sabbath. Both the theological and the sociological foundations of such a return have disappeared. Our goals must reflect devotion and imagination of our own movement as well as the springs of tradition. We will have to choose those elements from the wealth of past Sabbath treasures which may serve as the ingredients for a new and viable structure. They will be drawn from those ideas which we presented earlier (see above, II): there will be זכור and שמור, there will be emphases on home as well as synagogue, the individual as well as the people; our Sabbath must be celebrating the specifically Jewish as well as the broadly universal; and, last but not least, it must make demands and speak of עשה and לא תעשה.

No one's single thought can anticipate the multitude of ideas which will come out of such co-operative study. We merely make a beginning today, and this paper will now proceed to indicate some areas for discussion and some possibilities for new approach patterns.

Friday Night

I venture to say that a test of free association with the words "Friday night" would produce one overwhelming response amongst rabbis and another amongst our members. When you hear "Friday night" you think, quite naturally, of services. The majority of our members, if they think in Jewish terms at all, will probably associate Friday night first and foremost with candles and Kiddush, or more likely, with family, and only then with services. I have tested it often enough to state this with confidence, and I draw an important conclusion from it.

Friday night as a family night, with or without some mitzvot performed, is still a reality amongst many of our people. What have we done to give this feeling a meaningful mode of expression? Next to nothing. Our Union Prayer Book allots two and a half pages in the appendix to it and assumes *ab initio* that a Reform Jew will not or cannot recite more than one line of Kiddush.[47] The less said of our Union Home Prayer Book in this regard the better. We leave it to the National Federation of Temple Brotherhoods to devise a more effective home service, we leave it to the Joint Commission on Ceremonies to create a Havdalah service in experimental pamphlet form, and we leave it to the ingenuity of our colleagues to mimeograph, multigraph, or otherwise reproduce some substantive suggestions for other rich and prayerful home worship.

The reason for this studied underplay of Friday night observance at home is obvious: we do not want to compete with ourselves. We want our people to light candles, yes; we want them to say Kiddush and a prayer or two, yes; but not too long, not too much, because we also want them to get through with dinner and hurry to Temple. We even put our emaciated ברכת המזון some place else, lest they spend too much time at home.[48]

But suppose they do not want to come to Temple or cannot come for valid reasons? What do we do for them? Nothing, they are left to their own devices. So are the families of those congregations which do not have a late Friday night service. And what happens during the summer when we don't even want the people at Temple? Nothing.

I suggest that we create a full book for use on Friday nights at home. It should contain a service to be used by people who that evening — for whatever reason — will not come to Temple. It should have appeal for young and old; it should speak about the Sabbath and its opportunities; it should contain some guidance for Sabbath observance; and it should contain diverse readings. In other words, just as we have been able to produce a Haggadah for our movement, so can we produce a Sabbath Book and then set about with all our persuasive power and energy to get it accepted.

But, you will say, what happens to our service? Our service will not be affected, certainly not adversely. The 10 or 20 percent of our congregants who now put in an appearance will continue to come and, if need be, eat a little earlier. I am thinking of the 80 or 90 percent who rarely come and whose Sabbath needs we have almost completely disregarded. We have said, in effect, "Temple or nothing, take it or leave it." Yet, where is it written that one can truly observe the Sabbath only at Temple on Friday night? We owe our people an alternative for Temple attendance, especially since this alternative is steeped in Jewish tradition and sentiment.

Even if I would be convinced that a concerted Friday night home service program would be superlatively effective and eventually diminish my Friday night attendance to the vanishing point, even then would I gladly proceed with my efforts, in fact I would redouble them. I would then happily abandon my Friday night services and concentrate on Shabbat morning, as my traditionalist colleagues in Toronto have done. There, all Conservative and Orthodox synagogues have closed down their late services on Friday and instead record increased attendances on Sabbath morning. Their members come from the same neighbourhoods as mine and belong to the same occupational and social strata. For them Shabbat morning is a possibility — but only because they no longer have Sabbath Eve services. Meanwhile, for most of us, this will not be the immediate problem, although I think that we ought to consider the re-ascendancy of Shabbat morning most seriously.

In any case, our Friday night worship hours are in no danger from a resuscitation of home observance. Of course, there will be no overnight success in this effort. But we must start. Our Brotherhoods are already on record as favouring this enterprise and surely we can enlist our Sisterhoods for a task which is so well fitted to their purposes. What is needed, and I repeat it once more, is for us to cease considering Judaism a Temple activity. None of *us* believes that it is, but by inadvertence and circumstance we have led our members to accept this as תורה למשה מסיני. In the area of social action we have already magnificently demonstrated our capacity for making Judaism effective beyond the synagogue; now let us do for Jewish observance what we have done for social action. Instead of making our congregants come to us, let us go to them into their homes with our treasures of Jewish life. And if we go to them they will also come to us.

"The matter is not too far from thee." We do not start from the zero point. Friday night still has reality for many whom we never see at Temple. Perhaps the subject is, like Torah, dependent on *our* mouth and *our* will: כי קרוב אליך הדבר מאד בפיך ובלבבך לעושתו.

Saturday

Again, I will not treat here of our worship services nor of the bar mitzvah conundrum, nor of related problems, such as the holding of religious school on Saturday mornings. I will address myself now to the question of Saturday as a part of Shabbat. We are here, alas, at the point of unawareness. If our people still remember Friday night on some level, they no longer grasp that Shabbat has twenty-four hours. They have, in the style though not the sense of the ancient rabbis who reduced all commandments to one, reduced the Sabbath to Friday night, if not worse. The morning, the afternoon, no longer carry even a reflection of holiness. They are part of merely another weekday. To this especially, my colleagues, we need to address ourselves.

I do not blame the people. I need look no farther than our own movement to find a שעיר לעזאזל. We have failed to give direction to our people. How can they know what is expected when we steadfastly refuse to tell them? Vague pronouncements about "observing the spirit of the Sabbath" are about as efficacious as talking about "being good" or observing "a spirit of charity." I am of course talking about a guide for Shabbat. Say no to such a guide and you will by your negation condone our present הפקרות.

We have talked long enough about the pros and cons of a Reform guide, its advantages and its dangers. I belong to those who strongly feel that without a clear presentation of some Reform Halakhah we will have ultimately no Reform Judaism left. But I am also aware that this Conference is not ready to undertake a far-reaching project. I therefore suggest that you consider nothing else but *the creation of a Sabbath guide*. It will serve as a pilot project for the larger, more comprehensive guide. It will tell us much about the potential of discipline in our movement; its success or failure after a decade of application will instruct us about the expansion, alteration, or abandonment of similar experiments.

The often heard objection that a guide will establish minimum norms which will therefore reduce Reform Judaism to a level of minimal practice is surely not applicable in the area of Sabbath observance. How much more minimal can we become?

It will be objected that it is impossible to create a guide which would not be motivated by a clear philosophy or theology and which would be able to define its position. True, this Conference could not at this time reach agreement on such motivation. Some of us would say, "This is how we understand God's will for us," for there can be no מצוות without God, and no God of Israel without מצוות; others would speak of such practices as "sancta" in Kaplan's sense, as means for our people's survival; still others would plead for personal discipline; others would appeal to a historic sense of unity; and we certainly have scores of colleagues who would advocate such rules as good mental health measures. Some would support the rationale offered by Doppelt and Polish or the Reconstructionist *Guide*[49] and others would not. No matter — in order to create a Sabbath guide our Conference could present all of these motivations in a preface and leave the theology to the individual, or it could omit such a statement altogether. We only need to agree that in our opinion this ought, and this ought not, to be done.

We have ample precedent for this. The Joint Commission on Synagogue Activities in 1954 published a volume called *Responsa* in which no fewer than 229 official pronouncements made by the CCAR between 1890 and 1950 were collected.[50] Our last ten *Yearbooks* have carried further decisions. What are these responsa but guides to rabbis and congregants? And what of specific resolutions of the Conference on scores of matters, some of which are reprinted in our *Rabbi's Manual*? Are these not guides, are these not Reform Halakhah? Few of these decisions make any reference to their theological foundation.

My colleagues, *the so-called absence of a Reform Halakhah is fiction, not fact.* Without adding a single resolution, our present Halakhah would occupy a good-sized volume. In denying ourselves the full effect of calling it by its proper name we also rob ourselves of the most distinctive element of Jewish existence. Mitzvah is an indigenous part of Judaism; there can be no Judaism without mitzvah. And there can be no Shabbat observance without definable and therefore observable מצוות עשה and מצוות לא תעשה.

To return to a concept of Reform Halakhah is not to falsify Reform Judaism but to return to its fountainheads. All the early Conferences and synods were concerned with Halakhah. It was never a question of whether to have rules, but what rules to have. I cannot claim to be the first to advocate a Sabbath guide. Our best tradition advocates it.

Item: Max Lilienthal in 1854. "We wish to know when religious ceremonies have to yield to the necessities of life and when they have to be kept at any price, subjugating life and its exigencies. In a word, we wish to know what in our law is God's command and what is the work of mortal man."[51]

Item: Jacob Voorsanger in 1903, when he reported to the CCAR as chairman of the Conference Sabbath Committee. "We have perhaps, in years past, put too much stress on the popularity of the public rituals in so far as they represented diversity of opinion and the individuality of their authors; and perhaps we have put too little stress on the great fact that Judaism, in whatever historical form it presents itself, must be more a discipline than an official system; more of a factor in character building than a theology. The great need of our people at the present time is that of a strong and correct definition in what, aside from official service, charity, and the natural manifestations of virtuous conduct, Judaism really consists. To punctuate the necessity for such a definition we need not travel beyond the environments of the great Sabbath question." [52]

Item: Joseph Krauskopf in his presidential address in 1904, urging a synod to be called for the purpose of creating a guide. "Where there is no such deliberative body there is no authority, and where there is no authority we have a repetition of what we read in the closing words of the Book of Judges. And the result of each one doing what is right in his own eyes is only too patent to all."[53]

Item: Felix Levy, in his President's Message, 1937. "1 am not prepared to say how we can recover the abandoned ground and go back to some form of Halakhic authority and practice.... I recommend however that a committee be appointed ... [to] draw up a code of rules for guidance in practice."[54]

Item: Samuel Schulman, in presenting his own Reform platform that same year. "For the average individual, pure individualism is anarchy and, therefore, is in the deepest sense, anti-social and irreligious. Without liberty our religion ceases to grow and develop. Without authority, it disintegrates and dies out. In time of excessive authority, liberty must assert itself. In our time of excessive liberty, some form of authority must be re-established." And Israel Harburg, in his Sabbath lecture: "We will never get out of the wilderness as far as the problem of Jewish observance is concerned unless we stop catering to the passing fancies of our age and go back to the use of the Hebrew term מצוות."[55]

Our people are looking for a catalogue of מצוות, and it is our duty to supply it. But it must not be just another circumcised Shulhan Arukh. It must bear the best imaginative qualities of our movement.

We recognize that "rest" in a society which is already surfeited with useless leisure cannot have the meaning which tradition gave to it. The thirty-nine categories of labour have but a faint relationship to needs of our time. We lack the theological and psychological premises for taking seriously the Sabbath questions which presently agitate our Orthodox brethren here and in Israel: whether to make ice cubes in the refrigerator on Shabbat; the ערוב in Manhattan; turning on your hearing aid before Shabbat; or the fascinating question of what happens when a *mohel* drops his knife on a public thoroughfare on the Shabbat. Answer: he can retrieve it with a magnet. We are all Jews, but in this respect their references are not ours.[56]

There are, however, areas of new concern to which we Reformers can make our contribution. The fragmented metropolis with its proliferating suburbs renders family gatherings more and more difficult and hence infrequent. Sabbath — either Friday night or the day — might be our new family times, as in fact they already are for many. We have something to build upon and can fill a need which formerly did not exist.

We have, for reasons which must be evident to all, treated Saturday afternoons as "empty" time. We have here, however, a splendid opportunity for study, both formal and informal. If it is true, as the Talmud says, לא נתנו שבתות וימים טובים לישראל אלא ללמוד בהם תורה, that Sabbaths and festivals were given us only for the sake of study,[57] then why be satisfied merely to recommend this, like good deeds and love, to our congregants? Why not provide opportunities in the synagogue or at study groups in homes? (This would also help us to revitalize the practice of Havdalah, which is lovely and evocative of much sentiment and which, incidentally, should be regularly made at Saturday night bar mitzvah and wedding parties. It would serve, if nothing else, the purpose of זכור; even an ex post זכירה is better than none.)

Study and Shabbat — have we not recaptured this union for many of our children? They have religious school classes in the morning. Why not try adult classes as well?

The possibilities are many once we start to think about them seriously. We might well revive the old rule that activities למען הצבור are not only permitted but desirable. לא תבערו אש בכל משבותיכם, said the Bible, but it only said "in *your* habitations," not in God's habitation. One could and would light fires in the Temple on Shabbat, for it was for the sake both of God and the people.[58] We might well focus on the Sabbath as the day on which one serves the community.[59]

In the very multiplicity of opportunities will lie the attraction of our new Sabbath guide. It can no longer be an either-or, do-and-don't; and we must be specific, not vague. We will point out the mitzvah of having a guest and the mitzvah of abstaining from chores and shopping, and even from mourning. And we will, last but not least, speak about the mitzvah of worship.

I have understressed this latter mitzvah up to this point, simply because we have so often tended to identify Shabbat and services. This does not however obviate the obvious. Prayer is a mitzvah, public prayer is a mitzvah, and קל וחומר, so is public prayer on the Sabbath. Here too we have ways we have not trod and avenues we have not explored. When we have the authority to demand this mitzvah from people we usually do not hesitate to use it. We apply it to confirmands, not so much מיראת שמים but מיראת רב. Our logic is impeccable: we do not force our children, but if they want to be confirmed they have to comply. We mean well and express it poorly. We mean mitzvah and don't use the word. Why not say what we mean: that a young person who cannot fulfill the mitzvah of worship on a minimal basis cannot be admitted to the privilege of confirmation?

And why make the mitzvah applicable to defenceless confirmands only? Why not tackle your not so defenceless confirmation parents or your boards of trustees? The Union is already on record with a resolution demanding spiritual excellence from the latter. Our boards will be readier than we give them credit for. Why not tell a nominee that standing for election implies the fulfillment of certain mitzvot? It does say [60]לעשות את השבת and R. Ephraim Shlomo ben Aaron comments: כי לא יזכר טוביו כי אם בקום ועשה, one does not begin to know the rewards of Shabbat until one seriously does something about it.[61]

As we multiply the opportunities so will the means for their use be increased. Some of us have experimented with the old-new concept of חבורה and found it appealing to both adults and young people. The saying from Proverbs, ראשית חכמה קנה חכמה, applies here too: to make a beginning we have to begin. The revitalization of the Sabbath for Reform Jews starts with us; *we* have to take it seriously.

Our battling predecessors were fond of quoting the talmudic Shabbath dictum: היא מסורה בידכם ולא אתם מסורים בידה, "Not you are given into the hands of the Sabbath, but the Sabbath is given into your hands." [62] We have stressed the second half of R. Jonathan's saying, now let us stress the first: *the Sabbath is given into our hands*. The time will never be more propitious. Earlier Reformers challenged us to similar tasks, but neither we nor our people were ready to listen. I think that today we are more inclined to listen *and to do*.

I close with an exhortation from one of the founders of Reform. Leopold Stein, in his guide תורת חיים, wrote almost a hundred years ago:

> Therefore, all of you dearest comrades in faith, brothers and sisters of the house of Israel, who are so fortunate still to possess this holy day — maintain it, save it; and thereby you will assist, more than by anything else, to erect anew and to strengthen anew religious life and law in Israel. [63]

The Ambiguity of Reform

(Based on the Tintner Memorial Lecture, New York, 1974)

*I*t ought to be stated at the outset that even a few years ago the phrasing of my subject would have been unlikely, if not impossible. Certainty, some fifty years ago when the first Union Haggadah was published, and when Reform Judaism was still in what is generally referred to as the "classical" period, few ambiguities were discernible. To be sure, there were some Reform rabbis who stubbornly insisted on being Zionists, but the vast majority of their colleagues, as well as the lay membership, were convinced that Reform Judaism preached a universalism which excluded Jewish national aspirations. The Pittsburgh Platform is perhaps most remarkable in its sense of certainty. Its fifteen framers knew precisely where they were going, they knew what Judaism, as they conceived of it, demanded of them, what its perimeters were, its origins and its directions. There were flurries of debate on such issues as the nature of revelation, but everything was disposed of in three days, and the draft submitted by Kaufmann Kohler was approved with minor amendments.[1]

Contrast this with the deliberations and the notable lack of a single definitive statement produced so far by the contemporary version of the Platform Committee. Established in 1972, it was expected to formulate a new Reform platform in the fall of 1973, in time for the centenary observance of the Union of American Hebrew Congregations.[2] The present platformers are slowly and painfully coming to the conviction that a platform in the image of Pittsburgh or even Columbus is no longer a possibility. It is my prediction, therefore, that if we produce anything, it will be a series of essays rather than statements. They will outline the ways in which Reform Judaism is attempting to meet the spiritual, intellectual, and social challenges of our day. There will be in every case — whether they be essays on the existence of God or the nature of the Jewish people, the meaning of Israel or our approach to Halakhah — more than one answer. This is the change which has come over our movement. We have moved from the unequivocal to the equivocal, from the clear to the ambiguous. It is the purpose of this paper to show that ambiguity is in fact closer than its opposite to the real nature of our movement. At its inception Reform was, and now has once more become, an ambiguous movement. Therewith it is likely to attain a new dynamism, for while the unambiguous frequently becomes static, the ambiguous tends toward the dynamic.

I

How did Reform Judaism begin? This simple question is not asked often enough, for if it were, some of the problems which many reformers experience during these days could hardly exist, or at least they would be reduced. *Reform Judaism started as an attempt to reform the Halakhah.* It wanted to do no more and no less. The first decades of the movement were given to scholarly investigations of specific Halakhic problems. They dealt with the nature of the service, the permissibility of a sermon in the tongue of the land (this was the reason for Zunz's monumental work in 1832), with the legitimacy of organ music, and the like. This attempt to reform Halakhah was by definition ambiguous: to maintain the *spirit* of Halakhah while breaching some of its *prescripts* in the name of Halakhah. Ambiguity was therefore built into Reform from its beginning.

The first rabbinic conferences at Brunswick, Breslau, and Frankfurt dealt primarily with Halakhic questions. The first conference, in 1844, concerned itself first with mixed marriage, thereafter with liturgy, and it then turned to a discussion of Shabbat and its laws.[3] At the end of the first conference, the chairman, Joseph Maier (who later on became ennobled), warned his colleagues not to be impatient in their drive for Reform. "Let us not force from time that which it cannot give us," he said. For "he who forces time, time will force him" (*mi shedohek et hash'ah, hasha'ah doheket 'oto*). The subsequent synods in Leipzig and Augsburg had the same purpose: to develop Halakhah in a variety of ways. It is now just a little over one hundred years ago that the latter took place. The year was 1871, and it will be well to look at its final statement.

While fully appreciating and venerating the past, said Article III, Judaism strives, in accord with earnest scientific research, to set aside what is obsolete and antiquated, so that it may unfold itself in the spirit of the new age. Note the word *research*. Clearly, this referred to the development of Halakhah, a process conceived by the conveners as continuous, or, as they called it, "unfolding." The synod paid due respect to the past and reiterated time and again that the purpose of the assembly was above all to preserve traditional Judaism, but maintained that this could be done only when dynamic principles were applied. The final statement is equally revealing: "The task of the synod is not concluded by these preceding declarations or principles."[4]

That was a little over a hundred years ago. One need hardly emphasize that the development of Reform did not follow along the intentions and declarations of Brunswick, Frankfurt, Breslau, Leipzig, and Augsburg. In America especially, Halakhah became less and less an issue for the reformers.[5] Substituted for it was a new approach based not on the ambiguities of process but on the certainty of abandonment. *Reform Judaism no longer reformed the Halakhah but abandoned it.* This had one great advantage, or at least it appeared so: it made it possible to speak with certainty — not out of a process of ambiguity but from the clear and unfettered standpoint of philosophic and theological principle. Now, in hindsight, we can see that even the vaunted certainty which the successors of Augsburg (or in America, of the 1869 Philadelphia Conference) tried to achieve involved them in new ambiguities. What is commonly called the "classical" period of Reform Judaism — that is, the period after 1869 and 1871, which reaches up to the time of the Columbus platform in 1937 — *was in fact not classical at all*. It was not a culmination of the ideas of the founders but rather a radical departure. It was radicalism, not classicism. It was the relation of revolutionary excess to the purposes of the revolution itself, the relation of a Robespierre to a Diderot and a Montesquieu — that is, the radicalism of the guillotine to the searching pen of the philosopher. The year 1871 concludes the first period of Reform. In North America, the ambiguities of renewing the Halakhah which were inherent in the founding of Reform were abandoned for the ideological certainties, or presumed certainties, of a new radical vision.

Of course, these new certainties were in themselves debated and not always accepted by all reformers, but there was little question in the minds of most that with proper argument and persuasion one could reach some basic agreement. There were three anchor points:

1. Reform Judaism is Judaism purified.
2. Reform is prophetic Judaism.
3. Reform is in consonance with the spirit of America.

II

1. "Reform is Judaism purified." The banner-bearer of this theme was Samuel Holdheim, to whom Halakhah became ceremonial law and eventually identified with the dead letter of the Talmud. "Reform," he said, "must avoid as much as possible pressing the banner of progress into the rigid hands of the Talmud. The time has to come when one feels strong enough vis-à-vis the Talmud to oppose it in the knowledge of having gone far beyond it."[6] This was a cry of war: Halakhah was to be abandoned and no longer developed. By a strange happenstance, the victorious proponent of this anti-Halakhic point of view was none other than a rabbi who had first come to public attention in the early 1840s with a brilliant responsum in the Tiktin-Geiger controversy. He was David Einhorn. His responsum on when a rabbi can be removed from office was replete with scholarly references based soundly on Talmud and the Rambam. His summation read in part as follows:

> A Rabbi can be removed from his post if he rejects a talmudic interpretation and if the rejected talmudic interpretation and the disputed traditional law concerning tradition which in the Talmud is described and recognized by everyone as genuine and undoubted. Maimonides in his introduction to the Mishnah enumerated such traditional interpretations.[7]

Yet it was this same Einhorn who more than a decade later, upon his arrival in the United States, could propose that Tisha B'av should be turned into a day of joy rather than remain a day of mourning. For instead of weeping over the dispersion decreed by God one ought to he glad of it.[8]

That was 1855, the same year that Isaac M. Wise, along with eight other colleagues, issued an appeal to the American public asking them to attend a convention in Cleveland which would discuss the articles of a Union of American Israel. The result of that Conference was an unequivocal endorsement of the *original* principles of Reform — that is, a movement aiming at a development of Halakhah. "*The Talmud*," said the statement, "*contains traditional and legal explanations of the biblical laws which must be expounded and practised according to the comments of the Talmud.*"[9]

Wise saw himself as a classical reformer, as indeed he was. Einhorn was now the leader of the new radicals. There was hope for an understanding between Isaac M. Wise and conservative Isaac Leeser.[10] There was none between Leeser and Einhorn. The latter criticized the Cleveland conference bitterly:

> The said Platform would condemn Judaism to a perpet-
> ual stagnation, consign its countless treasures available
> at all times, to the narrow confines of an exclusive Jew-
> ish nationality, and expose to derision its entire histor-
> ical development, as well as the incontestable results of
> a wholesome biblical research. The declared legitimacy
> of talmudic authority cannot heal, but on the contrary,
> will render permanent, our unhealthy religious condi-
> tion, which consists not in the present conflict of par-
> ties, but must be sought for in the demoralizing effect of
> an antagonism between theory and practice, and in an
> opposition between descriptive rules and the unyielding
> nature of religious and social wants.[11]

Wise was a spiritual disciple of the early Geiger, and both were, on the whole, classicists in the sense that they recognized the ambiguity of Reform because Reform to them was a development of Halakhah. Einhorn had essentially given up this position and could now be considered a disciple of Holdheim. Einhorn's views prevailed in subsequent conferences and even more so in the actual lifestyle of North American Reform Jewry. Isaac M. Wise is usually called the father of American Reform. The historian must conclude, however, that he should be described as the father of American Reform *institutions* — that is, the Union, the College, the Central Conference of American Rabbis. The true father of American Reform, in the period which in the past was identified as the core period of our movement on this side of the ocean, was David Einhorn. He founded no institutions, but his philosophy gained the day and his *Olat Tamid* was the foundation of the Union Prayer Book — and not Wise's far more traditional *Minhag Amerika*. He was relatively unambiguous. He was certain that Reform Judaism as he saw it was Judaism purified. His chief disciples were Kaufmann Kohler and Emil G. Hirsch, who also happened to be his sons-in-law. And although Wise gave assent to the Pittsburgh Platform, it was the assent of a man who was theologically defeated — or, we might say, deflected from his original purposes.[12] Radical Reform Judaism was espoused by Einhorn, was anti-Halakhic and largely unambiguous. By implication it espoused a total eclecticism, which became the hallmark of the movement. The trend to oppose or even condemn the strictures of tradition was raised to the level of principle. The radicals abandoned Halakhah and no longer made themselves subject to the vagaries and ambiguities of its development.

2. Another way of phrasing the essence of Reform Judaism became popular during the latter part of the radical period. Reform, it was said, is "prophetic Judaism." That, of course, as Professor Shemaryahu Talmon has pointed out, is at best an idealized version of prophetic teaching, but had very little relationship to the Prophets themselves.[13] The reformers chose to quote selected passages, mostly from Amos and Isaiah, which stressed social and universal concerns. They tended to bypass the Prophets' intense nationalism and were never known to quote Ezekiel at length. Yet, for better or worse, the Bible has preserved more of his writing than those of any other Prophet, and though his book is replete with elaborate references to ritual, it says little about war and peace, or other matters usually referred to as "prophetic." "Reform is prophetic Judaism"— that was but another and temporarily more convenient shorthand for saying, "Reform is un-Halakhic, it is Einhornian and not Wiseian."

The radicals took a similar point of view with their exaltation of Psalms, selecting those they liked, and disregarding the others. It is noteworthy that even in 1974, the new Haggadah published by the Conference[14] failed to reintroduce the verse from Psalms which says, "Pour out Your wrath upon the nations that do not acknowledge You."[15] It was "too narrow" and thus continued to be excluded — a heritage of radical Reform. This omission highlights a continuing process of selectivity which does not as yet exhibit the sturdy developmental principles that were part of the truly "classical" period of the early movement and aimed at the development of Halakhah.

3. Finally, in this critique of the middle period of our movement, one needs to confront that now fortunately obsolete identification of Reform Judaism with Americanism.[16] Despite the protestations of the radical reformers, the vaunted policy of integration did in fact assist the process of assimilation, especially so since Reform Judaism became during this period the way of life and belief for a particular, upwardly mobile, social class, and in that it became a Jewish form of the Protestant way of life. Reform is usually approached, reproached, and defended in terms of ideology. The class nature of the movement is rarely discussed. Yet it was a potent force, especially in the radical period. This can be illustrated by the inner development of the Reform congregation in St. Paul, Minnesota.

> Until 1881 the great majority of the 75 families of St. Paul, Minnesota, belonged to the old and established Mt. Zion Hebrew Congregation of that city. The Congregation had exhibited moderate liberal tendencies, and had joined the Union of American Hebrew Congregations, but as late as 1879 a motion to remove hats at worship services was roundly defeated. Then, in 1881, the first large group of Russian émigrés began to arrive in the city. The first trainload brought at one time 200 people who were poor, hungry, disoriented, and did not speak a word of English. These too were Jews — and in the eyes of the Gentile community no distinctions were made between the newcomers and the older established families whose children were now in high school and some of them at University. While the St. Paul Jewish residents extended charitable help to the newcomers who began to arrive in ever larger numbers, there arose among the former a

need to differentiate between themselves, the acculturated members of Mt. Zion, and the "others." This need expressed itself dramatically in the rapid radicalization of pre-existing liberal religious tendencies, and this in turn was highlighted by a renewed motion to remove the head covering at worship. Where formerly the issue was decided in favor of tradition, the motion now won overwhelming approval and Mt. Zion henceforth became a member of the radical Reform wing. The confluence of this development with the arrival of East European Jewry is hardly coincidental.[17]

This is but one illustration of how what today in retrospect we are wont to call "ideology" was in part a function of social pressure and status. The appearance of large numbers of East European Jews in America strengthened the earlier residents in their sense of responsibility and charity, but at the same time fractured their sense of peoplehood in its social and political dimensions and eventually turned most Reform Jews into anti-Zionists.

Reform Judaism was in fact a "Protestant version of Judaism." This judgment was often pronounced upon it by its detractors — and vigorously denied by its adherents — the implication being that "Protestant" meant "Christian." However, once the word *Protestantism* is deprived of its emotional content, and seen it for what it was historically — a particular way of protest against the Roman Catholic Church, a way which then took on its own direction — we see that indeed that there are many parallels between this Christian protest movement and Reform Judaism. To be sure, because Reform Judaism flowered in North America, where the Protestant ethic and way of life held sway, it took on the additional coloration of the environment and was severely subject to its influences. These may be seen, for instance, in the shaping of Reform temples. Gone was the bimah in the middle, the worshippers were arranged like Christian audiences, and the preaching pulpit became the focus of the structure itself. Where formerly the house of God was also a *beth kenesset* and even served as a night lodging for transients, the elements of sociability were reduced in the modern Reform temple, and rarely did a synagogue building have either a lobby for socializing or an adequate hall for get-togethers. The former was deemed unnecessary — what Protestant church, or what church in general had a gathering lobby? — and the latter was frequently superfluous because the members of the congregation belonged to "Harmony" and "Progressive" or "Phoenix" clubs, or later to country clubs, where they could obtain all necessary social contacts. The service had hymns patterned after Protestant song; responsive prayers — quite unknown in this form to Jewish tradition — silent meditation, the inclination of the head by the devout worshippers, the centrality of the sermon — all these are instances of the protestantization of the Reform service. The abolition of the cantor, the introduction of organs and Christian choirs, made the picture rather complete.

Related to these aspects was what may be termed the "internalization" of Judaism. By internalization I mean the emphasis on faith and attitude rather than on *mitzvot*, an emphasis that was pioneered by Christianity, which, with all its cross-streams, continued to stress internalized faith over externalized works. It was a standard Reform phrase of the radical period to say, "I don't have to show my Judaism, as long as I am Jewish at heart." One did not have to eat matzoh on Passover or have a mezuzah on the door. Consequently, the prophetic attitude which the leaders tried to foster remained all too frequently an attitude only. The ideal place for the internalization of Judaism was, of course, the synagogue, where one studied and prayed. Both were activities of the mind rather than of the hand, of thought rather than of deed. In the past it was the males who had been the primary internalizers of Judaism — which they could safely be, because they combined with it an extensive practice of *mitzvot*, and neither they nor the women had any problem externalizing their religion as well. But now, with the advent of Reform, a strange reversal took place: the women moved from the home into the synagogue, and with it moved their Judaism as well. The women were the last practitioners of externalized Judaism, that is, of *mitzvot* practiced at home. Now the women, too, abandoned this and in time became the prime movers in the synagogue, where they too now internalized their faith. Men, in turn, having no further province of their own, moved out of the synagogue altogether, and frequently out of Jewish life in any meaningful way.

The identification of Reform with America found its expression in many other ways. I mention only three more. One was Reform's unhesitating approval of the rational or scientific approach to all matters of religion, which meant in time the gradual and complete elimination of the religious mystique, which, in its turn, made way for an expansion of humanism within the movement. The identification with America also meant an incorporation of the "pragmatic" into the religious enterprise. One began to ask of innovations in the synagogue, "Will they work?" If they did, they were deemed worthwhile, for the end was worthwhile. This, in turn, steered the movement onto the shoals of very dangerous reasoning. For instance, it was believed that improved mental health would come to congregants from regular attendance. The premise was, of course, wrong, because religious services may at times impart to the worshippers a profound sense of disquiet, for a meeting with the living God is not necessarily identical with peace of mind. But then, not only was the premise wrong, the conclusion emphasized unwittingly that religious services were important because they produced certain pragmatic results, measurable in medical and psychological terms. Of course, religious services were not subject to such pragmatic evaluation, nor did most people ever respond on that basis. If that had been the case, air conditioning, soft seating, good lighting, and all the rest should have improved attendance at religious services, something that manifestly has not happened, and if it has happened, certainly not for these reasons. But Reform was so caught up in its unequivocal acceptance of the American ethic that rationalism and pragmatism permeated the movement, which began to lose sight of the need for religion to deal significantly also with the nonrational and with the nonpragmatic so that it would in fact often run counter to much of the culture which American society values so highly.

Finally, Reform in its radical phase gave its unhesitating endorsement to America's optimistic approach to social and political problems. It was an American axiom that, given enough time, money, and willpower, one could achieve almost any end, and this became a Reform axiom as well. The innate limitation of man, which is part of the religious stance, was not popular in America's manifest century. Rather, American semimessianism foresaw the early achievement of universal brotherhood and so did Reform, despite its new social anti-Semitism which established itself during the 1870s as part of the American way.

Professor Alvin Reines drew a logical conclusion from this period of radicalism. Reform Judaism, he held, could be many things. In fact, it could be all things, for there never was any "Judaism" as such, only "Judaisms."[18]

Everything to which Jews responded was, therefore, in line with the thinking of the radical period, legitimate. This point of view represents the inevitable climax of the radical period, though it was formulated after its conclusion.

III

Since 1935, and increasingly since 1948, Reform Judaism has evinced signs of trying to find its way back to fundamentals, of loosening itself from the assumed certainties of its radical period, and of coming back to the ambiguities of its origin. That is to say, Reform Judaism once again began to concern itself with Halakhah and the need for its reform. The radical period produced some magnificent examples of idealism and ingenuity, especially in its commitment to social and esthetic values. In its third, post-radical phase, Reform Judaism has begun to deal once again with *mitzvah*, without posting God as the only *mezavveh* of tradition. It acknowledges the demand, yet does not make it in the name of any one source of authority. This tension is now seen to belong to the ambiguity of the movement.

Reform is thus once again understood to be pledged to the development of Halakhah, to the recapture of its meaning and its practice. Because it deals with the certainties of Halakhah and at the same time with the uncertainties of its reform, it is ambiguous by nature. For the process is filled with the tensions between authority and freedom, the uncertain relation of *mitzvah* and *mezavveh*, and thus the very process is in itself ambiguous. This ambiguity is both the inherent difficulty but also the potential strength of Reform. It is a movement which deals with questions rather than answers, with partial answers rather finalities. As it returns to its original purposes and its beginnings, it is again dynamic rather than static, and therein lies its abiding vitality.

The Four Phases of the Reform Movement

A Personal Statement

*T*he editor of the *Journal of Reform Judaism* has invited a number of
CCAR members to provide an assessment of Reform Judaism and its
institutions as we find them today, and also to prophesy what is likely
to happen in the days ahead. Prophecy is, of course, a risky business, but
fortunately Amos gave us a framework for procedure. The first response
he made to the challenge that he act as a *nabi* was to say that his father
was not a prophet. To speak in contemporary language, he averred
that whatever he would be able to do or not to do was influenced by
his upbringing and ancestry. So, in approaching my subject, I will take
guidance from the ancient preacher (who for a number of decades was
the prophet par excellence for the Reform movement) and begin by
stating my spiritual patrimony.

Our household in Berlin in the 1920s and 1930s was Liberal, using the
word in the European meaning of the time. In Berlin there was only one
Reform congregation that was comparable to its American counterparts;
the rest of the community was divided into Orthodox and Liberal, a
division which also spilled over into communal elections, in which both
religious factions were represented as parties. The Liberals in Berlin and
most other German communities of same size were, by today's American
standards, Conservative in their religious services. *Siddur* and *Makor* were
abbreviated. The synagogues had pipe organs. Many members might keep
a kosher home but ride on Shabbat. While the members were eclectic in

their observances, the rabbis (much as in Conservative synagogues today) would be expected to lead a fairly traditional life.

Thus it was with us. We had a kosher household but ate out. Theologically speaking, my father was close to being a radical reformer who approached his Judaism from a thorough knowledge of classical Jewish sources. Our library at home was filled with volumes on Jewish history and biography. It was taken for granted that we would be familiar with the *Tanakh* and attend services every Shabbat. (This meant Friday nights, because on Saturday mornings we went to school, for classes met six days a week.) I wrote on Shabbat. Among the five Jewish students in our high school class, there was only one who was Orthodox and who postponed his exams if they happened to be given on Shabbat.

Going to the synagogue on a Friday night was not a matter of choice; it was part of our family pattern. When I came home from school on Friday afternoon my Shabbat suit would be laid out for me; even if I had forgotten which day of the week it was, the suit reminded me that it was time to prepare for synagogue. Later, when I was a student at the university, where we had no Shabbat classes, I went regularly to morning services, a habit which was bound to fix in one's mind not only the prayers and psalms but also substantive portions of the Torah and Prophets. In 1928 I was taken to the second session of the World Union for Progressive Judaism and thus, as a sixteen-year-old, was introduced to many of the great figures of the Liberal movement. My father was a member of the Rabbinical Selection Committee for the city of Berlin and for that reason I, too, was exposed to many trial sermons, which were then still the custom. Leo Baeck was, from time to time, a guest in our home. Our Judaism was lived as a matter of course, with set patterns but without rigid insistence. Shabbat was Shabbat, and *yom tov* was *yom tov*. Yet, at least until the rise of Hitler, there were rarely extended discussions in our home on Jewish issues. More likely I would hear about the political scene in general and most often about the literature of the day.

I decided to go to law school and finished it just as Hitler came to power. It was then that Dad suggested I might take some courses at the Hochschule "until the passing of the Nazi madness." He provided me with a young, bushy-haired, and slightly emaciated student who had come from Warsaw to study philosophy in Berlin and who was to teach me Hebrew, at least enough to follow the courses at the Hochschule. The young student turned out to be Abraham Joshua Heschel, who tried valiantly to elevate my *siddur* Hebrew to an acceptable level of comprehension. Alas, he did not succeed too well, but our association was lasting.

I persisted at the Hochschule, especially since law as a career was now permanently closed to Jews and, while I was helpless in Chanoch Albeck's classes on Talmud, I enjoyed Leo Baeck's lectures on homiletics and Fritz Bamberger's classes on Mendelssohn. In April 1935, after a little more than two years of Hitler's rule, Dr. Baeck produced an invitation from the Hebrew Union College signed by Julian Morgenstern, which gave five of us the opportunity to study in the United States. However, the letter stated emphatically, the invitation did not obligate the college to seek employment for us; it was strictly an invitation to study.

In September, five of us — Wolli Kaelter, Leo Lichtenberg (*zichrono li-verachah*), Herman Schaalman, Alfred Wolf, and I — arrived in Cincinnati. By this time the conviction had dawned on me that even were the opportunity for my return to law to present itself, I would decline and give my life to the Jewish people. The unreasonableness of being Jewish was forcefully borne upon me in those days, and my decision partook of the category of "and yet." If Hitler was to persecute us, I would do my share to maintain our essential traditions and help to save Jews. Thus a Liberal background and a love for my people shaped the convictions which were to inform my years in the rabbinate.

Shortly after my arrival to Cincinnati, in a class by Dr. Abraham Franzblau, we were asked to write a paper on the following theme: if a young man comes to you and asks, "Why should I remain a Jew?" what answers would you give him? I was totally nonplussed and had no clue about either the nature of the question or any possible answer. My experience told me only one thing: a Jew was a Jew was a Jew. I wrote something to this effect on my paper and I forget Franzblau's comment (anyway, I passed the course).

No one had prepared my Berlin classmates and me for the nature of Reform Judaism in America. We did not know of its radicalism: we did not know that people worshipped without hats and that the rituals of daily and weekly life were largely absent. On the first Shabbat morning in Cincinnati the five of us went to Rockdale Temple, blithely unaware that our big hats would cause an enormous stir, especially in the breast of the venerable Dr. David Philipson. Since we were seated in the first row we noticed nothing except the absence of *talleisim* on the two rabbis and that they did not wear the preacher's headgear worn by German officiants. But everything was quickly put in focus as soon as services were over and we offered a *Shabbat Shalom* to the rabbis. "If you ever come to my service again," Philipson said to the five bewildered refugees in a magisterial voice, "and come to this temple wearing hats, I will have you bodily thrown out." Fortunately, most of us did not fully comprehend this tolerant welcome of five ignorant refugees, and I will not record my answer (at least not here). It was our introduction to American Reform, and who is to say that it did not have an impact on all of us?

The Holocaust and my first-hand encounter with it during the war (it was my dubious privilege to be present as a US Army chaplain at the opening of the first concentration camp) forced me to reassess my theology and deepened my identification with our people. In the course of time these twin bases of my outlook became one in the conviction that somewhere at the root of my Jewishness lay an obligation to my God and to my people. I did not accept tradition as immutable, but neither was I prepared to overlook it or discard it as irrelevant or nearly so. When in 1948, in an address to a regional UAHC biennial convention, I raised the question of *mitzvah* (actually using this term, unusual for Reform at the time), I was met with less than ready acceptance. Someone stood up and said, "Reform does not accept the concept of *mitzvah*; to my mind, it is purely Orthodox." I rejected that interpretation and I reject it today, aware that *mitzvah* as term and concept does raise serious questions. But without some commitment there can be no viable Judaism — that remains my basic point.

We are today, it seems to me, in the fourth phase in Reform history. In order to assess the past, understand the present, and project the future, it is essential that the four phases of our development be clearly understood. I have phrased their characteristics as responding to four questions, each of which has a different respondent.

PHASE I

The first period may be described as asking *mah yomru ha-avot*? "What does Tradition say?" This phase lasted for two generations, from 1819 to 1881, that is to say, from the establishment of the first Reform congregation in Hamburg to the arrival of large numbers of Eastern European Jews in the United States, after the assassination of Czar Alexander II. The period was dominated by what may be described as a "traditional" approach to Reform. It stood under the banner of an emerging Jewish historical science: *the past was explored so that it might shed light on the present.* Leopold Zunz's great work was more than a historical study of the prayer service; it was also meant to provide warrant for the preaching of understandable and meaningful sermons in the vernacular. The first responsa issued by the liberalizers dealt with such questions as the use of the organ and were closely reasoned on the basis of biblical, talmudic, and post-talmudic sources. However, unlike today's authors of responsa (who expound past decisions but state quite clearly that they will not necessarily be bound by them), the first Reform decisors derived their rulings on the basis of what they considered to be valid past precedent. This attitude is clearly observable in the early rabbinic conferences at Brunswick, Frankfurt, and Breslau, and at the Leipzig Synod. As long as this view of the essential continuity of Reform with its past was regnant the movement could contain both those who strove for a more radical interpretation and those who eventually emerged as the Conservatives. Both parties could still be found at the Cleveland Conference of 1855, and both parties co-operated in the founding of the Hebrew Union College. To be sure, the Philadelphia Conference of 1869 gave warning of changes to come. But, on the whole, the Reform movement in Europe remained traditional in outlook, and even in the ambience of America, where religious radicalism and experimentation were the order of the day and antinomianism was popular, radicals of the Holdheim and Einhorn type were still in the minority and the followers of Isaac M. Wise controlled the emerging institutions.

PHASE II

This time span may be set for the next two generations, from 1881 to 1933, and can be characterized by the consideration *mah yomru ba-hutzot?* "What does American culture say?" It was a period in which *the demands, the ideologies, and the opportunities of the environment were dominant* and when, at the same time, a distinct (though unconscious) shift away from the new Orthodox Eastern European immigrants was observable. America became the great model on which the movement moulded itself, and Jewish practices were adjusted to the American pattern. We removed our hats, we diminished the use of Hebrew, we experimented with Sunday as our main day of worship, we built our synagogues more like Protestant churches with the preacher as the focus rather than the bimah where the Torah would be read — and the Torah reading itself was reduced to the symbolic recitation of a few verses. While for some years the masses of Eastern European immigrants continued to cherish the old ways, the second- and third-generation German Reformers made it clear to themselves and to others that there was a palpable difference between the newcomers and the old-timers. Furthermore, it was in the nature of immigration patterns that the Reformers were distinctly middle class or upper middle class, whose children were receiving a higher education and whose professional and business enterprises laid a solid economic foundation for their communities. Not for them the radicalism of New York's Lower East Side, not for them the continued, visible identification with the past which many of the older immigrants sported in public — with their beards and kapotes and stubborn adherence to the Yiddish language.

None of this analysis is intended to derogate the great contributions which the Reform movement made at the same time: the intellectual expansion and exploration of the foundations of Judaism and its contemporary heritage, the intensification of a sense of responsibility for the needs of the poor both in America and abroad, and a growing concern with broad social issues. The major Jewish social institutions which are still the foundation of our communities today were created by Reform Jews during this period. Yet, when the sum is drawn, it was not to the past and its approbation that Reformers looked, but to the environment and especially to America the Golden. The widely quoted expression, "America is our Zion and Washington our Jerusalem" did epitomize this sentiment, and the historian must admit that we were staunchly anti-Zionist and that only a minority amongst us differed from the Reform mainstream. Toward the end of this period, especially after the First World War, a change was observable. This, however, became dominant only with the emergence of Hitler as the head of Europe's most dynamic nation.

PHASE III

This period lasted from 1933 to about 1965 and may be characterized as the phase in which Reform Jews asked *mah yomru ha-banim*? "What will my children say?" Shortly after its beginning, Phase II was characterized by the Pittsburgh Platform; Phase III was epitomized in 1937 by the Columbus Platform. Although the document did not say so, *the issue had now shifted away from the environment and its culture to the issue of survival.* I entered the Hebrew Union College at the beginning of this period, and I can follow its course in North America.

The word *banim* stands for our future, which we saw endangered. We focused primarily on the survival of our people. Anti-Semitism, the war, the Holocaust, and then the emergence of Israel moved to the forefront of the concerns of our movement. No longer was the issue, How do we adjust to the impact of the environment? Now it was, How can we save our people and secure a future for our children? Israel was one answer, and another was Jewish education, which came fully into its own with new ideologies, new techniques, and a renewed emphasis on prayer. While in the Orthodox and later the Conservative segments of North American Jewry the day school took centre stage, among us it was the congregational school and, with it, the synagogue itself as an educating institution. Congregations flourished and expanded. New congregations were founded, new synagogues were built — all expressions not so much of a newly found prosperity (which was real enough) as the symbolic expression of the synagogue as the spiritual survival factor of the era.

There was yet a third way of securing our future: through our actualized impact on society at large. Clearly, some of the values which America had provided and which in the previous generation seemed to have the stamp of divine approval were found to have ambiguous foundations. No longer would these values shape our Judaism, but now it was to be the reverse: spurred by religious impulses, *we would change society and help to make it over to fit the ideals of our prophets.* Social action was the cry. Congregations took it up, and the new president of the UAHC, Maurice N. Eisendrath, gave it vigorous leadership. We roared into the 1960s following the flag of social justice; we would build securely for our *banim*, with an added emphasis on the *banot* who had now, at least within our movement, come to claim full equality.

PHASE IV

I choose 1965, admittedly with some arbitrariness, as the starting point of this period, in the midst of which we find ourselves at the present time. I call this phase *hayyay — mah homru?* "What will my own life say?" Beginning in the middle 1960s, the North American Reform movement began to address this dimension of Jewish life. In 1965 the Central Conference of American Rabbis took an unprecedented step: it devoted one entire day of its sessions to an exploration of making Shabbat once again a life-giving force in Jewish life. In the past we had battled for its recognition in the synagogue, but now the direction was different. Shabbat belonged not only in the synagogue on Friday nights and Shabbat mornings, but above all in the home. For the first time the attention of the Conference was riveted upon making the life of the individual Reform Jew more meaningful on a personal level. We began to address our lifestyle, the lack of Jewish symbols and landmarks in our day-to-day existence, the absence of personal prayer, the altogether minimal character of personal observance. Shabbat was our flagship, no less and no more. In the middle of the 1960s, with their marches and revolutionary songs, the change of dress, sexual habits, and marital practice (or non-practice), we chose a hallowed Jewish symbol to give us anchorage. Survival was still significant and would remain so. Israel, education, social justice — these would remain part of our concerns, but they were not enough. Somehow the individual, too, had to re-emerge as a Jew in his own ambience. Shabbat was to be the paradigm.

We began to emphasize serious study. The Union launched a wide-ranging project to make Torah accessible to the movement and commissioned a new commentary. The Conference created a *Shabbat Manual* — still calling it a manual and not a guide, for the word had been proscribed in past discussions and the accusation of a "return to Orthodoxy" still lingered in the minds of many older members. But this was not Orthodoxy, this was a frank recognition that ideals too needed form and that without commitment, without *mitzvah* (however defined), Judaism would move totally away from the home and individual into the outer shell of institutions. A few years later even the proscription of "guide" disappeared when *Gates of Mitzvah* was published by the Conference and

was now without embarrassment called *A Guide to the Jewish Life Cycle.*
The Conference overwhelmingly voted to accept the book as its own.

It was not surprising that this direction would find vigorous
opponents. These felt that the new trend had led us away from the
authentic content of Reform, that it restricted individual freedom and
especially the freedom of the Reform rabbi. In its radical manifestations,
this opposition eschewed the guidelines of the past altogether and gave
to each Reform Jew leave to devise his or her own perimeters of Judaism.
If, for *me* (so the proponents of this ideology proclaimed) Thursday was
sanctified as my day of rest, then this sanctification had the same validity
as Shabbat had for others. Samuel Holdheim, paragon of early radical
Reform, had his comeback in the fourth period of our movement.

It was over the rising tide of mixed marriages that the opponents
clashed. While the Atlanta convention of 1973 reaffirmed the Conference's
old opposition to mixed marriage, it recognized its rising incidence and
the already wide divergence of rabbinic practice. In Atlanta the freedom
of the Reform rabbi became the paradigm of the inner struggle of the
movement. It was his or her freedom to act that was debated, his or her
limits within the context of Jewish tradition, sentiment and peoplehood
that were invoked time and again. There was agreement on the need
of the Jewish individual (rabbi or non-rabbi) to make a meaningful
decision about living in the midst of history's gathering storm. The core
of the struggle was over the location of the problem: was it to be found
in greater commitment and the assumption of *mitzvot* by the individual
Jew, or was it to be found in the assertion of his or her greater freedom?
How could a marriage between the two be effected? How were authority
and freedom to be wedded in Reform?

Another of the changes which marked Phase IV of our movement
deeply affected our synagogues. If it is true that the *siddur* is the
window to our people's soul, then the spate of liturgical publications
we have produced should give us a clearer insight into Reform's state of
mind. Indeed, in Phase III the Newly Revised Union Prayer Book had
reintroduced more Hebrew, had made a tentative mention of "Zion
restored," and especially in the High Holy Day liturgy had stressed social
action as a crucial commitment of the Jew. Its most often-quoted prayer
began with the words, "The synagogue is the sanctuary of Israel...." There,
in its halls of education and the fields of social action, lay the future of

our faith — not in the home which might still be a sanctuary in theory but had in practice lost all but the reputation assigned to it by outsiders. A Union Home Prayer Book was published, but it was promoted only tentatively and widely disregarded. The time was not ripe.

But in Phase IV it was. *Gates of the House* was a success. The two new prayer books (*Gates of Prayer* and *Gates of Repentance*) had come to terms with peoplehood and now unequivocally and unabashedly used *mitzvah* as a key term. Commitment was now part of the Reform parlance and had become a notable factor in its new theology. To be sure, services were provided also for those who could not pray or meditate in such an ambience. The inclusion of *mitzvah* and related concepts came at a price: multiple choices were thought to be necessary for those who could not go along. (It was, a contemporary rabbinic sage has been quoted as saying, "a weighty development.")

Large congregations began to form smaller units; the new movement of establishing *havurot* showed significant signs of promise. But while on the whole our congregational membership remained stable, the synagogue as an institution became weaker — added reason for shifting the emphasis of Jewish life to the person and the home. In American and Canadian communities the synagogue was no longer the primary institution. Federations and Israel-centred activities now claimed the best minds and absorbed them into the new power structure. In northern communities, older members, who heretofore had been the mainstay and core of the regulars at Friday night services, were absent on prolonged vacations in the south or southwest. Frequently they also encompassed the upper levels of the economic scale, which meant that they too were now missing, along with academics, the young, and singles. The latter highlighted the new frontiers of society and with it new tasks for the synagogue. The Conference began to deal seriously with problems of sexual behaviour, with gays, abortion, euthanasia, and now increasingly with geriatrics. The family was endangered, and all were affected by the ever-increasing mobility of North American society. If Gentiles were highly mobile, so were Jews — only more so.

In Phase IV the outstanding characteristic of the movement has been its willingness to deal with a multitude of new challenges and at the same time confront the basic problems of a movement that eschews final answers even in a time of insecurity. It is often said that the attraction of

Orthodoxy lies precisely in this: that it can provide some certainties and erect a fence against the onslaught of a thousand forces from without. That is true as far as it goes, but we who are not Orthodox should not overlook that Orthodoxy, too, requires a commitment. It is different from the kind we are willing to make, but it is a commitment, nonetheless — a sober reminder in our current phase when a meaningful commitment is asked of those who call themselves Reform Jews.

PHASE V — A TENTATIVE FORECAST

We are in many ways the avant-garde of Judaism. We have always tried to face the future in order to deal with it. In doing so we have made some serious mistakes but also had some glorious and memorable successes. The fruits of our ethical impulse are a prime example of the latter. While the resuscitation of an eighteenth-century pietism is surely inappropriate, some turning inward is necessary, and commitment or *mitzvah* are its twin anchors of expression.

Clearly the "American religion" of Phase II no longer can provide the spiritual basis that once we thought it gave us. No longer can we measure Judaism by the values which our environment has spawned. It is we, forming a vanguard of dedicated people — however small this vanguard may be — who can and must address ourselves to building lives that matter, in a society that is worth the struggle.

In this process there is always the danger that our twin directions — the social impulse directed outward and the individualized impulse directed within — may split our movement. It is possible that those who would stress internalization will link up with what may be called the left wing of Conservatism and that our "classicists" will form a new radical wing of Reform. History does not always move in directions that are deemed desirable by those affected by its changes, and so I have no way of predicting what may come to pass. (In the long run, I think, there may be a different kind of alignment in the next generation: first a moving together of the Rabbinical Assembly and the CCAR, and thereafter a split along different lines — but that is in the future.)

And that future may see us move from Phase IV into Phase V. How long our current period will last I cannot say, but I do not think it will survive the century, that is to say, it will last for about a generation. Since everything nowadays is compressed, it may pass even more quickly. What will Phase V have in store for us?

I know what I would like it to be. I would like it to respond to the urgent question *mah yomru ba-meromim?* "What do they say on high?" If that were to happen, Reform would move into a period where its impact on Jewish life would match the splendour of its early years and would give a new face to its meaning and thrust.

Meanwhile, however, we are suspended between the after-effects of the 1960s and the anticipation of 1984. We search within, at least tentatively, but we do not wish to give up on our potential impact on the world. We are not certain of ourselves, and that in itself is no shortcoming. We are at this moment a movement in search. Perhaps we will indeed be blessed by the challenge and promise of the prophet: *Dirshu Adonai b'himatzo.*

Religious Discipline and Liberal Judaism

I

Jewish history is replete with debates of various kinds on issues of importance to the contending parties. Some of these exchanges were profound, others were not; some were bitter, others were pleasant. In some, the participants were willing to let logic settle the issue, in others they were not. Thus, the opponents of the Rambam put his *Moreh Nevukhim* in חרם, doubtlessly because they were afraid that the master was about to turn his *Guide* into a code; while the opponents of Spinoza voted to cancel the rebel's membership in the Central Conference of Dutch Jews and expelled him forthwith. Rabbinic conferences in general have had their share of debates, and our Central Conference has been no exception — but what are all these compared to the great *vikkuhim* of earlier days, which merited the attention, and sometimes the interference, of the Lord Himself!

The first debate recorded in human history ended, alas, in murder. While the Torah does not report the argument between Cain and Abel and merely reports that "Cain said to his brother Abel...." (omitting the substance of that deadly debate), Targum Jonathan fills us in and records that the brothers argued *inter alia* about the justice of God, Abel affirming it saying אית דין ואית דיין and Cain denying it, saying לית דין ולית דיין.[1]

Or shall we consult the argument between Miriam and Aaron on the one hand, and Moses on the other? Quite evidently it was about the nature of prophecy which, as the Midrash tells us, related to Moses' sexual practices, or rather their absence.[2] Unlike in the Cain and Abel confrontation, this time God took a hand, with temporarily disastrous results for losing the team of debaters.

A similar interference ended the debate between Korah and Moses. Again the Midrash has to fill in the lacunae, for while the Torah seems to be satisfied to suggest that Korah wanted political and priestly leadership, the rabbis tell us that the argument between the two opponents was really about *zizit* and *mezuzot*.[3] And so it goes on and on, to Hillel and Shammai, Akiba and Ishmael, Kabbalists and anti-Kabbalists, Mitnaggedim and Hasidim, down to our day.

All of these debates had one thing in common: their telling and, even more, their interpretations, were to a significant extent functions of the political and social context of their time. Thus the statement that Moses and Korah were arguing about *tsitsit* was an obvious hyperbole pressed into the service of rabbinic Judaism; it was to underscore that the authority of the rabbis derived from Moses, and that even as God had taken the side of Moshe Rabbenu in dramatic fashion, so could his successors claim to speak in the name of Divine authority — and woe to their doubters! In this respect the theology of the Midrash is no different from that of the Rambam or of Mendelssohn: each addressed the Jewish people under very particular circumstances, which were limned by environment, education, and civic condition. The Rambam could not have written his *Moreh* in the period of Enlightenment any more than Mendelssohn his *Jerusalem* in medieval Egypt — and that brings me to a consideration of our Reform movement in its historical and contemporary settings.

My view of history is based upon two major premises. One, that while we act within and in response to a historic context, a movement worthy of its name should attempt to overcome history and master it. It will eventually be judged by whether it fails or succeeds in this respect. Secondly, that it is an error to speak of Reform as if it were something static that can be described as a firmly delineated ideology. Reform is a process rather than a state, a becoming rather than a being, a liberal mood and mode rather than a system.

II

Having stated these premises I now will attempt to outline for you the Reform Judaism of the past, the framework within which it operated and the needs it fulfilled, and contrast it with the needs which we have to meet today.

The battle-cry of the earlier stages of Reform was adaptation. *Adjust the Jew to the modern world.* היה אדם בצאתך ויהודי באהלך "Be a human being in the street and, a Jew in your home." The famous dictum of Yehuda Leb Gordon which came out of Eastern European Haskalah was already being put into practice by our movement's founders and their successors. Even across the distance of a hundred years one cannot help but marvel at the elegance of their thought, the verve and vigour with which they approached their tasks, their sense of mission. The weighted words they used came easily to them and were fraught with glowing promise. Above all, they preached freedom from the shackles of rigid laws which appeared to them to belong unequivocally to the past. They envisioned, in this land, a synthesis between Judaism and Americanism, and in Germany, with the same enthusiasm, between Judaism and *Deutschtum*. It was these great syntheses which gave rise to magnificent dreams and social visions, the conviction that the messianic age was but a few steps away, and that America and/or Germany were the harbingers of the future. To this future our forefathers gave themselves heart and spirit. No one can read the records of the past, nor even the early records of our Conference, without being touched by the splendour of speech and the depth of conviction which buoyed it up. Those were great years of battle when Reform was to its protagonists the banner bearer of hopes almost achieved.

But at the same time it was also an encounter weighted down with disappointment and frustration. Reform Judaism first and foremost sought to reform the traditional Halakhah. All early pamphlets and rabbinic conferences were primarily devoted to this purpose: justify the sermon in the vernacular on the basis of long-standing precedent; justify the education of girls, the shortened service, the introduction of the organ, the abolition of the second day *yom tov*, on the basis of the *original* intent of the Halakhah. Talmud became in time equivalent to human obscurantism, and Torah, in contrast, to Divine enlightenment. The early Reformers naively believed that once the historical origins of

Jewish practice would be clear, the community would adjust its lifestyle in accordance with new insights. It would be, so it was hoped, just as Jewish and fully observant — albeit of the essentials of Torah and not of Talmud and Shulhan Arukh. It was, truth be told, a quasi-Karaite position.

Alas, this first attempt at Halakhic reform failed. There were two major reasons. One, the denigration of the Talmud meant in effect the denigration of Jewish historical forces. Our modern Karaism did not reckon with the advance of rationalism and of biblical criticism which removed the remaining vestiges of compulsion from Jewish life: not only Talmud but Torah too was considered a human and, therefore, no longer a compelling document. Two, because having isolated Reform from history we also isolated it from the Jewish people and its practices, which often were the undergirding of Halakhah. Minhag, too, was relegated to the shelf of outmoded forms — and thus the whole structure of Halakhah crumbled for us with the crumbling of the ghetto society. Halakhah as word and concept disappeared from the Reform vision and neither the Pittsburgh nor the Columbus Platform mentions even the term.

To be sure, there were compensations — or so it appeared. Only sixty years ago such true stalwarts of Zionism as Martin Buber and Shmuel Bergmann spoke of the indestructible link which bound Jew and German together. The names of those who translated this vision into the American idiom are legion. They believed in truth that Zion had found a home on this continent and Jerusalem a new locus in the national capital. Reform beat to the pulse of America, its messianism, its spirit of the frontier resplendent with the romance of sectarian liberation, and its antinomianism redolent with the gunsmoke of the West. Here as nowhere else was Reform a function of the adaptive process. Caught between tradition and modernity we became, in John Murray Cuddihy's words, the "assaulted intellectuals" who launched their mission to Gentile Europe and entered the "ordeal of civility." [4] The very word *Jewish* disappeared from the names of our Temples and institutions. We became Americans of Hebrew or Israelite faith, and Germans of Mosaic persuasion. We embraced the rationalism of the environment and shed the drama of mitzvah as sterile formalism or sentimental baggage that we could well do without. For ours was a *religion*, and a religion only, which could be expressed much as the Christians around us expressed theirs. Bareheaded, we became seated in ordered rows to listen to the instructions issuing from the pulpit. It was on Sundays more often than on Shabbat that sounds of the organ (which after all was the church instrument par excellence) filled the splendid Temples (which were no longer "synagogues"), where for many years the language of instruction was German; while Yiddish, and let alone Hebrew, were languages of the past, if not of degradation.

Still, we would be less than fair to the early Reformers if we would not also recognize that within this framework of adaptation they tried to maintain something that was distinctly Jewish. But it was all too often vague and verbal, declamatory rather than concrete. Because of this, they failed ultimately to win the masses of our people, for in the process the Reformers had separated themselves from *amkha*, whom they treated at arm's length as objects of *zedakah*.

We became a religion of the middle class and not what we had hoped to be, the liberating standard-bearers of all Jews. To be sure, in time they too became non-observant, but for other reasons, and did not gather to our banner.

Now, gifted with the prophecy of hindsight, we can see that adaptation and acculturation would eventually have to become the handmaidens of assimilation. While the Reform Jew indeed became אדם בצאתו, the human being par excellence, he forgot that it was his duty also to be יהודי באהלו, a Jew at home. Adaptation had been the battle-cry of Reform. It broke first on the shoals of Nazism and the Holocaust, when the great synthesis between Judaism and Germanism was exposed as historically impossible. And even though America remained a free land in which Jews and Judaism could flourish and build a great community, the identification of Americanism and Judaism was also slated for the ash heap of failure. For America could no longer lay claim to moral imperatives after submitting for too long to the immoralities of Vietnam and Watergate.

Be a human being in the streets, adapt to your environment, make Judaism relevant to the world in which you live — these were the chief slogans of yesterday. They cannot be ours today.

III

The new Reform is already underway. It turns the old vision to its opposite: no longer does it try to adapt the Jew to the world, but rather to adapt the world to our vision. Make it our task to reform the environment, rather than the environment being granted a license to reform us. Our task is in truth תקון עולם.

The conditions through which we have lived, and which form the framework of our life today, are different from those of our fathers. The Holocaust destroyed whatever messianic illusions we might have had. It faced us with the bitter reality that we are still very much living in a world which lacks redemption, which we cannot bring into the purview of our time. Since 1945 the world has experienced a hundred wars; killing and cruelty, deceit and oppression, are still the daily fare of our age.

If the Holocaust destroyed our illusions, the birth of Israel inevitably brought us back to our people. To be sure, great leaders had arisen from amongst us and had led the masses toward the standard of Zion. But our movement as a whole, and the members in our congregations, were still at unease in Zion. The platform which we fashioned in 1937 began to formulate this process of return and rejuvenation. The Holocaust and the State of Israel became thereafter the new co-ordinates on our Jewish grid. Thus we recovered our people. To us, Judaism was no longer a mere religion, it was the living expression of that historic nation which had stood and still was standing at Sinai. The demise of the congruence of the spirit of Judaism on the one hand and of America and of Germany on the other, signified that the period of adaptation had now given way to its opposite. As we recovered our inner essence, we also discovered our innate strength. If ever there was a time to take seriously the mission which our forefathers had enunciated, that time has now come.

We have much ground to make up, old hang-ups to overcome. Why else would we still be so hesitant to offer aliyah as a viable option to our youth? Are we still afraid that it is "un-American"? I for one have no hesitation to urge young people to consider joining our new Reform Kibbutz, and I urge the CCAR and UAHC to accept aliyah into their panoply of goals. I do not hesitate to proclaim Zionism as a necessary expression of our particularity. I am a Zionist, even as I am a Reform Jew. I will not permit anyone to sully these terms of honour. I affirm Israel even as I affirm Diaspora. I stand with Elie Wiesel who said, "Whoever attempts to oppose Israel to the Diaspora or vice versa will inevitably betray both in the end."[5]

If we want to be the missionaries of our age we have to begin with ourselves. It is we, first of all, who stand in need of redemption. We stand in need of rejuvenation as much as mankind. We need new threads for the multicoloured coat of emancipation, and we need the fires of spiritual revolution kindled once again. The voices of Amos and Isaiah, nay the voice of a Moses himself, have to resound in the halls of Jewish life.

What then do we need to do what we must and what is given in our hands to achieve?

To begin with, we must recover the prophetic *spirit of dissatisfaction*. The smugness of yesterday and even today must give way to the straightforward recognition that too many of the people who are given into our charge are ignorant of Jewish values. They are drifting because they are being led to seek pleasure rather than duty; the acquisitional instincts of the environment have become theirs. They foster them with verve and vigour. The superficial religious services to which we invite them and to which they say a polite no are exercises rather than celebrations. The God whom many of us still proclaim is manifestly absent from these encounterless assemblies. Above all, our people lack a Jewish lifestyle. They live like goyim; they have adapted themselves so completely that they have forgotten what it is they left behind. To defend the emptiness of their lives, they shout "Freedom!"— but they mean הפקרות, license to carry on with as little as possible, or at best with what is convenient. We have forgotten to tell them that Israel left Egypt not merely to obtain physical freedom but to celebrate the Lord's festival in the wilderness and that Sinai was the goal of liberation. Sinai meant covenant, and covenant meant demand. We must never forget, and we cannot let them forget, that if a Jew ceases to stand at Sinai, he ceases to stand within the context of Jewish tradition. It is well to remember that from whatever side we approach the interpretive treasures of our religion, we find that freedom has its limitations in the divine command and is bound ineluctably to it.

Our tradition says that the commandments were engraven upon the tablets and that we should not read *harut* but *herut*, not "engraven" but "freedom." However, my colleagues, remember that freedom was not written into the air, it was written *upon the tablets*, and the tablets contained the commandments. In the Jewish conception of existence, freedom and commandment are inextricably intertwined.

There was a time when we forgot this. The founders of Reform certainly did *not* forget; they wanted to make the demand operative in their lives. That they failed — for reasons previously delineated — is no reason to discard their vision. That vision remains valid: to take Jewish demands and examine them in the light of free inquiry, then to decide what is and is not applicable to us, thus to combine the authority of the past with the freedom of the present. What a great and noble dream! I for one believe that it is a dream essential to the survival of our movement as a force in Jewish life. I repeat: the fact that for a hundred years it failed in its objective is no reason to abandon the dream itself, to live a meaningful Jewish life in the context not of the ghetto, but of a free society. Knowing the reasons for the failure we can now turn the dream into reality. We know the humanness of Torah as well as its divinity and therefore approach discipline from the starting point of self-discipline. We are no longer separated from *amkha*, and therefore have another chance to make Reform work for them. However difficult it will be to overcome opposing political and social forces, it will be worth the effort. It is to this that I would challenge our movement and especially the leaders of the movement, my colleagues of this Conference.

IV

I do this because the times are urgent upon us. Our people are like David's men at Mahanaim: העם רעב ועיף וצמא במדבר "The people are hungry and faint and thirsty in the wilderness" (2 Samuel 17:29). They exhibit a hunger we dare not disregard. They want to know how one can live as a Jew today; what kind of options and opportunities exist; how Judaism can help to rescue them from the mediocrity of our acquisitional civilization. *They want to be guided, and guidance we owe them.* Dare we stand by when they cry out for meaning and substance? Dare we let their voice find no answer except in the hollow reverberation of their own cry? We dare not, we cannot. Having found our people once again, we must not only embrace them with words, but give them sustenance: הוי כל צמא לכו למים "Ho, all who are thirsty, come for water!" Isaiah 55:1). We will give you living waters, ideals after which to strive, and social visions that you can make your own; we will put you in touch once again with the foundations of our faith. That foundation is the Covenant, for without the Covenant we are nothing. We will put you in touch with the God of the Covenant.

This is what we must say, and this is what we must guide our people to do. We must teach them the contours of piety, teach them not to smile at the word "holy," but to say, "I too belong to a people that calls itself holy." We have to create for them an environment of Jewish living that is both Jewish and alive. It must have the touch of the historic people, and it must also test the waters of tomorrow. This is the marvellous nature of our movement, that in the integrity of our thought we can try to find new avenues to salvation. But guidance we must give; this is what our people seek and need. I do not know what terminology will ultimately arise from our efforts. Some will prefer to use the term *mitzvah*, which transmits to Jews the traditional sense that something is demanded of them, or we might invest *hovah*, duty, with a new sense of urgency. But whether it be *mitzvah* or *hovah*, both convey to Jews that being Jewish they are commanded; that their freedom is limited and not total. By placing ourselves through בחירה in touch with the God of Israel we enter into the vortex of some commandment. In the final accounting, if God is not demanding, He is — as it were — not God. Leo Baeck once said, "God does not give advice, He demands."

Those who consider the creation of a guidance system to mean the beginnings of new Shulhan Arukh are very wide of the mark. None of us rabbis who has attempted to speak of this to his members has ever dreamt of forcing anyone to do anything. But people are hungry, they want opportunities, and we in turn must say to them, "Here are your opportunities for mitzvah." Do not denigrate them by saying that they are looking for cheap ritual comfort. The woman who raises her hand in blessing the Shabbat candles and feels that thereby she is in touch with the Divine presence is not merely engaging in rites and ceremonies, she is striving to stand in the context of holiness. That is no small matter which can be put aside, any more than prayer can be put aside as a convenient ceremony. It can be that, but it need not. We must give our people choices and opportunities and above all Jewish information, so that they can make these choices intelligently and in the freedom which is theirs. Help them be desirous of piety, make them strive for holiness, lead them again to become the children of the Covenant and place them at the Sinai of our time. They are tired of being merely lodge members in our Temple fraternities. Give them something of the excitement of living with the uncertainty of making decisions, without necessarily reaching the sureness of spiritual ease. Tell them that being a Jew is a near impossible task, and being a Reform Jew a difficulty twice compounded. For we Reformers must take autonomy and marry it to discipline. Perchance we ask the impossible, but when has history ever asked less of us? This is the glory and also the burden of Reform Judaism, to ask our people to discipline themselves in freedom. It is not we who will force them, it is they who will choose to do what they sense they ought to do. Only let us guide them to make their choices Jewish, within the perimeters of Jewish existence. They should be moved to combine *behira, hovah*, and *yahadut* (choice, duty, and Judaism) into a life-acronym which reads and is בח״י, standing in the context of living.

In whose name will such guidance be issued? In the name of rabbis who pray that their guidance may lead Jews to meet their God. When we speak of *mitzvah* or *hovah* may we not hope that in the doing a Jew will meet the God of the Covenant? I will not pursue this subject here; I only plead that we not get hung upon definitions on which we cannot agree, for both we rabbis and our members occupy too wide a variety of theological positions. But we can say, "I must because I will. I will as a Jew, and being a Jew I live in the context of some obligation." We must now, as Liberal rabbis, give reality to this obligation. As a start, we must exhibit it in our own lives. לא המדרש עקר אלא המעשה. We teach, above all, by example.

V

Before I close I must issue a warning: Once before we nearly separated ourselves from our people. Never again! Remember always that as Reformers we are the cutting edge, the avant-garde of our people, but we are *not* כלל ישראל, the whole people of Israel: we need our brethren. We must continue to seek them even if they do not seek us. We need those who take a different stance, who guard and nourish tradition in a different way. We who are more open to the world, who do not fear to go out and meet it, we must always be aware that we cannot and dare not lose touch with the armies of Jewish history. We cannot accept the Halakhah of tradition, but we must relate to it. We can veto it, but we cannot overlook it as if it did not exist. Reform is Jewish continuity, not discontinuity. We do not, we dare not, go it alone or as if there were no *amkha*. But we can march out in front, knowing who we are and what we are: visionaries of our people, bold, entering arenas not heretofore trod by our fathers, but always as Jews first and foremost. We look at the world not with Gentile eyes, but the eyes of *Am Yisrael*. We look at the heights of history always through the visions of Sinai. We want to take our people and make them ready for change and for עולם תיקון, and therefore must first give them a firm foundation that relates them to the Jewish past and makes them ready for the future. That past demands of us knowledge and love, a knowledge of history and of the Master of history; it demands that we embrace our people and its ancient language which rings to new sounds amid old accents.

This is how I see the Reform synagogue of tomorrow: diversified, different in its various stages of search, no longer committed to the walls of the Temple, but a living community reaching out to its members, going into their homes, into their places of work, in an outreach program of great spiritual and physical proportions. No longer will our synagogues merely be the service stations where members come to fill up when they need us, but from whence we take our spiritual nurture and bring it to our people. It is our holy task to mould them into members who will love Israel in all its habitations, who will affirm the worth and importance of Diaspora yet love Israel and the land of Israel with total love and devotion unrestricted by apology or excuse:

- members who are willing and eager to study;
- members who are willing to commit themselves;
- members who will not shrink from calling themselves partners in a holy enterprise;
- members who will take the risk of shaping their environment to the social and physical visions of Judaism;
- members who will not flinch when they are called to piety;
- members who will come forward and say:
  "Since I want to be a Jew, I must live like one"
  "I must because I want, and want because I must";
- members who are not above fearing a God who demands;
- members who will listen to the voice of a rabbi who interprets to them his vision of the Holy God of the Covenant.

For ultimately I see our rabbinate, too, moulded anew: rabbis, leaders of our people, who will guide them not with codes — these are gone without chance of return — but truly with visions of *hovot* couched in words of *persuasion*, who will make the doing of Jewish duties the great and holy goal of our people. To this I challenge you without fear, in the full acceptance both of our past and of a present that challenges us gloriously. Thirty years from now other men and women will stand in this place to reinterpret our movement. For today I stand here and I say yes to my people, yes to self-discipline freely assumed and freely practised as a way to God, as an identifying means of living in this world, so that my people may remain its continuing conscience.

That is my vision, and I pray it may be yours as well.

בחירה

חובה

יהדות.

בח"י! In the spirit of Jewish life!

Prophetic Judaism Without Prophets

$\mathcal{T}$he long association that my dear friend and colleague Rabbi Dr. Walter Jacob has had with Rodef Shalom has encouraged me to touch on some aspects of the temple's history.

The name Rodef Shalom clearly denotes that the synagogue was most likely the result of a split in the original congregation. In most communities the name Shalom or Temple Shalom is usually attached to the congregation that splits away, and I understand that such was the case with this Rodef Shalom as well. I further conclude that the quarrel must have been bitter, for the secessionist party saw itself as a veritable *rodef shalom*, chasing peace.

No wonder, therefore, that one of the early functionaries of the congregation, back in 1854, was a Reverend Armhold, whose name was an interesting wrestling term. Anyone called "Armhold" could doubtless keep his pugnacious responsibilities, for he had to act as *hazan*, *shochet*, *melamed*, and *mohel*. Such combination was custom in those days, and Holy Blossom Temple in Toronto (founded at about the same time as Rodef Shalom) also had as one of its first ministers a gentleman whose duties were exactly the same as those of Reverend Armhold. His name was Goldberg, and he came from Buffalo.

Although the early minutes of Rodef Shalom are missing, and the historian cannot find out the reason why Mr. Armhold left his employ, the minutes of Holy Blossom are in good shape and show that Mr. Goldberg had become the target of complaints launched against him because of his circumcisions. The temple struck a committee to see how well or poorly he performed these delicate operations, and the minutes say the following about the findings of the committee. "Rev. Goldberg, when he performs circumcisions, is more like a *shochet*." The report, not surprisingly, led to the discontinuance of Mr. Goldberg's services. Let me speculate that Reverend Armhold left Rodef Shalom for more ordinary reasons.

In any case, the Pittsburgh temple went on to play a leading role in the history of Reform Judaism, as did the city, and I now turn to certain aspects of Reform development during the years since the Pittsburgh Platform was fashioned 112 years ago. Incidentally, the representative of the congregation who played the host at the time was Rabbi Lippmann Mayer, who can be said to have assisted his colleagues in the metaphoric circumcision of the Halakhah, the body of rules for Jewish life that the assembled committee of fifteen rabbis considered contrary to the modern spirit. In its place the creators of the Pittsburgh Platform put what was then and later on called "Prophetic Judaism." In their view the real future of Judaism lay with the religious ideals of the prophets of yore. They often quoted Isaiah, Jeremiah, Amos, Hosea, Micah, Zechariah, and their colleagues to buttress the Reformers' concern for social justice. They loved Isaiah when he said in God's name,

> Is this the fast I have chosen? A day of self-infliction?
> Bowing your head like a reed, And covering yourself with sackcloth and ashes?
> Is this what you call a fast? A day acceptable to the Eternal?
> Is not this the fast that I have chosen: to unlock the shackles of injustice.[1]

They cited Amos as an advocate of racial equality: "Aren't you [Israelites] like Ethiopians unto Me?"[2] The prophets went on to expound his theme that although God had a special love for Israel, this did not give it the right to feel safe and superior. Human equality before God was the core of Prophetic Judaism.

Or take the saying of Zechariah, "Not by might, nor by power, but by My spirit, says the God of Heaven's hosts."[3] It isn't the physiological exercise of power, but rather spiritual strength, that makes for true religiosity. That was the spirit that underlay the Pittsburgh Platform of 1885, and with it went regular references to the prophets of Judaism.

I have looked for a summary expression of Judaism that conveys this vision. The person who wrote and spoke about it most insistently was Emil G. Hirsch, rabbi of Temple Sinai of Chicago, whose love for social justice expressed itself in vigorous public action. He was the founder of some of the great social institutions of the city of Chicago that have survived to this day. It is worth noting what he wrote nearly a hundred years ago:

> Sacrifices, the phylacteries or talismans, in fact all that Oriental pomp and circumstance which of late days has been urged as a very life air of Judaism cannot show credentials to this distinction when examined before the forum of comparative ethnography.
>
> In what was Judaism original? ... [It] was the contribution made to humanity by the prophets. Not sacrifices, not rituals, not holy convocation as such are religious. They are inconsequential, and if urged as final and essential, cease to be religious and sufferable. In the stead of the religion that operates with sacrifices and rites, the Prophets taught a religious view of life and world in which the Holy God could only be revered by holiness on the part of men. And this divine-like holiness of men consists in doing justly, loving mercy, and so forth.[4]

No other religion, says Hirsch, had known of this interpretation. From Israel's seers the larger world learned a revolutionary philosophy, and ethical monotheism was the original and essential content of our faith. Similarly, British liberal Claude G. Montefiore found more to affirm in the prophetic literature than in the Torah.[5]

Social action is still a major preoccupation of our movement, and I am happy to acknowledge this. But I am sad to say, at the same time, that nowadays most social action efforts in our movements are bereft of the prophetic presence. We still call it Prophetic Judaism, but the prophets have left the presence of those who sail under their banner. In part this is the result of the pervasive secularism of the North American cultural scene, which has produced what is often called "American's civil religion." Its reference is the U.S. Constitution, but not God.

This detour, unfortunately, has infected our movement. Where formerly our love affair with social action was grounded in Prophetic Judaism in the literal sense — that is to say, in the knowledge of prophets who invoked the presence of God and proclaimed, "Thus says the Eternal, and God spoke to me saying...."— our modern-day reformers base themselves on other sources. Ask the average member of a Reform congregation in North America about prophets and he or she will most likely think of profits. Prophecy is something that has to do, so it appears, with palm-reading and astrology but not with "Thus says the Eternal One."

There is a remarkable aspect to this development. The prophets were formerly ever-present on Shabbat morning, because after the Torah reading came the haftarah, and the haftarah was largely prophetic teaching. Today, all too many of our congregations omit the haftarah or no longer have a Shabbat morning service unless they have a bar or bat mitzvah celebration, and consequently — aside from our depletion of worshippers — most members of our congregations never listen to a haftarah save on the High Holy Days. If they hear of Prophetic Judaism they are probably not sure what that term betokens.

Even the social action pronouncements of the Central Conference of American Rabbis during the last fifty or sixty years made few references to the Bible. Instead, their prime inspiration was the American Civil Liberties Union, and it was its authority that was quoted, not that of biblical prophets. This was one of the reasons I was moved to write a commentary on the haftarot, to let my colleagues and the public know that there is a readily available source book that will undergird the social activism to which we have subscribed and that remains a chief endeavour of our movement. Reform Jews once dwelt proudly in a God-oriented spiritual Garden of Eden, but they have left it, and an angel with a flaming sword stands at the gate and says, "You cannot enter here, you belong elsewhere. You have subscribed to a civil religion that has left God's prophets behind. This Garden is no longer for you."

Does that really matter? It does, indeed, for what the prophets have to say is often incompatible with what North American culture says to us. That culture is highly individualistic, whereas Prophetic Judaism was highly collectivist. North American culture allows each person to determine what is right and wrong, because right and wrong are considered relative. *I* determine what is moral and immoral, which is an attitude that stands in direct opposition to the teachings of the prophets. It is safe to assume that Dr. Solomon Freehof would never had bothered to write his commentaries on Isaiah, Jeremiah, and Ezekiel if he had not been convinced that they were counterweight to American civil religion. He wrote these books to make it clear to his readers that for the prophets, as for God, there is a right and a wrong, as there is an authentic Judaism. All true religion must in the end be countercultural if need be, and rabbis are there to lead their flocks.

The rediscovery of prophecy, therefore, is for us a religious must. I should like to think that the kind of service that the rabbis of Rodef Shalom have rendered to our movement is an ideal held out before all of us. It has been the seminal teaching of Rabbis Freehof and Jacob that Jewish idealism must have a religious basis and that at the same time there must be boundaries to our behaviour, Jewish boundaries, which we call Halakhah. That is why both Rabbi Freehof and, following him, Rabbi Jacob combined their study of our religious tradition and prophecy with a study of Halakhah. They have taught us prescriptions for Jewish living, and this combination of prophecy and Halakhah represents to me the acme of Reform Judaism. It is Prophetic Judaism at its best. The prophets railed against inauthentic sacrifice but not against sacrifice, against inauthentic prayer but not against prayer.

Rabbi Dr. Walter Jacob has been devoted to the pursuit of such ideals. It is a heritage worth honouring and, I might stress, worth recovering, because we need the dual recovery of spiritual ideals and Jewish living. Unbound ideals together with guides for Jewish living have been the core of his ministry and thereby mark the essence as well as the future of Reform Judaism.

The German-Jewish Experience

The Elusive German-Jewish
Heritage in America

*W*hen German Jews awoke on the tenth of November 1938 their lives had been radically and irretrievably changed. Their nearly 2,000-year-long sojourn in Germany had come to an end. From here on theirs was the age-old cry: *Rette sich wer kann!* Jews scrambled for the exits, only to find few countries willing to receive them. But some still managed (or had already managed) to come to the Western Hemisphere and primarily to the United States. I was amongst them.

This article will attempt to discuss two questions: one, is there still a recognizable German-Jewish heritage in America?[1] and two, what are its components?

I

In 1988, fifty years after *Kristallnacht,* the traces of German-Jewish influence on the American continent are no longer as clearly visible as they had been fifty years before that seminal event. In 1888 there were three identifiable Jewish communities: the Sephardim on the East Coast; the Germans spread throughout the country all the way to the West Coast; and the Eastern Europeans now arriving in ever larger numbers and for the time being preponderantly concentrated in the East. There was no question then that the German Jews were dominant; they had already "arrived" and had joined the middle class; and their rabbis were the spokesmen for all of American Jewry. Their local institutions were highly developed, their national organizations firmly in place, and their thought patterns clear transplants from the old country. They were mostly (though not exclusively) Reform Jews; integration into the American pattern was a basic aspect of their striving. The way in which they described themselves provides a key to their goal: while other ethnic groups would put their ethnicity first and their American identity second (German-American, Spanish-American, Irish-American) Jews from Germany called themselves American Hebrews and not Hebrew Americans — a direct mirror of their past. For in the land of the Kaiser too they had been *deutsche Juden* and not *juedische Deutsche*.[2]

Today the role and identity of these Jews have become nearly invisible, and without the events of *Kristallnacht* and the attendant emigration of German Jews to America they would have become an historical footnote only. Yet they are still there, though one needs to look rather closely to detect them. Two contrasting incidents will illustrate this point.

I remember the day when the Beth Ha-Tefutsoth museum was dedicated on the campus of Tel Aviv University and Abba Kovner and Nahum Goldmann cut the ribbon. Goldmann, of course, was the *spiritus rector* of and prime fundraiser for the institution, and when I had once asked him how he would define his own cultural identity he had identified without hesitation, "German." But it was Kovner, the East European Jew, who was responsible for the content of the Diaspora Museum. It was evident then (though this may have changed since) that in Kovner's view German Jews had played no worthy role in European Jewish history and that in America too the likes of Isaac M. Wise and David Einhorn had paled before the Lubavitcher *rebbe*. No mention of the fact that the chief religious movements of our time — from Reform to Conservatism to Orthodoxy, all the way to the Agudah — had been invented and shaped by German Jews, and though of course Herzl, Wolffsohn, and Shapira received their due as founders of political Zionism, they appeared disconnected from their own background.

Contrast this with the year 1983 in America. In Los Angeles, at the annual convention of the Central Conference of American Rabbis, a German-born president (Herman Schaalman) was yielding the gavel to another president of like origin (the writer); and at the same time, the presidents of the three other Reform institutions were all German-born as well: the Union of American Hebrew Congregations (Alexander Schindler), the Hebrew Union College–Jewish Institute of Religion (Alfred Gottschalk), and the World Union for Progressive Judaism (Gerard Daniel); since that time the president of the Jewish Theological Seminary (Ismar Schorsch) has also joined this surprising constellation of German-Jewish influence. One might be tempted to apply the well-known words coined in a different context: *anachnu ka'n*, we are still here.[3]

Was this mere coincidence? Possibly, yet the confluence was startling enough to make one wonder. Perhaps there is a heritage which exerted a motivating influence and which in this late moment surfaced long enough to pose the question. But while its traces are still there, its characteristics are like covered tracks which await the discovery of the searcher.

II

The nature of German-Jewish influence has been described in terms of *Bildung*, a view of priorities which gave to education in the broadest sense a place of primacy. To be called *ein gebildeter Mensch* was a greater accolade than being described as rich or successful. A German doctor or lawyer was not just a good specialist in his field; he was expected to also be *gebildet*, and usually was. He would be conversant with Homer and Virgil, and would know the difference between Aristotle, Archimedes, and Aristophanes. He would properly quote the date and significance of the French Revolution. He would have studied Racine and Shakespeare along with Germany's own poets and thinkers. (To be sure, he would also think that Germany was the heart of the world, but that kind of self-perception was paralleled in other nations.) In addition, he would have a sense of order and obligation. In this respect the Jewish heritage with its emphasis on mitzvah blended perfectly with its German counterpart, as Moses Mendelssohn had tried to show long ago. Not surprisingly, almost all German rabbis obtained their doctorate in some field before they assumed congregational posts.

One is therefore safe in describing German-Jewish influence abroad by this kind of cultural apprehension. In Israel, the *yekkes*, though they have all but disappeared in person, survive as popular characters who are ridiculed and admired at the same time. While their pedantry gives rise to jokes, their constancy is held up as a goal worthy of imitation.

And in America? Here too the traces are all but gone, but the aforementioned confluence of "presidential" office holders gives rise to a fascinating inquiry: what was it that propelled these men — who after all were but a few brands plucked from the fire — to their positions of leadership in their new environment? The answer is not as easy as it may appear, for several of the men, while born in Germany, were not raised there. Yet they too give evidence of this German-Jewish inheritance.

A hundred years ago the question did not arise, for there was a predominantly German constituency in our congregations. In a few of them, as in Baltimore, the rabbi[4] had to be able to preach some of his sermons in the German language, and his listeners would likely be less patient with bad German than with faulty English. Their culture was still German-based, and in a number of communities such fraternal orders as B'nai Brith and the Free Sons of Israel conducted their meetings in German. Isaac M. Wise, Bohemian-born and German-speaking, had come to America in the late 1840s, and when in Cincinnati he began to plan a national journal he decided on a German version (*Die Deborah*) and an English one (*The American Israelite*). Both publications were replete with *Bildung* — literary references and academic discussions and a pervasive belief that knowledge and moral education would bring about not only a higher level of Jewish commitment but also a readier integration with and acceptance by the Gentiles, for they would see the Jews in their true role: as a light unto the nations. In many ways David Einhorn and his two sons-in-law, Emil G. Hirsch and Kaufmann Kohler,[5] put their stamp on what has become known as "classical Reform," with its emphasis on the spirit rather than the form of Jewish existence.

But in the 1930s, when the first five refugees from Nazi Germany arrived at Hebrew Union College, the constituencies of their future congregations had already changed drastically. Men of Eastern European background were now in the majority and the control of the old German founders and their offspring had already disappeared or waned drastically. Yet what these five men brought with them still had relevance in America and would afford them and those who followed them from Germany in the next few years a disproportionate influence on American Reform and the larger environment.

What then precisely did they bring with them? The answer I propose is two-pronged: those who had gone to school in the old country had been shaped by their high school education; and they, as well as those who had never attended a German educational institution, had been raised with a set of identifiable expectations.

I mention the German high school and not the university, for the latter (as I can testify from my own experience) served as a trade-and-technical training institution rather than one which would create and foster a broad appreciation of the liberal arts. These were taught in high school, which began at an age when in America students would go into Grade 5 of their elementary schools and lasted for nine years of a six-day school week. High school ended with comprehensive written and oral examinations in all subjects and proffered the so-called *Abitur*, or "going away" diploma. Possession of the *Abitur* meant readiness to go into law school or medical school or whatever further training one chose to pursue. On the average, we were nineteen years old when we graduated and had been exposed to a wide spectrum of knowledge. Its details depended on which of the three major types of institutions one had attended: the old-type *Gymnasium*, which specialized in the classical humanities and taught its students a thorough knowledge of Latin, Greek, and ancient history; the *Realgymnasium*, which combined the classics with some natural sciences; and the *Oberrealschule*, which stressed the sciences as well as a knowledge of French and English. All three school systems had extensive courses in literature and history, and in my time they still insisted that memorization was a worthwhile part of education, for it would allow a person to cite many literary passages from memory and lace one's speech with them. That practice extended also to the biblical text. In the rabbinical seminary over which Rabbi Leo Baeck presided,[6] we had to learn fifty Hebrew psalms by heart, as part of our first-level requirements.

Teaching followed a rigorous schedule with lots of demanding homework. All subjects save athletics were academic, and once one had chosen the type of high school to which to go (a choice usually made by parents for their children) all courses were compulsory. Failure in any two of them meant that the whole year had to be repeated. The school day lasted from eight until two, and on Saturdays until one o'clock, with a twenty-minute break at ten o'clock to consume the "second breakfast" one had brought along.[7]

I mention these details because my education outside the home was fashioned in high school.[8] All five of us carried this background to the United States. It meant, *inter alia*, a respect for ideas and the conviction that education had salvational aspects.[9] To be sure, the Nazis had shown that this was not enough, for they had turned the "land of poets and thinkers" (as the Germans liked to call themselves) into an obscene caricature of the ideal. Education could be perverted, they proved, unless it had its moral component. For us this was provided by our own Jewish tradition.[10]

But what of those leaders who had been born in Germany but had not gone to school there? They shared with us a home background in which there were certain standards and expectations. They might not have been to a German school, but they were taught by parents who brought up their children in an atmosphere where *Bildung* had a primary place. Add to this the "immigrant factor"— the added incentive to make it in the new world — and you have the ingredients which may help to explain the role which German Jews played in their new environment. Quite aside from rabbis who achieved positions of leadership there were scores of German-born academics who contributed significantly to American thought and the national polity, from the likes of Kurt Lewin, Hans Jonas, and Hannah Arendt to Bruno Bettelheim and Henry Kissinger.

In this way the final destruction of German Jewry which was set in motion on *Kristallnacht* made its unplanned contribution to the New World. Hopefully history will judge it to have been worthy of the opportunity. As for me, my own fate was inextricably intertwined with the event. For during that very day when in Berlin my father was hiding from the enemy, my bride and I — not knowing of the events in Germany — were married in Cincinnati.

The Yom Kippur That Never Was:
A Pious Pictorial Fraud

*O*f all the things in my grandfather's house, I remember most vividly a large print. It was entitled "Service on the Day of Atonement by the Israelite Soldiers of the German Army before Metz 1870." Later I was to learn that this print hung in many Jewish homes both in Germany and wherever the Jewish children of the Fatherland had migrated. Sometimes the print had German, English, and Hebrew subtitles, and the picture varied slightly from edition to edition. (Rabbi Arthur J. Lelyveld of Cleveland presented me with his copy. It measures 27 x 31 inches and was published in 1871 by H. Schile of New York. The printer was G. Schiegel.)

It was reproduced on postcards, on cloth, and on silk scarves. The large prints were embellished by a lumbering patriotic poem (in German) which began with the verse:

> Encamped at Metz in the waning sun
> Were German soldiers.
> One by one
> They left their ranks, glad, brave and hale,
> Marched and descended toward the vale,
> There in a solemn festal mood
> Twelve hundred German soldiers stood.

In all the variations of this popular print the basic theme was the same: in an open field before Metz, hundreds of Jewish soldiers were shown at prayer. Assembled around an Ark and cantor they presented a colourful group, with their peaked helmets and blue and red uniforms. Many of them wore *talleism*, were holding prayer books, and all were shown in reverent attitude. To one side stood high-ranking apparently Gentile officers who observed the proceedings with pious dignity. In the background guns were firing on the besieged city of Metz. It was all very sentimental and, in retrospect, a very possible representation of what might have happened. For several generations the picture was a reminder of the strong link between patriotism and piety, a striking recollection of an occasion which was to be duplicated in similar fashion in later wars and other armies.

There was only one trouble with this picture. What it showed never happened, at least not in the way shown. To be sure, there *were* services on Yom Kippur before Metz, but they took place under circumstances quite different from those portrayed in the ubiquitous parlour piece. No open-air services were ever held; the 1,200 soldiers who found their way into print were never there; the German Gentile officers made no appearance; in other words, *the picture was a pious, patriotic fiction.*

The real facts may be gathered from an article written a generation later, after the outbreak of the First World War. Its author was the redoubtable dean of German organized liberalism, the Frankfurt rabbi Caesar Seligmann.[1]

Seligmann describes how on August 25, 1870, General von Manteuffel was approached by the rabbinical offices in Mannheim with the request to allow a rabbi to conduct field services on the following High Holy Days. There were then no regularly assigned Jewish chaplains in the German army. The general replied that, circumstances allowing, Jewish soldiers would be excused from duty and that the arrival of a Jewish preacher would be welcome. Consequently, Rabbi J. Blumenstein, later rabbi in Luxembourg, went to Metz.

He came too late to make arrangements for Rosh Hashanah but he was given permission to arrange services for Yom Kippur in St. Barbe, which was at the centre of the Metz encampment. A portion of his report reads as follows:

> After an interview with the latter (the Adjutant) the time for services was set for Tuesday evening from 6 to 7:30 p.m., for Wednesday morning from 8–11 a.m., and for

the afternoon from 3–6 p.m. Soldiers were to go back to their quarters immediately after the conclusion of services. The Major did not at first understand the necessity for an afternoon service in addition to one in the morning, especially under the prevailing circumstances. He said that this would create additional kitchen and feeding problems. I assured him that this was a worry which, at least for Yom Kippur, need be of no concern.

A considerable difficulty arose in relation to the place for services. Open air services were deemed impossible for Tuesday night because of darkness and were also ruled out for Wednesday for obvious reasons. It is worth mentioning that I was offered the use of the Catholic church, although it would at first have to be cleared by the large number of soldiers who were then camping in it. However a physician from Koenigsberg, my immediate neighbour, was most willing to grant me the use of his room so that the service took place in our two adjoining chambers.

On Tuesday, on the eve of the Day of Atonement, almost all Jewish soldiers of the 1st, 3rd, and 44th Regiments appeared. They gave as their homes mostly the communities of Thorn, Kulm, Danzig and Tilsit. Several of them had been proposed for the Order of the Iron Cross. Most of them were stationed in the surrounding villages of Colombey, Ogy, Servigny, Retonfy, Flonville and Laquenexy. A few minutes before six o'clock I began the services. A non-commissioned officer sang the prayers with great dignity. Before the final Alenu I preached on the text from Jeremiah 31:15 and 16:

> Thus saith the Lord: Refrain thy voice from weeping and thine eyes from tears, for thy work shall be rewarded, saith the Lord, and they shall come back from the land of the enemy. And there is hope for thy future, and thy children shall return to their own border.

There was a truly exalted devotion throughout the service. Rarely were people moved as deeply and prayed as fervently as they did that evening. When I spoke of the prayer of the patriarch Jacob for a peaceful return to his own hearth, I was interrupted for several minutes by the weeping and sobbing of the audience.

With the exception of a few soldiers who were attached to the hospital and therefore remained in St. Barbe, all the others went back to their quarters at the conclusion of the services. Some had to walk for three hours.

Next morning all appeared at the arranged time. The cantor of the day before sang the *Shaharit* and *Mussaf* prayers, and since we lacked a Torah scroll I explained the contents of the assigned portion as well as the Haftarah from Isaiah. At three o'clock the pious worshippers assembled once again, with the exception of the few who had to return and prepare themselves for sentry duty. We prayed all the prayers of *Minhah* and *N'ilah*; a non-commissioned officer volunteered to be the cantor for *Minhah*, and I myself chanted *N'ilah*.

After services were finished at sundown, I addressed a few additional words to those present and thanked them for pious and lively participation in the prayers which would remain for me a sacred remembrance throughout my life. Thereafter Mr. Hirschberg, a non-commissioned officer from Culm (who, I understand, is about be made a Lieutenant) arose and expressed his comrades' most cordial thanks to me. He said that they had long yearned to come together in worship and open their anxious hearts before God; that they had fulfilled this desire now and were therefore ready to face the future in a happier mood and with greater confidence. In the name of all the comrades Mr. Hirschberg asked me to return soon and hold another service for the Third Army Corps. I parted from the devoted group in a highly elated mood.

Dr. Seligman then proceeds to quote a report from the abovementioned cantor, Mr. L. Hirschberg:

> Probably not even in the most magnificent temple of anyone's home town was there ever witnessed such intense prayerful devotion us in the small low-ceilinged room with the broken door and the glassless windows and the walls pierced by Shrapnel. From time to time we could hear nearby artillery firing towards Metz, and in the deepest recesses of our hearts we felt as never before the ephemeral nature of our existence and the need to reconcile ourselves with our God, for soon it might be too late.
>
> Many of us, who until then were strangers to the real meaning of Yom Kippur, now experienced it clearly and unforgettably.
>
> Of the 71 Jewish soldiers in the Corps some sixty had appeared. Amongst them were several physicians, a few members of military government, all of them joyously moved to be able to celebrate Yom Kippur. The place of prayer consisted of two small rooms. The lights placed in bottles were burning on a Mizrah table and were flanked by several rifles. The congregation itself, consisting of service men of all branches, was in full military regalia since an alarm could be sounded at any moment. The duties of the cantor were filled by a non-commissioned officer (who in civilian life is a well known merchant from Thorn), who sang simply but with profound understanding. Dr. Blumenstein spoke deeply moving words which fitted the circumstances and which made many of those present shed tears. We parted from each other in an exalted mood....

Dr. Seligmann adds that Yom Kippur services were also held near Paris, in the Synagogue of the Rothschilds' castle at Ferrières. Dr. Seligmann concludes his account with the observation that these services opened the way for the eventual appointment of regular German Jewish chaplains, but not until another war broke out, over forty years later, did anything come of it. Shortly after the beginning of hostilities in 1914 six rabbis were appointed chaplains. One of them was Leo Baeck, and another, Georg Salzberger, formerly of Frankfurt am Main, who now lives in London, England.

Who perpetrated the pious fraud? The suspicion is large that enthusiastic German-Jewish patriots on the American side of the ocean may have exaggerated the original account and may have commissioned a New York engraver to recreate the scene freely. If such was the case, it was a unique American contribution to German nationalism.

The Common Folk in Mendelssohn's Days

$\mathscr{T}$he history of eighteenth-century German Jewry is dominated by the towering figure of Moses Mendelssohn, who is properly regarded as a major influence in advancing and directing the emancipation of his fellow Jews. But it is well to remember that Mendelssohn and his Berlin followers moved in rarefied strata — a number of them even attaining an advanced education and considerable wealth — while the vast majority of German Jews lived in an entirely different universe which for many years was hardly touched by the famous savant. Their life had a character all its own, and it is this, more than Mendelssohn's model, that defined the nature of a community which a few decades after Emancipation would become the seedbed of enormous changes and the birthplace of modern Judaism in all its varieties.

Yet we have heard little about those Jews who were dispersed over Germany's villages and towns. Some Hebrew sources are available, among them Hayyim Joseph David Azulai's travel impressions[1] and Jacob Emden's responsa reflecting social and religious conditions.[2] There is, however, another and in most respects far richer source at our disposal in published form which so far has not been sufficiently exploited — a series of some seventy-odd volumes of reports by Christian missionaries who travelled the land attempting to bring the Gospel to the Jews.

These emissaries were sent out by the Institutum Judaicum, founded and directed in Halle by the Reverend Johann Heinrich Callenberg,[3] a Protestant divine who mounted a lifelong effort to convert the Jews by spreading the faith through full-time missionaries who would meet Jews face to face, even in the smallest villages, in order to bring them the Good News. Though the success of these missionary efforts was modest when measured in actual conversions, the enterprise unwittingly created rich historical materials, for the missionaries faithfully sent reports back to their employer who in turn printed them in order to justify the Institute's existence to its financial backers.[4] No less a personage than Mendelssohn himself was a subject for the Institute's conversionary efforts.[5]

Of course the missionaries' observations were coloured by their goal of conversion and the optimistic notes which the emissaries frequently entered into their correspondence must be seen in that light. After all, it would not do merely to report failure and only a very occasional success.[6] Despite the missionaries' bias, we can learn much from these reports, for the writers had no reason to be less than accurate when they related how Jews lived. Their reports cover all aspects of Jewish life, from people's occupations to housing and business practices; from family affairs and charities to language, education, and religious practices. Drawing upon these reports, this study will concentrate on the social conditions of ordinary Jews in various parts of Germany,[7] a subject until now fairly inaccessible to the student of history.[8]

Even though the Callenberg volumes span more than sixty years, from 1730 to 1790, they reflect remarkably little social change. The intellectual and social ferment of the outside world apparently did not touch the vast majority of German Jews. With few exceptions, poverty and isolation were their common lot, especially in the small communities where they lived in a world apart. Most cities had identifiable Jewish quarters and streets. Only if the number of Jews was small did they live interspersed among the Gentiles, though usually as close to one another as possible and always in easy reach of their synagogue.[9]

Their language has been characterized as "Western Yiddish" by some, and "Judeo-German" (*jüdisch-deutsch*) by others. It was closer to High German than Eastern Yiddish (today referred to simply as "Yiddish"), which became a separate language with its own identifiable grammar and lexicon. German Jews, unlike those in Eastern Europe, lived among German-speaking people and therefore were reasonably acquainted with their language and understood and spoke it, however imperfectly, in its various dialects — while at the same time expanding it with a vocabulary and grammatical variances of their own. The intermingling of these two linguistic streams was precisely what Mendelssohn's biblical translation tried to resolve, and therefore he wrote High German in Hebrew characters. His intention was not, as has often been misstated, to teach German Jews the German language *de novo*, but to teach them *proper* German, a language with which they, who knew street German and spoke Judeo-German, were less familiar.

West German Yiddish was not as distinct a tongue as was (Eastern) Yiddish and possessed an additional feature: a kind of "secret" speech which Jews used among themselves when dealing with Gentiles in a commercial relationship. These linguistic idioms, easily understood by other Jews in the trade, in time became outmoded, though not entirely forgotten, because the Gentile parties learned to understand them.

Elements of Judeo-German itself persisted into the twentieth century as a kind of familial seasoning to Jewish speech, especially in the western reaches of the country. Every Jew whom I knew in my youth in Germany spoke High German but would also understand expressions like *ausgebackene lecho-daudis*, *schmontzes barjontzes*, or *emes bajazzo*.[10]

How did the missionaries view these Jews who spoke a different language and lived a different life? One missionary's judgment was reflected throughout the collection: most Jews were "poor and humble and would be repressed in the presence of a well-groomed man," he wrote.[11] Life was hard for them. The outside world was unfriendly, often inimical, and business relations were governed by mutual caution. A continual refrain runs throughout the missionaries' chronicles of the Jew's response to their fate: times are bad, and we can't remember when they were good.

Despite this response, the missionaries found that Gentiles believed that Jews had money. Though the number of wealthy Jews was very small, these few exceptions were taken to represent the whole.[12] In reality Jewish hardship was intensified by the high cost of living, not only because Jewish ritual needs required special foods and clothes,[13] but because Gentiles would charge Jews higher prices. One writer estimates that the Jewish cost of living was twice that of their neighbours, an exaggeration perhaps, but apparently a common perception among Jews.[14]

As for the Jews' occupations, the missionaries noted a number of craftsmen and professionals, but the majority made their living in petty trade; they were storekeepers, peddlers, and cattle dealers.[15] Agriculture was generally closed to them as were those crafts that required guild membership. Where Jews were restricted from owning land they occasionally got around the law by arrangements with Gentile farmers who were made to appear as the owners. The missionaries rarely saw the peddlers or those working outside the towns, but interacted mostly with Jews who awaited customers in their shops and loan establishments. All too often they found them alone, waiting, and therefore concluded that "all Jews were lazy" and unfit for physical labour or even "regular work."[16] One report even quoted a Jew as having said, "If I really could get an apprentice, and even if I would offer to teach him for nothing, I wouldn't get anyone, for they are too lazy."[17]

The missionaries found tailors, silver and goldsmiths, bookbinders, glaziers, barbers, shoemakers, bakers, dealers in old clothes, an occasional farmer, and entertainers such as musicians, magicians, and acrobats. Travelling preachers would receive pay for their sermons and itinerant booksellers would purvey works which they or others had written. In Halberstadt a Jewish numismatist specialized in old Roman coins[18] and in the Meissen district another bought defective pennies.[19] Other occupations encountered were brewing and distilling of spirits, wine growing, tobacco, and leather works. The reports also noted that Jews dealt with Christian items in business life. A Jewish seal maker filled an order which specified the image of Jesus on the seal,[20] and another even was found selling missionary literature.[21]

Among the professionals, the *melamed* (teacher) was most frequently mentioned; he would either teach a group of children or serve as a private tutor for some wealthy family — the kind of work that gave Mendelssohn his start in Berlin. Teachers were often poorly trained; it was deemed sufficient if they could read, write, and had a reasonable knowledge of prayer book and Torah. Larger communities were able to support full-fledged rabbis, but cantors often needing an additional occupation might be ritual slaughterers or circumcisers as well.

The missionaries did discover a few Jewish physicians with academic training and mentioned this as extraordinary, for instance, when they identified one doctor who studied at the universities of Giessen and Leiden.[22] Occasionally the local rabbi would function as a physician, as Maimonides had in his day.

Women too worked when they could and when their assistance was required. The missionaries noted that women minded the store while their husbands were asleep, buying supplies, attending to religious duties, or away on other business.[23] This might indicate that such caretaking was not a regular occupation for Jewish women, as it frequently was in Eastern Europe. One reference to Jewish cottage industry notes that lace making was "the commonest work" of the women.[24]

In Germany, as in Eastern Europe, Jews were innkeepers, and the missionaries found that the lower-class Gentiles who most often frequented these places could be a source of friction. One amusing report describes some drunks who late in the evening asked for some more alcohol and were refused. As tensions rose the innkeeper's wife began to recite the evening prayers, inducing the raucous guests to depart.[25]

The Jews sometimes used these local inns as a place for assembly or prayer services, especially when they had no synagogue building, a practice which confused the missionaries, one reporter believing that this practice made the innkeeper into the "rabbi" of the village.[26]

We also learn about money-lending from the missionaries. One report quotes interest charged at one Kreutzer a week for every gulden, which would amount to a yearly rate of 52 percent. Another speaks of a rabbi who earned his living loaning funds but enjoyed little standing among his fellow Jews because he lent to Gentiles as well as to Jews.[27] But the reportage is not altogether trustworthy because the missionaries would often not know who was or was not a rabbi. Any literate and bearded man might mistakenly be believed to fit the role.

The majority of Jews whom the missionaries encountered, or chose to encounter, were poor. The disadvantaged have historically been the target of conversionary efforts and therefore the reports should not be taken as the basis for statistical data. Still, they do convey the impression that these poor whom the roving reporters found were not a discrete underclass but a substantial portion of the Jewish population who complained incessantly about their wretched condition.

In addition, a "professional" class of beggars, the *schnorrer*,[28] created problems. Begging was widespread, with children often panhandling for the elderly.[29] A number of communities felt so beset by itinerant beggars that they tried to hustle them out of town before they became a public charge. In Wasserbüdingen there was a Jewish poorhouse outside the town where wandering charity seekers would be accommodated, and in Dessau, Mendelssohn's birthplace, a special poorhouse existed inside the city's gates.[30] The itinerants travelled considerable distances, some of them wandering through Bohemia, Moravia, and on to southern Germany and Holland. In some localities Jews were advised not to give alms to such "travelling Jews," as they were known.[31]

However, many Jews faced the constant threat of being reduced to beggary. If one could not pay the annual head tax one might be forced to leave the community, and join the "travellers," a constant fear at the lower end of the economic scale. In contrast, the few rich assumed the role of princes, the famous court Jews kindling the imagination of many a Jew who naïvely likened their influence to that of the Emperor himself.[32]

But the famous "Jud Suess"— Joseph Suess Oppenheimer, a powerful court Jew who was hanged in 1738 — was not their favourite, for his disastrous fate demonstrated the fragility of Jewish life. Besides, he was said to be a quasi-renegade who did not even observe Yom Kippur. All of this did not prevent him from being a constant topic of discussion, even arguing whether he had a share in the world-to-come.[33]

The rich guarded their shaky position jealously, causing the missionaries to draw some unflattering parallels between them and similarly placed persons in the Christian community.[34] Wealthy Jews would often imitate the habits of their rich Gentile townsmen by ostentatious displays and thereby attract the envy of both Jew and Gentile.[35]

Riches also became a pathway toward assimilation. Of one rich Jew it was said that his major occupation consisted of eating, drinking, and gambling with his non-Jewish associates.[36] It need hardly be added that if such a person eventually "converted," it was likely not from conviction but simply an outflow of his social ambitions and the desire to escape the severe restrictions still placed on Jews in most German areas.

Though Jews tried to live as close to one another as possible, they were not generally ghettoized but dwelled among their Christian neighbours, which made missionary work among them more difficult and which also made for greater caution among Jews. They would not leave their doors open. Even during the day a visitor might pull the bell cord several times before he was answered and might then be asked for an identification before being admitted.[37]

Since in most places in Germany Jews were not allowed to own real estate, they generally inhabited rented and, more often than not, overcrowded and unsanitary dwellings. There were exceptions,[38] but typically the missionaries found Jewish families living in one room where they would eat, sleep, and also do business. In Leipheim a visitor even encountered people selling meat in a room where a sick man was bedded on straw in the corner. In addition, one single room might be the site of sundry occupations, such as two tailors working in the barbershop.[39]

Usually more than one family lived in each house, and in the larger cities, with space restricted and expensive, Jews would enlarge the building by adding storeys, if permitted to do so, one report relating that five storeys were not uncommon. Altogether, Jewish living conditions reflected the economically and socially depressed status of the Jews.[40]

Not surprisingly, it required all their wits to make a living. Even meagre success would lead Gentiles to accuse them of sharp dealing. The missionaries also were quick to point out Jewish shortcomings and note their unethical business practices, to which Jews would reply that Christians generally cheated them and thus forced them to adopt survival tactics. One such report has a frustrated Jew explain his poverty by saying that he could do much better "if he would cheat like other Jews."[41]

Jewish criminals were also part of this society, especially among the *schutzlose Juden*, Jews with no state protection who were, by definition, extra-legal persons. For some reason forced to leave their original homes, they roamed the countryside, being refused admission everywhere and having no way of earning a decent livelihood. They might join bands of thieves, as they did in southern Germany.[42] In Jena two Jewish thieves, Emanuel Heinemann and Hoymer (Hayim) Moses, whose Gentile sobriquets were Carbe and Ingolstädter, were executed for their misdeeds and a special booklet was issued describing their low life and their end.[43] In Frankfurt-am-Main two Jews were accused of having murdered for revenge and a man was broken on the wheel for having slain one Mayer Gabel of Heidelberg.[44] One report tells of a Jew seeking conversion to lighten his punishment and another of a Jew being kept in jail because he had stolen from his *shul*.[45]

Yet, we know from other sources that for the most part Jewish ethical teaching permeated Jewish life, despite the marginal conditions under which these people lived; given the opportunity in the New World, their exemplary ethics attracted special praise from their Gentile neighbours.[46]

These fragments about Jewish existence in eighteenth-century Germany reveal nothing about the success and failure of the conversionary efforts of our reporters, a subject addressed in some of the later, less accessible volumes. The missionaries' reports do provide, however, a glimpse into Jewish life not readily available elsewhere — a small contribution to an understanding of the background of a people who, a hundred years later, would attain middle-class standards, higher education, and widespread integration into German economic and cultural life.

An Interview with Moses Mendelssohn:
The Christian and the Jew

$\mathcal{O}$n June 22, 1784, less than two years before his death, Moses Mendelssohn granted an interview to an unusual visitor named Litsken. He was a travelling Christian missionary who, by his own admission, came to learn from and listen to the great philosopher, rather than try to convert him.

Mendelssohn, who was most reluctant to discuss matters of faith publicly, was quite willing to elucidate his views about Christians and Christianity in this private conversation. He had apparently no inkling that his visitor would set down and later on publish what was said. Of course, there is no assurance that the published record precisely reflects Mendelssohn's views and words. But the very frankness of the interchange has the ring of authenticity. Moreover, where Mendelssohn discusses biblical passages he reflects throughout the comments of Rashi, Ibn Ezra, the Radak, the Ramban, and other pillars of Jewish tradition. Of interest also is Mendelssohn's intimate acquaintance with the New Testament and especially his higher criticism of Mark 16:16. Scholars today have generally reached the same conclusion as Mendelssohn did 175 years ago.

The interview probably lasted several hours. The 10,000-word German text was printed in an obscure collection of missionary letters and remained largely unknown thereafter. It appeared in the so-called Callenberg series as Volume 12 of *Fortgesetzte Nachricht von der zum Heil der Juden errichteten Anstalt, nebst den Auszügen aus den Tagebüchern der reisenden Mitarbeiter*, edited by Justus Israel Beyer (Halle, 1788). The excerpt that follows is in my own translation.

MENDELSSOHN: If we really cared for people we would condemn no one. You claim to be a disciple of Jesus, whom the Scriptures show to have loved everything human and to have taught naught but love and mercy.... How can you deny eternal bliss to those who teach differently from you? I think I am the Christian, and you just bear the name Christian.

[The discussion turns to Mark 16:16 which Mendelssohn believes to be an interpolation. The disputed passage says, "He who believes and is baptized will be saved; but he who does not believe will be condemned."]

MENDELSSOHN: But let us even assume that the passage is a genuine statement by Jesus.... It could, however, never be meant for those who are not Christians, but only for those who are convinced of the truth of Christianity and yet do not act accordingly.... How could the heathen, for instance, believe in Jesus if they never heard of him? Your apostle himself says this and admits that it is not possible for all people to believe in Jesus. How then could God ask the impossible of human beings? How could He condemn people for whom there was no way to believe in Jesus? Why does He not send them apostles as in the beginning?

LITSKEN: There is no dearth of Christian missionaries to the heathen, but unfortunately the preachments find no believers.

MENDELSSOHN: If you were a heathen you would not believe them either. Just imagine that you lived in pagan ignorance, and there came a Catholic, a Lutheran, and a Herrnhuter[1]— every one a missionary who wanted to persuade you to accept Christianity. What would you do? The Catholic teaches one thing of Christ, the Lutheran another, and the Herrnhuter a third. Which of the three parties would you join? I rather think none, and you would remain what you are, namely, a heathen.

[There is a further exchange on missionary activities and then Litsken takes up Psalm 16.]

LITSKEN: If your time permitted I would show you that the whole content of Psalm 16 fits Jesus perfectly. But I came here to learn, not to teach.

MENDELSSOHN: ... I do not doubt for a moment that the passages which you would quote could be interpreted in such a way as to appear as prophecies which were later fulfilled. Many a sword is put in a sheath which does not really belong to it....You don't extract the true meaning from your passages; rather, you superimpose your meaning. You find that your apostles in their writings apply many Old Testament passages to Jesus. Consequently you conclude that all these passages are prophecies about Jesus. In reality the apostles thought of something altogether different. All they meant to say was this: what happened to Jesus is exactly what happened in this or that verse....If someone whom we have befriended repays us with meanness, we might say that David's words apply to us: "Yea, mine own familiar friend, in whom I trusted, who did eat of my bread, hath lifted up his heel against me" [Psalms 41:10]. But who would be foolhardy enough to claim that David was prophesying about us?

[Psalm 22 is discussed next. Litsken gives it the traditional Christian interpretation, applying it to Jesus.]

MENDELSSOHN: Your convictions are not mine. You are a Christian and you ought to have your convictions. But tell me, how can the beginning of the Psalm refer to Jesus? How can Jesus say, "My God, my God, why hast Thou forsaken me, and art far from my help at the words of my cry? O my God, I call by day, but Thou answerest not; and at night, and there is no surcease for me."

It is impossible for this to have been spoken by Jesus, for according to your teaching Jesus *had to suffer*. He knew this and suffered willingly. Now, if I undergo suffering voluntarily, without force and because I want to do so, then how can I complain to others about my predicament? How can I object or even call for help from others? Yet this is precisely what Jesus does, when he wants to be helped by God, his Father. How can Jesus complain that his help is far if he needed no help, since in assuming his role of suffering he knew what it implied? He who complains and calls for help does not suffer gladly....Can this complaining person who cries for help be Jesus? No, I am convinced it could only be David....

...But how could Jesus have been forsaken by God? Do you not teach that this same suffering Jesus was God Himself — how then could he have been forsaken by God? If until he expired he was God, he could not possibly cry, "My God, why hast Thou forsaken me?"

You said before that Jews living as they do among Christians could read the New Testament and thus convince themselves of the truth of the Christian faith. Yet, when we meet such inconsistent teachings which utterly contradict our own divinely revealed principles, how can we acquire your convictions by way of reason? You see, as long as these obvious contradictions in your Christian religion remain as stumbling stones, how can you wonder that an honourable Israelite will stand firmly by his Judaism? For if a thinking Jew would find some reasons to accept Christianity, these reasons would dissolve as soon as he learns that Christians multiply the Godhead. The teaching of God's unity is the foundation of our worship and, it would seem to me, of all true worship. A real Jew would rather suffer death than to forsake his faith in the one indivisible God. Christians cannot find any way in which they can make us understand and comprehend their trilogy — and certainly they cannot do it by declaring it a mystery which must be taken on faith and which reason cannot fathom....

...The teaching of an unchanging un-multiplied God is the noblest and most precious jewel which Judaism has preserved amidst all trials and tribulations. Should we exchange this jewel for an uncertain, self-contradictory dogma of a triune God, and give up our heaven-secured faith in the One God? Never! And if God will damn us, He will do so because of our misdeeds, but not because we find your religion unacceptable....

...Pressing affairs will not permit me to prolong our conversation. God did not use the Old Testament to reveal a natural, general, universal religion, nor did He use it for the exposition of dogmas and prophecies. Rather, through the Bible, God merely gave the Jewish people a human law by which it should be governed. Biblical law applies to the exercise of religion and is therefore of an external, earth-bound nature. It belongs to the realm of human conduct, not to the spiritual realm of reverence for God. The true religion of the soul is suggested to us by our common sense. It is this natural religion which, as I read it, was preached by Jesus. Not mysteries and idle speculations. No! His teachings were not meant to exercise human reason and memory, they were designed to train the heart and to express themselves in good, noble, virtuous works, in a love of man which is unpretending, active and universal. The morality of your Jesus is the finest and most perfect which I have found anywhere in the books of wisdom and he who would criticize it is not worthy of being called a man. Happy and blessed indeed is he who lives in accordance with this morality, be he Christian or Jew. For methinks that God will someday ask us what good we accomplished in this world, not what we believed.

That is the express teaching of your Jesus, that one should love all men, even one's enemies; that one should feed the hungry, give drink to the thirsty, clothe the naked, visit[2] the prisoners. In one word: do good for those who are in need; for God looks only to this, and He will grant man eternal bliss only because of such works. This is true religion and the right way to honour God — not through faith in mysteries, but through works of love. He who follows this religion can rightly say that Jesus is his saviour and that he will attain salvation because of Jesus....

I wish that all Christians would make love of man their first obligation. Instead of bothering their heads over systems of faith and method, over prophecies and mysteries, they should strive to cultivate and practice the spirit of goodness and service toward everyone — even toward non-Christians. Would that Christians had always thought in this fashion and had made the love of man their first law! Millions of people would not have lost their lives. No one would have heard of exile and expulsion, of Crusades and Inquisition, of the Thirty Years' War, and of uncounted evils which blind fanaticism and the spirit of persecution have spread across the earth. Nature is horrified over the history of suffering, the tribulations, the unheard-of cruelties....

In many countries matters have not improved up to this very day. Frederick the Great has contributed to the betterment of the world, for with his policy of religious tolerance he has re-introduced the love of man in his state. This philosopher and enlightened Christian grants to all the liberty to reach heaven in their separate ways, if only they consider the love of man their duty and act accordingly. Nothing else is asked of them; and Jesus, if I am right, asked nothing else of his followers. Love man and you please God, whether you are Christian, Jew, or heathen, for the name does not matter. You see: on this I build my religion.

Please forgive me now, we must leave off here, my affairs await me.

Germans and Jews:
The Symbiosis That Failed

$\mathscr{I}$was born in Münster, Westphalia, a pleasant university town where my mother had also been born. When I was very young, our family moved to Berlin, and I remained there until my emigration to the United States in 1935.

Strange to contemplate: the first memory of my life that has stayed with me is the waving of flags and popular jubilation. It was, my parents told me later, the celebration of Germany's victory at Tannenberg over the Russians during the First World War. But other childhood memories are more sombre. My father was in uniform, two of my mother's brothers died as officers in the German army, the country suffered from a blockade which restricted our diet severely, and my selective memory of childhood recalls also that during the summers I did not wear shoes, leather being in short supply.

When the war ended, and Germany had been defeated and the Kaiser had fled to Holland, there was fighting in the streets of Berlin. For a young boy, those were exciting times, but, of course, the deeper implications of the events then unfurling were unknown to me. I did not know about the Hitler *putsch* in Munich, but what I do remember is the shock and agony created in our household by the murder of Walter Rathenau, Germany's foreign minister and the first Jew to be elevated to such high position. My father was more deeply upset than I had ever seen him before. It was the summer of 1922.

Much later did I comprehend what went through his mind: a descendant of an old Hessian-Jewish family that had come to Germany probably

314

before 1500, Father considered the country his natural habitat, as it had been for his forebears. In the murder of Rathenau — a Jew more in name than in substance — he felt that a direct blow had been struck at German Jewry, and thus at himself, by people who wanted to warn all Jews that their place in the country could never be secure. He knew that Rathenau was killed not so much because of any policies that he had instituted, but because he was a born Jew, and, therefore, fundamentally unacceptable. To be sure, the murderers were apprehended and convicted, and one of them later even wrote a book asking for forgiveness, yet the wound left a scar on the soul of German Jewry, and my father never forgot it. Neither did I and, as I grew up, I began to understand what it really betokened.

While my grandparents on both sides were Orthodox, our small nuclear family lived a Liberal Jewish life, which in American terms may best be described as Conservative: *kashrut* flavoured with ritual permissiveness and a theology which was Reform in all its aspects. We always went to services for Kabbalat Shabbat, while on Shabbat mornings I, like all young people in Germany, attended public school. That was one of the things we took for granted, for school lasted for six days. While we had one student in class who did not write on Shabbat, and was given permission to take his exams on some other day, my parents allowed me to write and also to ride to school. We were moderate Liberals, with the emphasis on Liberals.

In high school I knew that we five Jewish students were somehow set apart, and we took that, too, for granted. We took it for granted that we were different. We were living in Germany and were German citizens, but it was clear that we were not like "them." Political and cultural anti-Semitism was an accepted backdrop to our lives, and with the rise of the Nazis it invaded our classroom. Still, it was the shock of my young life when I found that the boy who had sat next to me for the last six years one day sported a swastika in his lapel. I never spoke to him again.

I entered law school in 1930, and refused to join either of the two Jewish fraternities. For that matter, I joined no other group at first. I suppose I was an unpolitical person and my interests lay more in sports and chess. In time, though, I was attracted to the Social Democrats, and participated in some of their street battles with the Nazi student federation. Somehow, even this left no permanent impression on me. Perhaps the main reason was that I was simply too immature to take a wider view.

But, certainly, I never possessed any German national sentiments. Those were clearly reserved for non-Jews. To be sure, there was a small segment of the Jewish population that was super-nationalistic, but they were laughed at by the people I knew and not taken seriously, and their numbers remained insignificant. In our home, all forms of nationalism — which at that time included Zionism as well — were looked at with a good deal of suspicion, for in Germany, nationalism was then, and had always been, the property of those who considered the nation their exclusive possession, something that by definition excluded all foreign elements, and especially Jews. When I grew up, the Republic's flag, black, red and gold, was never accepted by the right-wing element. For them, the true German colours were black, white, and red.

As I look back, the symbolism of the flag revealed a good deal about the state of the country: it had no perception of itself and it was divided in its very heart. And we, as Jews, though we fervently supported the fragile democracy which was then ours, had no real share in the country's decision. It was "they" who would have to chart the direction of the land. We, as Jews, seemed to stand aside. We were in Germany, and had been there for a long time. We were citizens. But we were not like "them"— we were not of Germany in the full sense.

Much later I read the discussion then going on in the intellectual Jewish and Gentile circles. German writers, from Fichte on, had spoken with increasing enthusiasm and conviction of *Deutschtum*, which may best be rendered as "the essence of being German."

Just what this betokened was hard to describe. Certainly, it has a *völkisch* element to it, a belief that there was something inherent in the German people that was good and noble. The intellectuals of the pre-Nazi era would describe it as a combination of pride in reliability and industriousness, the freedom to think, to have a world vision; it meant esthetics, both cultural and social, a progressive social policy, a sense of order, correctness, and obligation. In our day, it is hard to think that these values were once ascribed to Germany by its best citizens, including the Jews.

It is not my task to describe why and how the German nation came to identity itself in this fashion, or how the French did it in theirs, or, for that matter, how Americans came to consider themselves as bearers of a manifest destiny. Let it be said merely that, in fact, there were markers by which Jews could measure themselves in Germany, and it is important to remember that the Jews of Eastern Europe looked at their Western neighbour with admiration and at its universities with the greatest respect. Germany was the intellectual mecca of the world. It had a musical tradition second to none, and a scientific establishment that was clearly the world's leader. It was here that the major Jewish movements we know today had their origin. Not only Reform was born there, but so were Conservatism and Orthodoxy as well as Agudat Yisrael, and so, in large measure, was political Zionism. It was in Germany that the Jewish National Fund was organized. It was a Jew of the German cultural realm, Theodor Herzl, who was the father of the State of Israel, and when I once asked Nahum Goldmann, the principal spirit of recent Diaspora Jewish leadership, what he, a child of the East and a world citizen, considered himself to be *culturally*, he unhesitatingly said, as late as 1970, "a German, of course."

Leading Jewish intellectuals held that there was an inner link between being Jewish and the essence of German culture, between *Judentum* and *Deutschtum*. This relationship was often debated and discussed, both by anti-Semites and by Jews. In order fully to comprehend the depth of this sentiment, it is instructive to listen to Hermann Cohen, who, in the early stages of the First World War, when the United States had not as yet joined the conflict, appealed to American Jews not to believe the stories then circulating about German atrocities in Belgium but, rather, to look at the German record, at the real nature of that land, its ideals and accomplishments, and, above all, to understand the close link between *Deutschtum* and *Judentum* — between the essence of being a German and of being a Jew.

Cohen's letter projects for us, through the mind and pen of a man who was one of the keenest thinkers of his time, the depth of the belief in the reality of the German-Jewish symbiosis. He wrote:

> Moses Mendelssohn was a German, a German thinker, a German writer, the genuine equal friend of the great Lessing. Like Luther, Mendelssohn translated our Pentateuch out of his German soul, and made it possible for us to enter the world of German culture through the German language. The entire rejuvenation of our worship occurred first in Germany and through the German spirit. It is the work of German culture and German religiosity

to which our own sentiment felt itself drawn at once, be-cause the historical spirit of Protestantism has also been the vital nerve of our own medieval religious philosophy since Saadya Gaon. The reform of Judaism became a Ger-man reform, and, from Germany and through Germans, it migrated to you [in America].

Dear brethren in America! You will understand me now if I say to you: every Jew of the Occident must, in addition to his political fatherland, recognize also the motherland of his religiosity as the basic esthetic force and centre of his cultural sentiments — and that is Germany which he must honour and love. I have the conviction that even in every educated Russian Jew there lives this admira-tion for German education; therefore, I also have the con-fidence that the Russian Jew follows our armed struggle with Russia with special hopes in his Jewish heart....

It is difficult to resist the temptation of being a prophet. If often we despaired of Russia's future, still to-day, because of its machinations, a great hope has risen. Germany, the homeland of humanitarianism, of the free-dom of conscience and of social welfare policies, has been called to battle by its enemies all around, who, though they are civilized nations, have made a compact with Rus-sia. I have the feeling that some day a divine judgment will come on Russia, not in the least because of its un-disguised measures for the extermination of the Jewish people. Every Jew who is convinced of the cultural power of his religion and, therefore, of its right to life, must deem himself happy if his patriotism accords to him at least neutrality in this war, but he must envy us German Jews who can battle for our Fatherland, borne at the same time by the pious conviction that we will obtain human rights for the greater part of our co-religionists. Germany, the motherland of Occidental Jewry, the land of intellectual freedom and ethics, Germany will, by its victory, found justice and peace amongst the peoples of the world. We trust in the logic of our fate and of our history.[1]

The liberals, many of whom clustered around the *Centralverein* (C.V.), firmly believed that Cohen's philosophy provided the best basis for the fight against the persistent outcroppings of anti-Semitism. In 1914, shortly after the outbreak of the war, Ludwig Hollander wrote:

> Just as those on the battlefield who belong to the Jewish faith strike a blow for the honour of Jewry as they struggle for the honour of Germany, so, too, those Jews who remain behind on the home front can be certain that everyone who lives and works quietly and modestly for the wellbeing of the German fatherland and its inhabitants also contributes today to the honour of the Jewish name. Such Jews will cause many of the aspersions of the past to be cast aside, and the German way of life will permit the rays from the bright light of its justice to shine ever more strongly upon Germany's Jewish children.[2]

Three years later, in 1917, Rabbi Felix Goldmann of Oppeln, addressing the general assembly of the *Centralverein*, declared that the organization's primary mission was the education of the German public concerning German-Jewry's "membership im *Deutschtum*."[3] Hugo Sonnenfeld voiced a similar opinion:

> The Jew has been rooted in Germany since long ago. Jews already lived along the Rhine during the time of the Roman Empire; no one has the right to declare them foreigners upon German soil. Yet, we have been treated as such; our children have had their rights curtailed, and discrimination and evil against us have been tolerated. It is precisely because of this, however — precisely because prejudice, deprivation, and humiliation have not been able to impair it — that our love for our German fatherland distinguishes itself.... Yet, precisely at this time of danger and suffering for our fatherland do we feel above all how precious our German fatherland is to us.... We swear before everyone that at this time the Jews will forget all that

has been done to them; they will show the fatherland that for them, no sacrifice is too great.[4]

Cohen himself believed anti-Semitism to be a non-malignant, transient phenomenon, and suggested that the idea that Jews were equal citizens had taken deeper root in Germany than anywhere else.[5]

Cohen's statements on the nexus between *Deutschtum* and *Judentum* exerted a deep and lasting influence upon the Jewish defence leadership, which employed them consistently during the final years of the war in support of time strategy of non-confrontation. But not everyone shared his view. Thus, the Zionists would agree only that Russia was the enemy. Heinrich Loewe wrote in early August 1914, even before war had broken out:

> We are confronted by the harshest tyranny, by the bloodiest cruelty and darkest reaction.... Our armour will secure not only the security of our women and children against the enemies of the country; we protect not only home and hearth of our own families; they are at the same time the only hope of millions and millions of the oppressed in the Russian empire.... As Jews, we have still another reckoning with the barbarians of the east.[6]

But, otherwise, the German Zionist movement rejected the notion that a shallow patriotism would be a means of integrating *Judentum* and *Deutschtum*. Kurt Blumenfeld, mentor of the movement, put it strongly:

> Jewish circles who are primarily concerned with the battle against anti-Semitism have never made a serious attempt to understand the inner reasons for anti-Semitism. The courage to understand that anti-Semitism is not only a misunderstanding, not only a haphazard, temporary attitude, can never be understood by people who do not have the courage truly to be Jewish.... Never has a battle been fought with poorer means than the so-called battle against anti-Semitism. In truth, it is nothing but a battle against Semitism, against the Jewish particularity

itself.... By capitulating continually before anti-Semitism, one pretends to defeat it. Cowardly mimicry is the standard weapon in this struggle. [7]

A classic debate between Martin Buber and Cohen exposed the opposing views in their full intellectual dimension. While Buber, an Eastern European Jew by birth and tradition, had also come to believe that "the German spirit" had a particular attraction, his Zionist conviction pointed him in a different direction. He criticized Cohen's insistence that Jews were "German citizens of the Jewish faith," and that such a definition would be a proper base for the fight against anti-Semitism. He argued that it was the primary task of the Jew to find himself and his roots, and not to seek integration with another culture, however prized it might be. It was Cohen's thesis, put forward in his rejoinder to Buber, that *Deutschtum* embodied supreme Jewish religious values, and that Jewish amalgamation into German society was a necessary condition for the realization of the Jewish messianic ideal.[8]

Franz Rosenzweig, then still a soldier, also disapproved of Cohen's identification of *Deutschtum* and *Judentum*, and wrote:

> To be a German means to be *fully* responsible for one's nation, to harmonize not only with Goethe, Schiller, and Kant, but also with the others, and especially the trashy and mediocre ones, the assessor, the fraternity student, the petty clerk, the pig-headed peasant, the stiff schoolteacher; the true German must either take all these to his heart or else suffer from them.... Cohen, however, has only Europeanism; there is no genuine Germanism for it to combine with, and Judaism, of which he has plenty, is notoriously incapable of cross-breeding. So, in the man everything remains merely juxtaposed, while in his writing we find the mad acrobatics of *Deutschtum* and *Judentum* in which Cohen, after speculating upon the Christian element in the German, proceeds to pronounce this element Jewish.[9]

After the notorious wartime census of the Jews he wrote:

> We are Germans; this you can safely say about our pol-
> itical affiliation, as long as this state which "counts" so
> wonderfully still recognizes us amongst its citizens.... The
> people, however, in contrast to the state, do not count us
> among themselves.[10]

George Masse avers that, while most German Jews succumbed to the almost irresistible temptation to share to the full the German war experience,

> after the war, many had a rude awakening and recap-
> tured the liberal and Enlightenment tradition. At that
> time, establishment figures like [Leo] Baeck had more
> in common with the left wing Jewish intellectuals than
> they might have cared to admit. Both believed that man
> must be the end and never the means, and that war per-
> verted the inherent virtues of man.[11]

As soon as the conflict was over, and the dogs of war had been reined in, anti-Semitism, which during the conflict had been confined to right-wing writings, now became vicious and violent. The frustrations of the German people over Versailles, and the destruction of the middle class in the wake of unchecked inflation, prepared a fertile ground for Hitler's propaganda. And, while the earlier Cohen had talked of the German-Jewish symbiosis as a reality, the popular German novelist Jakob Wassermann saw a new reality and took a directly opposite view. It reflected a view which abandoned the euphoric hopes that the common war experience had engendered. Written in 1921, a mere six years later than Cohen's appeal, Wassermann's disappointment with Germany was as profound as it was memorable to young people like me.

> *It is in vain* to adjure the nation of poets and drinkers
> in the name of its poets and its thinkers. Every prejudice
> that one believed overcome brings forth a thousand new
> maggots like a carcass.
> *It is in vain* to present the right cheek after the left
> one has been struck. It does not make them hesitant

in the least, it does not touch them, it does not disarm them: they will strike the right cheek also.

It is in vain to cast words of reason into the raving tumult of words. They say: "What, he dares to make sound? Shut up his face!"

It is in vain to be an example. They say: "We know nothing, we have seen nothing, we have heard nothing."

It is in vain to seek obscurity. They say: "The coward! His bad conscience forces him to hide away."

It is in vain to go amongst them and offer them one's hand. They say: "How dare he with his Jewish impudence!"

It is in vain to be loyal to them, either as a fellow-fighter, or as a fellow-citizen. They say: "He is like Proteus, he can be anything."

It is in vain to help them break the chains of slavery from their arms. They say: "He has probably made his profit doing so."

It is in vain to neutralize the poison. They brew it afresh.

It is in vain to live for them or to die for them. They say: "He is a Jew."[12]

Without knowing it, or understanding its deeper implications, I became aware that the German-Jewish symbiosis had failed. I should add quickly that this did not mean that therefore I would contemplate emigration. Not at all. Living as a Jew with, and amongst, Germans was a condition of life that had been with my family and the rest of German Jewry for many centuries. It was an accepted fact, and one became accustomed to it as a natural aspect of daily life. In pre-Nazi days, during the Republic, all positions were theoretically open to us, and I firmly contemplated becoming either a career diplomat or a judge.

As for being Jewish, this, too, was a natural part of my life. It meant that I had a certain ethical and religious tradition which was different from "theirs"— one that in my everyday existence was, in those days, secured by law. I don't ever remember saying or thinking that I was "a German"— I was simply a German Jew. Being a Jew was the noun and carried the weight of my self-definition. "German" was merely the adjective that described the special aspect of my Jewishness. I was first and foremost a Jew.

Then came the ascent of Hitler to the chancellorship, and the torch parade of the storm troopers through the streets of Berlin. Even then we believed that, in the course of time, there would be once again a change of government, and extreme German nationalism would give way to that steady, though, at times, unpleasant, relationship between Germans and Jews.

All this was, for me at least, shattered on April 1, 1933. That date was my mother's birthday and had always been celebrated with great aplomb, but in 1933 it became the day also of the Nazi boycott of all Jewish establishments, the day of the official degradation of the German Jew, and his official separation from the German people. The symbiosis which had never fully succeeded was now being publicly dissolved and declared not only to be a failure, but an existential impossibility. Four days later, the Zionist weekly, *Die Jüdische Rundschau*, carried an editorial by Robert Weltsch. It was entitled "Tragt ihn mit Stolz, den gelben Fleck" (Wear the Yellow Badge with Pride).

The badge of which Weltsch spoke was not as yet affixed to our clothing. That came later. It was, however, from now on the ineluctable mark of distinction affixed to the soul of every Jew simply because of his Jewishness.

On that day, Robert Weltsch became our prophet, speaking with a voice as incisive as one for whom the title *navi* is usually reserved. The last paragraph of his editorial read:

> The mark of the Jew was pressed upon all Jews of Germany on the first of April. Everyone knows who is a Jew. Evasion or hiding are no longer possible. The Jewish answer is clear — it is the short sentence which the prophet Jonah spoke: *Ivri anokhi.* Yes, a Jew. To say "yes," to be Jewish, that is the moral sense of the present events. The times are too agitated to allow for argumentation. Let us hope that quieter times will come. We Jews, we can defend our honour. We think of all those who for 5,000 years were called Jews and were stigmatized as

such. We are reminded that we are Jews. We say "yes" and wear the yellow badge with pride.[13]

But there were still the voices amongst us for whom the breach between Jewishness and Germanness was only temporary. For them, the essentials of being a Jew were paralleled by the best that was inherent in true German culture. They felt that the symbiosis had suffered a temporary but not a permanent setback. Amongst these was none other than Martin Buber, who wrote during those days:

> With all the national relationships into which the Jewish people has entered, with all the problems implied thereby, none has been as fruitful as the German-Jewish tie. The living together of *Deutschtum* and *Judentum* has in our day reached its crisis. Out of this we must grasp the present task of Jewish popular education in Germany. Today we need not disassociate from *Deutschtum*, with which we have had an inner relationship which nothing that Germans do can change.... To say this has nothing to do with those empty declarations of love and loyalty which we in our days hear occasionally amongst German Jewry. It means, rather, a concentration on Judaism, a new binding of the first bondedness in the hope of a covenant. We must make necessity the father of a great virtue.[14]

In this respect Buber was much like Weltsch. Both wanted to use the crisis as an opportunity for deepening Jewish knowledge, Jewish pride and Jewish identity. In many ways, Buber represents the paradigm of the symbiosis that failed, but which until the last moment remained an ideal for him. He, a lifelong Zionist, who had already participated in a Zionist Congress in 1899, and was a child of Eastern Europe, had nevertheless come to identify himself with *Deutschtum* — without thereby losing anything of his Jewishness. On the contrary, he always considered one to reinforce the other.

Today, with the shadow of the Nazi experience hovering over our perception of what Germany was like, such an identification seems almost incomprehensible — yet it was there. There were many Jews like

Buber and Cohen who believed that there was something in the German soul that spoke to the highest ideals of humanity, intellectually as well as morally. And it was with that aspect that Jews would — and could — feel an affinity. Therefore, one should not be surprised that it was not until 1938, literally the last moment, that Buber the Zionist took up the opportunity to make aliyah.

In retrospect, one should not blame German Jews for being short-sighted or unduly nationalistic. The symbiosis which they felt was a reality did not have any "rah-rah" quality to it. There was much less identification of Jews with Germany than there has been of American Jews with the United States. In America, the Jews saw the opportunity for living freely and untrammelled, without the strictures of the Old World, and so they made America their own, with an enthusiasm and abandon quite unknown anywhere in Europe.

In Germany, in pre-Hitler days, the identification was of a different nature. It had to do less with liberty and free access to any opportunities than with intellectual aspiration, with a way of treating life in an orderly and thoughtful fashion, of valuing education and of making *Bildung* the foundation of one's worth. The symbiosis of which German Jews dreamt was not of the material kind and it was not political. It had to do with intellectual affinity and with an outlook on life which had an identifiably worthwhile character. That the symbiosis failed is not a blot on Jewish memory. German Jews were not any less farsighted than American Jews — and it is well to remember that there are many, especially Israelis, who continue to preach the concept of *shelilat hagolah* (the worthlessness of Diaspora) and include in this dire warning American Jews as well. They, too, say, "Get out before it is too late."

I cannot here discuss the oft-studied and debated subject of the reasons why the German-Jewish symbiosis never had a chance. For this, I refer the reader to the works of Peter Gay and George L. Mosse.[15] The latter, especially, described the nature of the *völkisch* current in German self-perception, which excluded the Jew, which exclusion found its virulent expression in the anti-Semitism of the late nineteenth century and forward. In Fritz K. Ringer's words, "Mosse describes the anti-Semites' hero as 'the settled farmer, the traditional burgher, the provincial — the philistine. National Socialism, says Mosse, was the ultimate victory of the 'philistine with a soul.'"[16]

Peter Gay therefore disputes the oft-heard idea that the advent of Hitler was an historical accident:

> Hitler was neither an unwelcome invader nor an un-caused accident. Much in the German situation of the nineteenth and early twentieth centuries pointed to him, or to someone like him.... There is no need to exchange the tendentious condemnation of the whole German past for an equally tendentious denial of all antecedents, in that past, for the Nazi trauma. There was significant continuity between the Germany of the nineteenth and that of the twentieth centuries, but there was equally significant discontinuity.[17]

Because there was both continuity and discontinuity, says Gay, one cannot speak of Nazism as a predictable event that grew out of its antecedents. Rather, it was both unique and, at the same time, founded solidly in German history.

We who grew up in Germany did not know of this scenario. I had no idea that "they" considered me the antithesis to rootedness, that I was the representative of an intolerable modernism which the German *Spiessbürger* — the quintessential philistine — was unable to comprehend, much less to conquer. It was Nazism that helped him do just that, but what Jew was there who lived his life in Germany with the comprehension of today's analysts?

Seen from the latter-day perspective of history, there were, indeed, landmarks which signified danger and discontinuity.

For one, Germans were part of an essentially homogeneous nation, in language and culture. To be sure, they had regional differences. Bavarians were not Prussians; still, their German bondedness was clear and historically unmistakable, despite the multiple divisions which had marked the country during the previous century. It was this basic homogeneity that made it difficult for Jews to be accepted. Cultural pluralism was, in Germany, a non-starter.

But, in addition, Germans were more than a nation, they were a people, a *Volk*. And Jews, too, were a *Volk*, and, therefore, *other* by definition. They, too, insisted on being who they were, and the misconceptions about

German Jewry as being highly assimilationist are a gross misreading of their true history.[18] Of course, there was assimilation, especially in the large cities, as it existed and exists everywhere in the Diaspora. But, as a whole, German Jewry was also the fertile soil from which the great Jewish spiritual and political movements of these last 150 years sprang. Jews never abandoned the notion of Jewish peoplehood, and most were aware on some level that a fundamental tension existed between being Jewish in Germany and being part of the nation.

A further consideration relates to the intellectual heritage of Germany. Its leadership considered itself to be the bearer of a world mission which was salvational in nature. They thought and taught that Germany was unique, which was, in its way, a competitive claim with the Jewish insistence on specialness.

Therefore, taken all in all, the symbiosis was doomed, although no one could have predicted the excesses of anti-Semitism which wrote such a terrible conclusion to the failure.

Franz Rosenzweig had his own way of describing this riddle-laden relationship. When he was asked whether it should be "Germans and Jews" or "Germans or Jews," his answer was that, in the final analysis, this would have to be left to God. Perhaps, he ventured, sometimes it was one, and another time, it was the other. The symbiosis will both succeed and fail, and Jews will be at times part of their environment and then experience a fracture.

The German-Jewish relationship was a troubled and, in its heyday, a glorious one as well. The fact that it dissolved in a river of blood and misery was not, and could not have been, foreseen, and the basic problem which it betokened attends us and any Diaspora community as well. The question of German Jewry was solved by history. What it might be for us is something that we need to contemplate in our day.

The Legal Dimension

Hate Propaganda

(Review of The Report of the Special Committee on Hate Propaganda in Canada, Ottawa, 1966)

In January 1965, after a good deal of public controversy, the Minister of Justice appointed a special committee to study and report upon the problems related to the dissemination of varieties of "hate propaganda." Professor Maxwell Cohen, dean of the faculty of law, McGill University, became the chairman of the committee, members of which were Dr. J.A. Corry, principal of Queen's University; L'Abbé Gerard Dion of Laval University; Mr. Saul Hayes, QC, of the Canadian Jewish Congress; Professor Mark R. MacGuigan of the University of Toronto; Mr. Shane McKay, editor of the *Winnipeg Free Press*; and Professor Pierre Elliott Trudeau of the University of Montreal.

Ten months later they submitted the report which is here under review, and early in 1966 the Report was printed and made public. There can be little question that the 327-page document represents a milestone among the inquiries into a complex legal problem, which has been under consideration in many countries, and especially in the United Kingdom. The report's breadth of approach, its scholarly apparatus, and its amassment of relevant documentary material will render it a classic reference work — and this regardless of the law that will or will not be based on its recommendations. For here perhaps more than elsewhere, the law meets not merely altered economic, political, and social conditions, but it confronts that subtle and yet decisive element in the regulations of social relationship, the psychology of interpersonal behaviour and its effect on the common weal.

"Hate," says the report, "is as old as man and doubtless as durable. This report explores what it is that a community can do to lessen some of man's intolerance and to proscribe its gross exploitation."

The authors of the report freely acknowledge that not every use of human communication could or should be controlled by law. Yet every society must from time to time draw certain lines where the "intolerable and the impermissible coincide" and, in the opinion of the public as well as the government, the time to do so had come. The committee tackled the difficult job of defining such limits in an area both sensitive and resistant to ordinary definitions: the power of human speech. In doing so the committee has produced a substantial and, what is unusual under such circumstances, a readable document.

I

Before proceeding to an evaluation of its contents it might be well to survey briefly the areas covered by the report. The document starts with a brief analysis of the scope of the freedom of speech, then turns to an examination of hate propaganda in Canada, past and present, and surveys the recent increase in hate materials in various provinces. In a brief but worthwhile chapter, the document deals with the socio-psychological effects of hate propaganda and the role of law and education as controls. Then in its most important section the Commission turns to a discussion of the ability or inability of our present laws to deal with the present exacerbated conditions of inter-group tension, and it concludes with a series of recommendations. Principally they are the following:

The advocacy or promotion of genocide should be an indictable offence and liable to imprisonment for five years.

Incitement to hatred or contempt against identifiable groups, where such incitement is likely to lead to a breach of peace, should be either an indictable offence (liable to imprisonment for two years) or in some cases an offence punishable by summary conviction.

Those who wilfully communicate statements which promote hatred or contempt against any identifiable groups are liable in a like manner.

No offence will have occurred if proof can be brought that the statements communicated were not only true but that they were relevant to a subject of public interest and that the discussion was in fact for the public benefit, and that the one who makes the communication had reasonable grounds to believe it to be true. The recommendations make it clear that in such a case the burden of proof lies on the accused.

What is an identifiable group? Says the report in its list of definitions: "Any section of the public distinguished by religion, colour, race, language, ethnic or national origin."

The report then turns to six appendices of which the first three are the most important: a discussion of seditious libel and related offences in England, the United States, and Canada; a survey dealing with socio-psychological analyses of hate propaganda (including a highly relevant examination of the effects of hate propaganda upon members of the target group); and a survey of hate propaganda in Canada. There is also a discussion of private members' bills introduced at previous times, and a survey of hate legislation in other countries, including the United Nations. It was unfortunate that the British Race-Relations Bill was presented too late; its inclusion in the Cohen report would have made a valuable contribution.

The report has of course become more than an exercise in legal scholarship and philosophy, since Bill S–49, which on November 7, 1966, was introduced into the Senate of Canada by the Honourable Senator Connolly, PC, was based upon the committee's recommendations. This bill, representing the intent of the Canadian government, in substance reproduces the recommendations of the Cohen report, albeit with a few changes, one of which we shall have occasion to comment upon. All discussions of the Cohen report must therefore be coloured by the introduction of Bill S–49. However, this is as the framers of the report would no doubt wish it, since it was their hope that suitable legislation might ensue from their recommendations.

II

While on the whole the report has received widespread praise, it has been attacked, predictably, on the issue of free speech. Usually the argument has been phrased in philosophic language when it should have been couched in practical terms. The cry is raised that the committee's report endangers the exercise of free speech, when it is precisely with this issue that the report deals very carefully and when it is precisely in order to guard free speech that the report was framed in its present form. "Freedom of expression is a main cornerstone of our way of life," says the committee, and it adds that in any discussion of placing limits upon this freedom "the case for restraint must be shown to be very strong indeed."

Freedom of speech never was unlimited, is not unlimited now, nor will it ever be. There is indeed very little support for individual freedom as an absolute right, to be protected at all times, at all costs, and under all circumstances. The most that can be said is that there is a strong presumption in favour of freedom of expression, stronger than in any other of the important civil liberties; to say therefore (as it has been said) that the committee rode roughshod over precious Canadian liberties is an argument which cannot be taken seriously.

What can be taken seriously, however, is the question whether the restraints suggested by the committee are, or are not, already covered by present laws. The committee thinks they are not, and it proceeded to prove its point and does so cogently.

III

The reason for a gap between existing laws and present public needs is not hard to find, for the political and social circumstances which governed our past legal practices have been profoundly altered since 1933. The widespread introduction of laws forbidding discrimination in employment practices and the limitation of "freedoms" with regard to the incitement to group hatred which have been imposed in a score of states around the world is vivid testimony to this change in human society. Canada's creation of the committee and the subsequent introduction of Bill S–49 are merely the belated recognition of an existing sociological and psychological condition. Here as elsewhere, changed conditions necessitate a change of law.

Yesterday freedom of speech was deemed to be one of the primary safeguards of the individual vis-à-vis the incursions of a restrictive and potentially repressive government. In the tradition of Rousseau,

Montesquieu, and Paine it was a primary function of the law to protect the individual citizen from authority. But during the past generation we have experienced a profound alteration in our social structure. The "individual citizen" still exists in theory and in law. But because of the vast growth of urban centres with their concomitant anonymity and debasement of individual significance, men have found it increasingly difficult to identify themselves either as individuals or as members of a total society and have looked for intermediary groups from which they could derive their identity. In a sense we have returned to the kind of stratification operative in medieval days, when guilds, for instance, far more than modern unions, were that medium through which the individual both made his livelihood and gained his sense of public identity. Under vastly changed circumstances, this is the kind of internal social regrouping which we experience today. Consequently, what happens to the group with which a person identifies himself most intimately is of more than passing significance to him. If the group is threatened, his very identity stands in doubt; if the group is secure, his personal freedom is more secure.

This new stratification antedated the Nazi deviation of 1933-45, but it was dramatized in those years as never before, and the attending tragedy left its marks upon the post-Nazi generation to which we still belong. The introduction of group libel laws and hate propaganda regulations in so many countries during the last ten years shows vividly the increasing appreciation of the changing relationships between individuals, groups, and total society or government. It is against this background that the issue of free speech must be understood. To use fifteenth- and nineteenth-century terms of reference will simply not do.

IV

Everyone is aware that the special experience of the Jew gave rise to the report and to Bill S–49. Jews are of course not the only ones who have been persecuted or severely discriminated against or against whom genocide has been practised. Armenians and Gypsies are cases in point, but it is the persistence of violent anti-Semitism with its spectre of neo-Nazism which has made the matter urgent upon so many nations and now also upon Canada.

The bitter and bloody realities of anti-Semitism are general knowledge, and to reduce their effects was evidently an important objective for the committee. Its recommendations included, as we noted above, the word *religion* in its definition of distinguishing aspects by which a group could be identified (others being colour, race, language, ethnic, or national origin). Bill S–49 omits the mention of language and religion. About the former there may be some question in view of current intra-Canadian controversy. But the omission of religion as a mark of group identification strikes me as an overprotective caution. The Cohen report was clear and unambiguous in this respect. By implication it stated that amongst many groups, and at present chiefly amongst them, the Jews had to be protected, so that they might enjoy the full security and freedom of Canadian citizenship. The government, by omitting the word religion, weakens the intent of the report and appears to hide from public view what need not and should not be hidden. The Jews *are* concerned — even if they are not mentioned in the report — why then raise any doubts about it? It seems to me that in this respect the report is superior to Bill S–49.

There have been questions concerning the so-called escape clauses. I see no basic fault in them because ultimately they provide that needed protection which no one would eschew. It must also be clear that the operation of these clauses is limited. For if a court would ever hold that group libel is "in the public interest" or "for the public benefit"— then Canada's cultural setting would have changed to such a degree that the present foundations for a hate law would have crumbled and consequently the law would be inoperative in any case. This consideration applies also to the question whether in the process of proving his allegations as "true" the accused could use the courtroom procedure as a sounding-board for hatred. I think it is essential that we trust the court to provide proper safeguards in this regard, and past procedure gives us no reason to doubt that this will be done. Also, the application of the British law, insofar as we have had occasion to observe it, should lay such fears to rest.

At this late date, one need hardly expend ink and effort to argue the educative effect of legislation. Long ago, Dr. G.W. Allport stated that the establishment of law creates a public conscience, a standard for expected behaviour that helps to check overt prejudice. At the other end of the scale the law aids the member of the minority group who receives a much-needed assurance that the liberties under which he now lives are sufficiently secure against all incursions, and that whatever else may happen, genocide will never again be a problem for him and his group.

For when all is said and done, genocide is unlike any other offence. Its magnitude exceeds description and analysis, as the Nuremberg trials and the judgment of Eichmann have amply demonstrated. The United Nations has seen fit to deal especially with genocide, and so now will Canada. The report deserves our cordial endorsement when it stresses the general desirability of preventative and punitive measures, and when it aims to create a social climate that is uncongenial to hate propaganda.

The Report of the Special Committee on Hate Propaganda in Canada — the title might well have added a reference to genocide also — will be a landmark in Canadian law and, it is hoped, will provide an incentive for other nations to deal with this urgent subject.

Refuge or Asylum:
The Canadian Perspective

The Refugee Phenomenon: A Brief History

*T*he act of people fleeing lands of their nativity or habitual residence is as old as humanity itself. Sometimes just a single individual would seek refuge; at other times, large groups of people would embark on an exodus. The reasons for such migrations are as varied as the times and lands where they took place.

There were mass expulsions of Jews from France in the twelfth and succeeding centuries, from England in the thirteenth century, and from the Iberian Peninsula in 1492 when the Jews of Spain were faced with a decision to convert or to emigrate. The majority chose to do the latter; most settled in Italy, Greece, and Turkey, while a minority travelled northward to the Netherlands and Germany. No special term or word was created in Western languages to describe Jewish migrations because Jews were already classified as strangers. It was when Christians began to expel other Christians that language began to reflect the special needs and status of migrants.

With the exception of Jewish refugees who received only a qualified and clearly circumscribed acceptance, other refugees could settle anywhere in Europe. This is exemplified by migrant Christian groups in the wake of the Reformation who, because they contributed to the working population and significantly increased the tax base of the country, were considered an asset. For this reason, mercantilist doctrine tended to encourage immigration. Frederick William of Prussia, for example, invited the Huguenots to settle in his kingdom, and Poland-Lithuania, which was starved for immigrants, welcomed Jews.

Until the middle of the nineteenth century, these groups were simply considered migrants and as long as borders were open to them, they neither required nor received special juridical treatment. This held true also for individuals who left their countries for political reasons after having engaged in revolutionary activities. Such individuals were received in countries of refuge in accordance with prevailing ideas of political asylum.

Terminology: The Origin of "Refugee"

The development of language can be an indicator of historical trends. The word *refugee*, for example, is of relatively recent origin. Derived from the French *réfugié*, it was used originally to refer (like its French model) to Protestant Huguenots expelled from France after the Édit de Nantes was abolished by Louis XIV in 1685. For some time, the word continued to be used as a term meaning Huguenots, but its definition has since been expanded. A similar linguistic growth can be traced in the development of the Roman word *barbarian* which originally simply meant a person who seemed to babble (i.e., a stranger). It was first used to describe the invading Goths in the fourth century and later came to mean uncivilized people in general. Thus, too, the meaning of the word *refugee* broadened from its original, particular sense into a general term denoting people who had left their home country under duress. The third edition of the *Encyclopaedia Britannica* in 1769 noted this broader meaning: "In Germany, where many of the Huguenots fled, the existing word *Flüchtling* assumed the additional meaning of Huguenot." Even as late as 1911, the Sachs-Villatte French dictionary notes this use of the word *réfugié*.

The Refugee Explosion

True international concern about refugees began when the number of people fleeing oppressive conditions reached vast proportions. At the beginning of the twentieth century, some 2.5 million Jews left Eastern

Europe after the pogroms of 1881, 1903, and 1905. This was followed by large population displacements after the Ottoman retreat in the Balkans, the revolution in Russia, the devastation of the Armenians by the Turks, and the rearrangements of national borders at the end of the First World War. A few years later, the rise of Nazism and the Second World War created displacements of even greater dimensions.

One new element of these migrations was their vastly increased size. Equally important was the fact that twentieth-century refugees no longer found the borders of other countries as open as they had been previously. Nation-states had replaced the multitude of principalities and bishoprics of former centuries and these new political entities now zealously guarded their territories. While there had been attempts at international arrangements to care for the displaced after the First World War , these plans were postponed during the Great Depression and after the subsequent outbreak of the Second World War. It was only after then that an international refugee crisis triggered by the vast number of displaced persons prompted the drafting of the 1951 UN Convention, which encompassed concepts of international protection for refugees and *non-refoulement*. In response to the international refugee crisis, nations displayed reluctance to give up any of their own powers, agreeing only to minimal standards of protection and leaving a great deal to be determined by the internal procedures of the various states. An internationally accepted definition was eventually agreed upon, and the office of the United Nations High Commissioner for Refugees (UNHCR) became the first permanent structure on the international scene to be responsible for refugees.

Asylum

Although the phenomenon of refugees has existed since the beginning of (and doubtlessly prior to) recorded history, the complexities of the modern concept denoting and giving juridical dimensions to the term did not arise until modern times. Formerly, refugees found automatic asylum somewhere; today, with borders closed and controlled, they no longer can.

The original Greek word from which *asylum* is derived denoted a place of refuge. Later, it came to mean not so much the place itself as the protection afforded by that place. Scholars agree that while there are early records of asylum provided by secular authorities, the origins of the concept lie in the religious realm. It was assumed that there were areas which stood under the special protection of divine authority and upon which human beings must therefore not infringe. The Hebrew Bible (Numbers 35:9 and following) provides for a number of "cities of refuge" to which a person who has committed involuntary manslaughter might flee from the blood avenger, and where he cannot be touched by extra-legal proceedings. The principle of extradition too was touched upon in the Bible (Deuteronomy 23:15): an escaped slave was not to be returned to his master. It was also dealt with in a number of other ancient documents from the second millennium BC. The ruler of the Hittites, in a treaty with another monarch, stipulated: "Concerning a refugee I affirm on oath the following: when a refugee comes from your land into mine he will not be returned to you. To return a refugee from the land of the Hittites is not right." However, some modifications of this principle were made by the Hittites when faced not with a weaker contract partner, but with the Pharaoh of Egypt: "When a man flees from the land of Egypt... and comes to the great ruler of Hatti, the great ruler of Hatti shall arrest him and have him brought back to Egypt.... However, the man who will be brought back to Ramses, the beloved of Amon, the great ruler of Egypt, shall not punish him for his crimes. His house, his wives and his children shall not be exterminated, he shall not be killed. Nothing shall be done to his eyes, ears, mouth or legs; no single crime of his shall be punished." It is not clear why, under such conditions, extradition would be sought in the first place, but this treaty provision remains as an interesting instance of an ancient and persistent problem.

Rights of the Person vs. Rights of the State

There is some doubt as to whether these ancient precursors of secular asylum and extradition influenced the development of Greek law, but there is little question that the Greeks had a direct influence on Western legal concepts in the ensuing millennia. The creation of independent city-states resulted in interstate arrangements which eventually included also the protection of certain groups of people. It is noteworthy that the

Greeks considered the right to asylum not as a subjective right of the asylee but as a right of the city that granted it. This stood in significant contrast to the right of an individual who sought religious sanctuary where the refugee had that right as a divine rather than a secular prerogative. It may be said that throughout the history of Western civilization, this tension existed. The Church would maintain its prerogative to secure the rights of individuals (guaranteed in that sense by God himself), while the states, when displacing the power of the Church, also substituted the right of the state to grant asylum for the right of the individual to secure it.

By the mid-eighteenth century, and especially with the French Revolution, the power of the Church was broken and with it the right of an individual to asylum. The stronger the state became, the less important religious asylum was bound to be. Yet, at the same time, there remained some voices emphasizing that the right to asylum should adhere to the individual. We have already mentioned Grotius, and we may add the voice of Wolff who in 1764 noted of exiles that they "do not cease to be men ... nature entitled them to dwell in any place in the world which is subject to some other nation."

While this right was in fact tempered with its recognition by existent sovereignties, the exercise of sovereign prerogatives was clearly not contemplated in the absolute manner in which it is perceived today. It has become axiomatic to assert that the right to grant asylum belongs to the realm of national sovereignty, and that persons seeking it have no right to have it granted. No one can force a nation to conduct its asylum practice in any way other than in accordance with its own political and opportunistic goals.

Even in legal discourse, the interest of the asylum seeker would rate second place to the interest of the state. In 1908 John Bassett Moore stated that the "right to grant asylum is to be exercised by government in light of its own interests and of its obligations as a representative of social order." After the Second World War, the tone became even stronger, and Felice Morgenstern asserted that it was an undisputed rule of international law that every state had exclusive control over individuals in its territory including their protection and expulsion and their admission and exclusion.

It remains an historical irony that by the very act of insisting on their own prerogatives, nation-states created the *de facto* practice of *non-refoulement*. In the absence of specific extradition treaties, a nation would generally not heed the request of another to return a political refugee, for it considered the right not to return the refugee to be an exercise of its own sovereignty.

In one other respect, modern developments have shown a marked singularity. Where asylum and extradition were once closely linked, today this linkage has been greatly diminished. The linkage was strongest when national borders were open and asylum meant primarily the *protection of a refugee from refoulement* (usually in the context of extradition), but with national borders closed everywhere, asylum primarily became an opportunity *to enter and/or remain* in the land of refuge. The right to grant asylum was — and is — deemed to be the prerogative of the state, and most nations (with few exceptions) deny that persons in search of asylum have any right except that of *non-refoulement*. Put another way, in earlier days the right to reside anywhere was not in question, and the right not to return a prisoner formed the concept of asylum.

Today, because closed borders exist everywhere, the refugee must primarily seek asylum in the sense of a new home as well as protection from *refoulement*; the state, however, will generally grant the latter, but not necessarily the former. Refugees today, therefore, enjoy a far less favourable position than they did throughout most of history. In the past, they were at least able to find another place to go (although occasionally they were returned to their land of origin), whereas today political refugees are not likely to be returned only if they can find a place to rest. This plight of the modern refugee is caused by a combination of closed borders and the axiom of national sovereignty, and, while *refoulement* remains a problem, it is not the major one. Today, what most refugees desperately need is durable asylum — a permanent home in which they can rebuild their lives.

The axiom of national sovereignty leaves it to each nation to grant or refuse durable asylum. There is, however, a developing trend of opinion that juxtaposes a universal human right to find such asylum over and against the presumption of sovereignty. This would mean the assertion of individual rights vis-à-vis state rights. Thus, the German constitution provides that every political refugee, regardless of his/her political opinion, has a right to be granted asylum, and the constitutions of Portugal and Austria have similar provisions, although they are not as widely drawn as Germany's.

Asylum and International Law

Despite the recent improvements of the individual's right to asylum, the international community remains far from accepting any fundamental changes. The Universal Declaration of Human Rights states that everyone has the right "to seek and enjoy asylum." A proposal to substitute the words "to seek and enjoy..." with "to be granted..." was vigorously opposed, even though the Declaration imposes moral, not legal, obligations on state parties.

A similar reluctance may be seen in the history of the Convention. Although the French delegates had submitted articles that addressed the issue of asylum and admission into countries of refuge, the final text of the Convention omitted these issues and referred to them only in the Final Act. The Convention itself does not even specify any procedure by which the entitlement of a refugee is to be determined, so it may be said that the document is only a minimum response.

There can be little question that the refugee in search of asylum is the most serious international problem today. Attempts by the United Nations to respond properly have not met with success; in every case, party states have asked that the principle of *non-refoulement* be divorced from the notion of asylum, especially when mass movements of refugees might mean that some states would be obligated to accept large numbers of refugees already present in their territories.

There are many refugees, especially in Southeast Asia and Africa, who cannot find admittance anywhere and thus remain in their insecure and often dangerous condition. In addition, there is the plight of the "refugees in orbit" (persons without rights) who, shunted from one country to another, are denied asylum everywhere. Countries have responded to these new problems with various degrees of generosity. Portugal, the Federal Republic of Germany, and Austria grant asylum as a matter of legal right upon the recognition of refugee status. Other countries such as Canada usually grant asylum, yet consistently avoid making it a legal obligation.

It is important to remember that when Canada ratified the Convention in 1969, we did so with some reluctance. The United States had ratified the Convention the year before. Our reluctance was more noteworthy — in the two decades preceding, we had shown a highly liberal attitude toward the admission of refugees, in contradistinction to our practices during the days of the Hitler regime in Germany. But, while the whole content of the Convention was incorporated into internal law in the United States, Canada incorporated only a portion of the definition as well (as Article 33) into the 1973 amendments to the Immigration Appeal Board Act and the present (1976) Immigration Act. Apparently, we were prepared to do only the minimum in legal terms, while in practice we are often far more magnanimous — especially with regard to selecting refugees abroad. A visit for instance to our immigration office in Rome, where many applicants are processed, will confirm this tendency. It has been suggested that this liberality is directly related to our own capacity to select the refugees (immigrants whom we want in Canada) and to our continued opposition to any movement which would interpose international agencies or principles into this process of selection.

The Convention is not a part of Canadian domestic law, with the exceptions noted above. Asylum seekers who come to our shores are considered not so much persons in need of protection as potential lawbreakers who must be confronted with enforcement procedures. Many in Canada are concerned that we project an attitude of hostility toward refugees whom we have not selected but who find themselves nonetheless in our midst claiming refugee status. As adherents to the Convention, we observe the principle of *non-refoulement*, but nonetheless we insist that anything further be discretionary and voluntary.

One may also view this trend against a backdrop of attitudes that have developed in industrial nations during the past decade. These attitudes reveal a discernible xenophobic trend which reflects a variety of demographic, economic, and technological pressures. Unfortunately this is happening at a time when the plight of refugees is worse than it has ever been before, and the number of refugees is greater than has been experienced for some time.

Closing the Gap: Policy vs. Practice

In Canada, we have frequently done the right thing, but students of Canadian refugee and immigration history must come to the conclusion that we have done it unevenly and often without any perception of long-range policy. The time has come for us to look at the factors which today give rise to refugee movements and to our appropriate responses. We should examine these as well as the interrelation between refugee law and asylum and between national sovereignty and international individual rights. The result of such an examination may well re-affirm our present practices and policies, but it may also do otherwise.

Following the Supreme Court decision in the case of Singh et al. vs. the Minister of Immigration, a technical argument can be made that we in Canada have in fact acknowledged Canada's role as a land offering asylum. After all, it is now established that any person who reaches our borders has the full protection of the law, as if he/she were a recognized resident. But there is still a distance between legal recognition and administrative attitude. It is the responsibility of the academic community to help narrow that gap.

Four Points of Law:

Notes on the Relationship of

Law and Religion

*A*llow me to begin my address on a personal note. You see before you someone who was educated both in the laws of the state and in the laws of religion. To be sure, my graduation from law school occurred more than forty-two years ago, but much of the subject matter remains clearly in my mind, because in fact the transition from law to theology was not as radical as you might at first blush suppose. Quite on the contrary. In my own tradition, religion and law, faith and justice, are so closely intertwined as to make them mutually dependent. In fact, this relationship is the subject of my address this noon.

An ancient interpretation deduces this relationship from the opening of the Bible, the first two chapters of the book of Genesis. Were you to study them in the original Hebrew you would note that in the first chapter, when we are told of the creation of the world — a creation that ended with the formation of humanity — the Creating Power is called *Elohim*, which we translate as God. In the second chapter, however, when we hear of the creation of the human race in a more detailed and personal way, the divine cognomen is no longer "God" but "Lord God." In older Christian Bibles this has usually been rendered as "God Jehovah," while in Jewish transcription Jehovah is read *Adonai*, representing what the Hebrews considered to be God's personal name. This difference between the chapters raised a question. Why, when the creation of the world and of humanity is discussed in the first chapter, is the Creator only called God; while in the second chapter, when humanity's specific origins are explained, He is no longer God but *Adonai Elohim* — or Lord God or

God Jehovah? The answer which tradition gave is instructive and speaks to my theme: "God" (*Elohim*) represented the principle of *justice*; God's personal name (*Adonai*) represented the principle of *love*. At first the world was established with justice alone, but the Creator realized that that a world resting only on justice could not be sustained, and so He added His personal unique quality, the quality of love and mercy, and under the merciful *and* just God, *Adonai Elohim*, Creation could endure.

Thus, since very ancient days, already both justice and love were seen as the twin foundations of the world, and indeed the relationship between them remains close, even though in a society that tends towards emphasizing secular values this relationship is often obscured. But it is precisely on this inner relationship that I would speak to you, and coming from the particular background that is mine, I will take leave to speak on it as a loving friend of both. I will proceed from the philosophic to the pragmatic, from the general to the specific. In my view, to give a person the advice that he or she ought to be just rather than unjust, is worthless advice. It would be much like the sermon on which President Calvin Coolidge is reported to have commented. When he was asked what the preacher had talked about, he said, "Sin." And when further pressed what the preacher had said about sin, he simply replied, "He was agin it." To be against sin is about as worthwhile as to be for justice, or motherhood, or God and country. General asseverations avail us nothing; only the specific application of the principle will prove us to be either serious or spurious in our intentions.

I address myself today to four areas in which the nexus between law and religion is particularly observable and important.

Proposition Number One: A God who is generally unavailable cannot be my God; and similarly law unavailable cannot be my law.

I am reminded of the story of Chapter 18 of the first Book of Kings where we are told of the prophet Elijah who was engaged in a divine contest with the four hundred priests of Ba'al. They had built an altar and put a sacrifice upon it and surrounded it with wood; now they needed a sign from Heaven to ignite the sacrifice with the divine spark. Alas, despite all their incantations the Heavens were silent, and Elijah taunted them with images that were filled with sarcasm: "Why don't you call a little louder," he said, "maybe your god is asleep and needs a little rousing." What Elijah was speaking about was the unavailable God who is too busy or too tired, too preoccupied or too fatigued, to hear the human cry. Such a God is not the God of the Jewish and Christian traditions, who believes in a Divine power that is available to the call of the heart and the cadences of prayer.

Even so it is with the law. When the courts are unavailable, when they appear to be, in Elijah's terms, too busy or too tired, they have lost an important aspect of that very justice in the name of which they were established. Centuries ago, if I may draw this self-serving comparison, another clergyman, the famed Bishop Burnet (in his *History of His Own Time*) wrote: "The law of England is the greatest grievance of the nation, very expensive and dilatory." Expensiveness and dilatoriness are two sure ways to make the law unavailable to the people. It therefore appears to me as one of the greatest problems of our society — as great as the control of inflation and the cure of economic ills — to make the law available more evenly and more quickly. We therefore need an updating of our judicial administration, and not only more courts and more judges to relieve them from their own overburdened schedules. The problem lies in no small measure at the prosecutor's end, where additional manpower is needed badly. At the same time we have to make the legal process more readily available to those who cannot afford its mounting costs and do so to a far greater extent than our hitherto tentative attempts have managed to accomplish. The law, like God, must be available and readily so.

Proposition Number Two: Religion, like law, must be understandable. Judaism and Christianity eschew obscure and incomprehensible religions which are the sole prerogative and property of a priestly caste. Neither must the law be Delphic and intellectually out of reach to people gifted with ordinary reason. This is why we read in the biblical lesson from the Book of Deuteronomy: "This commandment which I command thee this day is not hidden from thee, neither is it far off. It is not in Heaven that thou shouldst say, who shall go up for us to Heaven and bring it near unto us that we may hear it and do it.... But the word is very nigh unto thee, in thy mouth and in thy heart that thou mayest do it." This is what Edmund Burke meant when, in his *Vindication of Natural Society*, he said, "Where mystery begins justice ends." Therefore it seems to me that we must begin to repair one of the significant lacunae in our education structure. The basic knowledge of the law and its principles must be as much of the common heritage of the nation as is the knowledge of its national history, or of any other civic subjects commonly taught. Law is not for judges and lawyers alone, law is for and by the people. Our human laws, to quote James Anthony Froude, are but "the copies more or less imperfect of the Eternal Law so far as we can read them." No student should be allowed to graduate from high school, no university student receive his Bachelor of Arts, without having demonstrated some knowledge of a basic understanding of our judicial system and its principles. Law, like religion, must never be Delphic; else it ceases to be law.

Proposition Number Three: I proceed to enunciate it with some hesitation, for I fear I may be misunderstood. In our religious context the human species, once it had lost its innocence in the Garden of Eden, was stamped as rebellious by nature. In fact, the entire Bible is a record of human rebellion against the laws of God. The laws of God were instituted precisely to educate man, so that he may find his way to higher levels of moral behaviour. Religion then comes into society as an educative force against the human tendency to rebel against the commanding presence of God and His will. Similarly it is with law. We are, if I may draw the parallel, given to lawlessness. *We are not born to be law-abiding, co-operative, and gentle.* I recall to you the words of the redoubtable Montaigne: "There is no man so good who, were he to submit all his thoughts and actions to the laws would not deserve hanging ten times in his life." Law therefore is not instituted merely to restrain the exceptional but rather to educate all of society. *Law is essentially an educative force.* It is natural that we should be preoccupied with crime and crime prevention, but I make bold to suggest that our whole direction of thought has been in reverse gear. We always ask, "What makes a person a criminal?" when instead we should ask, "What makes the majority reasonably law-abiding?" In the same sense we should not ask what makes a person irreligious, but rather what it is that inclines so many to be religious. Following along this line I would say that should we begin to understand what causes people to be law-abiding, we will perhaps understand better why others revert to their more natural state. Law, like religion, is a means whereby humanity corrects its natural impulses.

Fourth and last proposition: Judges, like God, have both their freedom and their limitations. In our common conception, God is not only free, He is also limited, limited by the very laws He has instituted. That is why the Psalmist said, "That which is a law for Jacob is also a statute for the God of Israel."[1] But at the same time we believe in a God who is free to grant grace or not to grant it, to bestow His presence or to withdraw it. It is this combination of freedom and limitation which is both a glory and puzzlement of the religious quest. So it is also with the law and especially with those who are called to administer it as judges. Abraham already called God a judge, and to many a person standing before the bar there is little distinction between you who sit in the judges seat and the Divinity itself. Therefore give me leave to compare your powers, which have been granted to you by society, to the powers of God Himself. *Quite obviously judges are limited by law, convention, and precedent, yet at the same time like God they must have an area of freedom*, and this freedom exists not merely to admit or reject evidence, to set dates for trial, to pass judgment or sentence. Law must always be a reflection of Divine imperatives, and the judge sworn to administer and interpret it must never lose sight of them. Ultimately, there is for each judge an area impossible to define in advance, in which he, like God, has freedom albeit within limitations. *A judge must be creative in the very execution of his duties.* A judge, of course, is not a law maker, but he is also not an automaton. The very area of his freedom also grants to him the possibility of responding to that which he considers to be the social or divine imperative, and it is this which is both the burden and the glory of the court, as well as the responsibility of the lawyer at the bar, to help the court develop this aspect. The judge, like God Himself, is bound by law and yet has his area of freedom.

The similarities between justice and religion go far deeper than my four examples can possibly signify. Yet even as I repeat them, they may serve to elucidate those areas which all too often are covered by the enormity of daily pressure and the endless accumulation of statutory precept and precedent.

> Justice, like God, must be readily available;
> Justice, like religion, must not be obscure, but be understandable and understood by the people;
> Law, like religion, must recognize that it is an educative restraint upon an essentially rebellious humanity, and we must therefore learn to understand what nonetheless makes people law-abiding;

And lastly, judges, like God Himself, are limited by
law and yet have freedom to act creatively, and by the
dynamism of their interpretation help to develop the law
in consonance with legal conscience and social insight.

It is to these parallels which bind the Divine and the earthly courts
together in common purpose that I would direct your thoughts today.
The opening of Her Majesty's courts in this province is every year a time
of supreme significance, when the demands of justice become concretized
in the words and actions of our courts. That these words and actions may
be blessed by the Divine Presence is our common prayer, and that the
natural relationships between the temporal and the Eternal may not only
be understood but also be exemplified by the execution of our laws is, I
know, the prayer of all the people of this province.

The Marshall Inquiry

*W*hen the administration of justice is brought into question, the very foundations of our political system are in fact questioned thereby. The issue, if not addressed in due course, may produce a crisis of legitimacy. This in fact has happened in the Donald Marshall Jr. affair.

I have been asked to provide a short submission on that well-publicized case and more specifically, to comment on the *Report to the Canadian Judicial Council of the Inquiry Committee.*[1] The committee's mandate was to review the judicial conduct of the five Nova Scotia Court of Appeal justices involved in the ultimate acquittal of Marshall.

As I was contemplating my response, a recent morning's newspaper caught my attention with two very different pieces of information. One was the report of the Moncton school board case, and the other the death of Friedrich Dürrenmatt — and both of them, in their different ways, have a bearing on the subject of this discussion.

The Moncton matter will still be fresh in the minds of readers: a public school teacher, Malcolm Ross, was accused of teaching hatred against Jews, and the family of a Jewish girl claimed that the Moncton school board, by not dismissing or re-assigning Ross, was colluding in making life miserable for the girl. Fellow students, apparently eager pupils of their racist teacher, had been persecuting her as a "Jew-bitch" who "deserved to die." Counsel for the school board, while professing sympathy for the plaintiff, nonetheless argued that the real victim of this whole affair was not the girl but her assailants — children from broken, poor homes who let their frustrations out against a girl who came from a good home and was secure in the love of her parents. The assailants were the real victims, counsel said, and not the plaintiff, an argument well known to judges and juries in rape trials: not the accused rapist but the victim is said to be blameworthy, for she led the poor, helpless man on by her seductive behaviour.

These are classic cases of role reversal: the victim is the real assailant, and the assailant the real victim. The application to the instant case will be made shortly.

The death of Dürrenmatt brings to mind his sharp and often bitter critique of how society handles the dispensation of justice. The author's latest play is in fact called *Justice*, and its theme too has a bearing on the matter before us: Justice, says Dürrenmatt, is not an abstract which is translated into fact by dint of impartial persons. Rather, by relying on judges, as it must, justice assumes the coloration of their experience. Since judges will generally stem from the same environment and have the same cultural likes and dislikes, they belong willy-nilly to a kind of club and in the long run their judgments will reveal this rarely talked about fact.

The last drama by the Swiss playwright was, needless to say, highly controversial, for people would rather retain their image of the judiciary as totally above the fray. Here we come yet another step closer to the core of our discussion.

We are asked to comment only on the Report of the Inquiry Committee, and neither on the Reference Court decision[2] nor on the findings of the Royal Commission.[3] In fulfilling this limited assignment I take my cue from the statement of Chief Justice Allan McEachern, that judges are free to say what they believe serves the cause of justice, but that, once they deliver their verdict, they hand it over to the public for its untrammelled comment. I will therefore treat the Report of the Inquiry Committee in the light of that observation, for its members acted in a judicial capacity.

In my opinion, the report, while well and clearly argued, does not go far enough because it leaves unsaid what should have been included. I say this with the greatest respect to its members, but I do not believe that they fully utilized their opportunity to let the public share in some uncomfortable truths — matters which, to me, are illustrated by the Moncton case and by Dürrenmatt's *Justice*. I believe that role reversal is a serious aspect of the instant case, and so are cultural prejudgments. While the former finds mention in the Inquiry Committee report, it is absent from the Reasons of the Chairman, and the cultural context of the case is glaring by its omission by both the majority and the minority.

I do not argue that the judges of the Reference Court should have been removed; I do argue that the reasons given by the majority of the committee left unsaid what in the 1990s should no longer be passed over in silence. In making my case I have had access only to the report and not the findings of the Royal Commission; if the latter already dealt with this matter, so much the better for having said it, and if it did not it is high time that the issue be aired.

One other source of information was available to me, and that was the media publicity which attended the Donald Marshall matter. It left me with one clear and lasting impression: that Marshall was a Native person and that as such he got the short end of the stick called "Justice."

Not that this was a surprise; it was not. After serving for seven years on the Ontario Human Rights Commission, I have come to understand that there are various kinds of justice: one is taught in law school and is an exercise in legal reasoning; another is practised by the cultural and social majority which controls the system of justice; and a third is meted out to certain minorities amongst whom are first and foremost our Native people.

Members of the judicial establishment will vigorously deny the existence of such distinctions, but once one begins to confront the uneven struggle for human rights in our country one cannot help but be struck by the fact that cultural prejudice is deeply ingrained in our social fabric. It is this recognition that I find lacking in the report.

In fact, the document reads like an earnest and well-constructed exercise in abstract principles. Thus we are treated to a consideration of what constitutes the limits of "legal error." Had I not been following the media, I might never have realized that Marshall was a Native person, for it would be easy to overlook the remark of Ebsary and MacNeil, "We don't like niggers and Indians.[4] In what follows, we deal with abstract human beings, not people of flesh and blood, with their likes and dislikes, preferences and prejudices.

To be sure, legal argument does of necessity proceed by abstraction, and the motivations of the participants, both on the Bench and in the court room, are of little concern. Therefore, I did not expect the report to examine the motives of the judges of the Reference Court — an impossible as well as improper procedure. Besides, the Inquiry Committee had a very narrow task before it, namely, to recommend whether or not certain judges should be removed from office. Still, I would have hoped that in the process, it might have said something of the social and psychological context of the Reference Court's judgment.

I will therefore try to note some aspects which the report passed over. I do this with the greatest respect for the Canadian judiciary and I assign no improper motives to any participant. After all, Donald Marshall was acquitted by the court. My comment is addressed to the *obiter dicta* and is therefore of a general, one might say generic, nature.

Marshall, at the time of the fatal incident, was seventeen years of age; I do not know of his schooling, nor of his level of intellectual comprehension. If he was an average Native boy of his age, he had a less than clear understanding of the white man's legal system and, to boot, harboured a fairly deep-seated suspicion that he might not obtain justice in the white man's court.

If he withheld information from his counsel it was done most likely because he was not sure that he could trust even him; after all, counsel are "officers of the court"; and though Marshall probably did not know the term, the dress and comportment of counsel make it clear that they are in some fashion part of the system. Having myself, in my own youth, lived as a member of a condemned class, I believe I can understand the young boy's basic mistrust. In addition, my experience on the Human Rights Commission has amply demonstrated instances of this kind.

I would have liked the report to have exposed something of this background, for it is not only the accused who was caught in the web of social misperceptions, it was the justice system itself.

The report is aware of this fact. It criticizes, in measured and careful language, the fact that the court put most of the blame on Marshall and that it "was not responsive to the injustice of an innocent person spending more than ten years in jail."[5] And it does take strong exception to the *obiter* remark that any miscarriage of justice was "more apparent than real."[6]

What lies behind this reversal of roles (despite the acquittal)? What caused the court to deliver itself of such language — language which in his reasons Justice McEachern calls "a bad mistake in the choice of words, but that is all it was"?[7]

I would have liked the report to have delivered itself too of some *obiter dicta*. For instance, it might have said that such remarks are really not all that surprising, given the perception which white people often have of Native persons: that they are not to be trusted, that they lie and that, given half a chance, they will get drunk and probably commit some crime. After all, goes this popular wisdom, Native people fill our jails in disproportionate numbers.

Translated into the instant case, this amounts to saying that a man like Marshall really deserved what he got, for if he had not been convicted of murder, he would have landed in the slammer anyway, because of attempted robbery or something like that. Sooner or later, that's where he would have ended up, so what's the big deal? He served for the wrong reason, to be sure, but the final outcome would not have been much different, which means that any miscarriage of justice "was more apparent than real."

No wonder, then, that the chief blame for the whole incident was affixed not to the two white men "from Manitoba," nor to the police who withheld crucial evidence, but to Marshall himself. This is a typical case of role reversal, which exculpates the majority at the expense of a minority. I would have liked the report to have given us something of this context.

As for the reasons of Justice McEachern, they partake of the shortcomings of the majority report and, in addition, present in essence a defence of "The System." This operates well enough when all parties are equal, but they were not in the Marshall case. Members of Dürrenmatt's "club" may see little wrong with that; I do.

Notes

The First Confirmation in America

1. New York, 1938, 16.
2. *The Voice of Jacob*, II (1842–43), 207. The report is signed, "The Correspondent from St. Thomas."
3. Ibid., III (1843–44), 45.
4. *The Occident*, 1 (5604=1843–44), 512.
5. The letter is handwritten, and the *a* is not quite distinct; it is possible that it should be read *er* instead.
6. Possibly *om* instead of *an*.

Jews in Seventeenth-Century Georgia

1. Chas. C. Jones Jr., *The Settlement of the Jews in Georgia*, I, 5ff; Leon Huehner, *The Jews of Georgia in Colonial Times*, X, 65ff.
2. There were three early Salzburg immigrations: in 1734, 1735, and 1736.
3. Johann Heinrich Callenberg in Halle founded, in the late twenties of the eighteenth century, an institute for the conversion of Jews and other nonbelievers. The reports of his missionaries were published in a large series of books, beginning with his *Bericht an einige christliche Freunde von einem Versuch das arme juedische Volck zur Erkaentniss und Annehmung der christlichen Wahrheit anzuleiten*, 2nd ed., Halle, 1730. This *Bericht* was followed by seventeen continuations and, in 1738, by a new series called *Relation von einer weitern Bemuehung Jesum Christum als den Heyland des*

menschlichen Geschlechts dem juedischen Volck bekannt zu machen, Halle, 1738, with twenty-nine continuations. Further series were published from 1752 on, and, after Callenberg's death, by his successors Stephan Schultz and Justus Israel Beyer. The fifteenth piece of the last collection appeared as late as 1791.

4. Concerning the identity of the author, see below, note 15.

5. op. cit., 76ff.

6. Ibid., 77, note 1.

7. i.e. Bolzius' *Journal*; about it see below, note 11.

8. Huehner, 77.

9. op. cit., 69, 70, 75.

10. Cf. *Jewish Encyclopedia*, V, 628; art. "Georgia."

11. *An Extract of the Journals of Mr. Commissary von Reck and of the Rev. Mr. Bolzius* (London, 1734) in Peter Force, *Tracts and Other Papers*, IV (Washington, 1846), page 20 of the *Journal*.

12. Huehner, 76.

13. See George White, *Historical Collections of Georgia* (New York, 1855), 436.

14. Joh. Heinr. Callenberg's *Dreyzehnte Fortsetzung seines Berichts von einem Versuch das arme Juedische Volck zur Erkaenntniss der christlichen Wahrheit anzuleiten* (Halle, 1735), 160.

15. This must have been Bolzius, for the Saltzburgers were accompanied by only one preacher, viz. Bolzius.

16. Joh. Heinr. Callenberg's *Relation von einer weitern Bemuehung Jesum Christum als den Heyland des menschlichen Geschlechts dem Juedischen Volck bekant zu machen*; Achtzehntes Stueck (Halle, 1744), 12–14.

17. i.e., missionary literature, printed in Halle or London.

18. op. cit. (note 16), Zwoelftes Stueck (Halle, 1742), 711.

19. See introductory note to the preceding letter.

The Israelites in Pharoah's Egypt: A Historical Reconstruction

1. Alan Gardiner, *Egypt of the Pharaohs* (Oxford, 1961), 228, 236–237.

2. André Neher, *Moses* (New York–London, 1959), 69ff.

3. Gardiner, 224.

4. *Targum Jonathan* on Exodus 13:17.

5. In the same way, the figure 318, which appears in Genesis 14:14, comes

from Mari culture and indicated that Abraham took with him "everything that he had."

6. Various sources are cited by Louis Ginzberg, *The Legends of the Jews*, vol. V (Philadelphia, 1955), 413ff, note 106.

7. See Rashi on Genesis 45:12.

8. Mekhilta Beshallah 1.

9. Mekhilta Pisha 5.

The Canadian Experience: The Dynamics of Jewish Life Since 1945

1. Canadian census figures are obtained at the beginning of each decade, and therefore mid-decade statistics are only approximate. These figures must further be interpreted in the light of the custom distinguishing, in the census, between religion and ethnic origin.

2. The influx of Jews from North Africa, which peaked in the 1960s, did not alter this substantially. Even though most of them were French-speaking, they identified first and foremost with the Jews already settled and, therefore, with a community that had culturally stood with the Anglophones.

3. The Jewish business establishment, however, soon moved away from political action and possible confrontation to the more acceptable realm of charities. Canadian Jews did not develop a counterpart to either the American Jewish Committee or the American Council for Judaism.

4. It was estimated that of the 300,000 Jews in Canada at this time (about 1.4 percent of the total population), Montreal and Toronto had about 120,000 each, with the former losing and the latter gaining in numbers.

5. Norman May and the writer. For further discussion of the Committee (generally called CIC), see pages 65–66.

The Wandering Aramean

1. Similarly, Ithra (Jether) is called both an Ishmaelite and a Jesraelite (I Chronicles 2:17; II Samuel 17:25).

2. Joseph de Trani, for instance, finds the key in God's appearance to Laban, and His prohibition to speak neither good nor evil to Jacob—and he has Jacob flee from Laban's *blessing*! Another over-imaginative comment looks

to Jacob's preference of Joseph as the clue to our mystery. Had Joseph been Jacob's first-born, his preference would have been justified and he would have been spared the punishment of famine and Egyptian migration. But why was Joseph not his first-born? Because Laban cheated him with Leah! Hence, Laban's deceit and Jacob's punishment are causally related.

3. It should be noted that the JPS translation of Deuteronomy 7:1 is inadequate and misleading. The nations which Israel will drive out of Canaan may be mightier and more numerous — רב ועצום ממך, but they are not "greater," as JPS has it.

4. אבד could, of course, also mean perdition or destruction, as in Numbers 24:20.

In Defence of the *Erev Rav*

1. Jeremiah 25:20 is followed, in verse 24, by both עֶרֶב and עֲרָב, throwing doubt on the earlier vocalization; and the Syriac version takes Ezekiel 30:5 to read עֲרָב instead of עֶרֶב.
2. The Masorah takes pains to note the vocalization of עֶרֶב, calling special attention to the *tzere* (which in its parlance it refers to as *kamatz katan*).
3. *Urschrift*, 71.
4. ... עֶרֶב אֲשֶׁר in *Kerovot* for the second day of Pesach.
5. Sforno believes that the cattle referred to in v. 38 belonged to the ערב רב.
6. Mekhilta Bo, Chapter 14; other midrashic passages reflect the same idea. There was also a tradition that at the time of the Exodus there were many converts to the God of Israel; see Exodus Rabbah 18:10 (where the "mixed multitude" is identified with Egyptians who celebrated the Passover with Israel); also Philo, *Vita Mosis*, I, 27.

   Targum Jonathan has still another figure, but he too makes the ערב bigger than the Israelites.
7. E.g., Deuteronomy Rabbah 2:23. See the copious notes in Ginzberg, *Legends of the Jews*, V, 106.
8. Exodus Rabbah 42:6. However, there are many other midrashic passages which take the mixed multitude to be the riffraff of Numbers 11:4 and name it as the cause of Israel's relapse into idolatry.

Pharaoh's Hardened Heart

1. Exodus Rabbah, Bo 13:3. The problem is also dealt with in Exodus Rabbah, Va'era 11:1, quoting R. Pinhas Hacohen in the name of R. Hama.

2. We need not concern ourselves with the legend in the pseudo-epigraphic Testament of Solomon where we are told that it was really not God but an evil spirit, Abezi-thibod, who hardened Pharaoh's and Egypt's heart. This evasion of the problem may have suited a popular fancy, but it did not become a dominant tradition.

3. Hilkhot Teshubah 6:3 (see also his introduction to the Pirke Abot). Migdal Oz is so impressed with Maimonides' argument that he feels it needs no comment.

4. Comment on Exodus 7:3. Biur repeats Nahmanides' exposition, as he often does. Similarly Sforno insists that, had Pharaoh truly wished to return to God, nothing would have stood in his way.

5. Abravanel also calls our attention to the problems contained in Isaiah 6, and to the use of לאין מרפא in Second Chronicles 21:18. Sifte Hakhamim introduces yet another variation by saying: people will ask whether it could be God's will to bring further misfortune upon a repentant sinner. Therefore, it was made clear that Pharaoh was unrepentant. Abravanel's main line of thought is taken up by Yehezkel Kaufmann, *The Religion of Israel*, 76.

6. See the detailed discussion in Hilkhot Teshubah 5:5.

7. My thanks to Rabbi Jerald Bobrow who first turned my attention to this possibility. S. R. Hirsch (Comment on Exodus 7:3) uses the variety of verbs in this story for his usual homilies, but this is not helpful for our purpose.

8. Torczyner's "Berlin" translation renders הכבדתי as *verstockt*.

9. See Eliezer Ben Yehudah, *Thesaurus*, Vol. VII, 6232, note 1.

10. Exodus Rabbah, Va'era 9:8.

11. See Cassuto, פירוש על ספר שמות, comment on Exodus 4:21; his further argument, however, is rather forced: that nowhere is it said that God's punishment was exacted of Pharaoh for hardening his heart. That is true, of course, but it weakens the main line of thought. *Interpreter's Bible*, vol. I, page 881, also stresses that not Pharaoh's free will but God's might are the theme of the story. This is also Nahmanides' final argument. "For the heart even of the king is in the hand of God." Hertz too follows this line of reasoning.

12. This point is made strongly by Kaufmann, *loc. cit.* Occasionally a traditional commentator also breaks through the scholastic fence; see *Yefeh To'ar* (Samuel ben Isaac Jaffe) in comment on Exodus Rabbah, Bo 13:3.

13. This is also the sense of the midrash which says, commenting on "I have set as a God to Pharaoh": Pharaoh thought himself to be God, therefore let him behold thee (Moses) and say (to a mere human): "This is God" (Exodus Rabbah, Va'era 8:1).

The Pillar of Salt

1. *Antiquities*, I 11:4, 203.

2. See *Views of the Biblical World* (Chicago-New York, 1959), 61; Pirke de R. Eliezer, 25; Philo, *De Abrahamo*, 27. The Arabs call the spot Jebel Usdum.

3. H. Clay Trumbull, *The Covenant of Salt* (New York, 1899), *passim*; Funk and Wagnall's *Standard Dictionary of Folklore, Mythology and Legend* (New York, 1950), *sub* "Salt"; Pauly-Wissowa, *Real-Encyclopädie* (Stuttgart, 1920), *sub* "Saltz"; James C. Frazer, *The Golden Bough* (London, 1918), Vol. IX, 278, 283; Robert Graves, *The Greek Myths* (New York, 1955); Chapter 28, note 3, where Greek sources are quoted. See also Ovid, *Metamorphoses*, Book X, 48-62, with a poetic account of the legend. In line 65 Ovid makes also reference to the man who turned to stone at the sight of Cerberus.

4. She is called עדית in Pirke de R. Eliezer, 25 (end); some readings have the name as עירית (see Ba'al Ha-Turim *ad loc.*). For the meaning of עדה, cf. Genesis 21:30; 31:52; Joshua 24:27.

5. See I Samuel 13:3, where the word denotes a symbol of oppression.

6. See Genesis Rabbah, 51:5.

7. See, e.g., Ibn Ezra, Nahmanides. The latter reads the verse as follows: "Lot was walking last; his wife looked back, past him." The Maharshal (quoted by Shabbetai Bass in his Sifre Hakhamim) speculates that nothing but wifely gratitude animated Lot's wife. Knowing that she had been saved on account of him she felt obligated to look after him. The question, of course, arises: why then was she punished?

8. So Pirke de R. Eliezer, 25; Zohar, Vayera 108b; of the moderns, see Kahana, on verse 17. The new (experimental) edition of the Jewish Publication Society translation avoids these difficulties by reading מאחריו as an apposition to "Lot's wife" rather than as part of the predicate ותבט: "But Lot's wife.

behind him, looked back…" This solution was also suggested by Abravanel; however, it too leaves our main queries unanswered.

9. Cf. Genesis 32:27, 31; Exodus 3:6; 19:21; 33:20, etc. Kahana adds that for this reason God's work is accomplished at night, i.e. out of man's sight (see Exodus 4:24; Judges 6:38ff; II Kings 19:35; Isaiah 17:14).

10. An opinion similar to that of Ralbag is cited (and disapproved) by Isaac Caro in his *Toldot Yizhak*. There has been at least one other attempt at a radical solution. Jacob Zvi Meeklenburg, in his *Haketav v'hakabalah*, suggests that we have here, in verses 24 and 15, two separate stories and that verse 26 must therefore be understood differently. This anticipates modern criticism by a good deal.

11. So Ephraim Solomon b. Aron of Lenczica, in his *Keli yekar* (1602).

12. Hayim ben Moses Attar, in his *Or Ha-Hayim* (Venice, 1742), strongly hints at a purely figurative interpretation. It is interesting to note that the New Testament (Luke 17:28–32) also interprets the story symbolically; see also 9:62.

13. See Pirke de R. Eliezer, 25, where Job 28:1ff is applied to Sodom; Zohar, Vayera l08b–109a.

14. The shalshelet over ויתמהמה underscores this hesitation nicely.

15. So Hertz and most Christian interpreters.

16. See Leviticus 2:13; Numbers 18:19; II Chronicles 13:5; also Josephus, *Antiquities*, 12:3 #3. Later ages made salt necessary for *ha-mozi*; see Isserles, *Shulhan Arukh, Orah Hayim* 167:5.

17. On the relation of unfitness and holiness in this respect, see Robertson Smith, *Religion of the Semites* (2nd ed.), 454.

18. Hirsch on Leviticus 2:13; see also David Hoffman's extensive comment on the same passage.

19. So Rashi on the phrase מלח ממון חסר (Ket. 66b); see also the alternative reading חסד quoted there; and Trumbull, op. cit., 115 ff.

20. This was not the original meaning, some etymologists claim. They say that the term arose from the custom of Roman authorities to give soldiers money to buy salt.

21. מלח סדומית, see Ker. 6a; Hul. 105a.

22. The parallelism to the Greek story is even stronger when we recall the Midrash which told that in Sodom a visiting stranger given silver and gold in abundance, but never any bread (Sanh. 109b).

Why Love a Stranger?

1. In the Bible גר is always a stranger, i.e., one from another place. Even Jews are in some instances referred to in this fashion. (Judges 17:7–13; II Samuel 4:3). Rashi (*ad* Exodus 22:20) explains the term as "someone born in another place," but there are many who disagree with him and want גר understood as proselyte (גר צדק). Mekhilta (Masekhta de-Nezikim, Chapter 18) and Talmud (BM 59a et al) intermingle the terms (cf. Lauterbach's notation in his edition of the Mekhilta, Vol. III, 138, and I. Goldschmidt's commentary on BM 59). Cf. also W. R. Smith, *Lectures on the Religion of the Semites*, pages 75 ff; A. Bertholet, *Die Stellung der Israeliten und der Juden zu den Fremden* (Freiburg, 1896); אינציקלופדיה מקראית under גר; Salo W. Baron, *A Social and Religious History of the Jews*, 2nd edition, Vol. I, part 1 (Philadelphia, 1952), pp. 155–56; and J. D. Eisenstein's invaluable article in the *Jewish Encyclopedia*, sub "Gentile."

2. BM 59b; Malbim *ad* Leviticus 19:34.

3. Rashi on Exodus 22:20. Lauterbach (*loc. cit.*) emends to סיורו the stranger "has a bad streak in him."

4. Mizrahi on Leviticus 19:34.

5. Commentary on Mishnah BM IV, 10. See other references in Kasher, Torah Shelemah, Vol. 19, 184, 130. See also commentaries on the parallel passages in Zohar II 99a, and Mas. Gerim IV, 1.

6. The new JPS translation on occasion drops the command to "love" the stranger and instead speaks of the duty to "befriend" him (see, e.g., Deuteronomy 10:18, 19). But in Leviticus 19:34 it retains the command to "love" him. The reason for this variation in translation is not clear.

7. BM 59b.

8. E.g. on Deuteronomy 10:19 and Leviticus 19:34.

9. See also the change of number in Leviticus 19:33 and 34 and S. R. Hirsch's comment.

10. Ramban *ad* Exodus 22:20. See the discussion of his viewpoint in Nehama Leibowitz, *Studies in the Weekly Sidra* (1st series), *Mishpatim*.

11. Abravanel *ad* Leviticus 19:34, actually uses the phrase: אני ה' אלהיהם. In his comment on Exodus 22:20 he advances a slightly different argument: don't oppress the stranger, for God may do to you what He did to the Egyptians.

12. *Ad* Exodus 22:20.

13. *Ad* Deuteronomy 10:19.
14. Ibid.
15. *Ad* Leviticus 19:33–34.
16. Quoted by Hertz in his commentary on Exodus 22:20.

The Origin of the Word "Yarmulke"

1. *Slownik Etymologiczny Jezyka Polskiego* (Cracow, 1927).
2. *Russisches Etymologisches Wörterbuch* (Heidelberg, 1952).
3. In private communication. Grateful acknowledgment is made to Dr. Noble, Research Director of YIVO, New York; and Mr. Heinz Frank, Canadian Jewish Congress, Winnipeg, Manitoba, for helpful information rendered.
4. "King-fearing."
5. Thirteenth to fifteenth century; see Felix Singermann, *Uber Judenabzeichen* (Berlin, 1915), 36, note 5.
6. Ibid., 36, note 7.
7. Ibid., 42.
8. Ibid., 38, note 10.
9. Ibid., 35, note 5.
10. Ibid., 24, note 3; 25, note 7.
11. "Sur la roue des Juifs," *REJ* VI, 268.
12. James Robinson Planché, *A Cyclopaedia of Costume* (London, 1876), 7; picture on page 8.
13. *Catholic Encyclopedia* (New York, 1907), Vol. I, 428–29, article "Amice."
14. Alexius Hoffman, *Liturgical Dictionary* (Collegeville, 1928), "almucia."
15. See Jacob and Wilhelm Grimm, *Deutsches Wörterbuch* (Leipzig, 1885), Vol. VI, 2839, "Mütze"; also *Encyclopedia Britannica*, 11th edition, Vol. I, 718, *sub* "almuce." A dissenting opinion is entered by Jas. A. Murray, *A New English Dictionary* (Oxford, 1888), Vol. I, 281, who believes that *almuce* was the secondary word, deriving from the German *Mutse*, later *Mütze*, and adding an Arabic title.
16. Grimm, loc. cit.

A Hebrew-Dakota Dictionary

1. The spirit of this unusual man reflects itself in this letter: "I have been here a long time and have not been the means of the conversion of one Indian, yet I am not discouraged. It is my earnest desire and prayer to God that he would give me the souls of these heathen as seals of my ministry; yet my eternal welfare does not depend on it. That, I trust, is secured by the promise of God 'I know in whom I have believed.'" Letter to his mother, undated, but perhaps 1838; quoted in Samuel W. Pond, Jr., *Two Volunteer Missionaries Among the Dakotas* (Boston, 1893), 127–28.

2. William W. Folwell, *A History of Minnesota* (St. Paul, 1921), Vol. I, 198, footnote 56.

3. Rabbi Simon Cohen of the Hebrew Union College Library was good enough to supply the following information:

    > A favorite book of that time was J. Parkhurst's *Hebrew and English Lexicon* which had been first published in 1762 in London and was several times reissued there. *The Gesenius Dictionary* had been translated into English and published in 1836. These were of course English issues and may have been available. I found no less than half a dozen treatments published in America....

    See also A. S. W. Rosenbach, "American Jewish Bibliography," *PAJHS*, no. 30.

4. Thomas S. Williamson, *Dakota Wowapi Wakan* (New York, 1865), renders *YHWH* as *Jehowa*.

5. Gideon H. Pond, "Dakota Superstitions," *Publications of the Minnesota Historical Society* (*PMHS*), Vol. II (St. Paul, 1902 [reprint]), 217.

6. Henry H. Sibley, "Reminiscences," *PMHS*, Vol. I, 377: "The religion of the Dakota is a mere myth."

7. Samuel W. Pond, "The Dakotas or Sioux in Minnesota as they were in 1834," *PMHS*, Vol. XII (St. Paul, 1908), 319.

8. Ibid., 404.

9. Boas does not use these terms, but this is in effect his general point of view. See article "Religion" in *Handbook of American Indians*, ed. by Frederick W. Hodge, Vol. II (Washington, DC, 1910), 365ff.

10. William H. Forbes, "Traditions of the Sioux Indians," *PMHS*, Vol. VI, 113.

11. James O. Dorsey, "A Study of Siouan Cults," *Annual Report of the Bureau of Ethnology*, 11th Report (Washington, DC, 1894), 361ff.

12. James W. Lynd, "The Religion of the Dakotas," *PMHS*, Vol. II (St. Paul, 1889 [reprint]), 159ff.

13. Ibid., 171; Edward D. Neill, "Dakota Land and Dakota Life," *PMHS*, Vol. I, 215ff.

    Between these extreme positions, Stephen Riggs occupied somewhat of a middle ground. He did not commit himself either way. In his view *Taku Wakan* comprehends all mystery, secret power, and divinity. Awe and reverence are its due. And it is as unlimited in manifestation as it is in idea. All life is *Wakan*. "The Indian exclaims in awe 'Wakan! Father, have mercy upon me!'" However, Riggs says, *Waken Takan* is the least of gods, and is not held in high reverence, and for that reason no worship is offered to him. He admits that he is not "... named except in the presence of white men, and then not as often as the interpreters indicate."

    He also points to the construction of the word *Waken Taken* and holds that it is of derivative rather than primary meaning. In 1869, he wrote, "Now of course, through the Gospel, *Wakan'-Tanka* has a Christian meaning. And many a Dakota now worships him as the only true God and Jehovah the God of the whole earth, the God of the Indian as well as the white man." Stephen R. Riggs, *Tah-koo Wah-kan* (Boston, 1869), 56–75.

Long-hand with Buber (a review)

1. Martin Buber, *Briefwechsel aus sieben Jahrzehnten*, ed. by Grete Schaeder, Vol. I (1897–1918), (Heidelberg: Verlag Lambert Schneider, 1972). The excerpts which appear in this article have been translated by Rabbi W. Gunther Plaut.

Assessing the Jewish Mind (a review)

1. Raphael Patai, *The Jewish Mind* (New York: Scribner's; Toronto: John Wiley, 1977).

The Sabbath as Protest:
Thoughts on Work and Leisure in the Automated Society

1. Margaret Mead, editor, *Cultural Patterns and Technical Change* (New York: Mentor, 1955), 70ff.
2. Akedat Yitzchak, Vayak'hel.
3. Mekhilta, Yitro.
4. See the comprehensive study by Max Kaplan, *Leisure in America: A Social Inquiry* (New York & London: John Wiley & Sons, 1960).
5. Josef Pieper, *Leisure, the Basis of Culture* (New York: Pantheon, 1952).
6. Edited by Moshe Davis (December 1956), mimeographed.
7. From *Paris Match*, reprinted in *Atlas* (May 1970), 22.
8. Holdheim argued that the true objective of the Sabbath was to achieve sanctification. Rest was but a symbolic means to the end of ethical sanctification, not an end in itself (see W. Gunther Plaut, *The Rise of Reform Judaism* (New York: World Union for Progressive Judaism, 1963), 190ff.
9. "Halachah and Reform Judaism," *Dimensions* IV:3 (Spring 1970), 20ff; also idem, "Shabbath as a State of Being," *CCAR Journal* (January 1967), 29ff. His suggestion that the Jewish Sabbath be shifted to Sunday and that the observance and the character of other Jewish holy days be changed has ample precursors in Reform History; see W. Gunther Plaut, *The Growth of Reform Judaism* (New York: World Union for Progressive Judaism, 1965), 269ff.
10. The new *Sabbath Manual*, to be shortly published by the Central Conference of American Rabbis, is structured on the principle of choice.
11. Kenneth Benne, *Conference*, op. cit., Part II, 74.
12. *Man Is Not Alone* (Philadelphia: Jewish Publication Society, 1951), 28–29.
13. Pantheon: New York, 1970.
14. *Imagerie mentale* (Paris, 1968).

Toward a Higher Morality

1. Maurice Stein et al., eds., *Identity and Anxiety* (Glencoe, 1960), 597ff.
2. Op. cit., 604.

The Un-Public Relations of Our National Bodies

1. On Sunday, May 30, 1965, Jewish counter-demonstrators clashed with the organizers of a neo-Nazi rally in Toronto's Allan Gardens. About a hundred police, some of them mounted, had to be summoned to restore order.

The Sabbath in the Reform Movement

1. על פרשת דרכים, Part III, Chapter 30 (new edition, Berlin: Jüdischer Verlag, 1921), Vol. II, 79. Ahad Ha-am's formulation was based on earlier statements such as Abraham ibn Ezra's polemic poem in his אגרת השבת:
   שמרתיך בכל ימים, למען שמרתני מאד מימי נעורים.
2. Union Prayer Book, newly revised ed., Vol. I, 31.
3. "The Sabbath and Festivals in Pre-exilic and Exilic Times," *Journal of the American Oriental Society* 37 (1917), 211.
4. For a review of current literature see *Die Religion in Geschichte and Gegenwart*, 3rd ed., Vol. V, 1258ff. (Tübingen, 1961); Salo H. Baron, *A Social and Religious History of the Jews*, 2nd ed. (Philadelphia: Jewish Publication Society, 1952), Vol. I, 359, note 13; Nathan A. Barack, *A History of the Sabbath* (New York: Jonathan David, 1965).
5. See, e.g., Isaiah 68:13, 14; Jeremiah 17:21; Ezekiel 20:12ff; Amos 8:5; Lamentations 2:6; Nehemiah 10:32ff.
6. תולדות העקרים בישראל, Chapter 6, 106. To phrase it in this manner was to modernize the scholastic interpretation of Maimonides (Moreh, II 31) who held that the Exodus passage established the Sabbath as a means of leading all men to a belief in creation and its Creator, and that the Deuteronomic passage commanded us to an *imitatio Dei*. In Egypt we had no choice and had to work at all times; now we have a choice and choose to be god-like in our Sabbath rest. "Accordingly the Sabbath is, as it were, of universal benefit, both with reference to a true speculative opinion (that God is the Creator) and to the well-being of the state of the body." (Translation by Shlomo Pines, *The Guide for the Perplexed* [University of Chicago, 1963], 360.)
7. עקדת יצחק, פ׳ ויקהל. His main line of interpretation is, however, that a Jew is bidden not only to remember the creatorship of God (Exodus) but also His historic role as Israel's Redeemer (Deuteronomy). The former, universal in nature, calls forth זכירה, the latter, particularistic in nature, demands שמירה.

8. Sab. 113a.

9. שם עולם, quoted in ספר השבת (2nd ed., Tel Aviv, 1938), p. 140. See also Nahmanides (on Exodus 20:8) who presents a great deal of classical material.

10. Mekhilta, Yitro.

11. The traditional saying, לא נתנה שבת אלא לתענוג (Pes. R. 22) was amplified by popular opinion that Sabbath slumber qualified pre-eminently in this respect. Hence the Sabbath acrostic: שינה בשבת תענוג

12. Betsa 16a.

13. Commentary on Ki Tissa.

14. Cf. Ibn Ezra, Sforno.

15. מגילת סתרים, on Ki Tissa; Sab. 118b.

16. See Sforno on Leviticus 23:2.

17. עקדת יצחק, loc. cit.

18. Exodus Rabbah 25:12.

19. W. Gunther Plaut, *The Rise of Reform Judaism* (New York: WUPJ, 1963), 188.

20. I have not found the source of Wechsler's quotation. In Mekhilta, Ki Tissa the text reads: חלל שבת אחת כדי שתשמור שבתות הרבה. See also Yoma 85b, and Mark 2:27–28.

21. Plaut, 189ff.

22. Ibid., 192.

23. Ibid., 195. Cf. *Proceedings of the Rabbinical Assembly of America*, Vol. XIV (1960), 112ff: "One should refrain from all such activities that are not made absolutely necessary by the unavoidable pressures of life and that are not in keeping with the Sabbath spirit, such as shopping, household work, sewing, strenuous physical exercise, etc." (Responsum by Morris Adler, Jacob Agus, Theodore Friedman.)

24. *Kol Kore Bamidbar, Über Jüdische Reform* (Chicago, 1859), 10. See Plaut, *The Growth of Reform Judaism* (New York: WUPJ, 1965), Chapter XIV, #5.

25. Plaut, loc. cit. See also I. M. Wise, *Reminiscences* (Cincinnati: Leo Wise, 1901), 285.

26. The German "Guide Lines" of 1912 were an exception. See below, at note 33.

27. *The Israelite*, December 31, 1869, 8. His later recollection (*American Israelite*, November 8, 1898) that Friday night worship was introduced in 1867 was erroneous. James G. Heller, *Isaac M. Wise* (New York: UAHC, 1965), 983ff, quoting a still later source, errs equally by placing the original date in 1865.

28. Ibid., December 31, 1869, 8.

29. Ibid., March 31, 1871, 8. Wise credits Mayer with this idea.

30. Ibid., July 11, 1873.
31. Ibid., March 25, 1870.
32. CCAR *Yearbook*, Vol. XII (1902), 145–46; Vol. XV (1905), 62. Kohler called it "an innovation of dubious character," and Silverman warned that "by some peculiar reasoning people believe that if they attended synagogue for thirty minutes Friday evening, they are then keeping the Sabbath." See also Eugene Mihaly's critique of evening worship, *Journal* of the CCAR (April 1965), 19ff.
33. Plaut, *The Growth of Reform Judaism*, Chapter XIV, #5.
34. Siegfried Gelles, "Ein Vorschlag zur Sabbath-Heiligung," *Liberales Judentum* (1914) 6:6–7, 152ff.
35. UAHC, *Proceedings of the 1st Council*, 1. Loth made his statement on October 10, 1872, in an address to K. K. Benai Yeshurun, of which he was president. He gave the observance of Shabbat equal weight with that of מילה and שחיטה.
36. Sifra on Leviticus 19:30. Enelow's address is found in CCAR *Yearbook*, Vol. XIII (1903), 168.
37. *The Jewish Reformer*, Vol. I, no. 1 (1885), 5 and subsequent issues. CCAR *Yearbook* XII (1902), 103ff.
38. CCAR *Yearbook* XX1I (1902), 103ff.
39. Ibid.
40. Ibid. XLVI (1986), 157.
41. Ibid. XLVII (1937), 824ff.
42. Of older responsa see, e.g., CCAR *Yearbook* XXXV1I (1927), 203ff (Lauterbach); XL1I (1932), 82ff (Lauterbach); LXII (1952), 129ff (Bettan); Freehof, *Reform Jewish Practice*, 2 vols. (1944, 1952); *Reform Responsa* (1960); *Recent Reform Responsa* (1963); all published by HUC Press, Cincinnati.
43. I want to express my sincere appreciation to Mr. Heinz Warschauer, Director of Education at Holy Blossom Temple, for assisting in the collation and interpretation of these data.
44. Ta'anit 8b.
45. Mo'ed K. 8b. In its traditional setting the principle refers of course to weddings during the festival week.
46. Mekhilta, Ki Tissa.
47. The first edition of our prayer book had the full Kiddush for home use; the second edition abbreviated it to one line; the last edition restored the full Kiddush—but in mutilated form and to the synagogue service only.

48. The first edition of the Union Prayer Book still had a respectable Hebrew ברכת המזון.

49. *A Guide for Reform Jews* (New York: Bloch, 1944), 12ff; *A Guide to Jewish Ritual* (New York: Reconstructionist, 1962). This latter guide deals in some detail with the Sabbath and does so from a liberal point of view.

50. Edited by Jacob G. Schwarz (New York: UAHC, 1954), mimeographed.

51. *The Asmonean*, 1854, 85. See Plaut, *The Growth of Reform Judaism*, Chapter XIV, #1.

52. CCAR *Yearbook* XIII (1903), 139ff.

53. Ibid. XIV (1904), 22.

54. Ibid. XLVII (1937), 183.

55. Ibid., 422, 336ff.

56. See the halakhic discussions in נעם, בימה לברור בעיות בהלכה, vols. 1–7 (Makhon Torah Shelemah: Jerusalem, from 1958).

57. Jer. Shabbat 15:3.

58. See commentaries on Exodus 35:3.

59. On the Sabbath as a unifying element for the people and the creation of loyalty to the community, see Mac. 1:30; Sanh. 65b; Genesis Rabbah 10; Pes. R. 23. See also M. M. Kaplan, *The Meaning of God in Modern Jewish Religion* (New York: Behrman, 1937), pp. 34 and 57 ff.

60. Exodus 31:16.

61. עוללות אפרים, #266.

62. Yoma 85b. In slightly different form, Mekhilta, Ki Tissa.

63. Stein, *Die Schrift des Lebens* (Strasbourg, 1872–77), Vol. II, 463ff, #17–19. (See Plaut, *The Rise of Reform Judaism*, 262.)

The Ambiguity of Reform

1. David Philipson, *The Reform Movement in Judaism*, rev. ed. (New York: Macmillan Co., 1931), 355ff.; W. Gunther Plaut, *The Growth of Reform Judaism* (New York: World Union for Progressive Judaism, 1965), 31ff.

2. In contrast to the 1885 Pittsburgh Platform and the 1937 Columbus Platform, both of which were framed exclusively by rabbis, the current committee consists also of nonrabbinical representatives of the Union and the Hebrew Union College-Jewish Institute of Religion. The author has been a member of the committee since its inception.

3. The second conference (Frankfurt, 1845) discussed the essentiality of Hebrew at worship services; the Halakhah concerning the Eighteen Benedictions and the Musaf; sacrifices; the triennial cycle of weekly pericopes; prescriptions for Torah and Haftarah readings; whether a Jew was permitted to play the organ on Shabbat; rules for the construction of a *mikveh*. The third conference (Breslau, 1846) dealt with the laws of marriage, the *'erubh* and other Shabbat observances; circumcision, especially *peri'ah* and *mezizah*; Passover, *halizah*, etc. See Plaut, *The Rise of Reform Judaism* (New York: World Union for Progressive Judaism, 1963), 74ff.

4. Ibid., 94.

5. On the reasons for this development, see ibid., xxii ff.

6. Ibid., 123.

7. Ibid., 119ff.

8. Ibid., 220ff.; see also Kaufmann Kohler, *Studies, Addresses and Personal Papers* (New York: Alumni of Hebrew Union College, 1931), 22 ff.

9. Plaut, *Growth*, 20.

10. Leeser had entertained serious misgivings about attending the conference, but in the end felt assured that the forces "positive historical Judaism," as Zacharias Frankel had put it, would win out (ibid., 221ff.).

11. Plaut, *Growth*, 23 ff.

12. Wise, like Leeser at Cleveland, was doubtful whether to attend the Pittsburgh Conference altogether; see James G. Heller, *Isaac M. Wise* (New York: Union of American Hebrew Congregations, 1965), 485ff. In the end, he decided to attend but was determined "to fall as a man rather than to rise as a renegade." Heller's analysis of Wise's attitude is as follows:

> It may be well to pause here and ask a few pertinent questions. Wise had declared that "nothing practical had been done at Pittsburgh, and that there was no truth in the charges, which began to be spread, that the Pittsburgh Conference had abolished the "Sinaic Sabbath and circumcision," or had denied the verity of revelation, or the "divinity of the Bible." And yet, as one reads its declarations, one finds it far from easy to understand why Wise went along with it so completely and so enthusiastically. We shall refer in a moment to the things he wrote of the Conference in the weeks and months that followed it. But it is strange to note that apparently he took no umbrage at the

resolution on a Sunday Sabbath, which did violence to all he had been saying and writing for many years—and with great passion. He did not argue about the second paragraph of the Platform, which could have been the words of a "higher critic," and which in the most cavalier fashion passed over the whole issue of the revelation of Scriptures. Some of the qualities and opinions that made the Platform a point either of rallying or of dispute for almost fifty years presented no difficulty for him, as far as it is possible to judge by what he wrote: the denial of the nationhood of Israel; the discarding of all hope of a return to Palestine; the sacrificial cult, etc. But it cannot have been so pleasant for him to have gone along with the specific language in the earlier paragraphs, with their reading out of considera-tion of the whole doctrine of the uniqueness of Judaism, and calling the Mosaic law only a "system of training."

Wise's whole course of action—at the Conference itself and in the period that ensued—is far from easy to comprehend. The only explanation that offers any degree of credibility is what he himself said, that he was once again willing to go very far in compromise for the sake of unity, in the hope that, by not insisting overmuch upon his own convictions, by not insisting upon issues, he might pave the way for complete rabbinic co-operation in the country.

13. Lecture before the 1974 (Jerusalem) meeting of the Central Conference of American Rabbis.

14. *A Passover Haggadah* (New York: Grossman Publications, 1974).

15. Psalms 79:6. It might be noted that the phrase occurs also in Jeremiah 10:25.

16. See Kohler, op. cit., on this identification.

17. See the author's *The Jews in Minnesota* (New York: American Jewish Historical Society, 1959), 181ff. The controversy can be followed in detail in the minute books of the congregation (microfilms available in American Jewish Archives, Cincinnati, Ohio); see, e.g., Vol. II, April 20, 1879 (page 146), as contrasted with the final victory of the radical Reform party (Vol. III, April 7, 1890, page 1).

18. See, e.g., his article "Halacha and Reform Judaism," *Dimensions* IV: 3 (Spring 1970), 20ff.

Religious Discipline and Liberal Judaism

1. See also Genesis Rabbah 22:8.
2. Sifre Num. 99.
3. Tanh. (Buber) Korah 4. Korah asker:
4. *The Ordeal of Civility* (New York: Basic Books, 1974), 169ff.
5. Address to the Jewish Agency assembly, June 1974.

Prophetic Judaism Without Prophets

1. Isaiah 58:5–6.
2. Amos 9:7.
3. Zechariah 4:6.
4. See W. Gunther Plaut, *The Growth of Reform Judaism* (New York: World Union for Progressive Judaism, 1965), 229.
5. Michael Meyer, *Responses to Modernity* (Oxford: Oxford University Press, 1988), 215; see also Kaufmann Kohler, *Jewish Theology* (New York: Macmillan, 1918), 330.

The Elusive German-Jewish Heritage in America

1. The article will use the terms "America" and "American" as a shortcut, to stand for "North America" and "North American."
2. In part this may also be a reflection of the fact that Jews saw themselves not so much as an ethnic but as a religious group and compared themselves to American Protestants and American Catholics. This self-perception tended to reinforce the integrationist thrust of their cultural and religious life.
3. I might cite another example. In 1961–1962 in Toronto—a city where only a handful of German Jews were to be found—the rabbis of the leading Orthodox and Reform congregations were German-born, and so were the rabbinical heads of two of the four major Conservative synagogues.
4. He was David Philipson, member of the first graduating class at Hebrew Union College.
5. Einhorn began his American rabbinate in Baltimore, in the 1850s, and his German-language prayer book *Olath Tamid* became the model for the

Union Prayer Book. Hirsch was rabbi at Temple Sinai in Chicago, a bold social reformer as well as a brilliant and erudite preacher. Kohler became president of Hebrew Union College and the author of the widely read *Jewish Theology*.

6. Originally called Hochschule fuer die Wissenschaft des Judentums, it was later (at the behest of the Nazis) renamed more modestly Lehranstalt.

7. One of the four Jewish students who graduated with me was Orthodox, and he was excused from writing on Shabbat and could take his examinations at another time. This, of course, was the era of the Weimar Republic (we graduated in 1930); shortly after the Nazis came to power all Jewish students were shifted to Jewish schools.

8. In law school I learned very little and like most other students attended only those courses which either were seminars or had outstanding teachers. I was prepared for my examinations by a professional *Repetitor* who drilled his charges with subject matters tailored to the questions that would be asked. Law school was, for me, a chance to do what I wanted; the basics of *Bildung* were provided by high school and home.

9. This idea had strong antecedents in Jewish tradition, best exemplified by the rabbi who, upon visiting a schoolhouse, declared its teachers and children to be the true guardians of the city.

10. Readers may wish to read more about this whole subject in George Mosse's *German Jews Beyond Judaism* (1985).

The Yom Kippur That Never Was: A Pious Pictorial Fraud

1. "Erinnerungen aus dem Kriegsjahr 1870," *Liberales Judentum* 6:9 (September 1914), 190 ff.

The Common Folk in Mendelssohn's Days

1. *Sefer Ma'agal Tov*, first published from 1753 to 1778, and edited by Aaron Freimann (Jerusalem, 1934).

2. *She'elat yavets*, first published from 1738 to 1759; a later edition appeared in Lemberg, 1884, in 2 volumes. See also Boas Cohen, *Kuntres Ha-Teshuvot* (Budapest, 1930).

3. Callenberg was born in 1694 and died in 1760. In 1791 the Institute merged with the Franckesche Stiftung.

4. The series has a variety of names. Originally it was called *Bericht an einige christliche Freunde von einem Versuch das arme jüdische Volck zur Erkenntnis und Annehmung der christlichen Wahrheit anzuleiten, 2d ed.* (Halle, 1730) (noted as Ber.). Subsequent volumes of this series entitled *Fortsetzung* are noted as F, F1, F2, etc. In 1738 the series appeared under a changed title: *Relation von einer weiteren Bemühung...* and are noted as R, R1, R2, etc.; in 1752 the title changed to *Fortwährende Bemühung...*, and its nine volumes are noted as FB, FBI, FB2, etc.; in 1754 the series was called *Christliche Bereisung...* (noted as CB). From 1760 on, after Callenberg's death, the editors were Stephan Schultz and after him, Justus Israel Beyer. The new volumes were entitled *Fernere Nachricht...* (noted as JAI, JA2, etc.). An index appeared in 1744 which makes the earlier volumes easier to analyze, but no index appeared thereafter.

5. I published this particular interview in *Commentary* 25:5 (1938), 428–30. Mendelssohn politely demolished his visitor's missionary arguments.

6. Reporting to one's superiors was then, as always, somewhat inflated, a practice to which this writer confesses with some embarrassment concerning his own military reports on his chaplaincy work during World War II. I am quite sure that I visited fewer soldiers in hospitals and had smaller synagogue attendances than my official memoranda reported.

7. "Germany" here is used as a broad term meaning the lands which were in 1871 unified into the German Reich. A century before, the principal states were Saxony (whose King Augustus served also as king of Poland), Bavaria, and Prussia, which was fast rising to pre-eminence. The rest of Germany consisted of numerous independent dukedoms, free cities and other principalities. Only occasionally would the missionaries roam as far as Hungary.

8. One should note, however, the highly useful study by Herman Pollack, *Jewish Folkways in Germanic Lands (1648–1806)* (Cambridge, Mass., 1971). Even though the author did not utilize the Callenberg reports, he explored much other material which enabled him to portray the general physical condition of their habitats, including descriptions of the interior of their homes and the extent of their libraries. Pollack's sources also describe areas such as Moravia, Bohemia, and Austria proper.

9. See Pollack, ibid., 1–3.

10. Freely translated: "As far-fetched as baked Sabbath prayers," "silly nonsense," "really true." See Werner Weinberg's collection and analysis of this material in *Die Reste des Jüdischdeutschen* (Stuttgart, 1971). The renowned linguist Uriel Weinreich, however, treats Judeo-German as a part of Yiddish; see his article in *Encyclopaedia Judaica* 16:790 et seq. See also Rudolf Glanz, *Geschichte des niederen jüdischen Volkes in Deutschland* (New York, 1968).

11. CB 365.

12. Ber 20.

13. In clothing, the prohibition of *sha'atnes*, the mixture of wool and flax.

14. F4:93.

15. Especially among the cattle dealers of Westfalen and Hessen, the Jewish "trade lingo" was common.

16. F4:31.

17. JA1:154.

18. FB2:3.

19. FB3:76.

20. F9:311.

21. F7:199.

22. 45.

23. F12:18; F8:336.

24. F6:29 et seq.

25. F5:89; R24.

26. F16:228.

27. R15:69, 78; F11, Vol. 2:32.

28. The word in time entered High German parlance as well. It is a corruption of the Hebrew *she-nodar[lo]* someone [to whom] one has pledged [a gift].

29. R4:17.

30. See Azulai, 15 and JA13:177.

31. R13:68.

32. R14:115.

33. R5:162; R10:6 et seq.

34. F3, Vol. 2:116.

35. F8:115.

36. F9:217.

37. F8:330; F6:17.

38. Such as recorded in F9:217.

39. JA 15:144; F6:42.

40. See R14:112, and note that what the report calls "first storey" is referred to as "second storey" in North America; see also Azulai's comment on housing conditions in a place called Buttenwiesen (page 13).

41. F9:178; F7:119; R21:62: R23:21.

42. R79.

43. R2:59 et seq.; see also R15:93 which describes a Jewish band in the Rhineland which stole 12,000 florins from a nobleman and burned down his house.

44. R6:61 et seq. and R7:2; R15:93.

45. F16:4; F11:33.

46. See Leon Huehner, "The Jews in Georgia in Colonial Times," *Publications of the Jewish Historical Society* 10:65 et seq.

An Interview with Moses Mendelssohn: The Christian and the Jew

1. A Moravian brotherhood whose members had fled from persecution and in 1722 had settled in Herrnhut in Saxony (Germany).

2. Litsken writes "visit" (*besuchen*). Mendelssohn more likely said "redeem the captives," which, while a long-practiced Jewish duty, may not have been familiar to Litsken.

Germans and Jews: The Symbiosis That Failed

1. *Jüdische Schriften*, ed. Bruno Strauss (Berlin, 1924), II, 229ff; see also 237ff. 319–40. Cohen frequently expressed this belief. "We love our German identity not only because we love our homeland as a bird loves its nest, and also not only because we received our spiritual upbringing from the treasures of the German spirit as much as from the Bible and Talmud, but rather because the way of the German spirit is completely and profoundly in harmony with our messianic religion.... The German spirit is the spirit of classical humanity and true cosmopolitanism." (*KC-Blätter*, May-June and July-August, 1916).

2. *Im deutschen Reich*, October-December 1914: 371–73. Quoted by Jürgen Matthaus in "*Deutschtum* and *Judentum* under Fire," *Leo Baeck Institute Yearbook* XXXIII (1988), 129–47, to whom I am indebted for this and other quotations.

3. *Stenographischer Bericht* (1917), 38–39.

4. *Im deutschen Reich* (November 1918): 433–34.

5. *Jüdische Schriften*, 279–80.

6. *Jüdische Rundschau* XIX (August 7, 194): 343. See Rivka Horwitz, "Voices of Opposition ...," *Leo Baeck Institute Yearbook* XXXIII (1988), 233–59; also David Engel, "Patriotism as a Shield," ibid. XXXI (1986), 147–72.

7. *Jüdische Rundschau* XX (July 23, 1915): 239–40.

8. Buber's article appeared in *Der Jude* (July 1916): 281–89, and Cohen responded in the *KC-Blätter*, quoted above. Buber replied in *Der Jude* (September 1916): 425–33.

9. *Briefe und Tagebücher* (Den Haag, 1979), 424.

10. Ibid., 349.

11. *The Jews and the German War Experience 1914–1918*, Leo Baeck Memorial Lecture XXI (New York 1977), 14. Masse goes on to say:

> To be sure, all Jewish papers exhorted young Jews to do their best, and called upon them to volunteer for the colors. Yet, there is enough meaningful difference that we can talk, if not consistently, about an ethical imperative which remained intact. If Jews were prone to accept Christian metaphors because ideas and rituals taken from the non-Jewish environment had penetrated to the heart of Judaism during the process of assimilation, so the ideals of the Enlightenment lasted longest among the Jews. The *Israelitische Wochenblatt*, as early as September 1914, warned against "unhealthy chauvinism" and appealed to reason instead. (Quoted in *Jüdische Rundschau* (September 14, 1914), 361).... The veterans' organization, Der Stahlhelm, for example, opposed the Republic in order to transmit "the spirit of the frontline soldier" to future generations. According to Der Stahlhelm, the new nation was to be built upon the "camaraderie of the trenches," yet the Jewish soldier was not excluded from such comradeship. As Jews formed their own veterans' organization, the co-operation between all faiths which had taken place on the front collapsed—Christianity had become too Germanized, all integral part of the *Volksgemeinschaft* embattled against the enemy (Masse, 18).

See also Binjamin Segel, *Der Weltkrieg und das Schicksal der Juden* (Berlin, 1915), and Ismar Schorsch, *On the History of the Political Judgment of the Jew*, Leo Baeck Memorial Lecture XX, New York, 1976.

12. *Mein Weg als Deutscher und Jude* (Berlin, 1921), 122ff.

13. *Jüdische Rundschau*, April 4, 1933: 1.

14. From an address delivered November 19, 1933; quoted in W. G. Plaut, *The Growth of Reform Judaism* (New York, 1965), 133.

15. See, especially, Peter Gay, *Freud, Jews and Other Germans* (New York, 1978); George L. Mosse, *Germans and Jews: The Right, the Left, and the Search for a "Third Force" in Pre-Nazi Germany* (New York, 1970).

16. See Ringer's thoughtful critique of Mosse's above-cited work in *Journal of Modern History* 44:3 (September 1972): 392ff.

17. Gay, op. cit., 8.

18. Why and how this misconception arose and was fostered as a "fact of history" is a subject that exceeds the limits of this article.

Four Points of Law: Notes on the Relationship of Law and Religion

1. Psalm 85.

The Marshall Inquiry

1. *Report to the Canadian Judicial Council of the Inquiry Committee established pursuant to subsection 63(1) of the Judges Act at the request of the Attorney General of Nova Scotia, August 1990* [hereinafter the Inquiry Committee Report].

2. R. v. Marshall (1983), 57 N.S.R. (2d) 286 [hereinafter the *Reference*].

3. *Royal Commission on the Donald Marshall, Jr. Prosecution*, Province of Nova Scotia, 1989 [hereinafter the Royal Commission].

4. Report of Inquiry Members Richard CJ, Laycraft CJ, Abella and Bellemarre, *supra*, note 1 at 5.

5. Ibid., 34.

6. Ibid., 32.

7. Report of McEachern CJ., *supra*, note 1 at 26.

Permissions

Grateful acknowledgement is made for permission to reproduce the articles by W. Gunther Plaut in this book as follows:

"The Wandering Aramean: A Commentary on Deuteronomy 26:5." First published in the *Central Conference of American Rabbis Journal*, January 1962. Reprinted with permission.

"In Defence of the *Erev Rav*." First published in the *Central Conference of American Rabbis Journal*, June 1964. Reprinted with permission.

"Pharoah's Hardened Heart." First published in the *Central Conference of American Rabbis Journal*, October 1962. Reprinted with permission.

"The Pillar of Salt." First published in the *Central Conference of American Rabbis Journal*, June 1961. Reprinted with permission.

"Why Love a Stranger?" First published in the *Central Conference of American Rabbis Journal*, January 1966. Reprinted with permission.

"The Origin of the Word 'Yarmulke'" from the *Hebrew Union College Annual* 26: 567–70 (1955). Reprinted with permission of Hebrew Union College.

"A Hebrew–Dakota Dictionary" from vol. 42 (September 1952–June 1953): 361–70, of a publication of the American Jewish Historical Society. Reprinted with permission.

"Long-hand with Buber." First published in *Judaism: A Quarterly of Jewish Life and Thought* 23, no. 1 (Winter 1974). Reprinted with permission of the American Jewish Congress.

"Assessing the Jewish Mind" (review). First published in *Queen's Quarterly* 85, no. 3 (Autumn 1978). Reprinted with permission.

"What I Believe" from *The State of Jewish Belief: A Symposium Compiled by the Editors of Commentary Magazine*, August 1966. Reprinted with permission of *Commentary*.

"The Sabbath as Protest: Thoughts on Work and Leisure in the Automated Society" from A. Leland Jamison, ed., *Tradition and Change in Jewish Experience*, 1978. Reprinted with permission of the Department of Religion, Syracuse University.

"The Four Phases of Reform." First published as "Reform Judaism: Past, Present and Future" in the *Journal of Reform Judaism*, Summer 1980. Reprinted by permission of the Central Conference of American Rabbis.

"Religious Discipline and Liberal Judaism." *CCAR Yearbook 1975*. Reprinted by permission of the Central Conference of American Rabbis.

"Prophetic Judaism Without Prophets" from Peter S. Knobel and Mark Straitman, eds., *An American Rabbinate: A Festschrift for Walter Jacob*. Copyright © 2000 Rodef Shalom Congregation. Reprinted with permission.

"The Elusive German-Jewish Heritage in America." First published in *American Jewish Archives* 40, no. 2 (November 1988): 73–79. Reprinted with permission of the Jacob Rader Marcus Center of the American Jewish Archives.

"The Yom Kippur That Never Was." First published in *The Jewish Digest* 12, no. 12 (1967).

"The Common Folk in Mendelssohn's Days" from Moses Richlin and Raphael Asher, eds., *The Jewish Legacy and the German Conscience*, 1991. Reprinted with permission of the Judah L. Magnes Museum.

"An Interview with Moses Mendelssohn." First published in *Commentary*, May 1953. Reprinted with permission of *Commentary*.

"Germans and Jews: The Symbiosis That Failed." First published in *Judaism: A Quarterly of Jewish Life and Thought* 40, no. 4 (Fall 1991). Reprinted with permission of the American Jewish Congress.

"Hate Propaganda." Review of *The Report of the Special Committee on Hate Propaganda in Canada*. Copyright © 1967 W. Gunther Plaut. First published in the *Osgoode Hall Law Journal* 5 (1967).

"Refuge or Asylum: The Canadian Perspective" from Howard Adelman and C. Michael Lamphier, eds., *Refuge or Asylum: A Choice for Canada*, 1990. Reprinted with permission of the Centre for Refugee Studies, York University.